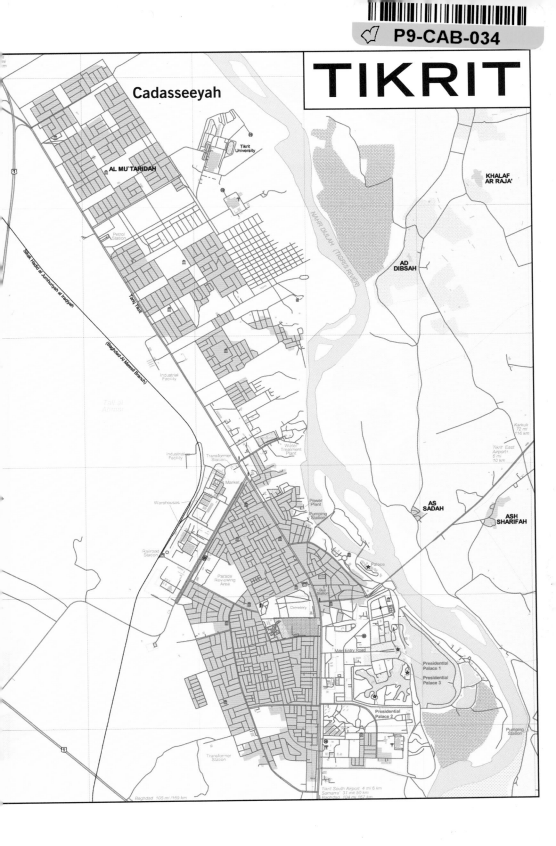

TIKRIT

Cadasseeyah

AL MU'TARIDAH

Tikrit
University

KHALAF
AR RAJA'

AD
DIBSAH

NAHR DIJLAH (TIGRIS RIVER)

Sikak Hadid ar Jumhuriyah al Iraqiyah

Tariq Turq

(Baghdad-Al Mawsil Branch)

Petrol
Station

Industrial
Facility

Tall al
Ahmar

Industrial
Facility

Transformer
Station

Water
Treatment
Plant

Market

Warehouses

Power
Plant

Pumping
Station

Railroad
Station

Parade
Reviewing
Area

Bus
Station

Cemetery

Palace

AS
SADAH

ASH
SHARIFAH

Karkuk
72 mi
116 km

Tikrit East
Airport
6 mi
10 km

Main Entry Road

Presidential
Palace 1

Presidential
Palace 3

Presidential
Palace 2

Transformer
Station

Pumping
Station

Tikrit South Airport 4 mi 6 km
Samarra' 31 mi 50 km
Baghdad 104 mi 167 km

Baghdad 105 mi /169 km

WE GOT HIM!

A MEMOIR OF THE HUNT AND CAPTURE OF

SADDAM HUSSEIN

LT. COL. STEVE RUSSELL (U.S. ARMY RETIRED)

THRESHOLD EDITIONS

NEW YORK   LONDON   TORONTO   SYDNEY   NEW DELHI

This book is as factual as personal experience, extensive research, author's personal journals, and interviews with participants will allow. Any errors are unintended, and the author apologizes for any omissions or errors.

Threshold Editions
A Division of Simon & Schuster, Inc.
1230 Avenue of the Americas
New York, NY 10020

First Threshold Editions hardcover edition December 2011

THRESHOLD EDITIONS and colophon are trademarks of Simon & Schuster, Inc.

For information about special discounts for bulk purchases, please contact Simon & Schuster Special Sales at 1-866-506-1949 or business@simonandschuster.com.

The Simon & Schuster Speakers Bureau can bring authors to your live event. For more information or to book an event, contact the Simon & Schuster Speakers Bureau at 1-866-248-3049 or visit our website at www.simonspeakers.com.

Manufactured in the United States of America

10   9   8   7   6   5   4   3

Library of Congress Cataloging-in-Publication Data

Russell, Steve, 1963-
   We got him! : a memoir of the hunt and capture of Saddam Hussein / Steve Russell. — 1st Threshold Editions hardcover ed.
       p. cm.
   Includes index.
   Originally published: Marietta Ga. : Deeds Pub., 2011.
  1. Iraq War, 2003—Campaigns—Iraq—Tikrit. 2. Iraq War, 2003—Commando operations— Iraq—Tikrit. 3. Iraq War, 2003—Personal narratives, American. 4. Hussein, Saddam, 1937-2006. 5. Russell, Steve. I. Title.
   DS79.764.T55 R87
   956.7044'342—dc23
                                                                                              2011027205

ISBN 978-1-4516-6248-1
ISBN 978-1-4516-6249-8 (ebook)

Photographs in the photo insert are used by permission of Efrem Lukatsky, and are from the author's personal collection.

Maps and other illustrations and charts are from the author's personal collection.

To the soldiers of the 22nd United States Infantry
who have given their lives in the defense of freedom

CONTENTS

CONTENTS

CONTENTS

FOREWORD

General Raymond T. Odierno

TIKRIT, IRAQ—DECEMBER 13, 2003, 8:30 PM

"Sir, this is Jim Hickey."
"Yes, Jim."
"We've captured Number One. . . . "

In my 35 years of uniformed military service, I've received many memorable reports from subordinate commanders. Many will remain with me for the rest of my life, fostering visions of families whose lives will be forever changed by the loss or maiming of a loved one fighting in a conflict thousands of miles from home.

This particular report from Colonel Jim Hickey, then Commander of the 1st Brigade, 4th Infantry Division, would have a profound impact. When made public, this news would have an immediate effect and induce mixed reactions within the city of Tikrit, from elation to violence. The news would provoke a spectrum of mixed reactions throughout Iraq, from relief and hope to fear of the unknown to come. The news would impact the Middle East and the world. What now? Will the Americans see this through? Al-Qaeda would view this news as an opportunity: "The Americans have been focused on Saddam, while we have been organizing. They will not stay. We will fill the gap created by the collapse of the government and the pre-existing fissures of multi-ethnic Iraq. This is our chance."

THE ENVIRONMENT

In June 2003, the environment in Iraq was volatile at best. In May 2003, the President of the United States announced the end of major combat operations in Iraq. The people of the United States were preparing to receive their victorious troops with open arms. Over the previous four months, televised live in their living rooms and offices, the U.S. Joint Force invaded, conquered and toppled a brutal regime, liberating the people of Iraq. However, the Multi-National Force on the ground was beginning to realize that much deeper problems remained. There were many underlying complications that had been building for years inside of Iraq: ethno-sectarianism, societal devastation, and economic underdevelopment, just to name a few that were not yet resolved.

So, while some believed victory was in our hands, we found ourselves, in fact, at a perilous juncture. How we handled the situation in the months and years to come would have a lasting impact on the nation of Iraq and on the Middle East.

Tikrit, Iraq, was Saddam Hussein's birthplace. It was also his final hiding place. In 2003, Tikrit was home to Saddam loyalists who unwittingly served as the first insurgents. Most of them were nationalists, not religious fundamentalists, loyal to their tyrannical dictator of thirty years and confident in their ability to restore him to his rightful place of power. They saw the Americans as they always had: enemies with great strength, but small hearts and no staying power.

1st Brigade, 4th Infantry Division, commanded by Colonel James Hickey, understood these nuances, as did many incredible and dynamic young commanders across Iraq. They understood what was at risk and, equally important, they understood what had to be done. The rest of the world, including many within our own government and our military, did not understand the dynamics or the reality unfolding on the ground. Many were quick to criticize the tactics of the ground force commanders as "heavy-handed," but the critics' understanding of the operational environment was marginal at best. For those of us who participated in this campaign and for many who have studied it in retrospect, we can appreciate the difficulty of culling irreconcilable enemy combatants, while simultaneously gaining the support and cooperation of the reconcilable population. It was an incredibly complex environment; complex in a way we had not anticipated prior to the invasion.

Each area of Iraq was unique and faced a unique set of challenges. Tikrit and Sal ah Din Province were vastly different from Mosul, Basra, Baghdad or Anbar. Each area presented unique challenges while demanding equally unique solutions. Additionally, to make matters more challenging, we did not appreciate the level of internal turmoil that existed in Iraq prior to our invasion. During the previous 30 years, Iraq was profoundly impacted by several key events, including: the Iran-Iraq war of the 1980s; its grab for Kuwait and resulting military defeat in 1991; the subsequent economic sanctions of the 1990s and the implementation of the no-fly zone; the intra-Shia rivalry; the Sunni-Shia issue; and the Arab-Kurd issue. However, we learned as a military and as a nation. I believe I learned as a commander at the division, corps and force levels. As a force, over time, our experience allowed us to understand the underlying dynamics of the Iraqi culture and we began to adapt to this complex environment.

THE TIKRIT APPROACH AND ITS LESSONS

To pave a solid path to a new future, Iraqis needed to believe that the brutal regime would never return to power. Talk would not achieve this effect. Deeds were necessary to enable them to follow that path. The best way we could reassure them was to permanently remove the threat of Saddam, his family and loyalists to the people and the country. Tikrit and Sal ah Din were a nest for loyalists. Twenty-two of the 52 original "most wanted" in Iraq would be captured or killed in the 4th Infantry Division's area of responsibility (Sal ah Din Province). Accomplishing this took a relentless pursuit of the enemy by organizations whose senior leaders were willing to underwrite appropriate levels of risk to accomplish the mission without handicapping their force.

This relentless pursuit of a path forward taught us all many lessons. These lessons would be revisited and sometimes, unfortunately, relearned over the years. We made mistakes and paid a heavy price, but never lost sight of our primary objective: a free and democratic Iraq, led by a government representative of its people and in strategic partnership with the United States.

The story of success detailed in this book resulted from the teamwork among many players. 1st Battalion, 22nd Infantry Regiment ("Regulars, by God"), commanded by Lieutenant Colonel Steve Russell, Jim Hickey's brigade, and the 4th Infantry Division cannot take sole ownership of the successful hunt for Saddam Hussein. It took a unity of effort between all partners to accomplish the mission in a very complex and evolving environment. I can say unequivocally, however, that Colonel Jim Hickey and Lieutenant Colonel Steve Russell were the two individuals most directly responsible for the capture of Saddam Hussein.

This time period served as a transition point for the way we as an American military will fight in the future. We have learned in

Iraq that success cannot be attained unilaterally. The transparency, cooperation and resulting relationships between the 4th Infantry Division (ID), 1st Brigade/4th ID, and our special operations forces (SOF) were unique and broke new ground. Initially built through strong personal relationships, this set the stage for future widespread cooperation between conventional and special operations forces which today is considered routine and necessary, both in Iraq and Afghanistan. In 2003, it was not.

Steve Russell's relationship with his SOF partners is indicative of the cooperation leading to success throughout the echelons of command in Iraq. Steve delivers the most accurate account I have read to date of the unprecedented partnership between SOF and conventional forces and the approach taken by both to accomplish our critical mission together. What Steve and his partners learned and demonstrated was that it takes a network to defeat a network. Steve vividly describes his interpretation of the enemy network he faced in Tikrit in the summer and fall of 2003. Through personal relationships, he successfully developed a network which included his SOF partners, Iraqi government officials, Iraqi police, sheikhs and elements of the Iraqi population. This friendly network, and our burgeoning ability (from platoon through Corps and the inter-agency) to collaboratively attack complex problem sets formed the basis of what would eventually yield one of the guiding principles for our success in Iraq: Unity of Effort.

Over time I have concluded that achieving unity of effort, operating on the ground among the population and maintaining constant pressure on threat networks are enduring characteristics of successful operations in a counter-insurgency environment. The operations of the 1st Battalion, 22nd Infantry "Regulars" in 2003 provided the basis for many of the tactics, techniques and procedures that were later implemented during the "Surge" of 2007-2008 and beyond. These principles enabled coalition forces to significantly reduce the impact of the insurgency, allowing us to transition to stability operations and turn complete control of security over to the Government of Iraq in 2010.

THE FUTURE

Some would argue that generals have demonstrated a propensity to fight the last war. I believe that we cannot afford to validate this assertion. We live in a dynamic world with diverse threats requiring flexible and adaptive leaders and organizations to deter and to defeat them. Two things we can be certain of about warfare in the future: First, our military will never again fight alone. There will frequently be a multi-national component and we must always take an inter-agency and whole-of-nation approach to warfare. Second, there will always be an irregular warfare component to any fight in which we may find ourselves. We cannot afford to relegate the Regulars' lessons to historical archives. Rather, we must keep them alive, learn from them and continue to grow.

It is an honor for me to introduce this personal memoir by one of the finest battalion commanders with whom I have served. His story captures the human dimension of this awful thing we call war, not often seen in the media accounts during the 24-hour news cycle, and usually overlooked during the search for the sensational. The brave and heroic actions of his soldiers, along with the countless sacrifices and actions by so many like them, have forever shaped the future of the world in which we live. It is humbling to serve alongside them and has been a distinct privilege to command them.

General Raymond T. Odierno
Chief of Staff
United States Army

PROLOGUE

After a wild ride spanning half the globe, the 1st Battalion, 22nd Infantry Regiment mobilized from Ft. Hood, Texas, in late March 2003 to deploy to Iraq in mid-April. I would join them in a few more weeks after a wild ride of my own. The original assault against Saddam Hussein and his army was to have been launched from both Kuwait and Turkey. The plan called for the 4th Infantry Division (to which the 1st Battalion, 22nd Infantry belonged) to attack northern Iraq from Turkey, but the Turkish parliament reneged and denied entry just before any equipment arrived. As negotiations waned, the war started without the 4th Infantry Division.

Their heavy equipment had bobbed on scores of vessels from the Gulf of Mexico across the Atlantic Ocean and finally to the Mediterranean Sea. The divisional army's "navy," larger than that possessed by many countries, now charted a new course south through the Suez Canal and the Red Sea eastward to the Indian Ocean and north through the Persian Gulf.

Porting in Kuwait, they off-loaded the ships and raced north. Their heavy mechanized and armored units churned hundreds of miles of Iraqi dust on roads and dunes. They bypassed the 3rd Infantry Division and Marines already fighting in Baghdad and other Marine elements that had briefly occupied Tikrit. Company

A split off the battalion to join a tank unit supporting the 101st Airborne in Mosul as the race continued toward the original objectives in northern Iraq.

Finally getting into action about the time Baghdad was secured, the remainder of the battalion fought the last vestiges of the Adnan Republican Guard Division near Tikrit by the end of April. The bulk of those remnants had collected near the village of Mazhem, wedged between the Tigris River and their home base known as the "Tikrit Military Complex," which headquartered the Republican Guard I Corps and the Iraqi Army Tank School. The 1st Battalion, 22nd Infantry fought some fierce battles from 26 to 29 April. Tragically, First Lieutenant Osbaldo "Baldo" Orozco, a fine officer and collegiate football star, was lost, and several more were wounded in an assault of a farm holdout near Mazhem cleared by their C Company and Scout Platoon. Lieutenant Orozco was the first casualty of the 4th Infantry Division in Iraq and, in an odd repetition of history, from the identical company of the division's first casualty in Vietnam.

Following these engagements, the battalion was given orders to occupy Tikrit around May 1 and relieve the 8th Infantry's 1st Battalion, also from the 4th Infantry Division. The 8th Infantry had relieved the Marines. Now the 22nd Infantry would take up residence for the occupation.

It was during this brief respite that I joined the 1st Battalion, 22nd Infantry Regiment, "Regulars, by God." The regimental moniker originated in the War of 1812, as described in the "The U.S. Army in Action" series from the Center of Military History: "The Battle of Chippewa—Chippewa, Upper Canada, 5 July 1814. The British commander watched the advancing American line contemptuously, for its men wore the rough gray coats issued those untrained levies he had easily whipped before. As the ranks advanced steadily through murderous grapeshot, he realized his mistake: 'Those are regulars, by God!' It was Winfield Scott's brigade of infantry, drilled through the previous winter into a crack outfit. It drove the British from the battlefield; better still, after two years of seemingly endless failures, it renewed the American soldier's faith in himself." One of the regiments in Scott's brigade was the 22nd. The name stuck and the uniform was adopted for West Point cadets in 1815. Thus began the long tradition of fighting excellence for the 22nd Infantry, a unit celebrated from Cuba to the Philippines, Normandy on D-Day, the Hurtgen Forest, the Battle of the Bulge, at Kontum, Suoi Tre and Tet in Vietnam, in Somalia, and soon—Tikrit.

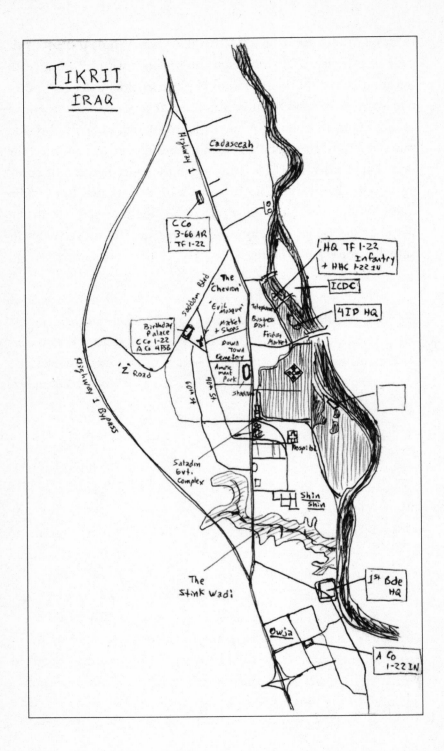

1. TIGRIS

Qais ("KAI-iss"), whose full name was Qais Namaq Jassim, settled down for a quiet evening. The air cooled slightly as long fingers of waning sunlight filtered through the trees in the orchard. He liked this time of year with its forgiving temperatures, blooming desert, and rich growing season. The citrus trees and towering date palms were laden with their bounty. In the near distance, the gentle ripples of the sun-dappled Tigris signaled a powerful undercurrent as the river swelled with winter rain. The fishing would be good.

There was still some work to do but the evening promised to be a pleasant one. He needed to prepare a meal for his guest now. That was his job. Qais and his brother, both caretakers who had served him for many years, enjoyed conversation with him, but were acutely aware of the need to be vigilant at every moment. The American patrols could appear at any time. Several close calls had taught them that seconds counted. In the last few months, the Americans had materialized undetected on his farm hut patio several times but had found nothing. They had been lucky thus far.

He was confident that their contingency plan was far too clever for the Americans. They would never find the guest. He looked weary. Still, there was a quiet strength in the guest's demeanor. He might have looked like a farmer with his common attire and unkempt beard, but one look across the river toward Auja was a reminder of his importance. Down at the riverbank, one could still glimpse the magnificence of his mansion standing stalwartly, even majestically, on the distant hillside.

Not even the American bombs could bring it down. Certainly it had been damaged. Even so, it remained. Just like their guest. The Americans had tried to break him for decades and could not. Now, though they occupied the entire country, their search for him had been in vain.

Qais was glad that, since their guest had begun life as a humble farmer on this land, the hardship was not intolerable for him. He and his brother could prepare meals and tend to their guest's needs until things got back on track. The setbacks were many, but they were substantial for the occupiers as well. Soon, they would leave, and their leader could restore power. He had endured similar hardship in 1958 under parallel circumstances and escaped from this very farm. Fate had brought him back. He would survive again.

With the setting sun obscured, the lights of Ad Dawr to the south and Tikrit to the north framed the horizon. As Qais prepared for the evening, the electricity failed. Again. This was not at all unusual, but it did cause him to wonder. Canting an ear to the distance, he could hear the low rumble of approaching vehicles. He strained his eyes through the latticed fence toward the wheat field to the east but could see nothing. Still, he didn't like the sound of things. He could hear too many vehicles in the distance. He began to hear what sounded like . . . helicopters!

Qais' mind began to race. (Quick! No time! Hurry! The carpet. Move it. Get the ropes. Please hurry! Be careful. Are you OK? Take this pistol. Get down. Brother, we must get this covered. No! They are coming! They are coming here. Run! Run!)

Qais and his brother snapped through the palm fronds and small branches lining the orchard. The sound of their crackling footsteps in the crisp evening air was muted by the rising furor they heard in the wheat field and over their heads. Propelling themselves forward at breakneck speed to avoid capture, they ran through the trees to the north, hearts pounding in their ears, every breath a painful gasp. If they could just get some distance from the hut, then maybe . . .

2. TOWNS

TREK TO TIKRIT

The Blackhawk helicopter blades fluttered with a breezy high-pitched clamor as I approached. I talked my way into a ride on the bird with a local and reasonable Air Force sergeant who did the manifesting. It had one seat. The other seats on the bird were filled with support troops. Support troops. Leaf-eaters, we called them. Though we gave them a hard time, we really did love 'em. They did the vital work of supplying meat-eaters everything they needed—everything but ammo in Kuwait, apparently.

"You can get it when you land north," a sergeant back at Camp Doha informed me. "If you draw it here, it comes from accountable stock. You will have to sign for it and return it."

All I needed was ammo for my passage north into a combat zone. I suppose in the sergeant's mind, a colonel had no need for ammo anyway. God help us! At what point did reality and regulation meet? To the admin types, they might as well have been as far away as the east was from the west.

I had scrounged an unclaimed rifle back in the arms room at Ft. Hood. It was a good one, an M-4 carbine that came in after the guys shipped out. I felt good about not pulling a rifle off the line. I had a pistol, but my first time in a firefight with one was the last. That's why I found a rifle.

It was in my hands now, muzzle end down with butt end braced between my legs, as I sat in the troop seats on the bird. Even though the rifle was empty, it was an old training habit to position it this way on a helicopter. It would be disastrous for a stray round to fire into the engine and rotors above. I tried to make myself as comfortable as possible on the cruel netting braced over aluminum that masqueraded as seats. I'm on my way to war again.

My mind raced back to the events that led me to this journey. Although slated for command in June, I had not been released from my previous job at III Corps Headquarters in time to deploy with the 22nd Infantry in March. Consequently, I took an "interesting" commercial flight from Ft. Hood, Texas, to Kuwait City some six weeks later. From the airport, I proceeded directly to Camp Doha in need of ammo and transportation, but was told that would have to wait for processing. Suddenly feeling very tired, I took advantage of the wait to get some rest. There was no time for administrative games, so I drew no linen and filled out no forms. I had my orders and I simply wanted to get north to my unit. I slept on my kit with a cap shielding my eyes from light in the cooler outside air. It sure beat sleeping with 600 of your closest friends in a hot tin warehouse.

Hurry up and wait—that's the army tradition. I tried to play by the book but found no one to comprehend the urgency of getting me to my unit. Taking matters into my own hands, I bummed a ride the next morning to Ali Al Salim airfield in Kuwait. I had stowed away from there many times before in my treks to Afghanistan. Something had to be flying north. I was in luck. A corps support commander had come from Tikrit to check on the flow of supplies into Kuwait, and I was just skinny enough to wedge myself and my kit onto his bird for the return trip. Now here I sat with blades whirring.

I could not help but think of that fast and furious last day at home. The uneasy sinking feeling began to come back to me. I never could understand it. Regardless of how often I reminded myself that things were usually better than the mind portended them to be, I found little solace. My mind blurred with the million little things that I might need, or might encounter, or might leave undone at home before I left. At the end of it all, I realized, as I always did, that I would just have to do the best I could and trust that things would turn out all right.

Goodbyes were always hard. This one was no different, but unlike the previous wartime deployment goodbyes, my wife and I both knew that the stakes were much higher and that my trade as an infantry commander put me at more risk than normal. I had just about packed up everything I needed. Then I added the toiletries and small comfort items that I held out for use that morning.

It was time to go. I hugged my five kids one by one. Hard. I smelled them and embraced them in the hopes of remembering their every detail. I knew from previous deployments that it was actually possible to forget the sharp details of what my loved ones looked like.

I shouldered my rucksack, tossed a duffle bag on top of that, carried another in one hand, and grabbed my assault pack with attached Kevlar helmet with the other. Burdened with the weight of my gear and of leaving my family, I shuffled out to the car. Since I was deploying after the main body of my troops to take command of a unit already there, I had to go to Ft. Hood and pick up my rifle and pistol for the flight. It always seemed odd to me to fly commercially with a weapon—and to war for that matter. Now, my M4 carbine would be neatly and innocently packed in a locked

Wal-Mart black rifle case and put in the cargo hold of a commercial jet. What if this gets lost? I thought.

When I went to the 1st Brigade headquarters to get my rifle, I
had a message to see the rear detachment commander, who had
been the adjutant before the deployment. What he said made me
angry. He asked me to carry a very large framed print with me to
Iraq.

Are you out of your mind? I thought and then followed ver-
bally with something very similar. "I have tons of gear and am
deploying to a war," I countered.

"It is for the brigade commander," he offered pathetically. "It is
his going-away gift."

Colonel Don Campbell, the brigade commander, was about
as fine a commander as anyone could wish. He was a soldier's
soldier and a leader. I could not imagine him wanting something like this to fumble with in Iraq. Further, I also could not
imagine how he could get the frame back without some degree
of difficulty himself.

"This thing could be shattered. And even if he gets it in one
piece, why burden him with getting it back?"

"You can talk to Colonel Genteel about it," said the adjutant,
retreating for safety.

Lt. Col. Gian Genteel was a fine man and one whom I would
come to greatly respect. But right now, I had dagger eyes for anyone who thought this was a good idea. After talking to him over
a faint phone line in Iraq, I consented and hated myself for it. It
was, in my view, dumb to send it over and dumb to bring it back
and dumb to ask me to do it. I was dumb to agree. I guess that
made us all even. As I fumed about it while securing my weapon,
I was informed that the gift was not ready. How terrible. I was
heartbroken.

I left the headquarters, satisfied that I did not have to run that fool's errand, and got into my car for the last time. Cindy drove me to the airport. The flight would be long. Very long. From Killeen, Texas, to Dallas to Chicago to London to Kuwait. Then I would catch whatever military transportation I could to Iraq.

Cindy and I embraced at the airport. We had done this before. Nothing made it any easier. It was hard to watch her walk away. It was even harder through moist eyes. I felt a wash of guilt flow over me for leaving my wife to shoulder family responsibility single-handedly for months on end. Left alone with five kids, worried about my safety, and staring at a long separation, she could scarcely relate any of it to friends and family at home. Like so many military wives, it was her burden to bear alone.

Soon the line was moving, and I had to get my boarding pass. Shuffling along with my gear, I began to focus on my mission. I braced myself for the responsibility of leading a thousand soldiers in combat.

During the flight over, I reviewed the high points of T. E. Lawrence's *Seven Pillars of Wisdom*. I found it helpful earlier when I had deployed to Kuwait and Afghanistan. But it seemed so much more applicable now. I also started and finished Alistair Horne's *A Savage War of Peace* about the French experience in Algeria. Something in my gut told me that any war with Arabs was bound to have insurgent problems. Little could I have known.

COMMUTERS AND CAPTIVES

The high piercing whine of a Blackhawk powering up brought me back to the present. The full colonel using this bird was gracious enough to let me strap hang. Frankly, I think he mistook me for an enlisted infantry soldier. It was a great compliment. I eyed the mixture of soldiers on board wondering which of them could fight if we landed unexpectedly. Opening an ammo pouch,

I brandished an empty magazine, shouting over the noise to a sergeant, "No ammo! Give me a magazine!"

"Sure thing, sir," he shouted back as he tossed me a 30-round mag and I tossed him the empty one. I instantly felt better.

Brown dust corkscrewed into billows surrounding the bird. With snout down and tail high, the Blackhawk nosed its way north into Iraq. I flipped on my handheld Garmin GPS to track our location should we go down. We crossed the big berm and anti-tank ditch Kuwait built as a barrier against another possible attack from Saddam's Iraq. War debris littered the landscape for many miles—charred hulks, flattened cars, and buildings in ruin.

Clipping along the Iraqi countryside, I absorbed the view. Every building was square with a walled roof, similar to those in Afghanistan but more highly developed. The entire population seemed to be clustered along the rivers and streams. Infrastructure connected the clusters in a constant flow of humanity tracking north toward our destination. Things were calmer now that the Iraqi army had been driven from the field. Still, the route struck me as risky given the ample supply of RPGs and shoulder-fired anti-aircraft missiles in Iraq.

Approaching Baghdad, we veered west in favor of a less populated route. The city was massive. Millions of Iraqis, about one-fourth of the population, lived there. As our flight path took us toward more deserted areas, the silhouette of the city faded on the horizon.

Suddenly, I heard the rotor pitch change as we leaned into a sharp bank. Peering out the Plexiglas window, I noticed two Iraqis with a pile of munitions in the back of their pickup truck. They were inside a square-bermed ammo storage bunker, one of many dotting the desert flats. The slapstick comedy act was about to begin.

I couldn't guess what was taking place as we touched down.

Once the swirling sand settled, I saw two aviators in flight suits moving with their pistols drawn toward the two Iraqis. Suddenly, the crew chief threw open the troop door.

"You and you!" shouted the colonel, pointing at two soldiers armed only with pistols. The two support soldiers followed the colonel as he moved toward the two military-aged Iraqi males already covered by the aviators. Whatever was about to develop, it seemed senseless to leave us on board as they developed the situation.

"Come with me," I ordered the only other rifle-armed soldier on board, the one who had given me a magazine. He seemed fit and perhaps able to fight.

"Yes, sir," he replied with energy as we left the bowels of the Blackhawk.

Chambering a round, I approached the colonel. "Sir, would you like me to search them? I'm an infantryman. I might be able to help."

"Sure! That would be great!" he gushed with a look that demonstrated my presence and rank had still not been noticed. Perhaps he believed two rifle-toters had just been beamed there for his benefit.

"Cover me from an open side, and do not let the Iraqi get between us," I explained as I handed my rifle to an aviator and instructed the sergeant.

"Roger, sir," he acknowledged.

I began my search. These were young Iraqi men, perhaps in their early twenties. Armed only with a wooden mallet between them, they appeared to be harmless. Like some characters from a Bugs Bunny cartoon, they were cracking the seals of stolen 57mm anti-aircraft shells, discarding the warheads and powder and tossing the brass into the back of their pickup truck. Spying a little teapot and two Turkish cups over a small fire, it appeared we had interrupted their coffee break.

Some soldier had handcuffed their wrists with plastic zip ties which were far too tight. I took note of their red and white checkered headdresses lying on the ground in the blazing sun. After my search, I knew they were both clean—no weapons or other contraband. I flipped out my Gerber "Gator" knife, a gift from the 3rd Special Forces in Afghanistan, and snapped it open. The Iraqis' eyes widened to the size of Eisenhower dollars as I carefully worked it under the zip ties to cut them free.

"Too tight," I offered by way of explanation to one of the soldiers nearby. "Redo them with a finger's width of slack to prevent permanent damage." I stooped to the ground, grabbed a checkered kaffiyeh and tossed it to the Iraqi to cover his head.

"Yes, mister!" He smiled, getting a modicum of relief from the heat as he reapplied it. "Thank you!" He nodded, giving a thumbs-up before being recuffed.

Once the two Iraqis were secure, I searched their truck for weapons and grenades. Nothing. As I emerged from the cab, the colonel expressed appreciation for my help.

"It's good to get more 'captives' on the 'scoreboard' for the support group," he announced.

I listened respectfully, trying to conceal utter amazement at this corps support group commander. Are you serious? Scoreboard? What scoreboard? Did he think this was some kind of grandstanding game?

"I called ahead for support since we are close to Tikrit," the colonel continued. "There is a QRF (Quick Reaction Force) on its way now."

Thank God, I thought privately, to save us from ourselves.

In the distance, I could see dust geysers rooster-tailing from Bradley Fighting Vehicles as they spotted our location. As they neared, I was relieved that fighting troops would be handling this "crisis" but wondered what important work they had been drawn from to do so.

First Lieutenant Matt Myer's platoon from A Company, 1st Battalion, 22nd Infantry had arrived. The support command colonel instructed Myer as he reported. I already liked the look of this unit. Their kit was practical; ammo was within fighting reach, their weapons were clean and oiled, and the Brads were stripped to no-nonsense fighting trim. Not yet in charge but curious about the unit I would soon command, I went to the rear of a Bradley to talk with the men. To my surprise, I saw Staff Sergeant Mark Dornbusch, a soldier I served with in Kosovo, leading his squad.

"Welcome to Iraq, sir. We heard you were coming." He grinned.

"Ranger Dornbusch!" I exclaimed. "Great to see you. Staff Sergeant, is it? Wow! It was private the last time. Thanks. It's good to be here. These guys don't look like much of a threat—just a couple of coffee-drinking looters melting down brass to make plates and teapots would be my guess."

"Roger, sir," replied Mark. "We'll take care of them."

I then talked with Lieutenant Myer briefly and asked him for a general update on his platoon. Speaking with confidence, he gave me a very thorough rundown of his mission.

"We've been guarding these ASPs (Ammunition Supply Points) out here," Myer briefed. "Tons and tons of stuff, sir. It's all pretty dangerous if it falls into the wrong hands. Every type of ammunition imaginable is inside these bunkers."

Matt said there had been some small arms contact with factions attempting to raid the ASPs. He told me his company was positioned in the village of Auja ("OH-juh"), the infamous birth village of Saddam Hussein, several kilometers to the northeast. A platoon had been rotated to this location to provide security.

"Do you have mortar support?" I asked.

"I don't think so, sir," he replied. "But we are within artillery range of the 4-42 across the river and attack helicopters."

Good answer, I thought. A stray platoon out here in the desert was a disaster waiting to happen without proper indirect fire support. As we talked, I realized I had served with Matt's father, Colonel Steve Myer. Suddenly, I felt old.

Not wanting to miss my ride, we parted company. I walked back to the bird with a very good first impression of the battalion I would soon grow to love in ways only soldiers can understand.

WAKE-UP CALL

Dust clouds billowed from the Blackhawk, sand-blasting the infantrymen who I am certain had nothing but "praise" on their lips for this unimpressive, ragtag element they had come to rescue. I mused at the whole thing, thankful we had encountered only coffee-drinking pot-makers.

The Tigris rose up to our right, connecting us to the village of Auja. Spectacular housing and palaces linked Auja with the city of Tikrit. Ornate mosques sharply contrasted with the squat, blocky, communist-style architecture below. Alongside the river to the right was a sea of military vehicles and a few helicopters on well-manicured, palm-lined avenues within an enormous, walled palace complex. To the left, the city sprawled in a crescent shape, each tip connected to the river.

The choppy sound of changing rotor pitch signaled the end of our journey. We landed on a flat, paved surface that made a decent airfield. To the east, several lines of 5-ton "expando van" trucks marked the headquarters of the 4th Infantry Division.

Duffles and kit in hand, sweat dripping from nose to kneecap, I made my way toward the vans to find a ride to the battalion. I recognized a few faces from Ft. Hood and was soon greeted all around. Someone made a call to the 1st Battalion, 22nd Infantry. They would come get me. I wandered toward the division operations truck for an update while I waited. Lieutenant

Colonel Mark Woempner, the current battalion commander, soon greeted me.

"It sucks to meet my relief," he asserted. "I'm glad it's you."

"I won't get in your way, Mark." I offered. "You're still in command. I would like to get around to the units, though, as much as possible to make my own assessment."

"Whatever you need, Steve," he replied. "You are welcome to come with me or have the run of anything in the battalion."

I felt like my entire life had been preparation for this moment in Iraq. While I could never have imagined the events to follow, I could sense something significant was taking place—an opportunity to shape events for the good of our nation and perhaps even the world. It was surreal.

One of the first things I did was get acquainted with the environment. I wanted to see what we were up against in the city and how our soldiers interacted with local Iraqis. I had the opportunity over a couple of days to do just that. The city struck me with a mix of sights, sounds and smells. Communist overengineered, square, squat, pre-fab apartment buildings sprouted above the flat-topped, Arab houses. Hanging laundry flapped with companion swirls of dust and fluttering trash. Rivulets of filth and greasy sewage kept company with dingy yellow and white candy-striped curbs. The burnt smell of diesel fumes mixed with other assorted odors. Young Arab men haunched everywhere, busy at nothing. To the casual observer, it appeared that the national occupation must have been sitting.

Women occasionally appeared but were always busied with some task. How they maneuvered in their black burqas while carrying loads in the oppressive heat was a great mystery. The locals believed the rumors that our sunglasses were x-ray capable, angering the men as they mentally accused us of lusting at their women. (Even if we possessed such technology, nothing could seem more repulsive to us than to ponder what lay beneath a few of these well-filled black sacks bustling their way along the sidewalks. Perhaps their modest attire was a merciful benefit to all.)

Men, young and old, wore kaffiyehs. A square yard of soft cotton, linen, or silk was folded diagonally and then turned and twisted to suit their various stations of life. The still-thin, young working men twisted it turban-like around the head. Sometimes one corner would be pulled across the nose to filter the dust, revealing only dark brown eyes. Those holding some tribal station in life framed their faces with the cloth in a neat arched fashion, topped with double ropes made of goat hair. If they held some special tribal importance, the ropes might be square instead of round with tassels dangling to further denote magnificence.

From the neck down on most men, a shirt of their favorite pale blue or cream color flowed down to near the ankles. We dubbed them "man dresses." Their feet were shod with flip-flops of varying simplicity, but some of the younger men wore tennis shoes. Some middle-class men wore pants and shirts, and some of the administrative and government types appeared in their best polyester brown or blue suit with a few daring to sport a Western trademark tie vice the open collar.

Kids, nearly all of them beautiful, were adorned in bright red, orange, yellow, and green shirts and pants. Some wore shoes. Many did not, but it seemed more a function of youth rather than lack of availability. They appeared smiling at the portal of every gate, allowing a glimpse to their houses within. Walls of cinder block and mortar, some finished and painted, some not, garrisoned the yards from the streets and public. Scuffed, underinflated soccer balls rested nearby. Standing vigil over the kids between gates and walls were the piercing but almost welcoming eyes of their mothers, tracking us as we passed.

These were the daily scenes of the city and surrounding villages of Tikrit, Iraq, as well as a thousand other cities, towns, and villages. Tikrit was where Saddam Hussein was spawned, its notoriety secured by a man rather than by important geography or natural resources. This made it an interesting place to secure, as many "diehard" old-regime loyalists populated nearly every section of the city. Most of their neighbors were not as committed but played the game with true Arab flair and deception. Many, regardless of loyalty, appeared to welcome our soldiers but their eyes betrayed this. They feared that their neighbors would kill them for desiring to work with us or for living privileged lives under Saddam. Consequently, nearly all wore a façade of hate as we occupied the city and surrounding desert villages.

In the brief span that followed, I also talked to hundreds of my new soldiers. Information was water, and I was a sponge. I scoured the countryside, absorbing the sights and sounds, looking for subtle nuances of trouble or opportunity as I considered how our soldiers would mesh with this city. In a few short days, I would shoulder the responsibility of nearly a thousand troops. I prayed that God would give me wisdom, confidence, protection, and clear thinking.

The phase of war unfolding before us seemed to be an insurgency. I noted in my journal how the signs of danger belied the false sense of calm governing the actions of many commanders in the division. The current discussion was focused entirely on submitting "wartime" awards. The cutoff was May 1, the date President Bush had declared as an end to major conflict. Plans and talk centered on governance, reconstruction, schools, and public works.

Mark Woempner presented a good assessment of his command team. I agreed with most of it. The Command Sergeant Major, Salvador M. "Pete" Martinez, was everything one could ask for in a battalion's top soldier. Pete was not built in the typical form of most modern infantry sergeants major, the type that usually comes with youthful, square-jawed seriousness, a great physique, lots of "scare badges," but not much experience. Pete was older and baldheaded. He sported a thick graying mustache and a thicker Puerto Rican accent. Having encountered nearly every situation that could come his way, he was an outstanding sergeant major, akin to the old regimental sergeants major of World War II. He had already been a brigade and battalion sergeant major. Rather than wait for a brigade when he was reassigned to Ft. Hood, he asked instead to return to the Regulars. Since he had been a platoon sergeant and first sergeant with the 22nd Infantry in previous years, some might view the move from brigade to battalion as a step down. Pete would tell you it was a step up. He preferred life with the troops.

The executive officer, Major Brian Reed, was second to none. Tall, laid-back and with a humorous nature, Brian was simply the best. The operations officer, Major Mike Rauhut, was the same. Although more serious, there was none more thorough or conscientious than Mike. Both were big men, with Brian standing even taller than Mike. Brian had close-cropped dark hair; Mike wished he had hair. Their long-standing relationship traced all the way back to their years at West Point. The friendship and love I would feel for these men after the trials we would face together cannot be described.

Two of the three rifle companies were well led. Ironically, the least competently led company seemed to have the most crucial mission inside the city. It didn't seem to me to be working. Perhaps this was allowed due to the experience of a very good top sergeant and a compensating aggressiveness found in the executive officer. Whatever the case, I believed that something had to change—the company, the leadership, or both.

None of this was so much a reflection on Mark Woempner as a

commander as it was a misinterpretation of the present situation. In May of 2003, no one in the entire command, from generals to soldiers, knew how the Iraqi people would react following the overthrow of Saddam Hussein and the defeat of his army in the field. It was assumed we would simply "transition" to better times. Neither Colonel Jim Hickey, who would soon be my commander, nor I believed the theory of better times.

Colonel Hickey and I sensed danger lurking within the city. Perhaps it was because we were about to assume command of a brigade and a battalion. We discussed the numerous concerns we had. I noted, at the time, the danger of the stability operations or "Balkan" state of mind among some of the Army's leaders. The people of this culture were decidedly different and would need to be handled with an understanding of their penchant for display, bravado, forcefulness, and magnanimity so common to the Arab culture.

Whether it was the mind-set of the time or lack of tactical awareness, the battalion seemed to me to be unprepared for the current set of dangers. The mortars were not being used for in-direct fire support missions, and a more incapable officer to lead them in that crucial task could not have been found. The scouts, while extraordinarily led, were not being used for reconnaissance; their mobility had been siphoned off for dubious escort missions. The battalion snipers no longer existed. They had been dispersed among the companies rather than being used with scouts and out-posts for battalion ambush missions.

The company missions were little better. The soldiers' strength and awareness seemed to wane as they guarded schools, banks, and other important static points. Consequently, there was little move-ment in the battalion and many seemed vulnerable to ambush. Some elements were assigned to guard areas beyond the range of indirect fire protection and that with only spotty radio contact.

There were no 72-hour observation posts; foot patrols were lacking in the town, and many of the hasty outposts that did exist had security gaps.

All the components for trouble were present. The Iraqi army had no formal surrender. Enemy soldiers were not officially processed anywhere. They simply dissolved into a hundred cities, towns, and villages—many with weapons carried from their armories as yet undiscovered. There had been much finger pointing in the press about the mistake of "disbanding" the Iraqi army. That was nonsense. The army disbanded itself.

Most of the Iraqi soldiers defected to get on with their lives. In Tikrit, however, there was a high concentration of Republican Guard, and, as we would later learn, actual Saddam Fedayeen units. These soldiers remained unconvinced and had even been instructed to prepare for the defeat. Saddam had them convinced that, if they struck back as resistance fighters, the Americans would grow weary with the rise of casualties and eventually withdraw. Then he could make a play for restoration to power. Consequently, the Fedayeen and some Republican Guard loyalists were now ready to take to guerilla warfare. They were already being supplied and funded with hidden stashes of weapons and money. This small minority, clinging to the past, began to attack our soldiers. Just before I would assume command, the activity began to escalate.

On May 25, 2003, I turned forty years old. I never imagined myself turning forty in Tikrit, Iraq. Though I no longer feel so today, I somehow felt I had been robbed of something. As the time to take the battalion colors neared, I prayed that the unit would be protected until I could assume command on June 11. Sensing an imminent threat and reading the danger signs in Tikrit as I made my way around, I worried we would be attacked before I could establish a more aggressive footing. My worries, unfortunately, were well-founded. The battalion was about to receive a brutal wake-up call.

In the first week of June, our soldiers would be attacked in a series of small hit-and-run skirmishes with rocket-propelled grenades (RPGs) and automatic weapons fire. The new insurgents were not afraid to engage our troops. One could call them many things, but cowards they were not. Their utter disregard for surrounding civilian life could be called evil, but not cowardly. They demonstrated a willingness to attack us with weapons and technology far inferior to ours.

On June 4, insurgents attacked a section of our Bradleys from Scott Thomas' B Company, attached to the 3rd Battalion, 66th Armor in the oil-refining town of Bayjii ("BAY-gee"). The enemy attempted to hit our men as they entered a residential area, but our infantry evaded the initial strike. As our patrol came around the village, insurgents lurking in the alleys and on rooftops popped out and fired a volley of four RPGs. One of them connected to the rear of B-13, the lead Bradley. The rocket swooshed in a direct line to the ramp door. These doors, while fairly robust, were neither intended nor designed to stop anti-tank rockets.

The rocket's penetrator sliced through the door, threading the narrow gap between the infantry fire team sitting on the bench seats in the back of the vehicle. Miraculously, none of Sergeant Charles Myers' men were hit directly. The warhead smashed some electronic equipment near the turret wall and exploded. The brilliant hot flash was immediately snuffed out by halon from the internal fire extinguishers, sucking the air out of the lungs of the men inside. The soldiers suffered flash burns, broken bones, fragmentation wounds, and asphyxiation but were miraculously spared serious injury. Armored vests and Kevlar helmets saved their lives. All five of them, Charles Myers, Devon Pierce, Hector Lopez, Joel Deguzman, and Timothy Moore eventually recovered. Some returned to duty within a few days of the attack.

The next night, B-34, also one of our B Company Bradleys, hit an anti-tank mine on the front left side of the vehicle. The blast ripped a hole through the driver's compartment and sent the front drive sprocket, a couple of road wheels, and the six-foot-wide armored hull access cover flying.

The driver, Private Joshua Schoellman, endured the shock of the blast. He instantly suffered two broken legs and a broken arm. His body armor and equipment saved him from more serious harm. Despite his injuries, Schoellman did not think of himself. He kept his head and immediately hit the fuel shutoff valve and the switch that dropped the ramp door, allowing his fellow infantrymen to escape out the back. His comrades came to his aid, pulling his broken body from the vehicle.

Schoellman would recover physically over the next several months but would have a much longer mental recovery after this episode. Whatever his struggles when we returned home, his bravery and selfless actions to cut off the fuel and lower the ramp quite possibly saved the lives of his fellow soldiers. The Bradley was out of action permanently. The resulting laceration in the armored hull floor was almost big enough for a man to climb through.

That same night an RPG also hit one of our C Company Bradleys as a section patrolled down 40th Street in Tikrit near the Women's College. The residential area was an upscale neighborhood built for Saddam's favorites. This street was actually called "The Street of the Forty." We would learn all too soon that "The Forty" were part of Saddam's inner circle of Special Security Office (SSO) soldiers who served as his bodyguards and functionaries.

As the Bradley headed past the college, an RPG rocket slammed into the upper hull area. The cone of the warhead hit a case of water bottles, causing it to malfunction. Astonishingly, the charge did not explode, and our soldiers were able to safely remove the fouled rocket from the water bottles. Thankfully, there would be no wounded in this attack.

About the same time this attack unfolded, the crack of mortar rounds impacting in another part of the city alerted everyone. Our men reacted quickly, capturing the mortar with 15 rounds of ammunition. Unfortunately, the enemy crew fled before our soldiers could seize them.

A FIGHTER TO THE END

Situated on the west side of Highway 1 at the northern tip of Tikrit was a group of buildings once used by the Iraqi police. A residential neighborhood adjoined the former Baath Party Headquarters across the street. The Baath Party building lay in a heap of rubble, obliterated in the opening attack on Iraq by the U.S. Air Force. Regrettably, it was unusable. We endeavored to use buildings once occupied by Saddam's government as we aided the establishment of a new government. Our goal was to avoid evicting residents or viable businesses occupying sound structures in the process.

A Civil-Military Information & Coordination (CMIC) office was established in one of the nearby police buildings. This would be a place for local Iraqis to make claims, receive or provide information, or just generally grumble about how bad conditions were. The latter use was most prevalent. The Army had begun to establish these CMIC offices in previous deployments, particularly in the Balkans. Lt. Col. Woempner had been ordered to provide a secure area for such a place to be manned by civil affairs soldiers and others, both from the brigade and our own battalion.

The Military Police battalion, the 720th, would man the police station while our infantry would secure the CMIC. It made sense to reopen the Iraqi police station and locate this new CMIC in close proximity for purposes of government efficiency. But civil efficiency was not always consistent with sound tactical position. Using HESCO Bastions (five-foot-high mesh boxes of fabric and cage wire filled with dirt), our soldiers positioned a perfunctory amount of defensive protection by connecting the existing walls with these sod contraptions. Scavenged wire further reinforced this minimal protection.

For Abdullah Ghalib Mahmood al-Khatab, the American outpost across from the former Baathist headquarters was too much to bear. There was already plenty of planning on how to strike the Americans with guerilla operations, just as Saddam Hussein had instructed. Abdullah was ready to answer that call. He had been in the Fedayeen and his family was intensely loyal to Saddam. He was related to two of the four Aces in the infamous "deck of cards" list used to help expose the most wanted in Saddam's regime. While not on the list himself, Abdullah's father, Ghalib, was married to Saddam's half-sister, Bissan Ibrahim al-Hasan. His brother, Fuaz, had a daughter married to Saddam's Presidential Secretary, Abid Hamid Mahmood al-Khatab. Abid Mahmood was also his cousin. The motivation to strike back was inherent, and the time appeared to be right as the American soldiers seemed to be relaxing.

Organizing a dozen former Republican Guard, Fedayeen, and Special Security Office soldiers, Abdullah was convinced he could inflict damage on the Americans. The best place to start would be with a nighttime strike on the former police station that had a coordination office set up next to it. They could move down the back alleys, hit the Americans from multiple directions and rooftops, and then make good their escape.

On June 6, 2003, Abdullah and friends launched a volley of RPGs into the CMIC's walled compound, rupturing the stale night air. Soldiers scrambled for cover as hostile small arms fire peppered the bastions, pocked the buildings, and chipped the pavement.

Fragmentation sliced into Staff Sergeant Darrell Patton's shoulder and Staff Sergeant Larry Taylor's leg. It also perforated the support company Humvee (High Mobility Multi-purpose Wheeled Vehicle) at the entrance. Sergeant Matt Lesau from C Company had wounds in the face and leg. Specialist Juan Cabral was also wounded.

The men continued to fight the dozen insurgents situated on the rooftops of homes across the main highway. At the police station, Military Policeman Jesse Halling spotted some of the assailants and opened fire with a .50 cal machine gun atop his Humvee. Private Halling walked the rounds along the rooftops, fracturing stucco and sending concrete sailing in all directions. His suppressive fire allowed the men at the other building to reach cover, organize, and energize Sergeant Jason Tatro in the turret of a headquarters Bradley.

Scurrying along the erupting rooftops, an insurgent buddy team fell back and then established a better position with an RPG grenade launcher. As Jesse Halling blazed away at the enemy directly opposite the soldiers at the CMIC, a rocket swooshed from a rooftop across the street and landed squarely in the MP Humvee. The deafening explosion hurled flame and debris across the small courtyard. The .50 cal machine gun immediately fell silent.

A struggling Private Halling collapsed in the truck amid scores of empty shell casings and steel links from an entire can of machine gun ammo he had fired before slipping into unconsciousness from loss of blood. His efforts allowed Jason Tatro to follow with machine gun and 25 mm cannon fire along the rooftops. This effectively decided the contest. All firing ceased at that point.

At battalion headquarters, the radio crackled with frantic calls. The battalion radio operators flipped to C Company's net to get a reading on the situation. Reports of wounded accompanied the distant sounds of the firefight. Major Mike Rauhut and Captain Matt Weber in the battalion headquarters ordered relief from C

Company and dispatched a battalion evacuation team for the wounded. The aid station began to fill with the realities of combat. Most of the soldiers brought to the aid station suffered from fragmentation wounds. Our field surgeon, reserve Captain Phil Billoni, managed to stabilize the badly mauled Halling. Despite Captain Billoni's efforts, nineteen-year-old Private Jesse Halling of Indianapolis, Indiana, died that night, a fighter to the end.

When reinforcements arrived at the CMIC, the enemy had vanished. Combing the alleys, dwellings, and rooftops produced two RPG launchers that had been ditched as the enemy fled the Bradley's fire. There were also blood trails. Four of the enemy were eventually captured; four others were wounded. Other enemy losses remain unknown.

This bloody encounter sent shock waves through the battalion. The slow reaction that night caused me no small concern. It is precarious to second-guess another's situation, but my own belief was now firmly cemented that this had been building up over the last week. The battalion had not been vigilant to this kind of activity, though the signs had been present. Small insurgent attacks had harassed our troops for several days without response on our part. There had been no increased patrols, no ground-walking infantry. During the fight, reaction had been somewhat better. It appeared that the troops had a clear assessment of the situation, and while a decent plan was formulated in the hours after the engagement, it was, in my view, far too slow.

As I assimilated the events of both this day and the previous week, it was clear that we had an insurgency on our hands. The CMIC attack was proof enough for me. It was a well-organized ambush using an effective combination of small arms in mutual support. My view was that we were now in the thick of it, despite questions in Iraq and denials at home. In a single week, in our battalion alone, we lost two Bradleys and had two others attacked with RPGs. We survived several mortar attacks without injury, but ten soldiers were wounded, and one was killed in action as a result of enemy ambushes. The enemy clearly had the initiative in our city. If major hostilities were now over, someone failed to tell Saddam's loyalists in the city of Tikrit.

The posture of the battalion had to change. We desperately needed scout observation posts coupled with snipers and infantry foot patrols. We currently had none. Our soldiers needed to be on a reverse operations cycle, with activity at night and rest during the heat of the day. Our troop layout in the city, while fairly decent, demanded reinforcement in the north. We needed to develop civilian ties in every sector and match them with existing police and government infrastructure. Absent that, we would need to cultivate our own informants.

It was agonizing to observe from the sidelines for the four days before I assumed command. I prayed for Mark Woempner and felt terrible for him as he ended his service with the Regulars on such a note as this. He had trained these men with skill, deployed them at the head of the division, and led the battalion capably in the fight against the Iraqi Army in late April. He had captured Adil Abdullah Mahdi al-Duri, who was on the Iraqi most wanted list and number 52 in the "deck of cards." Mark also had developed some precursory relationships with local Iraqis that later proved invaluable as we pursued those harboring Saddam. I hated to see him leave second-guessing himself. The transition from a full-scale fight to a fight with insurgents shrouded among the civilian population was something few could see at the time.

KEEPING TIKRIT BEAUTIFUL

Lt. Col. Mark Woempner responded quickly from this point. In essence, he locked down the city. While a curfew had already been in place, it would now be strictly enforced. Any movement at night would be regarded as enemy movement. Hopefully, this would convince the locals to stay off the streets. Mark and I discussed what action to take with violators. I suggested a penalty that we had used successfully in Kosovo. Those caught out after the curfew would be involuntary "volunteers" for community trash detail. The next morning he did just that. Scores of Iraqi men, both young and old, were pressed into service in full public view to pick up the greasy garbage matted to curbs. This attempt to help beautify Tikrit was optimistic at best.

The effect was immediate. The locals had no desire for such work, and the streets were eerily empty during subsequent nights. For the next few days, Mark focused his efforts on departure as I focused mine on the tasks at hand. Colonel James Hickey, the officer due to replace Colonel Campbell as the 1st Brigade Commander, and I met several times to discuss our assessment of the situation. He made some key points about standards and aggressiveness toward the enemy that were music to my ears.

Major General Ray Odierno, our division commander, also gave us some guidance. He, too, was concerned about what he sensed was a rising insurgency. He impressed upon us that fighting this type of enemy would have to be a decentralized fight. We must take risks and trust our junior leaders. We should underwrite risks of our leaders when they executed a plan. We should not be afraid to operate freely within the general's guidance. He ordered us not to label captives as Enemy Prisoners of War (EPWs) as we had done earlier when fighting the Iraqi ground forces. They would now be labeled terrorists, and their acts against our soldiers or the new Iraqi government would be recorded as acts of terror.

Having leaders like Colonel Hickey and Major General Odierno gave me confidence to aggressively propel the battalion forward and move quickly with what I knew would be necessary to defeat the enemy in our area. We needed to take an offensive stance. No recent action had taken the fight to the enemy. We had little to show for the efforts of the past week other than being scuffed up pretty badly.

TO THE COLORS

The air was filled with dusty heat and the foul smells associated with a dirty city. As I awoke and pulled on my faded desert uniform, I was fully aware of the responsibility I would wear by the end of the day. Nearly a thousand soldiers, including our attachments, would benefit or suffer directly from my decisions as we dealt with an immoral, elusive enemy bent on using the civilian population as a shield. People back home thought that our mission was coming to a conclusion. Even some soldiers believed it.

Those who entertained fantasies about our mission could not see the reality that I saw. We were fighting a homegrown variety of criminal insurgent that operated in direct violation of everything decent and moral among civilized societies. No scheme to regain lost power was beneath them. The insurgents used any expedient reasoning, whether newfound "religious" fervor, conveniently acquired zeal for nationalism, or a longing for the nostalgic "bad old days" of power. The Baathists under Saddam's sway had never surrendered. They merely disappeared. Now they materialized from the shadows and lurked among the innocent, hoping to strike a blow to us while shielding themselves from our response.

This had to end. How long it would take to thwart them was directly proportionate to the amount of nonsense that we would tolerate. I believed the most humane resolution for the Iraqi people, our own nation, and my soldiers would be to ruthlessly pursue the enemy. The old proverb about "removing the scoffer and contention ceasing" could not have been more true. The enemy had to be annihilated. I could do that with a clear conscience, though some Americans could never reconcile that concept. Fine. They were not in Iraq. We were, and all we wanted was support for the effort to which they had committed us. I prayed that morning for God's wisdom to be the leader that these soldiers and our nation needed and expected me to be.

After oiling my weapons and readying my kit, I joined Mark Woempner for the ride to Saddam's Birthday Palace. Our C Company and support company had occupied this infamous half stadium, half palace complex where Saddam once reviewed the Iraqi military on special occasions such as his birthday. No longer. Today, our soldiers would be on review.

The sergeant major assembled skeleton units to represent full-strength companies currently on point around the city. High palace walls framed the formation that centered on the bright and inspiring banners gently blowing in the intermittent breeze. A confident soldier with set jaw and proud heart gripped a pole made of ash on which was mounted our nation's colors. Some idiot in high command whose boots likely never walked on sand had deemed it unfitting to fly the American flag in Iraq at our outposts and troop concentrations. We were told it might offend Iraqis or cause them to think that we were occupying Iraq. It was little wonder that I got a bit choked up as our occupying soldiers held the Stars and Stripes high now.

Adjacent to the national flag, the weighty dark blue colors of the 22nd Infantry Regiment stood fringed in gold, adorned with an American bald eagle holding a scroll in its beak embroidered with the motto "Deeds, Not Words." Scores of brightly colored streamers dangled from atop the pole. Bold names somberly declared the reason they hung there: Chippewa, Pine Ridge, Santiago, Normandy, Huertgen Forest, Kontum, Suoi Tre, Tet, Somalia. Now these same colors unfurled on another battlefield—this one.

I wondered what would hang on these colors from our efforts. Would we achieve the same high standards as those who earned these streamers? I prayed we would.

Colonel Don Campbell, 1st Brigade Commander for yet a few more days, proudly marched our small command element to the colors. Major General Ray Odierno surveyed this minute component of his vast 4th Infantry Division with a look as reassuring as his commanding presence. I was not nervous. I felt ready, as though my whole life had been preparation for this moment. The moment would begin now. In the short span of an hour, we would resume our current operations. We were, after all, at war, and there was a war to be won.

With short recitations of orders, the battalion colors marched forward. Command Sergeant Major Pete Martinez forcefully snatched them from the soldier, as is the custom. Every soldier knows he must not waiver when the Sergeant Major grasps the colors. Martinez faced about and presented them to Lt. Col. Woempner. "It's been a pleasure, sir," Pete intoned in heavily accented English.

Mark's last act of command was to hand them to Colonel Campbell who praised him for his successful command. Campbell then entrusted the colors to me with this charge and encouragement: "A lot of people expect great things from you, Steve. I wish you every success."

So I took the colors under which tens of thousands of men have served in its rich history. Over three thousand American soldiers had died under these colors. I was determined that no dishonor would ever befall this banner. Not on my watch. Following a short march past the reviewing officers, the formation returned to war.

HIGH POWER

His face was framed with an intelligent brow, short, thick black hair, and a neat mustache. There was a trustworthy look in his eyes and facial expressions. He spoke with sincerity and gentle force.

"We face many difficulties," declared Major General Taha Achmed Mezher al-Ganaim, the Salah ad Din Provincial Chief of Police. "I have few vehicles. Much has been pilfered. We have to rebuild everything. Everything. I have few weapons. My police, some of them patrol with no weapon at all. You must help us."

I reserved judgment, knowing that there were always two sides to every sad story. He did indeed have challenges, but weapons were not typically in short supply in Iraq. Yet, I sensed he was being truthful. His appraisal actually was possible in that we had already intercepted many caches of weapons from raided armories. I knew I would have to earn Mezher's trust if this liaison was to be successful. In the spirit of T. E. Lawrence, I was prepared for the moment. Lawrence knew the importance of playing to the Arab sense of honor and penchant for display without belittling the essence of the people. Still, I never imagined the opportunity about to avail itself as two kindred spirits pondered the impossible security challenges facing my troops and his police in the city of Tikrit.

"I don't even have a weapon," he insisted with a shrug of his shoulders and open palms extended for emphasis. "I gave it to one of my men," he said with overemphasized resignation.

Looking to the ground and holding up my hand in an exaggerated gesture to stop, I interrupted, "Wait, you have no weapon?"

"Yes, it is true." He nodded, placing his right hand over his heart.

"I can fix this now. Please, take my pistol," I commanded as I unholstered a Beretta 9mm handgun, offering it to him, butt first.

With a shocked and puzzled look he insisted, "No, I cannot take your own pistol. What will you have to defend yourself?"

"I have my rifle," I answered, patting my M-4 carbine. "Besides, I have an entire battalion of soldiers. I can get another pistol, but we cannot get another Chief of Police."

General Mezher paused. Our eyes locked. I could detect a slight moistening in his as he realized that I was totally serious. "Please, General, we have a long road ahead together, and you must be protected. I will try to work on the other issues as well."

"Thank you, Colonel Rasool," he articulated in his best English. With a sincere nod he added another: "Thank you."

Thus began my long association and friendship with General Mezher. He didn't know the pistol I gave him had been captured from a Baathist big shot. It was identical in appearance to our own service pistols. I had grabbed it that morning for the change of command ceremony as Mark was still assigned the one that would become mine upon his departure. I had not foreseen giving my pistol to General Mezher that morning, but it was a most fortuitous opportunity. (It also protected some good soldier from the temptation of sneaking home a pistol identical to ours, thereby escaping scrutiny upon redeployment—whenever that might be.)

If there were only half a dozen decent, honest men in Iraq, Mezher was surely one of them. I would meet others, but my first day in command was rewarded with a bond to the provincial police chief that would have incalculable impact on future operations.

By the time the meeting with General Mezher was over, sweltering heat that can only be simulated by sticking your head in an oven had engulfed the area. I patrolled our area and checked the various companies, static points, food warehouses, and key public works in the city. Eventually, we made our way to the cluster of government buildings housing the Salah ad Din Provincial government.

While the security outside was unimpressive, the small personal bodyguard of Governor Hussein al-Jabouri was intimidating. Several fit and intelligent young men armed with MP-5 submachine guns looked more than capable. We had soldiers in the area, and the brigade had a liaison of soldiers on site as well should there be trouble.

Hussein al-Jabouri was an odd combination of former general, smiling politician, and tough soldier. Unlike his contemporaries, he made no attempt to blacken his thick silvering hair, but the obligatory Arab mustache was darkened so drastically that it lent a Groucho Marx-like appearance to his face. His smile was stretched but sincere.

Translating through his doctor, Ali, we carried on a remarkable conversation that drew me to the governor in short order. He hated Baathists. His tribe, the Jabouris, had a long-standing grudge with the Nasiris who were the tribesmen of Saddam and most of his henchmen. The Governor warned of certain locals trying to impersonate government officials and gave us a list of names to monitor. He linked a few of them with other names to flesh out more detail.

Soon a tray of shot glasses appeared. They were filled with two-thirds hot tea and one-third sugar. After engaging in this custom, we were offered what appeared to be canned Pepsi with Arabic lettering. An average-sized man, with many scars and eyes that bored right through a person, entered the room and joined the conversation. Colonel Mohammed Jassim Hussein was introduced as the governor's head of security. He offered his services, of course, as a matter of protocol. Only later would we realize what those services could deliver. After some business, he asked for a pistol for himself and his assistant. Not to be excluded, the Governor, of course, needed one as well. "High Power," he specified, referring to the superb Belgian 9mm Browning handgun.

My, how quickly word travels! At least they were not asking for U.S. service 9mm Berettas. Still, loyalty through firearms was a prospect we could probably maintain. They wanted legitimacy. We wanted loyalty and cooperation. A stockpile of captured handguns might put us on the same page.

Making my way back to headquarters, I checked with the ops center for the pulse of things. Their read was similar to my own observation on the ground. I passed on the Governor's list of names to Tim Morrow, my intelligence officer, and then prepared to attend a dinner hosted by Governor Hussein al-Jabouri in honor of Colonel Don Campbell, our brigade commander. The location of the banquet was an isolated farm in an area known as Allum.

That evening, the cooler air gave respite from the oppressive heat of the day. Our open-topped hummers magnified the breeze even further. One of my first acts of command was to strip our vehicles like a chicken bone—no canvas, no doors, no encumbrances. If called to fight, split seconds mattered. These changes allowed us to see in all directions and allowed us to provide cover with our rifles as we traveled.

My eyes were on heightened alert as we followed the narrow dirt tracks leading to the Governor's farm. If we were ambushed here, there would be no room for a maneuver of any kind. Thick green brush and tall monkey grass lined much of the path, gapped only by farm entrances. It was noticeably cooler here in the bottomland near the Tigris River. Ahead, guards and a few familiar faces from earlier in the day greeted us. We steered our vehicles into the Governor's fields and made our way to the first of many feasts we would dub "lamb grabs."

Transitioning from combat patrol to dinner party, we crossed a plush, green lawn that was garrisoned by the ubiquitous, white plastic chairs. Always, the white plastic chairs. I became convinced there were more of them in Iraq than there were Iraqis.

They doglegged from a large communal table, completing the arrangement. Lamb, fowl, fish, various vegetables, nuts, and fruits crowded the table. Bare hands reached into bowls and deposited generous portions onto plates. Noticeably absent was the fine instrument known to us as the fork.

After a satisfying "finger-licking" meal, the Governor made a presentation to Colonel Campbell. A barely translucent black robe trimmed in gold embroidery was set on the colonel's shoulders, and a red and white checkered headdress with goat hair ropes capped the presentation. Several of us were ceremoniously awarded a similar headdress. Instruction on application of the headgear followed, with smiles and laughter all around.

Before the evening was over, Brigadier General Abdullah Hussein Mohammed, former tank commander in the Iraqi Army, engaged me in conversation. He immediately struck me as intelligent, refined and altogether decent. His English was impeccable. As we discussed our backgrounds, I learned that he was a graduate of the Indian War College and had also been educated in Europe. His children were of similar age to mine. He was slightly older, about the same age as my brother. I discovered that he was fluent in German and our conversation drifted naturally to that language that I learned as an exchange student to Germany in high school. In time, this quite remarkable man would help us immensely and would become a close personal friend.

One had only to meet such individuals as Mezher and Abdullah to recognize the undeniable hope for Iraq's future. Men of influence, education, and intelligence with a genuine concern for the future of their families and country abounded. Our task was to ensure this hope prevailed through the nurture and encouragement of these honorable men. It would not be easy.

3. TIPS

WE HAVE SOME INFORMATION

"Mister, I must see Colonel Rasool," he said with a friendly face. His brother stood nearby, nodding and smiling.

"What is your business?" asked one of my soldiers at the CMIC.

"I heard the Colonel is here; we have some very important information."

So it was always "Mister, I must see . . ." or "Mister, I need . . ." or some such demand or query. The CMIC, despite its battered façade from the firefight a week before, appeared to be serving its purpose. Nevertheless, many Iraqis were fearful of initiating an encounter with the Americans, terrified of being branded as collaborators. Some countered this with the assertion of Arab tradition for "baksheesh," the cultural habit to demand favor and get it from those who have it.

I had already determined to not spend much time there, other than to check on security. Unlike Mark, I felt that we must secure the city before worrying about local relations. I believed the real key to local security was contending with emerging government, civic, and tribal leaders rather than broken window complaints, but I also recognized that the CMIC was needed as a place for Iraqis to redress grievances. I would grow to hate it and call for its abandonment in time, but for the present it served a purpose.

"Sir, sorry to interrupt but there are two guys out here demanding to see you," informed the sergeant, drenched in sweat.

"Yeah, I bet. Them and everyone else," I answered begrudgingly, also miserable in a sweat-soaked uniform.

"Sir, I think they are serious. They don't look like the others we've had here today," speculated the sergeant. "When I told them to pass the information to me so I could get it to you, they refused. They said they would leave first."

"All right," I surrendered. "Bring them in after they've been searched."

I was naively oblivious to the significance of this moment. Afterward, I felt completely stupid for nearly missing something so major it could have changed the course of history.

"Colonel Rasool," they smiled with extended hands. "We have heard so much about you. My name is Ahmed, and this is my brother Nahed."

"It is a pleasure to meet you." I smiled and shook their hands. "How can I help you?"

"Please, Mister, can we go someplace private? We have some information."

I had seen it all before, but these two intrigued me. There was something about the look in their eyes—a warmth, an honesty. It was hard to describe. "Yes, please, of course. Come this way."

We sat on battered furniture scavenged from buildings in various degrees of ruin. I called for drinks, mindful of the Arab tradition of hospitality. After learning more about them, I was curious about what they would tell me. The brothers were businessmen with a penchant for survival. They lived in Al Auja, Saddam's birth village. They were once landowners and men of influence, but

Saddam had killed their father and seized their land for the village as it now existed with its well-appointed houses for Saddam's closest cronies.

"They leave us alone now," explained Ahmed. "We stay by the river. We have a business in Jordan also, so we travel and are able to get by."

Nahed seemed to understand English but was much less confident in speaking it. Without a translator, I had to rely on the rudimentary English skills of the Iraqis who visited the CMIC and hope for the best. In a couple of days I would make a plea to Major General Odierno to obtain a translator for my task force. Being the kind of soldier and commander he was, he gave me his personal one.

Joe Filmore was an American born in Iraq whose father was on the Iraqi Supreme Court in 1968. His family fled when the Baathists came to power, and Joe would later serve in the U.S. Navy. He volunteered his language skills when we geared up for Iraq and was assigned to General Odierno. He would be a translator of the first rank but as of yet, I did not have him. Fortunately, Ahmed's English was excellent.

"You need to understand something," Ahmed whispered as he scanned the room and closed the door. "Saddam is still in the area. He is being protected. They travel in cars with dark windows. You need to stop all of those cars."

"What do you mean?" I inquired. "Who is protecting him?"

"There are many," he answered.

Great. Here we go—more Arab histrionics about having information and elaborate tales that will send us on yet another wild-goose chase.

"There are certain families," he declared flatly.

I was not expecting this. For the next hour and a half, the brothers explained Saddam's pre-war security apparatus. The network revolved around five controlling families who had known Saddam since his youth, roughly since the 1950s. They had inter-married and were trusted.

"The first group is called Saddam's Special Bodyguard," Ahmed explained about the group composed of Saddam's most trusted bodyguards. "There are twenty to twenty-five of them, and they are with him everywhere and every day. The bodyguards live here in white houses. We have seen them now back in Tikrit. That is how we know he is here."

The next group was called "The Forty." Only later did I learn that this group lived in a south-central section of Tikrit that we mistakenly called 40th Street. It was really called the "Street of the Forty," which explained why we had so much trouble there. These were a second layer of bodyguards who served as Saddam's func-tionaries, attending to his every need. They drove, cooked, gar-dened, machined, or attended while still being very much a group of bodyguards. They were completely trusted by Saddam.

The third layer was composed of groups known as "Saddam's Special Soldiers Units."

"They have maybe a thousand in each group," estimated Ahmed. "They go on the routes where Saddam travels and look for trouble. He may send several of the groups on different routes and then take only one."

The meeting wrapped up with an exchange of contact informa-tion and the assurance that I would not expose them to undue danger. I realized, if this information were true, they had risked much in coming there.

As they left, I remember thinking this was either the most elaborate lie ever fabricated or that it must be completely true. Shortly, we would become thoroughly familiar with these families as names like Musslit, Hadooshi, Hasan, Heremos, Khatab, and Majid began to emerge. As we commingled this information with the intelligence collected to date, information previously lacking coherency started to make sense.

Our missions to date had been largely dictated by what was called the "Black List." They were the names of the infamous fifty-two detailed on the "deck of cards," that brilliant piece of public relations work whereby Saddam's government officials and most wanted enemies were grouped together and pictured on decks of playing cards to aid in their capture. Additionally, the "Black List" had the names of those corps or divisional targets that various intelligence sections deemed important.

This was something entirely different. As I pondered the details the brothers had imparted, I began to speculate on the scope of our task by asking myself a series of simple questions I had learned to do in wars and training past: What did the enemy look like? How could he hurt us? How could we hurt him?

We knew that there were street fighters launching attacks on our soldiers. Someone had to be organizing them. I decided to reduce the possibilities in simple terms to communicate a strategy for our soldiers. I called it the "Three Tiers." The first tier was the "Deck of Cards" guys. These were Saddam and his henchmen. The third tier I called the "Trigger Pullers," those we were scrapping with on the streets. But who was in the middle? The brothers had not only given us the immediate answer but also so much more. This second tier I called the "Bodyguards." They were the conduit between Saddam, his personal protection, and the foot soldiers he would inspire.

If we could somehow identify and locate this second tier, then in theory, we could disrupt those organizing the attacks and perhaps find trails leading to the big guys. The problem was unearthing a way to expose their identity. With the brothers' information and the intelligence already possessed, we had enough to get started.

THE ENEMY IS STILL HERE

He came with a reputation for many things, and I had heard all the horror stories. I first met Colonel James B. Hickey, our new brigade commander, just before we deployed. He hailed from Naperville, Illinois, and was a graduate of the Virginia Military Institute. He had been wildly successful as a commander of companies and a cavalry squadron, and he had earned early promotion three times. Sitting at a small table surrounded with peanut shells, loud music and conversation, he asked probing questions to ascertain key background information, and I answered him assertively over a thick steak at the Texas Roadhouse in Killeen, Texas.

I left our meeting with the confidence that we were going to be commanded by a warrior. My evaluation was shaped long before we would work together. Therefore, I did not have the same shadow of foreboding I sensed in others. Perhaps it was because we were both in new assignments and were observing the same things concerning our commands and the enemy. We sat now at a different table, an elaborate furnishing with inlaid mosaics of exotic wood elegantly posed on the marble floor in one of Saddam's palaces in southern Tikrit.

"The enemy is still here. We are still at war," Hickey pronounced with tilted head, furrowed brow, and eyes blinking only occasionally for emphasis.

For an hour or more, Colonel Hickey outlined the strategy he would follow. I liked it. It may have been delivered with forcefulness that those of us serving under his command did not yet understand, but it made sense.

"They are waiting to attack our supply columns, combat command posts, and compounds," he prophesied. "We cannot allow them sanctuary among the population."

For Colonel Hickey, our mission was simple. It was to win the war. Thank God! While his mannerisms and management style were very much different from my own and often the butt of jokes, his beliefs were square on. I would grow to respect him, and in time, would do anything for him.

"The mission will come first," he continued in measured, articulate sentences with a bit of a cadence to them. "We must close in on the enemy and kill him. Reconnaissance will drive every action and will be the means by which to find him. We must stay alert and vigilant. Pass intelligence on to this command, to each other, and to your subordinate units, and keep it updated daily. When you make contact, you will send a contact report immediately. As you develop the situation, I expect a spot report. Later, I want a more detailed situation report. You must know this is how my mind works. It will never change.

"You command your units. I expect you to equip, man, train, and support your soldiers. Don't screw up the soldiers. We are the moral arbiters of our soldiers—tone and climate matter. Remain vigilant in this.

"You will use the chain of command. Staff communication will deal with staff channels. Command information will flow between commanders. Keep your subordinates informed. Pass intelligence on to them. Allow them freedom of action. It is okay to be decentralized and to move along multiple axes. I will judge a young officer by his initiative. It will be the big discriminator, especially for our captains.

"We are here for the long haul. We all wear stripes. Some wear the zebra stripes and some the tiger stripes. Be the tiger. Don't let your soldiers be culled from the herd. Excellence and endurance will be the key. I will be out and about, not to micromanage but to gain awareness. I expect you to be tough on the men. Be tougher on the enemy."

With that, Colonel Hickey gave some instructions for an

upcoming raid. Our brigade's name was the "Raider Brigade." The name was about to take on an entirely new meaning. Colonel Hickey wanted to stir things up a bit with a show of force on June 15. My troops were already on the move in many areas. The last several days had netted machine guns, mortars, ammunition, and more than a dozen Iraqis. Some would be released; some would be retained. I could not help but feel that we were netting some dolphins with the sharks, but as the enemy chose to hide among the populace, it was unavoidable.

Some reasoned that our approach with civilians was uncivilized. It was not. People forget the laws of land warfare are designed to protect community and property from undue destruction. When the enemy refuses to observe the laws of warfare, it is they who are responsible for the human suffering inflicted. They, after all, are the ones using the innocent as a shield. It's not possible, though, to convince the bleeding hearts back home, living in safety and comfort as they "armchair quarterback" our methods of separating the insurgent from the innocent population.

In a city occupied during war, the people are the terrain. Buildings and land are less important than the citizenry. If the people are won in the type of warfare we were now fighting, then the war gets won. But blowhards in 5th Avenue suits and pantsuits will point political fingers at soldiers, castigating us for "aggravating" and "abusing" the population. Few of them have ever had to contend with easing the pain and suffering of innocents, fighting bad guys, maintaining the delicate structure of public works, and providing for the welfare of hundreds of thousands of people. These political pontiffs fail to recognize that sometimes, the most humane approach to ending suffering in a war is to administer a swift and fatal blow to the enemy in the most expedient manner possible.

My biggest challenge was providing the manpower needed to

defeat our enemies and protect the people. As debates raged back home regarding the sufficient number of troops, I covered a massive area and was responsible for the city of Tikrit and several of its surrounding villages. We accomplished this with just two companies of Bradleys, one company of Abrams tanks, some engineers, and a mere eleven rifle squads. Perhaps our ranks should have been filled with some of those politicians or Rumsfeld staffers who were convinced that we had adequate troops. No matter. A good soldier marches with the resources available to him.

The big raid planned for June 15 had a silver lining. It had the potential of ferreting out some key objectives. The enemy was indeed still here. The night raid was to be a merger of my A Company troops under Captain Mark Stouffer in Auja and our Scout Platoon led by First Lieutenant Chris Morris. They would be attached to "Jack."

YOU DON'T KNOW JACK

We first met "Jack" after his men replaced a similar Special Operations Forces (SOF) team conducting the early entry operations. I met him when he and Matt, his operations man, came into my command post to observe our intelligence. Mostly, he came to introduce himself. The juxtaposition of my wiry frame next to his massive one was almost comical. I extended a hand in welcome, and it was nearly swallowed by his. While he was only slightly taller than I, his shoulder width rivaled my height. His assured and confident demeanor was anything but arrogant. It was genuine confidence. He conversed in a respectful tone and demonstrated his willingness to collaborate with us.

The SOF guys were, without argument, the best. It wasn't about the mystery behind them. Some of us had known some of them from earlier days. I had served in the same battalion with one of Jack's team members in Alaska in the 1980s. They were the best because they were the most fit, most dedicated, best-trained and best-supplied operators on the planet. They could do things that we could only dream about. These teams were commanded by majors, but rank was never part of the equation. Full names were almost never known to those outside the community unless you had previously served with one of them. Ranks were never used and were not necessary. Every man in the team had a job and was an expert in it.

"My battalion is yours," I offered. "Anything you need will be available to you. We're all on the same team. I understand your mission will be different from ours and focused on specific targets in a broader area. But any time you are here, whatever we have will always be welcome and available to you."

I had worked closely with Special Forces in Kosovo, Kuwait, and Afghanistan but had never worked directly with the SOF guys. Jack could sense that I was "friendly forces" to his team. It was the beginning of a friendship with his guys and a battle-bond few will understand. We discussed the latest news coming from our Iraqi informants plus my own assessment of the situation.

"I think we're fighting individuals organized in a layered structure," I speculated, taking a dry-erase marker to a whiteboard. "I call it the 'Three Tiers.' The top tier is the 'Deck of Cards' guys: Saddam, his associates, and maybe the 'Black List' guys. The middle tier is the 'Bodyguard' group."

This was the structure I had formulated in my mind after my soirée with the two brothers several days before. There had to be a way to visualize the enemy so we could gain access to him.

"This group is probably funded and inspired by the top tier, and a portion of them may even protect the top tier," I continued. "I call the third group the 'Trigger Pullers.' These are the guys we are fighting on the streets and in ambushes. I believe that they are inspired and funded by the middle tier, perhaps even led by some of them."

As we discussed the "Three Tiers," Jack interjected some thoughts of his own. We discussed the possible links and family relationships, though things at this stage were not nearly as clear as they would be in the very near future.

"I need your Scout Platoon," requested Jack. "We have a raid in Auja, and I would like them to help us hit a target we cannot cover alone."

As we looked at the area, it was obvious that this raid was focused on a big guy. When Jack identified the target, it was a big guy indeed.

"That shouldn't be a problem," I assured him. "I plan to cover the ops of tomorrow night's raid with A Company. They can handle the security cordon, and you guys can hit the inner cordon as needed. Just let us know what areas you need us to cover."

As Jack and I looked over the satellite imagery maps with Mike Rauhut and Brian Reed, my two majors, we pondered the two-square-mile village that had spawned Saddam Hussein. Its houses were well appointed, its occupants accustomed to luxury. Sitting on a western bank bluff on the Tigris River several kilometers south of Tikrit, Auja was in every way connected to Tikrit, except in privilege. According to Mahmood Neda al Nasiri, chief of the Nasir tribe, the area was simple farmland with a scattering of shacks when Saddam was born in the village. After Saddam's rise to power, it became the fashionable village of the privileged elite.

The plan was very straightforward. The SOF team would hit two houses on the east end of town believed to contain none other than Abid Hamid Mahmood al-Khatab, Saddam's Presidential Secretary, known as the Ace of Diamonds on the deck of cards. Chris Morris' Scout Platoon would augment them. Mark Stouffer's A Company would provide cordon, and more of my battalion assets would be brought to bear as needed: mortars, reserves, and aviation assets pushed down to me from Colonel Hickey. It would be the first of many raids with Jack's SOF team and the first of many raids in Auja. We would come to know them all very well.

DOLPHINS AND SHARKS

As Mark Stouffer's A Company soldiers already occupied the sports complex in the village of Auja, it would not be very difficult to gain the element of surprise. It would take just minutes to clamp down on the village. As we formulated plans, my majors readied the assets for the raid while we conducted combat operations throughout the city.

I felt no real anxiety over the raid. We had great soldiers and great equipment and we would be working alongside the finest soldiers in the Special Operations community. I felt excitement at finally being able to strike the enemy. For weeks, he had hit our battalion on his terms. Tonight would be on ours. From this point on, I determined we would never look back.

Dusk, there's something about dusk. The air begins to show mercy, the heat begins to subside, and the smells begin to retreat. The Cummins engines of the Hummers pattered. The diesel fumes mixed with the scent of oil on our weapons, the tang of canvas seats, and the stench of dust and body odor. Sweat continued to roll down every channel not matted with clothing. We rolled.

I adjusted the FBCB2 on the vehicle. This was a device that displayed every leader vehicle in my command and within our division. It worked most of the time and provided us with enough awareness of each other to be practical for speed of action and for "balling up" on a fight when contact was made. We were the only division to employ this new technology allowing us to "see" one another over great distances on a computer screen. Looking like an oversized fish finder, it had a bright display that had to be toned down so we didn't light up like a Christmas tree. Round "bubble-like" icons represented vehicles with varying symbols for the type of unit. I could see Mark's Bradleys. They were coiled and ready to spring.

We were a peculiar assortment of wheeled vehicles. I had a couple of our stripped command Humvees. Chris' scout Hummers were hardtoppers with machine guns and grenade launchers mounted on top, but they were the unarmored type. All of our Hummers were unarmored at this stage of the war. Jack's Hummers were different from ours. They looked like what we would do to ours if we had the resources with many extras not for publication.

Each group traveled on its own route with its own timing. The wind raced through our clothing, evaporating traces of sweat. Our eye protection had been adjusted with clear lenses for night. It protected our eyes from the wind but gave us a bug-eyed appearance. We scanned every rooftop, balcony, dark alley, and open lane as we raced through the city of Tikrit toward the objective. Rifles bristled from various corners of each vehicle as soldiers' helmets swiveled with the Cyclops eye of PVS-14b night vision goggles. The bubbles in the fish finder showed a converging of forces. I could see Colonel Hickey's command element closing in as well. Mark Stouffer's "Gators" of A Company had already grabbed the four corners of the town.

With the anticipation of a roller coaster that has come to the top of its climb and reached the tipping point, we swooped into town. Whatever happened at this point was simply going to happen. All the plans were committed. Only training, reflex, and action mattered now. As commanders, we could only anticipate and adjust. One could never hesitate.

The feel of pavement under my boots was much different from the shimmying of a speeding Hummer. I felt comfortable now. Though my radios would be limited on the ground, I knew I could call Mike Rauhut, who was standing nearby. He could relay any message I needed.

The flash-crack of explosions ripped through the heavy night air. Jack's guys were hitting the residence of Abid Hamid Mahmood al-Khatab, Saddam's Presidential Secretary. He was a significant objective, holding a position similar to our White House Chief of Staff. In fact, because of his importance, he was listed as the "Ace of Diamonds" on the deck of cards, number four behind Saddam and his two sons. Brief messages passed on the radio in response to the flash-bang grenades tossed by Jack's men. We watched the corners and the streets. My scouts under Chris Morris hit the second target simultaneously. It was going well. Flames began to lick out from the corners of Mahmood's house. Now all was silent.

Jack's men and my scouts came out with a couple of captives each. After a while, I relayed to Mark that the teams and targets were secure and ordered him to continue the cordon. Colonel Hickey and I conferred on the ground. Jack informed me matter-of-factly that Mahmood was not home but may be in the neighborhood. Since the cordon was in place, it made good sense to clear the area. If Mahmood tried to flee, he would likely be in the immediate area as nothing had moved since our arrival into town.

Colonel Hickey ordered more air support for me to replace that already fluttering overhead. The sophisticated thermal systems on an Apache helicopter could help us track any bad guys running from house to house. I ordered Mark to bring up his reserve forces; we would need the infantry if it became necessary to secure a city block. After all was assembled, it was time to determine who was innocent and who was not.

I was concerned that we would become targets if we lingered too long, but I had the confidence of having very good security. The night dragged on. More Iraqi males were flushed from homes for questioning. Women and children were separated. Jack's interrogator went to work. Sharks were kept; dolphins were released. Over fifty men in all were detained for questioning. Jack took a man with a Syrian passport. We nabbed Abdullah al-Kaleb, a Fedayeen general involved in coordinating recent insurgent activity. We also took two men believed to be involved in the CMIC attack from earlier in the month. We missed the Ace of Diamonds, Abid Mahmood, but all in all, it was a very good night.

ACE OF DIAMONDS

The collarbones suffered most. The armored vest with counterbalancing ballistic plates in front and back pressed into them. Hours of wearing the kit with senses on high alert added to the fatigue. In the early hours of the morning, I unclipped the rifle from my vest, dropped my helmet on my cot, ripped open the vest's Velcro flaps, and shed my armored exoskeleton weighted with rifle and pistol ammo, water, a small radio, mini binos, and other assorted items needed by a commander. I was soaked to the bone. I ran my fingers through soggy, matted hair to see if my scalp had any feeling left. My lungs, freed from containment, instinctively expanded with newfound freedom.

I wandered toward the operations center sequestered on the south side of the elaborate Salah ad Din main palace building. It was the primary structure in a complex of a half dozen and shaped like Solomon's Temple. It was very majestic, very rectangular, very sturdy, very marbled and very ornately decorated with carved teak paneling, massive columns and stained glass. I later learned from the locals that the temple sat on the exact site of a Crusader stronghold until it was taken by Salah ad Din, the Islamic warrior and hero for whom the province was named. Now it housed part of the 22nd Infantry Regiment of the United States Army.

Desperately needed sleep would have to wait until I ensured that all was in order. As my majors and I conferred, it was clear that we now had the initiative. I knew it, and Colonel Hickey knew it, too. He pushed us hard. Jack and I, excited at the prospect of the surge of new intelligence, worked together on the next round of suspects. We were getting some valuable tips from local Iraqis. Captain Tim Morrow, my intelligence officer, sifted through the new data.

Jack's men continued to focus on Abid Mahmood. He arrived with the news that Mahmood may have fled to the northern suburb of Tikrit called "Cadaseeyah." He asked for Chris Morris and my scouts again, and, of course, I complied. Jack left, and I gave instructions to alert Chris with a warning order.

I was comfortable with our plans to attack the enemy. So I was caught completely off guard when my staff relayed a myriad of senseless divisional and corps staff directives that would potentially impair our ability to pursue the adversary. I could hardly believe what I was hearing. One of my favorite directives introduced at that time was the "trip ticket." Some genius, whose backside was no doubt shaped like the seat of a chair, determined each and every patrol had to be cleared by higher. Higher what? Intelligence? Stupidity? What kind of blockhead, I wondered, believed their staff directives could override the authority of a commander engaged in fighting the enemy? Maybe some troop leader who likely used his armored vest as a doorstop? It would be difficult to respond spontaneously, either defensively or offensively, to the tasks of war if each soldier had to obtain a "trip ticket" to leave headquarters, rather like getting your mother's permission to play outside. No doubt the reason for leaving the compound in the first place would no longer exist after complying with protocol.

As I digested these new directives, I could feel the anger tempting me inside. This was an insane order for combat troops. It might work for the 3rd Leaf-eating Battalion or some such entity, but there was no way combat troops could endure such bureaucratic nonsense at our level. Once again, I lodged a complaint with Colonel Hickey and General Odierno. Once again, I was instructed to focus on combat missions and keep the enemy at bay. They promised to quash the protests of those who never ventured from protective compounds. True to their word, as always, they did.

The advantage of deploying with the first units into any war is that the volume of nonsense is far less than when the theater gets more developed. I had seen it before in Kosovo and Afghanistan. Still, there we were, not three months into our mission in Iraq, contending with such idiotic orders as wearing seat belts in combat fighting vehicles and needing a "trip ticket" to go on combat patrol. Insanity! The seat belt order was ludicrous because the strap couldn't encompass soldier, gear, and ammo. Furthermore, trying to release a seat belt when caught in an ambush could be fatal when split seconds mattered. With the cover of my higher leaders, I instructed my soldiers to be polite at the gates but to never slow down for such frivolity and to always ensure that they could fight instantly. They were to inform inflexible gatekeepers to take up any objections with me. Few ever did.

I needed to turn in. In just three hours we would start all over. I felt like my head had just hit the pillow when Captain Matt Weber awakened me three hours later. I rose from a rock-dead sleep to a day that promised great activity. Our C Company was already netting a lot of bad guys by setting up flash checkpoints. By evening's end, they would seize more than a dozen insurgents at gunpoint and haul in everything from AK-47 rifles to RPG components. As an added bonus, one of the captives was connected to a "Deck of Cards" guy.

As dusk fell, Chris' scouts readied for action. Jack gave us the hit times for the Mahmood raid. I arranged for tank support in the north with Jon Cecalupo's men while my rifle companies focused on the city. Cadaseeyah is more open than the tightly packed quarters of Tikrit proper. This allowed our tanks to use their optics and range to cover the operations. They would also be able to use speed for action when needed. My mortars stood ready, and Jack's team prepared special ops birds in support.

The raid was swift. The forces converged on a well-appointed expansive residence with a walled courtyard. The main exterior wall of the residence was adorned with an elaborate sculpture of gazelles. Flash-bang grenades concussed the calm night as gates snapped and troops moved in. Our scouts held the corners of the walled compound; SOF guys invaded the interior. Stunned and haggard, a gaunt and unshaven Abid Hamid Mahmood al-Khatab was nabbed and secured. Saddam's Presidential Secretary would perform no more administrative duties for him. The feeling of capturing the Ace of Diamonds was utterly euphoric, but this was no time to celebrate; much remained to be done.

The document guys went to work quickly. What a wildly successful night! In a calculated move, the news of Mahmood's capture, the biggest of the war to that point, was released in an effort to show that we had the upper hand. The news spread around the globe, and reporters in Baghdad and elsewhere made plans for increased coverage of Tikrit. News was being made there.

Success felt good. Nothing raises morale like success. All the comforts of home can do nothing to lift the spirit like success. Even if the comforts of home were available, they could do nothing for morale if the mission failed. Success is the only true thing soldiers desire in battle. It is the only thing that lends any kind of meaning to our suffering and sacrifice.

QUEENS AND CASH

We readied ourselves for the next mission based on the information Mahmood surrendered in his capture. That led back to his original residence in Auja, which was added to a list of two other suspected target houses. News of Mahmood's capture gave Iraqis enough confidence to tell us about a possible safe house for Saddam south of Auja near the Tigris River. I instructed Mark Stouffer to plan raids on the three dwellings in Auja since his command was there. To beef up his force, I attached Chris Morris' Scout Platoon to him for the raids. Chris' troops were needed because part of Mark's company was still attached to the 101st Airborne in Mosul and some were guarding ammo dumps in the south, which strapped his forces even further. Mark would be in overall command of the fourth target, but some autonomy would be given to Chris to provide the initial force to cordon the farm until Mark's troops could arrive following their house raids in Auja.

I alerted the battalion mortars and gathered what air support Colonel Hickey was able to secure for us. My other companies would continue their combat patrols of Tikrit. We would execute the raids at 0200 on the morning of June 18. Our forces planned to be in position on the evening of the 17th to avoid raising suspicion in the targeted areas. It was going to be another long and busy night.

Mark opted to use an infantry platoon on the Auja houses. Two of the houses were adjacent to each other and could easily be grouped together. By arranging his forces in proximity to the Mahmood house, he could provide mutual support to his forces and still hit each objective. Chris Morris announced that, after the strike in Auja, his scouts would move to cordon and monitor the farm as Mark's forces closed in from Auja. The idea was to display a lot of activity in Auja in order to catch the farm by surprise. Chris' men would surround it; Mark's soldiers would then raid it.

To better support the operation, I relocated two mortar tubes near Colonel Hickey's brigade headquarters to increase their range. We had seen the Auja targets before. Mark's troops lived among them, and his main compound, a sports complex in the village, was actually quite near two of the houses. The Mahmood house had been raided by Jack's SOF team and our troops a few nights before. These were all well-constructed and well-appointed houses. Most had eight-foot or higher exterior walls with a single point of entry. The two houses near Mark's compound were bordered on the back by a large wooded area, making the possibility of escape a major concern for the troops surrounding the locality.

A few miles farther south, the setting was very different. Resting below a bluff several hundred yards from the Tigris, the Hadooshi farm was sorely out of place. The main structure looked ordinary enough—a typical concrete prefab multi-room dwelling with a garage and garden, all facing the west bank of the Tigris. Cattle dotted the field within the wall to the east. A stable was nearby. South of the main structure was a large fish hatchery, and even farther south, and wildly out of place, was a square guest house that dominated the entire compound.

The guest quarters, constructed of fine Italian brick and marble, were elaborately trimmed and crowned with expensive chandeliers. It was designed on the order of Saddam's palaces in Tikrit. What was it doing out here, and why weren't the residents living in it? These questions would soon have answers.

We led the raid as Jack's guys were interested but still not sure of our intelligence sources. Still, with Saddam as a possible target, some of their guys joined us later, and we were glad to have them.

The tactical approach to Mohammed al-Hadooshi's farm was tenuous at best. The access road from the main highway led through a small village called Oynot (pronounced "Why not," the name a source of comic relief for our soldiers). Exiting town, it led downward into a carved-out bluff, which was ideal for an ambush. If we attempted to bypass the main road, which we did, we would have to traverse even narrower dike roads. Any navigational error would result in a fatal plunge into fetid, soaked fields. These were even more vulnerable to ambush.

We already had indication that a guard regularly patrolled the farm compound with other guard activity all around it. Satellite photos showed guard shacks at both the entrance and the back of the farm. Approach to this compound without detection was unlikely. Speed would, therefore, be essential. Chris' scouts would secure the outer areas while Mark Stouffer's A Company would strike the main buildings. Air and mortar support would stand by.

With successive raids planned and coordinated, we would wait for evening, but evening would not wait for us. About an hour after sunset, the explosive "dumpster crash" sound of an RPG rocket smashed the stale night air. The radio began to crackle with contact reports about an attack on Mark's troops in Auja. I was patrolling in Tikrit and ordered my driver to nose our vehicle south. In such a situation, the heart begins to race. The mind fills with a thousand "what-ifs" as you check your weapon and equipment while mentally trying to prepare for the unknown. I alerted my other companies but waited for Mark to develop the situation. He had a hundred guys to work it, and the last thing he needed was his commander breathing down his neck. We raced toward Auja from downtown Tikrit.

None of our men had been hit, but Mark's compound had. Two insurgents, armed with a rocket launcher, fired directly at Mark's troops who were occupying the security post on the northeast end of their compound. The rocket exploded just short of their post, showering flame, metal, and concrete, but hurting only the wall. The soldiers on security at this outpost spotted brief activity to the east in the woods just south of the very dwellings we intended to raid in a few hours.

Chris Morris' scouts immediately mounted up the scout gun trucks and spurred them into action. Chris was coordinating the final preparations with Mark at his company command post when the attack hit. Mark deployed his "Gators" into the woods and along the houses. They spotted two men running south from the market area into the woods. Chris searched farther south in an attempt to cut off anyone trying to flee into the fertile, overgrown river area.

I arrived in Auja to see Mark's Bradleys positioned around part of the area we intended to raid. Chris had a gun truck deployed with them. Soldiers watched walls, roofs, alleys, woods, and streets while I found Mark to get an update. He told me that First Lieutenant Eric Tapp's soldiers had cleared the two houses near the place attackers were believed to have fired the rocket. Our soldiers detained several males from the houses. I put Joe Filmore to work on them while Major Mike Rauhut relayed reports to Colonel Hickey. Mark said that the attackers likely headed south.

All our plans for the night had instantly changed. Any bad guys leisurely going about their business in Auja would be nervous about our presence and might have ideas of fleeing before our planned raids (which were still three hours away) could be carried out. While we could adjust our plans, it was obvious that the enemy had plans of his own that evening. Was this the end of the enemy's attack plans? Was it a diversion? Were there additional enemy cells afoot preparing for an ambush?

With these questions in mind, I quickly made a decision. I told Mark and Chris to execute the raids right then. While it was not the fight we anticipated, it was the fight we had, and I believed that we still had the advantage of surprise. The individuals at the target houses would not anticipate our interest in them based on the events that had just transpired and they would likely be hunkered down. Ironically, one of the houses that our troops had searched in pursuit of the RPG attackers was one of two target houses. We were able to find some very useful photographs, documents, and phone lists there even though our targeted individual was not found.

Mark adjusted his forces. Chris reset his own. Mike Rauhut radioed from my command Humvee to Brian Reed at battalion headquarters about the new plan. Colonel Hickey arrived, as he often did when activity spiked. I briefed him on our situation and told him that we were implementing the raids immediately. He agreed. He wandered over to the Iraqis detained by Mark's soldiers and questioned them with the aid of Joe Filmore, my translator.

Within ten minutes, our soldiers swarmed the remaining houses of our planned raid. Eric's men seized two individuals of note, one of whom we were specifically seeking. With the capture of Brigadier General Kafim Jasim Nafar, the night's effort was already worthwhile. Joe and Mark speculated that the men detained from the initial raid were not likely involved in the RPG rocket attack. We freed them. They were just dolphins among the sharks—wrong people, wrong place, wrong time. I ordered Chris to detach from us and set out for the Hadooshi Farm. He had already bagged one target, so speed was essential to prevent word from leaking to other possible targets at the Hadooshi farm.

I felt good about the evening and was proud of the way Mark's men handled the earlier attack, but I felt a bit of angst about the farm. If Saddam was using it as a safe house, the enemy contact may have decreased our chances of nabbing him due to our change of plans. Such is war.

Chris' scouts approached the Hadooshi farm from various points intending to cordon the area so that Mark's soldiers could search the grounds. It did not play out that way. Because of the difficult approach, the scouts were spotted. Using a fleeting moment of surprise, Chris decided to speed toward the front entrance. As the scouts approached, two Iraqi men ran toward their pallets on the ground. The soldiers acted quickly, drawing their weapons on the men. Within moments, the Iraqis were zip-tied and squatted near their pallets. A quick search revealed two AK-47 rifles under the makeshift beds.

Chris radioed Mark to tell him that he had detained two men running for rifles and told Mark to notify him when the front entrance was secured. He needed immediate backup to better cordon the area. I raced toward the farm, as did Mark Stouffer. Eric Tapp's platoon was already moving in that direction as Chris advanced into the compound. A large number of women and children were discovered inside the main dwelling, about fifteen in all.

Pablo Rivera, the Scout Platoon Sergeant, covered the front entrance on the north with his section while Staff Sergeant Brandon Walker's section moved on the east side of the farm. Staff Sergeant Sean Shoffner's section moved in to cover the other side. As the scouts thinly covered the farm, Mark's troops closed in. Staff Sergeant Brad Owens' troops linked up with the scouts and very quickly brought the farm under control.

When I arrived, Joe Filmore immediately went to work interrogating the Iraqis. We had definitely discovered something—but what? This place was odd—garages, stables, ornate guest quarters and multiple families. I ordered everything searched. This would take some time. With Eric Tapp's Bradleys on site now, we had ample firepower for any contingency. What we needed was to make sense of this objective. With armed guards already detained, the scouts and infantrymen probed the remainder of the compound.

Brad Owens' soldiers began to search a 20-foot trailer filled with hundreds of bags of grain. As Specialist Matt Summers and Private James Lusk removed the bags, they discovered a large cache of weapons. Soon, our soldiers would have submachine guns, foreign-make handguns, an SVD sniper rifle, more AK-47s, night vision goggles, cell phones, and many other high-end items not typically found among the average Iraqis.

Satisfied that we were onto something, I ordered Mark to secure the area until morning. I wanted every square inch of the farm searched in daylight. There was something irregular here, and I couldn't let it go. I conveyed this to Staff Sergeant Sean Shoffner. He was adept at finding things, so much so that I called him "The Bloodhound." He assured me the guys would be vigilant and uncover whatever was there. After conferring with Mark and Chris, I left Joe Filmore with them to continue grilling the Iraqis on site. As Jack's SOF men arrived to search through our discovery, I returned to downtown Tikrit where C Company was wrapping up the successful checkpoint operations that had yielded numerous weapons and insurgents.

The search continued on the farm over the next several hours. Documents, photographs, weapons, phone lists—it was a treasure trove that would direct us to even more bad guys. However, nothing prepared us for what happened next. At the first break of daylight, Chris Morris emerged from the back of the farmhouse. Even though soldiers had searched all around, Chris noticed a patch of bare ground in the garden. When he stepped on it, the ground gave in a strange way under his weight. He called for a mine detector. There was a strong hit on it.

The soldiers began to dig. They tapped into a metal box of some kind. It was a two-foot-square metal bank vault box containing more than $4 million in U.S. currency bundled in Chase Manhattan bank wrappers. Mark was alerted. The radio began to crackle. They relayed the information to me. By the time I reached the farm again, our men had discovered three such containers: two with $4 million each and one slightly smaller one with $2 million in jewelry. There was an additional $750,000.00 in foreign currency from Kuwait, Saudi Arabia, and Great Britain. The scope of the find was staggering.

Handling the incredible haul from the evening's raid made it clear that we had landed something big. Among the males detained was Sabir Abd al-Aziz al-Hadooshi, a lieutenant colonel on our main target list. It was the documents and pictures, however, that captured our attention. Joe Filmore was elated.

"Sir, look at these. This is from Sajida Kheralla Toulfak Hussein," he asserted while tapping what appeared to be a passport. Seeing my puzzled look, he clarified, "This is Saddam Hussein's wife!"

In the next few moments, Joe described the documents and items lying on the table before us—identity cards, papers, and the personal family photo albums of Saddam Hussein. Stunned, I called Colonel Hickey. He returned to the farm, and more of Jack's men came for a look.

The Hadooshi Farm Raid was one of the most important events that summer. From that raid, we not only depleted $10 million from Saddam's personal coffers, but we gathered intelligence from the papers, photographs, and documents that would prove invaluable in the hunt for Saddam. I have often wondered if Mrs. Hussein was among the women on the farm that night. Joe didn't think so. Considering how Saddam would later be captured, I can't help but wonder to this day if he was hiding below ground at the farm that night. We may never know.

News of the raid and its yield quickly spread around the world. As we sifted through the haul, one of the most important finds was a picture of former Special Republican Guard Commander

Barzan Abd al-Ghufar Sulayman Majid al-Tikriti, a relative of Saddam and number 11 on America's Most Wanted List. He was also known as the Queen of Hearts on the Deck of Cards. This was the first photograph anyone had of him and, as a result, he was captured shortly thereafter. Another high-ranking member of Saddam's elite expunged from the deck.

TRANSITIONS

After we withdrew our forces, we had a vast treasure to sift and sort through back at headquarters. I ordered the money and jewelry immediately secured by armed guard. After looking at the jewelry, I was concerned some of it might contain pieces of the Kuwaiti crown jewel collection still missing from the first Gulf War. While we were accounting for all the money next morning, Mark Stouffer's troops netted a cousin of Saddam's leaving Auja with a Samsonite suitcase containing $800,000. We added it to the $9.3 million worth of already confiscated booty.

The sergeant major and I formulated a plan to safeguard this loot. Ten million dollars would be an overpowering temptation for even the most honorable soldier. Each individual bill was a Ben Franklin. Each half-inch wrapper contained $10,000. Each stack contained ten such wrappers totaling $100,000. We had 84 of these stacks, not including the foreign currency or the money that Mark had just reported. Spread out, it was literally a bed of cash on which a man could stretch out.

Pete procured a black tough box, the kind one could purchase at Wal-Mart and throw in the back of a pickup truck back home. On the opening side were two hasps for locks. We placed a "Series 200" government lock on each one. Pete wore the key to one lock around his neck, and I wore the other around mine. Anyone wanting in the tough box would need both of us to open it, rather like nuclear missile guys collaborating for a launch. To make entry more complicated and to deter the curious, I ordered Sergeant First Class Milton Benson to count every bill each time the chest was opened. Benson could bench-press 300 pounds and looked like he could crush you with his thumbs. That would be enough to annoy him and keep the tough box closed to inquiring minds.

By late afternoon, division reported the media's interest in the fortune and jewels confiscated in our raid. We would later coordinate a press event for the purpose of displaying the currency and jewelry for the cameras. In the meantime, there was a war waiting for us.

My personnel officer informed me of the arrival and assignment of Captain Brad Boyd to our headquarters. He was a godsend. I planned to place him in immediate command of my C Company. The current commander was no coward, but in my estimation, he was not handling his company well. In early assessments, I rated them the weakest of the fighting companies.

Early on, I had several sit-downs with the soldiers and sergeants of the various units in my command. Clearly, there was much infighting within C Company. The soldiers, excellent material and with capable junior officers, were not being properly led. I was very candid with these men. At one such meeting, a sergeant asked me point-blank why I always gave the raids to A Company. I shot back, "Because they are better than you." War is no place to be concerned with feelings or fairness. A soldier can either carry the water or he can't. If he can't, he'd better learn to use a bucket quickly.

I had met Brad Boyd prior to my deployment from Ft. Hood. He arrived as I was about to leave. I had a good exchange with him and a young captain named Mike Wagner. My intention was to garner both of these excellent officers for the 22nd Infantry. While I was immediately successful in securing Brad, Colonel Hickey had other ideas about getting both of them. Mike Wagner was siphoned to brigade headquarters for a short time. Eventually, I was able to draw him in for command while still deployed in Iraq.

We experienced high turnover of personnel during this critical period. Major Brian Reed, my outstanding executive officer, would be pulled by Colonel Hickey to become the brigade operations officer. While good for the brigade, it was a loss for us. Nevertheless, it was a good move for Brian, and I was happy for him. He was first-rate, and the job for which he was selected was awarded only to the very best officers. I mused a bit that Mike Rauhut would be lost without his "twin." These two West Point classmates, who had served together on multiple occasions, would now be split apart. Even so, no one was more qualified to replace Brian as my new executive officer than Mike.

Replacing Mike as operations officer was a big unknown. My first choice prior to deployment was to snatch Brian Eifler. He had worked for me at the III Corps G-3 when the three of us were sentenced to serve in the basement at the corps operations center at Ft. Hood. Serving there was about as much fun as poking a sharp stick in your eye, but soldiers like Wagner and Eifler made it more tolerable.

I was not to get Major Eifler. He was pulled to shore up the operations in 2nd Battalion, 8th Infantry. Brian did outstanding service in Iraq with this first-rate unit. The choices remaining centered around the poor souls sentenced to service on the 4th Infantry Division staff. Major Bryan Luke stood head and shoulders above that crowd and was rewarded with orders to report to 1st Battalion, 22nd Infantry. Bryan was a brilliant and focused planner who had been working for Major General Odierno. With a gap of a few weeks before Bryan would be released to my command, Mike Rauhut was left with both jobs in combat. Not an easy task at all.

In the following weeks, I also made adjustments to my staff. Captain Craig Childs would become my adjutant, responsible for all combat personnel, replacements and casualty reporting. I moved the old adjutant, First Lieutenant Andrew Camp, who was a hundred pounds soaking wet and an annoyingly efficient West Pointer who would be great for shoring up the administration of C Company as their new executive officer. Few officers were more loyal. I received a lot of flack at first, but I knew Andy perfectly suited the needs of that company.

We received our first set of replacements for some non-returning wounded. Command Sergeant Major Martinez plucked from among these a new soldier to replace my driver. Specialist Pedro Martinez, once Mark Woempner's driver and now mine, was rotating back to the States. My new driver was a six-foot, seven-inch Crow Indian from Montana named Cody Hoefer. He was one tough, smart soldier that would endure a great deal with me. The bond we formed cannot be described with words.

The assessment of our operations thus far was substantial. The local population reports indicated that we had severely impaired the subversive elements. Even the Muslim imams expressed their appreciation for our efforts, but our work was not nearly complete. Numerous hostile elements lingered and would attempt to strike back with indirect fire and convoy attacks or whatever means they possessed to remain relevant in the fight. We had to remain vigilant.

Our soldiers were enjoying good morale and were flushed with recent successes. We were now living well for the most part, billeted as we were in former palace compounds. The weather remained oppressive, and every moment of the day our uniforms were soaked with our own sweat in the 115-degree June heat. The heat would increase another ten to fifteen degrees by summer's end, as we would soon discover. Nevertheless, we were eating well and generally had good hygiene and protection because of the hard billets. Our equipment was holding up pretty well given the operations and environment. The robust Bradleys and our body armor had already earned the unqualified respect of our men for their lifesaving protection.

As we contended with the issues of hunting Saddam and faced life-and-death situations each day, Americans contended with the possible prison sentence for Martha Stewart's investment fraud and suffered anxiety over who would win the Stanley Cup and the NBA Championship. We could not help but feel that we were an army at war and a nation at peace. The feeling only increased with the passage of time. When the War on Iraq made headlines, it was portrayed with words like "setback," "disaster" and "tragedy." We focused on what we were sent to do: fight to win a war. Success is the best silencer of critics.

BORDERS, REPORTERS, AND ORDERS

The call came as a complete surprise, as such calls often do. "Need your location ASAP for a face-to-face," said Brigadier General Mike Barbero, our Assistant Division Commander for Maneuver.

I ended my patrol in Tikrit, and we met on a flat area of the sprawling landscape inside the Tikrit Palace grounds. The pace of operations continued to be brisk, but the news General Barbero brought would heighten it even more. The division needed an infantry unit to support operations on the Syrian border for a possible high-level intercept. He asked if I could spare an infantry company.

"Yes, sir, but it will severely hinder our offensive capability," I offered.

"This will now be your number one offensive priority," he

countered. "I want to know how soon you can get them into action."

"Sir, I can assemble them now. I can send my A Company, use my scouts to secure Auja, and use my C Company and Tank Company to hold the city. You do realize that with this move I will have only three platoons of Infantry left?"

"I hate to do this, Steve, but we need more than this," he informed. "Can you beef up the company with an additional rifle platoon from your remaining company?"

My mind raced to make an instant assessment of my situation. I had a platoon of infantry on loan in Mosul that I would likely never see again. Two squads guarded a large ammo site far to the south. I was about to loan Mark's company to General Barbero, thereby leaving Auja and the hornet's nest we had stirred virtually uncovered. I was about to gut my city infantry company by one third. Other than that, things looked pretty good.

"Yes, sir," I pledged, knowing full well that General Barbero would not be asking this sacrifice were it not of utmost importance. I had worked for him at III Corps at Ft. Hood. He had a reputation of the highest order when it came to taking care of the troops. This was about trust, and thankfully, I had General Barbero and General Odierno calling the shots.

So it was that our Syrian border adventure began. Our A Company, along with a platoon from C Company, helicoptered hundreds of miles southwest to support operations along the Syrian border. The 3rd Armored Cavalry needed support for a containment operation, and our task force was given about 45 minutes' notice from alert to liftoff. I stood with pride as our "mechaneers" from a heavy infantry battalion climbed the ramps into the belly of the CH-47 "Chinook" helicopters. They pulled together as though they were light or air assault infantry. Most of our battalion leaders had all been in light infantry and airborne units anyway, so it was really just assembling the guys for a new mission. The birds were merely transportation.

The men operated out of rucksacks for about five days and performed superbly. The mission was somewhat successful, but in combat, opportunity is often created rather than delivered. I regarded the exercise as useful, if merely to keep our soldiers on their toes. The heat on the border was oppressive, as it was in the rest of the country, but the vegetation was a little greener, and the temperatures were actually quite cool at night. I had dispatched Major Rauhut as liaison so my troops' needs would be adequately provided. He took a tactical satellite radio known as a TACSAT so he could relay daily reports.

Back in Tikrit, we had to make do with reduced forces, and there was no doubt that the border operation gave the enemy in Tikrit a brief respite. When our battalion reassembled, we followed up on leads from earlier raids. Our intelligence led us to massive areas of farmland along the Tigris River. William Booth, a reporter from the *Washington Post,* spent about three days with our task force and wrote a nice piece (26 June 2003) on our operations. His purpose was to witness the reaction of a unit that had given and taken casualties. He was impressed at our ability to maintain the initiative with good spirits and good results.

He observed one operation that missed our target, but one of our Bradley Fighting Vehicles doing a forced entry into a farm courtyard made a profound impression on him. No danger would ever be risked with our men going through what all infantry know as "the fatal funnel"—the obvious entryway that channels them into a danger zone or ambush. On this raid, the BFV smashed through the gate, removing wrought iron, concrete, and mortar in a cloud of dust and was quickly followed by our Infantry shuffling down the ramp of the vehicle to secure the area as the Bradley's gun scanned like a metronome. I confess that it was magnificent to behold, something one never experiences in training.

Our troops were becoming weary from constant raids, operations, and routine combat patrols. The physical condition of the men remained healthy but the "Fedayeen Funk" began to seep through the ranks. It struck me personally as I received radio reports in an early morning brief. I suddenly had a tunnel view of my surroundings. I stood, handed the radio handset to Mike Rauhut and said, "Take over. I'll be back in a minute."

I took two steps. The next thing I knew, my staff was huddled around, and I was regaining consciousness, sprawled out on the floor. Talk about an embarrassing moment. There I was in command, the picture of poise and confidence transformed into a vomiting wimp on the floor, having had a needle stuck in my arm. Dizziness, vomiting, and diarrhea overwhelmed me for a miserable 24-hour period.

Fortunately, the battalion had an ample roster of talent who afforded needed rest for me. All of our men saw bouts of this type on occasion, and the soldiers even coined several entertaining terms to describe the maladies: "Saddam's Revenge," "The Two-Cheek Sneak," and the already mentioned "Fedayeen Funk." Fortunately, our medics and docs attacked these maladies with medication that would "shock and awe" viruses into submission within a day.

After springing back to health, I was privileged to brief Ambassador Paul Bremer and Army Secretary Les Brownlee on our recent successes. They were very complimentary of our soldiers and noted the important success of our operations. I tried to convey our resolve to maintain the initiative rather than hold static points while the enemy moved freely. I assured them that we were on the path to mission success in our area, both in terms of fighting the nascent insurgents and in terms of tracking down Saddam's henchmen.

I also conveyed to them the exasperation at the "poor soldiers" treatment articulated in the press. Some BBC reporters had arrived with a pre-written story in mind and were seeking to acquire sound bites to support it. They weren't the only ones. The popular notion at that time was that we were somehow suffering from a complete misunderstanding of the situation we had gotten ourselves into.

We could not concur with the media's estimation that operations had somehow turned for the worse in Tikrit. Every soldier knows this simple truth: pursuit of the enemy increases the chance of finding him. Never mind that Abid Mahmood and other significant targets had been captured in Tikrit. Never mind that Saddam forfeited wealth, personal property, and clues as he narrowly escaped our operations. The press preferred to focus on the violence because violence sells news. It was difficult to understand, then and now, why the media spotlighted the negative with political approval while each day soldiers witnessed positive results of the American presence in Iraq. I felt that we should all be on the same side—the side of freedom.

I did not view the press as the enemy. I was actually grateful to have media coverage of our soldiers in hopes of showcasing their success and reassuring Americans back home. I explained to reporters that the acts of violence perpetrated against us signified the actions of a desperate and defeated foe and that we would see the ring closed on Saddam. Some listened. Most did not.

I explained that cooperation with the locals continued to improve, and both the Iraqi government and police officials in our area had joined our forces in securing their future. I could not speak for all of Iraq, but I knew that we held the upper hand in Tikrit and made no apologies for taking a heavy hand with those who did not comply with our resolve to accomplish the mission assigned us.

To me it was black and white. In time, I would improve my relationship with reporters and learn to appreciate them, though I suppose I never became accustomed to the view that victory was not the best option. Our cause was certain because truth and justice must always prevail over evil. That should have been obvious.

During this period, I read a scripture from the twentieth chapter of 2 Chronicles. It encouraged me, and I made note of it. Just as Jehoshaphat emboldened the people in their struggle with the Edomites, I also took heart from his advice to his troops, "The battle depends on God and not you. . . . Just take up your positions, and wait, and you will see the Lord give you victory. . . . Put your trust in the Lord your God, and you will stand your ground." We could never have forecast the remarkable events that would ensue as we chose to stand our ground.

I was moody from the high-level briefs and "stump the chump" treatment from reporters, so the best cure for me was joining the troops on patrol. The command sergeant major and I went to Mosul to visit the portion of our A Company troops attached to the 101st Airborne there. The town is situated on the site of the ancient city of Nineveh. I found it fascinating to think that Jonah had walked and preached there. The scenery was a nice change as well. The hills, the taller trees, and greenery were a pleasant contrast to the austere area of our operations.

First Lieutenant Casey Lusk commanded the platoon there. Our men were making the best of the situation which was, in my view, a fine waste of infantry. I understood how they got there but I didn't like it. The original "handshake agreement" was between two esteemed commanders—General David Petraeus of the 101st Airborne and General Ray Odierno of our 4th Infantry Division. I imagined the conversation was something simple and meaningful:

"Hey, Ray, I could really use a bit of emergency firepower for my troops should we run into something big. Any chance we could keep a portion of the tank battalion that marched up here with us?"

"Sure, Dave, makes sense to me. You work out what you need, and we'll do it."

The translation of that honest and decent support was that a tank company team, the one containing our infantry platoon, remained in Mosul after the 101st took the city in April 2003. Fair enough. However, when I inspected the manner in which my soldiers were being used, it was clearly a good deal gone bad. My troops were reduced to providing a "mechanical gate" and gate guard. They were using my awesome Bradleys to block gate entries and would move forward and back to allow passage on command. My troops would rotate daily in shifts for this "arduous" and "skilled" duty that apparently only mechanized infantry were trained to perform.

I advised the troops to make the best of it. I told them to never relax their standards and to always stay in their gear. The enemy was looking for zebras to cull from the herd. They were to be hunters, even if their hunting spot was this menial outpost.

Upon my return, I raised the issue of the gate guard to General Odierno when I next saw him. With a wry smile, he placed his big hand on my shoulder and said, "Steve, you're not getting your platoon back. Make do."

I smiled and nodded back, "Yes, sir," realizing that this support was as much about relationships as about effectiveness. I never broached it again. Instead, I heeded General Odierno's order to make the best of it. I asked my staff if we could rotate the Bradleys back from Mosul by heavy transport and use the rotating duty as a kind of "R&R" (Rest and Relaxation). It was simply a matter of selling the duty to the troops in a positive light. They could view it as a waste or consider it an opportunity for reprieve from the front line in a safer environment. So it was. Our Mosul rotations resulted in needed rest for both troops and vehicles.

Part of "making do" was to exact better performance from my C Company through brilliant leadership. That was due, in no small part, to the skillful direction of Captain Brad Boyd. It was an odd journey that paved his way into a U.S. Army mechanized infantry battalion. As an enlisted artillerist in the U.S. Marines, he made non-commissioned officer and was selected for Marine officer candidate school. Passing with flying colors, he earned a commission in the Marines as an Artillery Second Lieutenant. Because he commanded a platoon well, he was selected to become a Marine instructor of re-cruits and was then awarded recruiting duty. Weary of training and recruiting, he opted for a service transfer to the U.S. Army Infantry. He came to Iraq upon completion of his captain's course. The 1st Battalion 22nd Infantry was his first taste of the real Army.

By chance, Brad's first day in our battalion was the event at which we displayed Saddam's cache of currency confiscated from the Hadooshi Farm Raid for the benefit of reporter ogling. There stood Brad with Brian Reed, looking the part of soldier-hero standing with the loot of his new battalion. He even got his name in the papers. Of course, we ribbed him about it later. But Brad hit the ground running. His aggressive style was precisely what we needed there. His top sergeant, First Sergeant Mike Evans, was an outstanding, if not youthful, first sergeant. Mike spent most of his time in the 82nd Airborne and had seen combat before. He was learning that infantry is what you make it, even mechanized in-fantry. He had all the makings of a great top sergeant but needed a firm hand. He would have it with Brad. The team these two would become was a sight to behold.

FIREWORKS

Long hot days greeted us, but not necessarily in the morning. Our men conducted operations at all hours. The average soldier in our task force was active 16-20 hours a day. Sometimes we got more rest but rest could not be scheduled. Operations drove activities and soldiers got snatches of rest when they could. They did not need to be told. As for me, I had never been so tired in my whole life. I would sleep a few hours in the early morning after coming in from patrols and would try to get an hour, maybe more, in mid-afternoon during the most oppressive heat of the day when activity was low.

Oppressive is a feeble description of the heat. The sun burned into our vehicles and clothing and eventually into us. Profuse sweating saturated our uniforms from shoulder blades to knee-caps. Our equipment absorbed even more sweat as it pinched and encased us like an exoskeleton, transforming us into stinky, sour, salty, drenched combat creatures. We had grown accustomed to the heat, but I found comfort in the vague hope that, since we were past the summer solstice, we would lose seven minutes of sunlight each day, which would gradually result in cooler temperatures. When we shed our equipment, we attempted to dry out. This being accomplished, our uniforms took on the appearance of stiff and badly starched fatigues, with salt stain maps delineating the shores where sweat had advanced into our clothing.

The sun also bored into the metal of our weapons. Sometimes our rifles were so hot to the touch we wore gloves to keep from burning our hands. But even the ruthless heat of the sun did not pierce our morale or diminish our ability. We were very much able to fight under these conditions, as our enemy would learn, to his own detriment.

The Fourth of July had come, but for soldiers it was simply another day of combat patrolling—no backyard barbecues, no baseball, no fireworks displays. However, the following day, soldiers from our B Company were greeted with a fireworks display of a different kind. A Bradley Fighting Vehicle, B14, was on patrol with a tank section on a dusty street in Bayjii. Sergeant First Class Joseph Walden, the platoon sergeant in the vehicle, noticed a tire in the road and, as this was unusual, told the driver not to drive over it. Private First Class Steve Fink, the driver, who, on a gut feel, had placed his armor plated vest on the floor below him that morning and wore a vehicle vest in addition to it, veered sharply to the right. When he did, a violent explosion erupted through the vehicle.

Thousands of pounds of engine lurched cock-eyed as the front hull-access cover on top sailed through the air, followed closely by the entire transmission of the vehicle. As the transmission completed its trajectory, road wheels, sprockets, and associated smaller hatches accompanied it. Walden's helmet was blown from his head and immediately consumed in flames, although his head was miraculously untouched.

Inside, Fink felt a searing heat. He smelled the halon fire extinguishers blow, which consumed the flames. He had his feet and legs bounced upward by his armored vest and felt a sharp pain to the back of his neck and left hand fingers. The soldiers in the back were consumed in a concussive shock wave of blast and heat that was extinguished as quickly as it had lashed at them. Private John Lyons' glasses were blown from his face, while Sergeant Charles Myers, Sergeant Andre Allen, Specialist James Blalock, and Private First Class Joshua Whitson were all nearly knocked out, but somehow maintained consciousness. Two of the men suffered severe concussions. In the turret, Sergeant First Class Walden felt sharp stabs at his nerve endings and had blood on one of his legs.

As the smoke cleared and the dust settled, the men began to come to their senses. Steve Fink, despite his wounds, was able to pull himself free, exit his station and help the others out. Everyone exited the vehicle, covered by the tanks in trail. The men could not imagine having been inside the vehicle they were now viewing in disbelief. This was the second time that B-14 had been destroyed. This vehicle had replaced the one destroyed in June. For Walden and Myers, this was the second time in a month that they had struck a mine in a Bradley, and it was the second time Myers had been wounded.

Now full of adrenaline, they accounted for themselves and their equipment and realized that God had spared them from what should have been certain maiming or death. They secured themselves, evacuated the wounded, and recovered the destroyed vehicle. Of the eight men aboard, five of them were wounded and all but one was able to return to duty. The Bradley was a contorted, twisted, mangled mess. It was hard to imagine that anyone could have survived that blast. I thanked God for sparing our soldiers' lives.

NOT TOO SHABBY

We continued to suffer some losses without replacement. When we deployed, the Army envisioned sending packets of soldiers to replace combat losses while also refusing to allow soldiers whose terms of enlistment had been completed to depart. Withholding newly arriving soldiers was called "Stop Move" while preventing soldiers leaving their units was called "Stop Loss." Now that policy changed. Soldiers scheduled to depart could be released, provided that they had replacements in addition to combat replacements for wounded or killed. Those due to rotate, in turn, would have some valuable combat experience for the Army to use as they prepared units to come to Iraq for the long haul. While these policies would later change again, it did allow some of our troops to go home. Some who had been extended to deploy were allowed to leave the service as well.

We were privileged to receive a visit from General Jack Keane, the Army Vice Chief of Staff. General Keane earned the love of every infantryman in the Army the first week he was assigned to the Pentagon. He said that a bunch of the Pentagon staff were fat and ordered them to go on Pentagon staff runs. That shook the place up. He was a huge man given to some theatrics, but what effective leader wasn't?

I asked the General if he would personally pin Purple Hearts on my wounded. He said that he would be honored. About a dozen of my return-to-duty (RTD) soldiers were awarded Purple Hearts on the spot. A couple of these fine soldiers would be wounded again. At least one of them would earn another Purple Heart after being killed in action. Others would receive their medals in the States while recovering from wounds. For still others, because of flaws in the system, we fought for their awards for years after deployment. Gone were the days of World War II when a young company commander could pin on a Purple Heart. Now, the authority for issuing awards had gone all the way to the Pentagon with consequential delay, nonsense, and red tape.

I briefed General Keane about our operations, our view of the enemy, and our plan for stalking him. As he and General Odierno walked away, not knowing I was following at a distance, he turned to General Odierno and said, "Not too shabby—that battalion commander. This is a good unit." It was a great compliment.

It was my honor to pin Combat Infantry Badges on some of our men before they went home. The CIB is a silver flintlock musket measuring a quarter of an inch tall by three inches wide, framed with a light blue background. It has a silver wreath of oak leaves around it and conveys to all that the bearer earned it by risking his life against an armed enemy in close battle. It was created in World War II, and veterans for the last 60 years nod at each other when seeing it on a lapel or ball cap. It speaks volumes.

The Command Sergeant Major and I pinned Combat Infantry

Badges on each of the qualifying soldiers and thanked them for their service to America and to the Regulars of the 1st Battalion, 22nd Infantry. I told them to walk tall for us back home. I challenged them to look people in the eye and to be proud of what they had accomplished. I asserted to them that every reason that brought us here was as valid today as it had been in March 2003. If not us, then who? Who would step up for these 26 million Iraqi people? Our resolve remained clear, and we would continue on to finish the job.

The men were becoming very proud of their service. They were seeing results from their tenacity and were aware the enemy's will was being broken. They were confident that we would win. Our reason for being there was as legitimate in that hot summer of 2003 as the day we arrived. We could never forget how vile this country's regime was under Saddam Hussein. The fool's notion back in the States that Iraq was better off before our intervention and that, "at least, Saddam made the trains run on time" was just that—a notion for fools. Iraqi testimonies were a constant reminder of the human suffering inflicted under Saddam, which could not be ignored with a clear conscience. To do so was to sanction the evil that oppressed the nation.

While the enemy was small in comparison to the combined forces present in Iraq, he continued to engage us, and the attacks increased in response to our raids. We faced an activity at this time not seen in other sectors of Iraq. The casualty lists bore witness to that as well. Most of those we were fighting were Saddam loyalists. In retrospect, it was clear that the opening rounds of the insurgency occurred in our area. What started as a Baathist-led, Saddam-inspired insurgent effort would be defeated by us, but the resistance would be hijacked by al-Qaeda in the spring of 2004.

This was yet unknown to us. We only knew that bad guys were trying to kill us and that Saddam and his henchmen were still at large. We felt then, and still feel, that it is better to fight those who hate America on their soil than on our own. Our immediate task was to seize the initiative, retain it, and weaken the enemy by driving into him relentlessly. To date, our efforts had been "not too shabby."

PEPSIS, RUBBER BOATS, AND GRAFFITI

Our driving into the enemy was not without response. In the days following, our positions were probed by a series of "pinprick" attacks, producing little but damage to the enemy. In acts of desperation, assailants made improvised bombs from Pepsi cans filled with gunpowder from artillery shells and packed with "creative" fragmentation such as glass or gravel. The tops were then sealed with tar and capped with a fuse. The attackers crept up on our positions behind walls at night and hurled the makeshift bombs at our troops. The flying, sizzling cans hit the pavement, looking like nearly spent cigarettes being cast into the street. The ensuing flash and bang caused little damage, and in most cases, our soldiers captured the inept manufacturers of these beverage bombs.

After a few days of "Pepsi" war, C Company thwarted a more serious attempt at injury to our soldiers by their alertness and swift action on July 7. Two men on a motorcycle followed First Sergeant Mike Evans' convoy, which was rotating troops from a position. The assailants intended to advance to the trail vehicle, shoot a soldier point-blank with a pistol, and escape down a side alley, as had been done in Baghdad.

Our soldiers, having had previous experiences with punks on motorcycles, carefully watched the riders. As they approached their turnoff, Mike decided to make the turn but use the vehicles as an instant barricade on the road. The tactic caught the thugs completely by surprise. The motorcyclists braked sharply and tried to jump their bike across the median to escape the soldier blockade. The soldiers fired warning shots. The passenger took a poorly aimed shot with a 9mm Beretta-style pistol. Our soldiers' next shots showed no mercy, hitting the armed man in the leg. The driver gave up but his passenger attempted resistance by continuing to fire. Specialist Ricardo Uribe's M-16 rifle put a shot into the jaw of the gunman that ended the engagement. Both Iraqi men were captured, and the wounded man struggled for life at our local combat hospital with tubes stuck in every opening of his body. Again, the ranks of the enemy were thinned.

The following day, our entire battalion ventured out from Tikrit to well north of Bayjii on a 50-kilometer raid of a house belonging to Saddam Hussein's first cousin, Fidel al-Asawi. This was the third major raid to directly target Saddam in as many weeks. The intelligence was decent and came from sources that had led to past successful raids. The intelligence claimed that Saddam was being harbored on this farm. Given that he had nearly been caught at the Hadooshi farm, this seemed plausible.

Our recon platoon, led by Chris Morris, along with the oft-attached Brigade Reconnaissance Troop under Captain Dez Bailey, scouted the initial objective area and provided an inner cordon. Mark Stouffer's A Company, with attached engineers, provided the assault forces, while Brad Boyd's C Company provided an outer cordon. Some tanks from Jon Cecalupo's C Company, 3-66 Armor permanently attached to our task force, reinforced them.

I selected Brad Boyd, being a former Marine, to lead elements of C Company in borrowed engineer RB-15 rubber boats, from the 74th Engineer Company, along the Tigris River to effect a cordon of the riverbank at the target house. Several of us had graduated Ranger School and trained with these boats so this was not over the top. C Company had a few Rangers to rally around for this movement. We would hit them from all sides.

Two new arrivals to our task force accompanied us on this raid. Brian Bennett from *Time* magazine and world-renowned photographer Yuri Kozyrev joined our battalion for a few weeks for a feature story on our Saddam hunt operations. Brian was a remarkable and relatively young man with whom I would form a deep friendship as time passed. He was of average height and build and looked somewhat like Johnny Depp when Johnny Depp was trying to look like himself. Brian was a reporter of the highest caliber who soon earned our respect. We considered him friendly forces.

Yuri was simply incredible. An award-winning photographer and veteran of countless wars, Yuri would march to the sound of the guns all over the globe to capture amazing pictures. With more lives than a cat, he would later snap incredible shots of our firefights. So it was, this unlikely assembly set out in the early morning hours of July 8.

Saddam's cousin, much to our disappointment, did not occupy the house we raided but had been there recently. We discovered this only after a grand entrance provided by Mark's "Gators" of A Company. Unable to gain access to the single entry behind the plush house, the men of Matt Myer's platoon, armed with a 10-pound sledgehammer, wailed on a system of sturdy anti-theft bars protecting the door to the kitchen and all the windows. After four minutes of sweaty work, the soldiers decided to use a door charge of C-4 explosives, using the "P for Plenty" method of measurement. The resulting blast remodeled the kitchen with a nice open-air view to the bluffs on the Tigris. It rearranged the dishes in the cabinets, as well as the cabinets themselves, and provided open windows for all of the rooms on the ground floor.

A continued search of the house revealed important documents, photographs, and small amounts of explosives. Hidden in the yard was a cache of RPG launchers, ammunition, a machine gun and several AK-47 rifles. Our mission was complete in a matter of hours, so we picked up our "Regular" navy from the Tigris and moved with the entire task force back to Tikrit. It was a remarkable testament to the flexibility of our soldiers and showed the versatility of infantry when properly equipped and led.

Back in Tikrit, we started what became known as the "Graffiti Wars" with the enemy. We wanted to counter an array of absurd and poorly written Arabic slogans that prophesied the return of Saddam and called for death to Americans and those who collaborated with Americans. A silhouette of Saddam's head often accompanied these slogans. We initially simply painted bayonets stuck in the Saddam heads, some even adorned with blood spurts or an eyeball popping out to incite effect. We also posted news that a $25,000,000 reward awaited the captor who brought him in, dead or alive.

Stirring a hornet's nest of sorts, we augmented our information campaign, thanks to Specialist David Haggerty, with whom I had served in Kosovo, with neat stencils and Arabic writing propagating the "Down with Saddam" theme. About this time, Greg Palkot, from Fox News, accompanied our task force and reported on our combat operations live from Tikrit. Fox News, *Time* magazine, and *Stern* magazine all began coverage of our operations.

The news people seemed to be amused and intrigued with our graffiti campaign. I assured them that we had not lost our minds. We simply refused to allow the enemy even the slightest advantage, not even with their slanderous graffiti. To prevent the opponent from returning to his venomous wall themes, we had snipers fire warning shots nearby. These slogans and symbols were the insignia of the Saddam Fedayeen, a silhouette of Saddam's head surrounded by the words "God, Country, Leader." The Fedayeen were the revolutionaries we were beginning to fight in large numbers in street battles and they were clearly marking their territory.

Some territory was more important than other territory. We

wrapped concertina wire around one major sign along the main highway and placed magnesium trip flares within the wire so that if the Fedayeen pulled the wire away to alter our handiwork, they got the scare of their lives. The graffiti campaign produced results. We noticed that more and more people cleaned it off their walls or replaced it with tasteful murals or professional signs. Either way, we won.

By July 12, we saw some Iraqis were targeted by hostile forces for working with us. The attacks were mostly threats, but some improvised explosives were thrown at people's farms. In one such case, a Pepsi bomb sizzled in a sparkly arc into a man's courtyard and rolled to a stop. His curious cat spotted it and immediately pounced after it. Its paw was raised for action just as the bomb detonated. I guess the old saying is true after all.

THE STRONG MAN

Constant movement and action from our task force characterized the days that followed. We planned, assembled, raided, exploited, reassembled, and set out again for the next operation. An area to the east of the Tigris, known for its love of mortars and an enemy willingness to use them, was the initial focus of our operations. As our soldiers moved through the farms and fields, fanning out across a wide area, we noticed little things that caused us to take a closer look. Before long, the farms and fields yielded a bounty from a different crop. Soldiers with minesweepers and shovels soon harvested rifles, weapons, and RPG launchers. Farmers claimed innocence but could neither explain the weapons nor their lack of weathered hands and feet that betrayed their disguise. They soon became unemployed.

Our operations continued with our mechanized infantry delivered to their objectives in Bradleys, trucks, V-hulled boats, and helicopters. We remained versatile, and the impact on the morale of the soldiers was very positive. Many of them had never used these techniques before, at Ft. Hood or any other location in their military careers. I saw them as infantry and employed them in the most effective means possible to accomplish the mission. And accomplish it they did. The impact on the enemy became steadily measurable, and we continued to impair him.

Our goal was to press the enemy until he realized that he could never sustain his operations, be as flexible as we were, match his will against ours or, most importantly, defeat our forces. We had to show him that it was better to abandon the Saddam legacy and align himself with the new Iraq—even in Tikrit. We were already beginning to see a lack of popular support for our enemy among their own population. I believed that the Sunni Arab would side with the strong man. If we showed ourselves to be tough and strong, they would cast their allegiance accordingly. If we showed ourselves to be weak, they would counter us. If we could contain the Sunni Arab resistance, I believed, the rest of Iraq would likely follow.

That was the hope for the future. For the present, the enemy clearly had fight left in him, and it was growing. He began to take advantage of our American code of ethics and honor. Not only would he hide behind his women and children, engaging us from multi-family dwellings, but he also attempted to kill those who cooperated with us, including the old and indefensible.

One such target was a man named Nathem who had worked with our forces since our arrival. He was the owner of the curious cat. On July 14, he was visiting his son's auto parts shop in downtown Tikrit. Four men came into the shop and began to threaten and argue with the 55-year-old man. Weapons were soon exposed. Nathem pulled a pistol and fired near the attackers to ward them off. He quickly emptied his pistol. When he was out of ammo, he was surrounded and shot point-blank, once in the head and twice in the chest.

Nathem's two sons came running to his aid. The younger one had an AK-47, which he promptly emptied into the man who had just killed his father. He then used the empty rifle to club another man senseless. His older brother, armed with only a hammer, nailed away at the head of the third attacker. Two of the four escaped. The engagement was effectively over, but nothing could bring back Nathem. He lay in a pool of blood next to his weeping sons before our soldiers were able to identify the direction of the gunshots and rush to them.

Nathem was a hero for the new Iraqi nation. He took a stand when others would not. Two days before he died, this man gave us information about activity in a village to the north of Tikrit. We used that information to target a series of selected farms and maneuvered our forces by tank, Bradley, truck, scout Humvee, and even boats in the Tigris River to access the banks of the village. Within four hours, our men had unearthed over 250 AK-47 rifles, 56 crates of Composition 4 (C-4 plastic explosives) totaling over two and a half tons, eight crates of blasting caps for the explosives (25,000 in all), surveillance equipment, and a variety of military goods and wares. The men felt proud, especially the brave tankers who discovered the largest cache, to have found a way to honor Nathem's death. We were all saddened by the loss of this poor, honest, and decent man. Their numbers were too few in the godforsaken town of post-Saddam Tikrit to lose even one.

But lose one more we did, a local national whose English skills made him an effective translator. He was a simpleminded, strong, humble man in his forties who had a penchant for the bottle. One night he drifted away from his dwelling. When his body was discovered floating in the Tigris River snared in the nets of our military float bridge, we recognized signs of a major struggle and a severe beating. No doubt he was rolled into the river to finish the brutal attack on his life.

THE RETURN

The enemy stepped up activity all around the city. Locals told us that they had been warned of Saddam's imminent return and that cooperation with Americans would exact a heavy penalty. This grandiose return would be on July 17, the day Saddam first came to power and a former holiday of the old regime. For weeks this rumor had been brewing. Every Iraqi believed that Saddam's loyalists might return and defeat us on this anniversary.

We first learned of the enemy's activity in Tikrit when he spread rumors that we had imposed a curfew banning all movement on July 17. We noticed on the evening of the 16th that many of the shops were closing early. We asked the locals why and soon learned of the rumor. We immediately countered with bullhorns and translators telling the people that the 17th was a normal day and that they could move about freely as they were now a free people. Saddam no longer had the power to control them. The cheers and applause that greeted these messages could easily be heard above the bullhorns. The next day the city was teeming with normal activity.

That evening, however, the enemy attempted to show his presence. I had posted several observation posts (OPs) around the city, manned by our scouts. Our troops would be alerted to enemy activity, preventing them from moving between sectors undetected. We still did not have enough men trained, but as it happened, on this night I did have three such outposts in critical areas. In time, teams of snipers, scout- and infantry-manned OPs, and roving combat patrols would give us a firm grip on the city. At this stage, my men were not yet trained well enough to survive should an OP be compromised.

One such outpost was posted on a public building dominating the south end of 40th Street known as the "Women's College." It was actually a school for girls but it provided an excellent field of view at a key intersection in the inner residential district. At this particular outpost, Sergeant Jesse Sample and Corporal Andrew Brokish established an excellent OP on top of the college roof. They were in good communication with Chris Morris and the rest of the Scout Platoon and reported our patrols along 40th Street.

At 11:50 on the night of July 17, I patrolled the city in my Humvee convoy that included a 5-ton truck that was tasked with collecting curfew violators. They would be an instant labor force for graffiti removal around the city. As we cruised around southern Tikrit on 40th Street near the Women's College, also known as "RPG Alley," the area once again proved itself to be aptly named.

My driver, Cody Hoefer, had always been instructed to follow his gut. If something did not seem right, he should act on his instinct. I did the same. On a whim, I told him to turn right at the last minute in front of the Women's College rather than proceed ahead. That was the exact moment that the enemy launched an ambush. Not anticipating our right turn, a volley of two RPGs narrowly missed our Hummer as they were expecting us to continue in a straight line through the intersection.

An RPG making contact sounds like a dumpster dropped from a fifty-story building. The volley struck in a prong with the left fork heading near Sergeant Sample's observation post atop the Women's College and the right fork just barely missing our convoy due to the spontaneous right turn. The sound was deafening as the concussion washed over us.

Sergeant Sample and Corporal Brokish were knocked off their feet by the concussion. Hunched over and skirting the rim of the building, they immediately made a run for the lower floors to link up with other scout elements.

My men and I immediately jumped the median of the multi-lane street and directed our unarmored vehicles back into the direction of the enemy. Every infantryman knows that the best way to survive an ambush is to turn into it. While not the reflexive thing to do, it may startle the enemy enough to let you get your bearings and have a fighting chance.

Our men deployed as small arms fire began to crack around us. The enemy had taken cover. I desperately tried to find the source of fire. Bullets aimed directly at a person make a distinct supersonic and deafening crack, not a "wisp" or "zip" as the movies portray. I could get a general sense of direction but not a precise location. The enemy was firing from dark rooftops and long shadows, and we were in the worst of all possible positions, a well-lit, four-way, four-lane intersection.

In a matter of seconds, I considered a hundred things. My men were behind cover, but they could not see the enemy either. I knew we could not stay there. Then the firing suddenly stopped. I was furious. We couldn't see them. I knew we had to reestablish contact with them or they would hit us again, now or later. My troops were not hit, and our equipment suffered no visible damage. It was time to act.

Angered at this point at the enemy's impudence, I walked out into the bright intersection and shouted oaths and epitaphs toward the enemy, taunting him to come out. "Sir, get down. You're going to get hit," someone called from behind.

"No, let's go," I ordered, sternly glancing sideward. "We have to reestablish contact with the enemy."

Suddenly, a few shots of small arms fire snapped. It seemed to come from the rooftop directly to the east. Good, I thought. They're still here. Gaining the cover of a low and crudely laid block wall, I saw Lieutenant Colonel Dave Poirier with a few MPs in a couple of Hummers across the way. He heard the gunfire and raced to our location.

"What do you need, Steve?" he questioned across the street.

"Can you cover the main road on the east side so we can cut them off as we wedge them forward?" I shouted to him. He gave a big nod. I asked if he could drop to our frequency, and he nodded again.

This accomplished, I began to make out a couple of Chris Morris' scout Hummers coming from the north.

"Chris, turn around and take this street back north while we go one block over, and we'll do the same," I ordered. "The MPs are one more street over for a backstop. We will drive them back north to the open area. Be careful. They have RPGs."

Mike Rauhut radioed our situation to battalion and brigade. A section of Bradleys was alerted. Along for the ride tonight was Major Bryan Luke. He was visiting from division to become acquainted with his new job as our operations officer when released to join us. I was glad to have him. We now moved on a residential side street parallel with my scouts who were to the left on 40th Street.

I began to feel somewhat better. We now had some extra forces, and more were coming, but timing was critical. I didn't want the enemy to escape. Without uniforms, it's hard to identify them and get them to commit. We clearly had contact with a pocket of them, and I wanted them dead. As we moved north on parallel streets, we came to a cross street that, if viewed from above, would form the bar of the letter 'H.' The streetlight painted us all too well. Our night observation devices (NODs) mounted on our helmets struggled to identify the enemy with the bright residential lights washing them out. If we flipped up the NODs we couldn't see anyone in the shadows. If we flipped down the NODs, we got the washout effect.

Suddenly, chaos erupted. Small arms fire chipped pavement all around us and pocked the walls near the sidewalks. The enemy opened up with automatic rifles and what sounded like at least one submachine gun. Bullets smacked the scout Hummers, and soldiers could not see where they were coming from. It is a terrible feeling. You know you are in danger but you cannot see where to shoot back. You are not helpless because you have a weapon, but to use it, you have to find the guys who are trying to kill you before they succeed.

I could hear the deafening crack of shots aimed directly at me as pavement chipped nearby. Still not seeing the fire, I at least got a decent orientation on the sound so I took a knee and began to fire at the rooftop of a small building about 75 yards ahead.

"I'm hit!" someone screamed.

To the left, I noticed someone fall to the pavement from the scout Humvee. A medic rushed to the injured soldier and grabbed the nylon strap on the back of his body armor. The sound of a man being dragged across the concrete could be heard.

"Shoot back!" I shouted and continued to fire my M-4 carbine.

Mike Rauhut grabbed the Q-Beam maintenance light we had in the Humvee. I had ordered these when I took command. We used them effectively in Kosovo to spotlight the enemy, not unlike spotlighting deer in season. Mike began to shine it along the rooftops.

"I think I see one!" someone else shouted.

"Shoot him! Shoot the son of a . . . !"

Thunk, thunk, thunk. The Mark-19 grenades sailed through the air. The rounds whacked another rooftop to the right of the one at which I was shooting.

"I think I got him!" Specialist Felipe Lazen called out.

The fire ceased. I took a quick look around. Specialist Percell Phillips was hit. Sergeant Richard Giardine, the scout medic, said he would be all right. Phillips had been manning a Mark-19 grenade launcher from the cupola of one of the scout trucks when a bullet grazed his right temple and lodged in his Kevlar helmet. The force of the bullet "cork-screwed" him around and tossed him to the pavement. While a bit bloodied, he would be mended with a dozen stitches, leaving only a nice barroom scar for future war stories. I thanked God that he was not seriously hurt. He would return to duty in a couple of weeks.

Not so the enemy. Our combined return fire had indeed eliminated one, probably more. Chris' scouts searched the area of the two buildings where we returned fire. Enemy shell casings littered the rooftops. A trail of blood led down from the roof where we fired the Mark-19. The blood trails tapered off until our men could no longer track them. They had no doubt been given sanctuary within any number of possible residences in the neighborhood.

We confirmed later the name of the insurgent we killed when a martyr banner appeared the next day. These were black muslin banners with hand-painted calls for a wake bearing a slogan about martyrdom. They looked very similar to regular Iraqi funeral announcements, but the lettering was different. Joe Filmore always alerted our men to them. We cut this one down, as we did all martyr banners. On it was the name of Arkan Najan Abdullah Hamza al-Duri. He was a relative of Izzat Ibrahim al-Duri, the King of Clubs on the deck of cards. Izzat was the former Vice Chairman of the Revolutionary Command Council and one of the original members of the coup that brought Saddam to power.

As we assessed the situation, the outcome was satisfactory. We had been ambushed and fought our way through it with one man slightly wounded. It was not pretty, but combat never is. We could withstand whatever they threw at us in RPG Alley. I told my men that we would never be unwilling to go into this neighborhood.

"Sir, are you okay? Did you get hit?" asked Mike Rauhut.

"No, I'm fine, Mike." I said, relieved.

"I don't see how," he replied. "I saw fire hitting all around you."

"God is good!" I offered with a smile.

As things settled, I noticed a reporter from what I believe was the European *Stern* magazine standing nearby. In the pandemonium, I had forgotten that he was on board with us that night. He had been a quite pleasant man when we visited earlier. Seeing a camera around his neck, I asked, "Hey, did you get any pictures?"

"Of the pavement!" he replied with the wide eyes and excited smile of a survivor. We all had a good laugh.

Scroll forward a few hours. Mark Stouffer's A Company had been patrolling the streets of a dusty farm village south of Tikrit, checking for anything abnormal. Rocket-propelled grenades flying toward you certainly qualified. The men brought their Bradley section into action but the assailants fled into a house. The "Gators" of A Company quickly recovered from the near misses of the RPGs and brought their force to bear on the house. Mark's infantry spilled out the back of the vehicles, joining others brought in by truck. The house was empty of attackers but not weapons. The enemy fled, leaving an RPG launcher and three rockets. Patrols arrested the attackers the following day when they tried to return.

Go forward another hour to northern Tikrit and the "Cobras" of C Company. A skinny man on a motorcycle cruised down the four-lane road with an even skinnier weapon. The silhouette revealed it to be an RPG launcher strapped to his back. He was still a good distance from the Birthday Palace but close enough to be deemed hostile. Fusillades of fire greeted the man, causing him to turn wildly and escape down a side alley. He was quickly absorbed into the city under the cover of night. His attack and, no doubt, his pride were thwarted. Unfortunately, we did not capture him. These were the events of July 17, the day of the "returning" enemy.

While certainly active, it was a pathetic effort to usher in Saddam's return to power.

While the enemy's boastful claims of Saddam's return on July 17 never materialized, something else was born on that date. On the morning of July 18, the people had a different view. Rather than Saddam and his henchmen, the Iraqis saw their own police, government officials, and American forces providing for their security. They seemed to accept it. They seemed, also, to acknowledge that Saddam would not return. Even his image on the Farouk Palace Gate was blown from its mount on that morning, providing a powerful visual to those who observed it.

The Farouk Palace was the massive complex of buildings adjoining the west bank of the Tigris and the wedge between river and city. The huge bronze statue sitting atop a 50-foot-high arched gate was soon laced with explosives. A fireball of flame erupted, followed by billows of brown smoke. The metallic body of Saddam holding a banner and sitting astride a charging horse flanked by rockets soon fell down the parapet, stumbled, and crashed with finality, symbolic of Saddam's former regime. As the dust settled, the people seemed to settle with it. The Tikritis became almost tranquil when they realized that the talk of Saddam's return was just talk. The evening of July 18, 2003, was calm but for a volley of mortar rounds fired into an insignificant patch of sand near our tank company, C Company, 3-66 Armor—the "Cougars."

4. TACTICS

THE HUNTERS

While the people seemed to cooperate more, we also saw a more developed enemy. I was working feverishly with my commanders, urging them to train OPs and combat outposts to secure points in the city and eventually to set our own ambushes. It was risky work, but if it was properly done, our men would gain the element of surprise and could cause some serious damage. Nothing stops enemy ambushes more effectively than being ambushed himself.

Captain Boyd was quickly getting his troops on a war footing, but I still required the outposts. I had asked Brad and all my commanders how quickly they could be ready. "We are an infantry battalion," I reminded them. "We ought to be able to do these things. We may have Bradleys to ride, but we must still fight like infantry. I want to know how soon we can be ready."

"Sir, it will take at least three weeks," Brad asserted. The other commanders agreed. "I have to take these guys through baby steps," he continued. "It's not that they can't shoot or fight; it's the patience and concealment part that needs work. I plan to give them outposts near the Birthday Palace for a few hours at a time until they improve."

The evening of July 19 was a good example of improvement. Brad ordered Sergeant Andrew McKnight, Sergeant Jarvis Gibson, and Sergeant Joseph Sheldrick to establish an OP ambush providing security and warning to C Company opposite the main entrance of the Birthday Palace. At 11:10 p.m., the men sighted a two-man Fedayeen team in long-sleeved black clothing with shemaghs drawn down to cover their faces. They had stealthily scaled a wall and were now in direct view of the soldiers across the street. They did not see the soldiers and began to work a corner near the Birthday Palace entrance, each with a loaded RPG launcher.

Sergeant McKnight whispered to the others and upon seeing the RPG launchers, he opened up on the insurgents. The first bullet struck two inches from an insurgent's head, perforating the rear flange of the RPG, and causing him to lose control of it. Startled by the shot, the enemy prematurely squeezed the trigger, wildly firing his RPG grenade into the street. The second insurgent also pulled the trigger of his weapon, sending a deadly blast into the compound wall 15 meters short of his intended mark. Metallic, echoed booms, followed by a patter of gypsum-starved concrete from the wall and pavement from the street, blended with the sharp pops of American rifle fire from Sergeants McKnight, Gibson, and Sheldrick. The soldiers at the gate hunkered behind sandbags and were not harmed.

The badly shattered enemy fled over a breach in the residential wall he was pinned against and into even darker shadows. Brad gathered a knot of men who had hastily assembled inside his compound. A Bradley Fighting Vehicle crashed through the gate and flattened it to the ground. Brad led his forces in the direction of the last known location of the attackers.

Chris Morris, hearing the sound of the guns, brought his forces on patrol, and I joined in with my command group and interpreter on patrol in the city. All of our forces began to cordon approximately four blocks of the city along a two-street axis. The enemy fled on foot, ditching weapons, grenades, and other items that would mark them as hostile. The soldiers weaved through city blocks, unable to find those whose attack had been thwarted.

That night, Brad Boyd, First Sergeant Mike Evans, and Sergeant Andrew McKnight presented a shot-up RPG launcher to me with the boyish and deserved pride of hunters showing off their game. In their hands was proof that this elusive, insurgent enemy was not 20 feet tall. He could be found, and he could be defeated.

The men were making progress. They were becoming alert and on the hunt. The enemy, on the other hand, found himself looking over his shoulder, worried about our ambushes rather than planning ambushes of his own. The tale of my taunting the enemy at the open intersection circulated widely through the battalion. The morale of the men shot up after these three days of combat as we began to hit the enemy hard and seized the initiative. Not only were we seizing it in raids against Saddam's inner circle, but in street fights as well. Patrols and OPs throughout our sector gained confidence. I told the men that we would be the hunters, not the hunted.

SALT LICK, CATFISH TRAPS, AND SPAWNS

On the morning of July 20, a command-detonated explosive, hidden in a pothole, erupted. A Humvee from a passing Military Police element was the target. The attack happened on Highway 1, the main highway that vertically bisected Tikrit and connected it with Bayjii in the north and Samarra in the south.

Three soldiers were wounded, but fortunately, they were very near one of our surgical hospitals. Jon Cecalupo's "Cougars" quickly loaded the wounded into their tanks and provided medical assistance. Thankfully, the men were not seriously injured. Sifting through the debris, our men noticed parts of a cell phone used to detonate the device. Also visible were parts of a mortar tube, apparently packed with C-4 and used to make a "super pipe bomb" in a very unconventional manner.

We used our own mortars in the conventional manner on the following day. Finally given permission for counter battery fire, the "Thunder" soldiers of our mortar platoon registered 120mm rounds, sending earth and stubble skyward from abandoned fields. For weeks now, the division compound had been harassed with enemy mortar fire. We begged to shoot back with our own counterfire but had been denied. Then we asked to fire Harassment and Interdiction fire (H&I) on the locations that we were able to trace back with radar. Those were mostly rural areas. The enemy could shoot from the eastern side of the Tigris River and lob shells into the huge palace compound where the 4th Infantry Division headquarters resided. Our logic was, if observed, the H&I fire would keep the insurgents out of the field altogether. General Odierno agreed and gave us the permission we needed.

We fired numerous rounds over several days to counter the enemy's indirect fire attacks. Once our fires began, enemy mortar activity declined sharply. This was the first firing of "Regular" mortars from the 22nd Infantry since Vietnam, and the men were proud to carry on the tradition of veterans before us while keeping the indiscriminately lobbed mortar rounds of the insurgents at bay.

Over the next few days, I sat down with Mike Rauhut and Bryan Luke to assess the situation. Still desperately short of needed infantry, both of my infantry commanders in Tikrit were doing what they could to help. Colonel Hickey relieved the Bradley section guarding his headquarters and replaced it with his own headquarters troops. This freed an additional patrol for us. He also relieved us from guarding the massive ammunition dump southwest of Tikrit, giving us an additional force. Colonel Hickey replaced our troops at the ammo dump with Lieutenant Colonel Mark Huron's 299th Engineers, who were blowing up hundreds of thousands of enemy munitions there.

With my rifle companies regaining their guard forces and with the relief from having to guard key infrastructure in the city, the liberated force allowed me to make my units more mobile and agile. Still, I needed OPs, combat outposts, and snipers. My scouts had the OP capability well in hand, and my infantry were learning the trade of combat outposts, as Sergeant McKnight's group had proven, but we still needed a tight net to track and kill the enemy lurking in alleys and city streets. We had snipers, but they were scattered throughout the battalion when I took command. I brought them back together but I needed a strong leader who could act independently and allow teams of two men to conduct operations over a three- to four-day period, if necessary, to get the kills. This would take the right kind of leader and Command Sergeant Major Pete Martinez and I worked diligently to find him.

To reform the snipers, we needed the absolute best and most resourceful staff sergeant in the battalion. I told my company commanders to submit their best because we would find them anyway. We interviewed some of the finest squad leaders in the battalion. While each was excellent in his own right, the man qualified to lead the snipers needed to possess resourcefulness, bravery, patience, assertiveness, and innovation . . . and perhaps a bit of insanity.

We found him in Staff Sergeant Brad Owens, one of Mark Stouffer's "Gators" from A Company. Brad had the mind-set needed for this mission and I knew Chris Morris could work with him in the Scout Platoon. While the snipers would work directly for me, they would also work hand-in-hand with my Scout Platoon. Chris' scouts would primarily seek, while Brad Owen's snipers would kill. The tasks and tactics were very much different.

Of the nine soldiers in the sniper section, four of them were graduates of the U.S. Army Sniper School at Ft. Benning. I instructed Brad Owens to build a fourth team with his headquarters element, even though we only had three sniper rifles. We were able to build another team by using the Russian-made SVD sniper rifle captured at the Hadooshi farm.

The soldiers needed to realize what I hoped to accomplish in Tikrit. In each district of the city, scout eyes, reinforced by sniper teams in augmenting locations, were needed to track enemy movement. The scouts would then pass off the enemy to roving combat patrols that would bird-dog him until he could be positioned for the kill. I estimated the need for about four scout OPs, three to four sniper teams, several combat outposts from the companies, and roving combat patrols. We would use these components like "bumpers" on a pinball machine, giving the enemy no place to hide. Once identified, he would be killed or ambushed.

I used two illustrations to convey the plan to my men. The first was called the "Salt Lick." In any typical infantry battalion, there are hundreds of soldiers with hunting experience. A common tactic in deer hunting is to place a salt block, during the off-season, in an area where deer are likely to travel. The hunter determines where the deer might move by observing lines of drift, water sources, wind direction, etc. He then places a block of salt called a "salt lick" in that area. The deer licks it until the hunter removes it during deer season. With a deer stand in place, the hunter is ready when the deer comes looking for the salt, and bang, he gets the buck.

I told my commanders we would use "salt lick" tactics to strike the enemy. We knew the areas in which he moved, his "lines of drift." He wanted to ambush us on known routes and choke points that we had to travel, but also in areas where he could readily escape into dense parts of the city. Knowing this, we would establish our own ambushes; when the enemy went in search of us—bang, we would get the buck. My commanders got it. So did our men.

The second analogy I used was the "catfish trap." Each trap is a box made of long slats, somewhat like a picket fence on each side, so the water can pass through the trap but not the fish. Ideally, it is laid lengthwise in the direction of the flow of water. There is a divider in the center of the box, with a funnel made of more slats that are sharp at one end. It funnels the incoming fish, like a street cone, but wide enough to let the fish pass through. The opening is not too wide so that, as the fish turns around and tries to enter through the nose of the cone, his whiskers touch the sharp ends of the slats and he refuses to swim back through. The second compartment is soon full of catfish waiting to be rolled in cornmeal and fried for dinner.

I told my commanders that the "slats" of our catfish trap would be our scouts, combat outposts, and OPs in the city. As the enemy advanced, he would be passed off from place to place until he was "boxed" in. We would then strike with combat patrols and snipers and soon have the insurgents rolled in cornmeal, frying for dinner. Combining this with the "salt lick" ambushes, our men could ambush or be focal points for obliterating the enemy.

It would take a few days to redirect our forces, but the men now perceived the basics well enough to employ the new tactics. On the evening of July 22, as we began to apply some of these sniper teams, scout OPs, and combat patrol tactics, we noticed that a strange mood had descended over the city. Every eye was glued to the television set as the breaking news of Uday and Qusay Hussein's deaths jolted the population like an electric shock.

Tikrit was eerily quiet, but not without danger. At approximately 10:50 p.m., we heard another familiar "dumpster crash," signaling an RPG attack, as we headed south in our command group convoy. We pressed northward along the main highway bisecting the town and saw a pall of bluish smoke. Local men gestured from balconies, giving us the general direction of the activity. A quick patrol from our men looped around the block, but we found nothing. The target was a photo shop wedged into a corner. It was all very strange. Perhaps the assailant didn't get his film on time.

BROTHERS, BROTHER-IN-LAW

As I rolled to my feet from a short, deep sleep in the early hours of July 23, I had no idea how long and violent the day would be. By dusk, it was clear that the enemy had become very active, given the scattered reports of gunfire and mortars throughout the day from all the subordinate commands. Even with such obvious activity, the enemy remained elusive, though his damage was negligible. Perhaps the news of brothers Uday and Qusay Hussein's deaths had ignited even more hatred and anger. Regardless of what may have sparked the evening's events, it was a day I would never forget.

While my team and I patrolled Tikrit that evening, my radio crackled with a report from Brad Boyd and C Company. At about 9:30 p.m., Brad's troops reported stopping a speeding car containing 25 million Iraqi dinar (about $15,000). Because it was an unusual sum and he did not understand the explanation the men in the car offered, Boyd called to ask for assistance. His men set up a checkpoint as we took my translator, Joe Filmore, to the scene to decipher the situation. There, Brad and I learned the Iraqis in the car were brothers who had made a legitimate business transaction on the sale of some property. Since everything in Iraq is on a cash basis, they were afraid of being robbed and hurried back to their house.

We went to the house they claimed to have sold and, after

verifying the documents, released them. I loaded my command troops in our Hummers and proceeded south in the city. Boyd's patrol withdrew their checkpoint and prepared to leave.

Simultaneously, but quite unknown to us, Ali Maher Abdul Rashid had been waiting for such an opportunity. Working with a number of men, former Special Security Office and Fedayeen leader Rashid was determined to avenge the death of Saddam's sons. He had already organized attacks in our area and would personally lead another on that night. After all, his sister, May, was married to Saddam's son, Qusay, and he was set on revenge.

With a group of willing followers composed of loyal Saddam families and a few students recruited from the University of Baghdad, Rashid was confident that he could continue to infiltrate after curfew, using ambulances to mask his cells' movements. Having had one such encounter with an ambulance already, we were expecting a recurrence of confiscated ambulances for aiding and transporting insurgents.

Spotting the activity of some American soldiers who had stopped a car near a residential area, Rashid himself found a good location to ambush the unsuspecting Americans at the checkpoint. With Salmon Khalid Faris, Leith Adnan Azawi, and Khalid Adai Aweed, he hastily organized an attack. Heavily armed with RPGs, grenades and automatic weapons, Rashid staged their pickup truck for a quick escape and took two men with him up a back alley.

Meanwhile, Rashid's other men operating in the city center camouflaged their movement in an ambulance on the main highway route for further opportunity. After making his way up the alley, Rashid noticed the soldiers leaving the area. If he was going to hit the unsuspecting Americans, the time had to be now.

As Captain Boyd's soldiers, now nicknamed "Cobras," left the T-intersection, a crash of RPG rounds thundered around them, accompanied by small arms fire. Though they were surprised and shaken, no harm came to the men inside the Bradleys or to the vehicles themselves. The attackers fled to points south as rapidly as they had fired.

The shock wave of explosions mixed with the rattle of rifle fire behind us jolted all my senses into high alert. We were heading south in complete blackout conditions when we heard explosions near the location we had just left. The first thing that flashed through my mind was the possibility that the enemy would attempt to escape along the narrow parallel streets to avoid contact with reacting forces. I had studied insurgent tactics such as those used effectively in places like Northern Ireland and Algeria. Since an open field to the north rimmed Boyd's checkpoint, I was certain that the enemy would not go there and would likely be on my side of the city block. I wanted to turn back toward the place we suspected the attack may have originated, but I needed to get some more distance for a "buttonhook" up the back alleys to intercept them.

"Hoefer, go down a couple of blocks and 'buttonhook' back up on the parallel street one block over," I shouted as we raced south. "We might be able to cut them off."

"Roger, sir," replied the calm and focused Crow Indian.

Ali Rashid and his men leapt into the small, white Nissan pickup. His driver was already moving, with the truck's tailgate open. Their faces were covered with headdresses as they hopped into the back with their RPG, grenades, and rifles. They raced south from their ambush, darting through the small residential side streets to safety.

"Regular six, Cobra six," crackled the radio.

"Regular six," I answered.

"Sir, our soldiers and Brads are OK. They attacked with RPGs. We're moving troops to that location," Captain Boyd radioed. He deployed his forces toward the ambush and called out another one of his platoons from the nearby Saddam Birthday Palace.

With wind racing, hearts pounding and fingers gingerly touching our weapons, we dashed at full throttle a couple of blocks south. "Turn left and cut back up the next street!" I yelled at Hoefer.

"Go one more street down!" shouted Major Bryan Luke, now fully on board as my operations officer. Cody Hoefer obliged. My guys had been instructed to act on their gut instincts while on patrol so this did not concern me. It was just one of those things we all could feel. Bryan's gut would have major consequences tonight. As we button-hooked back north, I could see we were well ahead of the other two vehicles in my command convoy. As we skidded around the second corner to head back north, my eyes locked in on a white Nissan pickup fishtailing around a corner, heading toward us, about 100 yards ahead. My mind raced as I processed the visible weapons and covered faces of the enemy poised for action in the back of the truck. The game was on. No time. No time to think.

I instinctively flipped the safety on my M-4 carbine to fire. I saw the shape of an RPG in the back. There were four men in the truck.

"Cut 'em off!" I yelled.

Cody Hoefer veered to the left to block the pickup. Looks of surprise flashed from beneath the Arab headdresses. Hoefer did not just cut them off. He rammed the Nissan head-on. Just before he did, I leapt from the Hummer. The enemy was startled by the impact. I was already on my feet charging the vehicle, aiming for the driver behind the windshield. He raised his hands as if to protect his face as I fired. I was not going to let them drive away. Spiderwebbed circles appeared on the glass. The back window shattered. Did I hit him enough times? The driver was slumped in his seat after my opening burst, so I shifted my attention to the two men in the back.

The second vehicle in my convoy rounded the corner, seeing enemy fire sail through the air from the insurgents in the back of the truck. Neither Hoefer nor I noticed it through our tunneled view, heightened senses, and pumped-up adrenaline. Bryan Luke, with radio hand mic stuck inside his helmet, ripped out the cord to make a quick exit as he moved up beside Hoefer on the sidewalk next to the vehicle.

I saw a blur of clothing and flashes from AK-47s and heard earsplitting sound from my rifle and theirs. I rounded the Nissan driver's door, crouching low to work my way under the guys in the back. I squeezed the pad for the tactical flashlight on the foregrip of my weapon and fired heavily into the pool of light it threw, point-blank on the torso of a man standing in the back of the pickup near the cab, firing his AK-47. He fell straight down as my rounds walked up, stitching him in the gut, chest, face, and head.

Specialist Hoefer cut down the big man riding shotgun as he attempted to fire an American M-79 grenade launcher while exiting the passenger side of the Nissan. The big man fell to the ground with bullets in the torso and face as his weapon fell with a thud and metallic clunk. With Hoefer on one side and me on the other, we had them trapped in an 'L' with no place to go.

I shifted fire to the other man in the back who was wearing a red and white checkered headdress. He seemed to hesitate. He could have raised his hands and lived. He could have fired to survive, but instead he tried to flee. I could see my rounds hitting him in the hip and torso as he and his AK-47 tumbled to the other side of the vehicle.

Working his M-16 with Major Luke firing beside him, Specialist Hoefer fired at the same man, now struggling on the other side of the pickup. He became a wadded-up heap beside the right rear wheel as we finished him off with our rifle fire.

Our other soldiers in the trail vehicles had come alongside to support, but the enemy lay scattered where he fell. A Fedayeen cell was destroyed. *Time* photographer Yuri Kozyrev captured the fight on film.

With the enemy appearing subdued, I instinctively let out a guttural yell at the top of my lungs. I don't know where it came from or why. It was an instinctive response as when one has suddenly won a contest. Catching myself, I glanced toward Hoefer and saw Bryan and him standing on the sidewalk with weapons up. I could hear boots thudding down the street and the rattle of flapping equipment as the men in the trail vehicles came running up.

Insanely, one of the trail men fired a shot at the last man killed who was obviously already dead. "Cease fire, CEASE FIRE!" I shouted. "We will show quarter." It was clear we had subdued them. In the heat of battle, when the blood lust is up, men will react in different ways. It is vital that leaders keep the men in check. The circumstances may be understandable, but it is imperative for leaders to exhibit total control to prevent immoral acts.

The worst danger had momentarily passed. I looked around to confirm that there were no other enemies nearby. We could still be in great danger. Magazine, I thought. Check your ammo. I pushed the magazine release with my trigger finger. One round left. Flipping my rifle safety with my thumb, I reached down and pulled the Velcro flap on a magazine pouch on my kit and slapped in a new magazine. I checked my rifle; it was still loaded with a round in the chamber.

"Search 'em." I ordered. "Let's get some security out as well."

Bryan Luke found a working hand mic on the radio and made the report to battalion. Soldiers throughout the city heard the explosions and gunfire of these two fights within minutes of one another. Soon, Captain Brad Boyd and First Sergeant Mike Evans rolled up with a patrol of their men. We conferred briefly.

I wanted Captain Boyd to continue to scour the area south of the mosque. There were likely more bad guys waiting there to play their dirty games.

Suddenly, one of the insurgents made a horrible groan. Bullet-ridden and lying in a pool of his own blood, he also had a bullet in his forehead. How could he possibly still be alive?

"Shut up!" a soldier screamed, followed by a string of curses.

"Knock it off!" I demanded. "We will show quarter. Medic! Get up here, and see if there is anything you can do." There wasn't. The enemy was badly riddled with gunshot wounds. In moments, he gurgled his last breath.

As we were wrapping up this scene and searching the dead, a blue car and an ambulance crept cautiously along Highway 1, the main city thoroughfare. One of our OPs reported the ambulance as it pulled out of the dispatcher's station. As the next OP picked it up, they spotted two men with AK-47s exiting the ambulance and getting into the car. We had waited a long time for this one.

Staff Sergeant Brad Owens' snipers had been situated at one of several "Salt Lick" outposts on the roof of a large building on the main highway. The blue car tried to race away as glass shards flew from its rear windshield as Owens, Specialist Juan Cantu, and Specialist Danny Harris opened fire with the Russian SVD sniper, an American M-24 sniper rifle and an M-16A2 rifle. The ambulance driver could not maneuver at all. Spiderwebbed circles the size of half-dollars sequentially dotted the driver's side of the windshield. The ambulance stopped. A badly wounded man struggled out of the vehicle and collapsed on the street.

Suddenly, explosions struck our snipers. A confused "friendly" force of Military Police attached to the division's Air Defense battalion mistook our men for the enemy and fired a Mark-19 grenade launcher at the rooftop. They had no business being there. Having heard the gun battles we were engaged in, they left the division compound assuming that our men were the bad guys. Our snipers kept their heads and attempted to gain the MPs' attention by shouting down to them that they were American forces. It was to no avail. Our three men remained disciplined, despite the American automatic grenades that impacted their location, wounding one in the leg, one in the side, and one in the head.

Chris Morris was furious. He had heard Staff Sergeant Owens' report that an unknown friendly force was shooting at them. Chris rocketed toward the location. He swore at the MP soldiers and forcefully disengaged the confused element with oaths and fists. Specialist Cantu at the rooftop sniper position, in a final act of desperation, was about to throw a grenade at the friendly soldiers to interrupt their stupid attack. When Captain Morris got the MPs to stop, Cantu was left holding a grenade with a handle but no pin. He radioed Morris of his intent to toss it over the side of the building in a vacant field. One more explosion was added to the night, echoing throughout the city.

The entire team was wounded, including Owens, but thankfully, their injuries were fragmentation wounds of the flesh only. Two would return to duty right away, and the other in a few weeks.

I was pumped with adrenaline as we searched the four insurgents from the pickup, and I took this latest development hard as I heard it over the radio. Our ambushes had been extremely successful. Now, they were clouded by the careless actions of well-meaning but idiotic non-infantry soldiers. I couldn't think about it yet. There was too much activity in the city.

Lieutenant Casey Lusk, recently rotated back from Mosul, moved his QRF to our location. Mark Stouffer had dispatched him on hearing the activity on the radio. He had been given instructions to find me. Typical Mark. Head in the game. Always anticipating. I ordered Casey to secure the area, informing him that Captain Boyd and C Company had their own forces out in the area. Casey secured the corner areas with his two Bradleys and an infantry squad.

We continued to search the dead. They were now soaked in their own fluids, lying in pools created from blood, urine, and a constant stream of fuel leaking from the bullet-ridden Nissan. We dragged the bodies up on the sidewalk, a greasy path leading back to where they fell. I called the battalion, requesting that they phone the Iraqi police and someone to retrieve the bodies. This mess had to be cleaned up by morning.

"Sir, look at this." Sergeant First Class Gil Nail motioned. He was holding Indian currency and French cigarettes taken from one of the bodies. What did it mean? We collected three AK-47s, two RPG launchers with rounds prepped and ready, two hand grenades, an M-79 40mm grenade launcher with six rounds, and several magazines of small arms ammunition from the truck and the dead bodies. Armed to the teeth, these men clearly intended to kill more Americans that night.

The radio crackled with the news that the Iraqis would not retrieve the bodies. The morgue had no one to dispatch and the medical emergency vehicles would not respond given the shooting of one of their insurgent-friendly ambulances. I turned to the police who had arrived. They didn't want to deal with the bodies either. I asked if they could get a police pickup truck to the location. They did do that.

There had to be no evidence of this fight by morning. The last thing needed was a bloody diorama to fuel more hatred toward Americans. Insurgents or not, they were still Iraqis, and the people might be sympathetic toward them. I asked Joe Filmore to tell the police that we needed a fire truck to wash off the street. In the meantime, we would have to remove the bodies ourselves. Not willing to order my men to do anything I would not, I walked over to one of the corpses and reached down to pick him up. "Hold on, sir," called Gil Nail, my operations sergeant. "I think I've got some rubber gloves."

Several of us strapped them on and proceeded to pick up the bloody cadavers and stacked them like cordwood into the back of the police pickup. Their blood smeared on my sleeves, but when it dried, the brownish red color blended with the desert camouflage of my tunic. Uniforms being in short supply, I continued to wear the tunic in the future, but each time I did, it would remind me of that terrible fight.

The gruesome work done, we pushed the perforated, leaking Nissan to the side of the street in a textbook parallel park. As I walked to the police truck loaded with the insurgent remains, I noticed the Iraqi policeman staring at them. He began to nod his head. Then he turned to me, gazed, and then looked back at the bodies, nodding some more.

"These men, no good," he asserted in broken English while wagging his finger side to side. I couldn't agree with him more. He and his partner got in the pickup and drove off to the city morgue. I now had three points of the city secured. The enemy's attack was defeated at every point with a heavy price exacted from him each time. A dozen insurgents had been killed and wounded by our actions that night. While three of our men were wounded, they would recover. I was enraged at the stupidity of the rogue MP platoon and incensed that it was Americans who injured my men.

Even so, I was pleased with the first concentrated effort to secure the city using the new tactics. We had taken a toll on the enemy, and word of it would spread widely by sunrise. We learned later that the four men in the truck were sons of Saddam Hussein's bodyguards or sons of his relatives. One, Ali Maher Abdul Rashid, joined his brother-in-law, Qusay Hussein, as well as Uday, in death. The sins of the fathers are visited on the next generation. Now, if we could only get the fathers.

I returned to battalion headquarters about 3:30 that morning, physically and emotionally exhausted. In a fight, thoughts and actions are reflexive. After the fight, additional stress is experienced as the mind attempts to process the reality. Even so, I slept soundly for the few hours I had until it would be time to start another day. The sleepless nights would come much later.

CONTINUED SUCCESS, DISCONTINUED SUPPORT

The next day, another insurgent cell attempted a daylight attack on C Company's Birthday Palace compound, in an open field abutting to the east. The engagement began with sporadic rifle fire from a residential area and a multi-story dwelling under construction in the field. Perhaps the enemy was attempting to draw out Brad's soldiers. Captain Boyd's "Cobras" obliged the enemy, but not in the manner he expected.

Boyd sent out Staff Sergeant James Parker with two Bradley Fighting Vehicles and an infantry squad to check it out, as gunfire in the city was a daily occurrence. Taking his section of vehicles to the southeast corner of the field, he began to receive fire from the unfinished house to the north. Parker opened with machine gun fire from his Bradley and moved in echelon toward the gunfire. Now the exchange picked up intensity.

Brad Boyd and Mike Evans were observing from their vehicles on the high ground at the Birthday Palace. Parker's men began to assault the house, and soon a man darted out, attempting to run toward the ubiquitous white Nissan pickup seen everywhere in Iraq. Parker's troops chased the man with machine gun fire, and Brad Boyd, observing the movement from his own Bradley, ordered his gunner, Private First Class Rodrigo Vargas, to light up the truck. Twenty-five-millimeter shells smacked into the pickup, which rocked from side to side, bumped up and down, and then burst into flames. The man changed direction, whereupon he was shot through the lungs by one of Parker's infantry soldiers on the ground.

As First Sergeant Evans covered with a Mark-19 grenade launcher, Brad decided to move out toward Parker. Boyd and Evans linked up with Parker's men near the house. As they approached it, a man came out with raised hands and fell to his knees. He was taken prisoner along with several others, but the fight was not over. The insurgents had managed to squirt out the back from blind spots and were covered by supporting fire from other insurgents positioned in residential balconies to the north of the unfinished house.

Bullets smacked the walls, followed by the swooshing of RPG rockets and ending with metallic bangs as the soldiers took cover. The men opened up on the residences from where the fire came. "Cease fire," Brad ordered his command, as it was clear that the enemy had withdrawn. He wanted to minimize the damage to people's houses in the area.

Brad's troops moved swiftly to close in on the enemy to the north, joined by additional C Company troops closing up from behind to reinforce. Sergeant First Class Stephen Yslas of Brad's 2nd Platoon provided cover while Brad moved with Parker's troops toward Highway 1 in an effort to maintain contact with the enemy. Although many of the assailants fled, one had been killed, three were wounded, and seven others were captured, along with a few weapons.

The contest was over. Another insurgent cell was shattered while C Company remained unscathed. I was very pleased with Brad's handling of his company. He led them. He fought. He inspired his troops and could read a situation as it unfolded. Soon his company would shake off the self-imposed stigma of not pulling its own weight. I now had a company that I could totally trust to hold the center of the city.

The damage to the enemy in the last twenty-four hours had been manifest. Anger and carelessness cost him in deficits he could not readily repay. So continued the last desperate gasps of a dying regime. It would be just a matter of time before we gained complete dominance over Tikrit. The city began to take on an apprehensive calm. Iraqis began to work with us and give us valuable information as we, in turn, helped them rebuild their lives.

Back home, while Iraqis began to gain heart, Americans were seduced into losing it. I wrote home assuring people that things were not nearly as bleak as the press would have them believe. While our wounded and dead were tragic to us all, we had good weapons, good equipment, and stout hearts. Those of us on the front lines understood our purpose. The Iraqi people had been held in the grip of evil for decades with no means of escape. With Saddam's government fallen, his army destroyed, and Saddam himself on the run, there was little to prevent the accomplishment of our mission—if public support at home remained firm.

Our morale was high, and I felt that success was certain. We were already successfully capturing some of Saddam's inner circle, fighting insurgents in the street, and interacting with the Iraqi people. We clearly held the initiative. Our actions of the last month had truly impacted the enemy. Even so, I would learn of a new threat to be fought—the threat of inaccurate reporting and the need for telling our story. Rather than shun the press, I opted to engage them as openly and honestly as possible. Stories would be written whether our view was presented or not. Better, then, to provide that view.

As August approached, the press would descend on us as Tikrit had become irrefutably newsworthy. We would meet many reporters, and I grew to respect them, eventually. I continued to base my plan for success in Tikrit on the "Three Tiers" strategy of henchmen, bodyguards, and trigger pullers while we braced ourselves for what would inevitably come as we endured the oppressive heat in the land of the two rivers.

TOUGH GUY

Hot, that's what it was. The burning, blistering, brutal heat seared our hands as we held weapons, picked up tools and handled parts. We wore gloves to prevent burns. In vehicles, the wind fanned us like a blow-dryer on the maximum heat setting, increasing the effect of the soaring temperature. Even our fingernails got hot.

Yet, somehow, we endured. The Iraqis became suspicious. They could not fathom our ability to operate in battle gear and armored vehicular kilns in the sizzling summer sun. Therefore, another explanation must be given for our endurance, some explanation beyond toughness and tenacity. Since we were Americans, we must surely have some technology allowing this capability. Iraqis inquired about our air-conditioned helmets and their source of power. The talk on the Arab street was about our cooling vests and air-conditioned underwear. Despite our best efforts, we were never able to find these items for issue or purchase.

The markets in Tikrit did offer some merchandise for reprieve from the heat, however. We traded greenbacks for underpowered, Chinese-made air conditioners and fans, with minimal benefit. Like most things in Iraq, they initially presented an impressive façade but worked with only marginal effectiveness and soon expired.

We had been extremely busy since the firefights of late July.

Time flew swiftly, but it was all so surreal. Every day was just another day, interrupted by too few hours of sleep. Days of the week blurred without weekends to delineate them. Were it not for our watches and incremental changes in the moon, there would have been virtually no awareness of time at all. We counted the days because they promised relief from the heat. We longed for autumn and the subsequent hope of seeing our families and friends one day in a world much different from this one.

The battalion experienced improvements in family contact during this time. A couple of satellite phones for the companies greatly improved communication. It wasn't perfect. The AT&T satellite phones did not always track properly, and the heat caused the keypads on the iridium phones to short-circuit. An AT&T phone tent served as another possibility, though the expense was a bit over the top. Phone cards were about five times the normal rate. Nevertheless, the calls we were able to make were wonderful. It was the first time that we had talked to our families since coming to Iraq.

The battle for e-mail was won as well. It took an immense effort but soldiers could now send a note every few days to their families. Three terminals were established in the battalion headquarters, which the companies used on a rotating schedule. Telephones and e-mail, taken for granted at home, were now the lifeline to family and friends. I vowed to keep improving communication to the extent it was feasible. In retrospect, August 2003 was generally remembered as the month soldiers were finally able to write and call home.

Beginning on July 27, Command Sergeant Major Martinez and I made the rounds to our companies to award the Combat Infantry Streamer to each Infantry Company guidon, a small flag representing each company. Its tradition was founded in the Civil War; its present form dates to World War I. The purpose of the guidon is to designate and mark lettered and headquarters companies in a battalion, regiment, or brigade. In World War I, company guidons received silver bands on their staffs for campaigns. In World War II, companies were awarded small streamers for battle honors and combat achievements. The Combat Infantry Streamer meant sixty-five percent of each company's soldiers had been awarded the Combat Infantryman's Badge. It is a great honor to the units and one of which they are very proud. It is rare to see company guidons fly these streamers as they usually only appear during or shortly after a war. As peace takes hold, those with combat experience disappear, along with the streamer.

During these visits, Pete and I took the opportunity to ask soldiers about their concerns. Their comments ranged from the need for mission-essential equipment to small comfort items for relaxation when not on patrol and better communication with their families. Improvements had already been effected in most of these areas. The acquisition of the newer body-armored vests for all our soldiers was one of them. We were 167 sets short upon arrival in Iraq. The older unarmored fragmentation vests made up the shortfall. Now, all of our soldiers were better protected.

After returning from one such visit on the evening of July 27 from Bayjii (north of Tikrit) where my B Company was located, we had activity that quickly reminded us that there was still much work to be done, even while we felt proud of the accomplishments that we had made thus far. Someone placed a bomb in front of a house in central Tikrit. The blast blew open the gate and damaged the courtyard wall. The victims of the blast, an Iraqi family, asked our soldiers to help them move in with relatives that night as it was after curfew. My operations officer, Major Bryan Luke, obliged. As the family was escorted a few blocks to the east, one of our soldiers noticed a shovel leaning against a wall. Specialist Gersain Garcia looked at the dirt and the shovel. He started digging.

Within minutes, he unearthed 44 anti-tank mines, 20 pounds of C-4 explosives and 200 pounds of propellant. More digging produced nine grenades, four mine initiators, an AK-47 and thirty 60-millimeter mortar rounds. This building had been cleared by our troops just days before.

As this situation developed into the early hours of the morning, a burst of gunfire erupted to the south in an arc across the main highway toward the governor's building. "Gators" from the A Company QRF raced into the night, enveloping an area with two warehouses. The soldiers entered the first warehouse and spotted five men, one armed with an SKS rifle. The Iraqi man immediately dropped the rifle when he saw the Americans. Our men quickly deduced that these men were merely food guards and left them alone.

They continued on to the next warehouse. Staff Sergeant Miguel Delosantos ordered his men to post on two corners of it to flush out the attacker. Specialist David Morgan led his fire team over a wall as they moved toward an even darker back alley to a post on the northeast corner. As he dropped to the other side and took a knee to cover the other men climbing the wall, he spotted a man standing in the shadows. "Come here!" Morgan shouted to the man in both Arabic and English.

As Privates First Class Matthew Rankin, Kenwaski Robinson, and Bryan Patenge scaled to the other side, Morgan fired a warning shot when the man darted inside the building. He reappeared, this time aiming an AK-47 rifle. Specialist Morgan was faster. His shots hit the man in the chest. Body and rifle tumbled to the ground. Morgan closed up on the assailant as he struggled for life. Brushing aside his weapon, he began to render what aid he could to the dying man who had just tried to kill him.

Sergeant Delosantos organized an evacuation for the mortally wounded attacker, who died before reaching the aid station. The Iraqi police at the governor's building identified him as the man who had just shot up their building. As night turned into morning, we had eliminated another enemy and captured a large quantity of deadly mines and explosives.

As we continued to thin the ranks of our enemy during the last week of July, we received detailed information regarding the location of Saddam Hussein's number one personal bodyguard who had served him for over 20 years. We had seen this man often in photos with Saddam and his family. He accompanied Saddam everywhere, a constant companion at birthday parties, outings to the beach, and the routine events of his everyday life. He was Saddam's most trusted personal bodyguard. The locals, however, knew him to be a vicious murderer.

With that information, we planned a lightning raid with my Scout Platoon and elements from A Company to secure three houses in residential Tikrit. Other elements provided a cordon. We were looking for three specific men: two bodyguards and an organizer for the former regime.

The main target was Adnan Abdullah Abid al-Musslit—Saddam's personal bodyguard. He was part of the "Five Family" network, in this case, the Musslit family. He was also a tough guy who didn't go down without a fight. When we struck in the dark morning hours of July 29, our scouts found him upstairs, reinforced with liquid courage, attempting to grab a Sterling submachine gun. Butt strokes, epithets and quick action by my scouts prevented it. Unable to grasp his weapon, Musslit swung wildly at our men, to no avail. Soon he was being dragged down a flight of stairs, his head hitting each step.

Subdued and blindfolded in his own courtyard, with slight bleeding to the forehead, Adnan endured camera flashes from the media who were present. The news spread quickly throughout Tikrit, to the elation of all. Within forty-five minutes, all three targets were captured: 1) bodyguard Musslit, part of the "Five

Family" network; 2) Rafa Idham Ibrahim al-Hasan, a relative of Saddam's half brother, also a part of the "Five Family" network and a Fedayeen general; and 3) Daher Ziana, a former Tikriti security chief under Saddam.

Reporters at the scene were curious about the raid, the targets, and the swiftness of action. This was the first time that large numbers of press had covered our raids. We filled in blanks as best we could, endeavoring to convey the profound importance of detaining these three. They began to ask a series of questions.

"How did you find them?" asked one reporter, as if we were going to tell them our strategy.

"Every photo and every document connects the dots," I told them, telling the truth without too much detail. We had been searching for Musslit since the raid on Barzan's (Queen of Hearts') farm. He turned up in scores of captured photos. We asked the people who he was, and Iraqis helped us find him.

"Were you surprised Musslit put up a fight?" asked Ann Scott Tyson, a reporter from the *Christian Science Monitor*.

"Were we surprised? He's a bodyguard. That's why we went in with our steely knives and oily guns," I asserted. "If everything else had failed and we just got that one guy, we would be happy." The press loved the comment, and it went around the world.

I learned that night that the key to getting our message heard was honesty and sound bites. I also learned that reporters were not the real target of interviews. The real objective was to reassure the home team that we were winning this fight—from Professor Highbrow at Educate U to Bubba sipping his Budweiser back in Chitlin Switch, Oklahoma. The enemy also needed to know he was losing and that we were hot on his trail. It was an important lesson I would not forget.

The raid made international headlines, and the captured men proved immeasurably useful to future efforts. News of our success spread across the worldwide media as well. Soon, several news services embedded with us and covered our operations with live broadcasts and daily press reports. Most were convinced, and accurately so, that we were on the heels of Saddam Hussein. The presence of news media didn't sway our focus.

Then something strange happened. It became eerily quiet on July 30 and 31. This was perhaps the first time in weeks that nothing happened. No gunfire. No attacks. Just absolute quiet. We used the respite to catch our collective breath and sift through the mountain of intelligence that we were gathering. Jack, with his SOF team, sorted through it as well to weigh his information with ours. He was impressed with the type of intelligence we were developing and recognized the importance of our strategy and the Musslit bodyguard raid. He also asked us to join him on another raid in Tikrit that was closely connected to that strategy. Unlike our nighttime raids, their surveillance suggested that the targets would be home in the heat of the day and we could literally catch them napping.

The raids continued with success. On August 1, we bagged three more men on Jack's raid. They all had ties to Saddam. The most significant detainee was Taha Yaseen Omar al-Musslit, part of the "Five Family" network of Musslits we were seeking that we believed would lead us closer to Saddam. Jack also hauled away two others who were drivers for Saddam Hussein. At this stage, each raid seemed to feed upon the previous one with encouraging results. As Colonel Jim Hickey told a reporter at that time, "We've unraveled a big ball of yarn in Tikrit, and I think we're at the end of it."

PAYING US BACK, PAYING OUR RESPECTS

As encouraging as these raids were, discouraging news shortly followed. Sheik Mahmood Neda al-Nasiri called on the civilian

telephone line set up at headquarters for locals we trusted to contact us directly. Sheik Mahood was head of the entire Nasiri tribe
and was an intriguing and comical character in the cast of the
melodrama entitled "Tikrit." A native of Auja, he balanced the
delicate tightrope of being acquainted with Saddam's closest associates while desiring the evolution of a better Iraq. Mahmood
stood six feet four inches tall in all of his sheik finery. His smile
was genuine, his manner was appealing, and his appearance was
reminiscent of a deep-voiced Groucho Marx in Arab garb.

I spoke to him on the phone through Joe Filmore, my translator. He was frantic.

"They are coming here!" he warned. "They are going to bury
Saddam's sons in the Auja cemetery. You must do something."

"What do you want me to do?" I asked.

"There will be anger and great danger, I am afraid. You must
prevent it. They cannot bring Uday and Qusay here. If you cannot
stop it, I do not know what will happen."

"What do you think will happen?" I queried.

"I am afraid. They want me to sanction it. If I do, as their sheik,
then maybe both sides now hate me and will not understand the
position I am in," he reasoned. "They could harm the people of
our village." Sheik Mahmood had a valid point and every reason to
be concerned.

The information was passed on to Colonel Hickey. Even with
all our advanced technology, it seemed that the speed of the sheik's
"grapevine communication" was faster still. His report proved incredibly accurate. Not pleased at the news, as my A Company men
under Mark Stouffer were in his village, we worked all evening to
validate this turn of events. We were instructed to do nothing. The
corpses were to be surrendered to the Red Crescent after being
flown from Baghdad to Tikrit. We were to provide no escort or
involvement.

I ordered Mark Stouffer to cover the area anyway and to observe the event through our best optics. This was a perfect opportunity to snag the "Who's Who" of Saddam loyalists, yet for political reasons, we were ordered to do nothing. We watched at a distance as three corpses were laid in the dirt. The third body was Qusay's 14-year-old son, Mustafa. He had been killed while firing an AK-47 at SOF soldiers from under a bed in the same Mosul house blown apart to get Uday and Qusay.

Arrogant men, some veiled, surrounded the graves in a theatrical display of counterfeit mourning for these murdering lifeless forms. They piled dirt mounds above their sunken corpses then secured an Iraqi flag to each mound with dirt clods and rocks lining the edges, the mark of a martyr's burial. The funeral passed uneventfully. Few tears were shed. Not a single box of tissues was needed for this occasion. The enemy, however, had other uses for tissue boxes.

In the early evening, we were introduced to a new tactic, the improvised explosive device (IED) attack. The first bomb attack was nearly identical to the second except in result. Each bomb appeared to be a box (first Pepsi, then Kleenex) packed with C-4 plastic explosives and mixed with nuts and bolts to serve as projectiles. The source of detonation was not clear to us at that time, but we became well versed in these deadly devices later.

The first attack unfolded as our Scout Platoon traveled the main highway north through the center of the city. Congestion by the telephone exchange offices narrowed the lanes to one. A median, elevated with decorative concrete box planters, served as a directional backstop for the Pepsi box bomb that the enemy had concealed among so much other trash in the unsanitary country. The first scout Hummer passed safely, but the second disappeared in a concussive mass of orange flame and brown smoke. Glass from the large plate windows in the telephone exchange building on the east side of the street exploded in every direction. Policemen inside were thrown to the ground. Shards of flying glass from the windows of a parked taxi sliced into the passengers, all of them children. As the dust settled, the pavement along the blast area took on the appearance of an unfinished mosaic of glass.

Sergeant Christopher Gardner in Scout Hummer 233 saw his fellow soldiers in Scout Hummer 232 disappear in a cloud of smoke right before his eyes. He told Sergeant Robert Eschenbacher, his driver, to close with them up ahead to see if they could help. The truck was gone.

Although briefly knocked unconscious, with an eye bleeding and an arm filled with fragmentation, Specialist Claude Goodwin threw the vehicle into low gear and nursed the heavily damaged Hummer with three flat tires out of the blast zone. His vision already impaired, he could not see at all through the shattered safety glass, now merely a striated pattern before him. Still unable to hear, he somehow managed to understand Staff Sergeant Sean Shoffner seated on his right.

"Keep moving forward!" shouted Shoffner, also deafened by the blast and unable to hear his own words. He instinctively performed a quick check of his men.

Specialist Stewart Simmons, in the backseat, took searing heat and fragmentation to his neck and left arm. His left eardrum would register no sound. The men yelled to each other, able to hear nothing. Specialist Jason Wells, up top, was bleeding from the face and neck but appeared to be regaining consciousness. Specialist Carlos Rodriguez, positioned behind Staff Sergeant Shoffner on the right side of the vehicle, though badly shaken, was not wounded.

The scouts continued their wobbly ride toward the battalion headquarters compound where the badly perforated vehicle was waved through the gate. The scouts cleared their weapons with bloody hands and made their way, with assistance, to the aid station. Two would return to duty. The third would need more time for his ear to heal, but he would recover. God, in His providence, had protected us that day.

Just twenty minutes later, about two miles north along the same road, a second bomb detonated. Military Police vehicles, similar in appearance to our scout vehicles, became the unintended target. The bomb, in this case, was built around a Kleenex box packed with plastic explosives in place of facial tissues. No major damage was sustained in the mistimed blast, only a few broken headlamps and minor cosmetic damage to the fiberglass hood of a single vehicle.

The attack was coordinated and seemed intended for our scout Hummers who were often main participants in our raids. Unlike prior mine attacks, these roadside bombs appeared to be detonated by some form of wireless device. Our study of these devices and the methods used to emplace or destroy them became a major focus of our tactical operations. I treated them as point ambushes and dealt with them in ways that initially drew controversy but later proved very effective.

After I ascertained that my wounded scouts were going to be fine, we persevered with several more hours of combat patrols. Though I was exhausted from a strenuous day, there was yet one more important task to accomplish before my day would be complete. I ordered Cody Hoefer to Auja's cemetery to locate the new graves of Saddam Hussein's sons. Pulling up alongside, adjacent to the mausoleum where other relatives of Saddam were buried, we found them. They lay in dirt mounds about nine feet long, four feet wide and two feet high. A smaller grave for Mustafa, son of Qusay and grandson of Saddam, lay next to them.

Iraqi martyr flags had been neatly spread and weighted with rocks on each grave, as is the custom. I approached the first grave, then the second, and yanked each flag from the mound. They would be afforded no honors. I left Mustafa's grave and flag undisturbed. Whatever mistakes he made could not be blamed on a 14-year-old boy who was merely the product of his upbringing. The sins were of the father.

RATS' NESTS AND ROCKS

August 3 was spent with Jack and his SOF team planning a simultaneous raid on each side of the river. The target was Rudman Ibrahim Omar al-Musslit, a major figure in the "Five Family" network and one of ten Musslit brothers. Early attempts to capture his brother, Mohammed, in May, met with negative results, but slowly the shadowy figures were becoming more visible. While we had thinned some of the Musslit family, we had yet to strike at the heart of the sons of Ibrahim Omar al-Musslit.

With Saddam's Presidential Secretary Abid Mahmood captured, we surmised that his role had passed to individuals in the family network, particularly the Musslit family. Rudman seemed most likely to inherit the mantle. We felt that he might reveal Saddam's location if captured. He and his nine brothers would be a major focus as we tightened the noose around Saddam. We had no photo of him, but our intelligence was good, and we found what we believed to be the locations of his family farms. For this raid, Colonel Hickey would be in overall command. Captain Dez Bailey's G Troop, 10th Cavalry would target some of the structures, while Jack's SOF guys would focus on the house in the multi-structure compound where they expected to find Rudman. Mark Stouffer's A Company and Chris Morris' scouts worked in tandem on the compound with Jack's men. I would accompany Jack to synchronize communication, as SOF used different equipment than conventional forces. We also had helicopter and close air support.

Brad Boyd's company was left to secure Tikrit, and Jon Cecalupo's tanks guarded Cadaseeyah. Since the armored vehicles were with us, the battalion mortars were assigned to cover the city should they be needed there.

As we moved stealthily on the Musslit compound, every available man was needed for the search. We had redirected as many of our forces as possible for the raid. I moved on foot with Jack and some of his SOF guys, clearing buildings and barns, rooms and stalls. The raid went precisely as planned, but Rudman was not found. His family was present, but he had either narrowly escaped or was hiding nearby. There was, however, one very interesting person on site. He was the 80-year-old Omar al-Musslit, the granddaddy of all Musslits. We did not detain him, but we confiscated many items from the compound, including Omar's national identity card. We later noted that "666" was his registration number, the infamous "mark of the beast" in the book of Revelation. It was appropriate as he had spawned so much evil. We also found important documents and photos revealing, for the first time, the identities of Rudman and many of his brothers.

In addition to the fruit of this raid, there was an added bonus. The following morning, Qais Shaban, one of Saddam's personal staff, was detained. Incredibly, he came to the civil-military relations office to complain about the raid on his undamaged house. We took him to our complaint department where he remained for quite a long stay.

We maintained combat patrols in the city with ambushes plotted for an elusive enemy. Assailants with RPGs fired on a C Company patrol near the Women's College but hit nothing. A Kellogg, Brown & Root worker driving a truck north of Tikrit was less fortunate. He hit a mine and lost his life in the ensuing blast. It was a terrible tragedy, illustrating the dangers of employing civilian contractors on the battlefield.

On the night of August 5, we shifted to the street fight with a network of "Salt Lick" ambushes involving Chris Morris' "Comanche" elements (scout OPs), "Badger" elements (battalion sniper teams), "Cobra" patrols (C Company) and "Gator" QRFs (A Company). The troops were becoming more adept "flippers" on the insurgent pinball machine in the city of Tikrit.

Our tactical setup was quite unknown to Omar Hadel Mohammed Ahmed and his fellow insurgents. In the morning darkness of August 6, our soldiers noticed a small group of men walking across the main street in town with an RPG launcher and AK-47s. They didn't have a clear shot, so they waited and reported. We were confident that if they continued to move, we would pick them up. Soon the twenty-year-old Omar appeared around a corner near one of our outposts, with an RPG at the ready. Our men fired first, wounding him in the leg. He shrieked in pain then calm settled over the alleyways. Soldiers searched the area but found only blood trails. Nevertheless, whatever attack this group had planned was now foiled. We would face several Ahmed family members in the future and would later capture Omar Ahmed, in December, sitting in his front yard smoking a cigarette.

As the day progressed, Tikritis informed us of a local recruiting effort by a Fedayeen leader nicknamed "Sami the Rock." Having never heard of him, we classified him as a "Trigger Puller" or possibly a low-level organizer. Jack's men were not familiar with him either. Taking the information, we diagrammed a raid on "The Rock" at the hotel where he was alleged to be staying.

Raiding a farm was one thing. Emptying a hotel was quite another. If our man Sami was there, sifting him from a crowd would be a challenge. It would be complicated work dealing with many civilians, mostly innocent. The potential that the hotel could be full of his cohorts had to be considered as well. I decided to go in strong with lots of force. We would bring Bradleys and tanks.

No chances would be taken. More is always better in any potential fight. If things went south, it would be better to clear rooms with one of Jon Cecalupo's M1 tanks than with our soldiers. The press, now numbering a dozen different agencies and outlets, knew something was adrift by the number of troops planning for action. I allowed them to accompany us. While our man Sami was not part of the Saddam hunt, he was a "Trigger Puller," a real and present danger to Tikrit and our soldiers. The reporters were embedded into various units participating in the raid.

The "hotel" was a squat, multi-story building that might be classified as condemned apartment housing in the States. Locals told us it was filled with temporary workers. These "rent-a-day" workers came from Baghdad and other parts of Iraq seeking employment. They would loiter on a main intersection in town hoping to be hired for some odd job. The "rent-a-days" caused us some concern, not so much for the economy as for the potential they might easily be influenced to hire on as instant armed forces for some concerted insurgent effort.

Chris, Jon, and Mark's troops cordoned the hotel, and we moved in with Brad's soldiers and some headquarters troops. Elements from Jack's SOF team, while not directly involved, came along, as they often did, to see what we stirred up. I believed that the only way to catch Sami was to cast a wide net and throw back anyone who wasn't him. This meant moving every person inside the hotel outside into a compound behind the structure and doing a quick sifting similar to those Jack's guys had performed in early Auja raids.

The sleeping residents of the Rat Nest Hotel did not know what hit them. They were benign and cooperative. Only an idiot or a zealot would have resisted the force we assembled. Thirty-nine individuals were ultimately detained; among them was "Sami the Rock." As he was led away to captivity, I decided to address the involuntarily assembled crowd of mostly "rent-a day" workers.

"I apologize for the inconvenience you have faced tonight," I stated as Joe Filmore translated. "You are going to be released. Sometimes when you cast a wide net to catch sharks, you get dolphins along with them. We are going to let you go as you have done nothing wrong. A Fedayeen insurgent leader was living among you, and he has now been captured. If you have done nothing wrong, you have nothing to fear from us. We need you to cooperate. If you don't, we will hunt you down and kill you."

With that, I ordered their release. Reporters had filmed and quoted my "dolphins and sharks" and "hunt you down and kill you" statements and sent them around the world the following day. It was exactly the message I wanted the local people and insurgents to hear, as well as Professor Highbrow and Bubba back home. We were already receiving thanks from the locals in Tikrit for removing "Sami the Thug," described by many as an outside troublemaker.

The overall effect was positive and must have had an impact on the recruiting effort in Tikrit. Two of "The Rock's" new recruits fled the following day, but Mark Stouffer's men got a tip from the locals and caught them motoring south toward Baghdad. Later, a merchant brought us their RPG launcher with three rockets. He said that he saw them hide it earlier and brought it to us once he learned that they had been captured. Iraqi support continued to increase with each success.

CRACKERS AND KALASHNIKOVS

It was clear that we were hurting the enemy. Street fights and raids were taking their toll. The insurgents attempted to enlist new recruits and resupply their arms but with much less success than they expected. Still, they were able to find enough of both to continue their efforts. Some of our best information about the source of arms flowing into the city came from Governor Hussein, General Abdullah, and the Governor's security chief, Colonel Mohammed Jassim Hussein.

"Why don't you do something about the Friday market?" asked Governor Hussein on one of my regular visits.

"What do you mean?" I responded.

"Everyone knows where the arms are traded. People from Baghdad bring them in and sell them at the market on Fridays. If you want to find them, you can."

Locals confirmed this information and told us that the merchants from the market had complained to the governor and police about it. They said that the weapons were being used to attack the Americans and them.

Rather than take on the fight himself, Governor Hussein wisely put us on the trail of the arms market. If he took action, it might bode ill for him should there be a mishap. If we erred, well, that was to be expected. We were Americans. It was good politics and good tactics to proceed in this manner.

Daylight ambushes were set on the Friday market to curb the flow. The first Friday produced no results. The second Friday was entirely different. Our snipers were positioned at two points within a large vacant building adjoining the vast market. The area was near the Rat Nest Hotel. Staff Sergeant Brad Owens controlled the teams who infiltrated at 3:30 a.m. on Friday, August 8. They encountered nine Iraqi squatters, who were released at 6:00 a.m. when curfew lifted. They prepared their mission, expecting activity between 8:00 a.m. and 12:00 noon.

At 7:30 a.m., we finally confirmed the complaints to be true. Owens noticed two men in a red car pull into the field surrounded by the market shops along the streets. The field was also used as a flea market where anyone could vend his wares or produce. These two decided to vend weapons. They laid out wheat sacks filled with AK-47 magazines and grenade launcher attachments. Next, they set up various other small arms items on the now empty sacks. Our men reported it but wanted to be absolutely certain these were weapons dealers. I gave them clearance to use their own judgment and to engage if they saw weapons.

Owens and the other snipers continued to observe. Finally, the suspects pulled an AK-47 Kalashnikov rifle from the trunk of the red car. After seeing small devices and electronic switches for bomb making and then more AK-47s, Staff Sergeant Owens called the shot and engaged.

The sharp crack of a sniper rifle drew little attention at first. A vendor selling crackers not ten feet from the arms traders took little notice, thinking the men were merely testing the weapons. But then he noticed that one man holding a weapon jerked and suddenly dropped it, his arm bleeding profusely. The driver of the red car, unaware of the activity around him, watched as one of two other men standing there handled a rifle. The man turned around with an AK-47 at the ready, seeking the direction of the fire. A round ripped through his groin. He ran forward, weapon still in hand. Another round smashed through his torso. He slumped to the ground, brought down by Owens and Specialist Juan Cantu.

The driver ran frantically to the car, attempting to flee. Owens gauged the approximate location of the driver through the rooftop (the car was facing away from him) and fired. The round perforated the top of the car and hit the man in the head. He stumbled out of the car and died. Specialist James Kelly began to place rounds in the dirt in front of a curious bystander contemplating whether or not to pick up a rifle. As dirt flew near his feet, he began to have second thoughts.

The last armed man stood little chance. Owens fired a round

through his leg and cut him down. Struggling on the ground, he dropped the weapon. The engagement was officially over.

When rounds began to hit the arms dealers, the Friday market crowd dispersed in a circular pattern, exposing a vacant area like a crop circle. Closer to the building, a crowd began to gather and peer up at the windows from which the snipers fired. Sergeant Jesse Sample and Specialist Danny Harris tossed a red smoke grenade down at the crowd. Though quite harmless, it had the desired effect of spooking the innocent to move out of the way.

The quick-thinking Owens then rushed to the site with his men. He wanted to secure the area before the crowd stole the weapons and components. He and the snipers "circled the wagons" until Chris Morris' scouts and the battalion QRF arrived.

A sea of confusion raged among the locals. A bystander had already stolen one of the AK-47s but everything else was still in place when the snipers and scouts arrived. Soon soldiers from A Company cordoned the market and we secured the scene. The two wounded were transported to the Tikrit Hospital. Iraqi police appeared to assist in crowd control and body recovery.

The press arrived, wanting a full account of the ambush once things had settled. Most could clearly see what had happened, but Theola Labbé from the *Washington Post* was puzzled by our actions.

"Did you give them any warning?" she asked.

"No, ma'am." I replied.

"Your men just opened fire?" she continued.

"Yes, ma'am," I explained. "We will not allow people to carry weapons in the city. We had received complaints about these arms dealers from the people and the governor. When someone takes up a weapon openly in public, he is considered a combatant at that point."

"Do you think that is fair?" she pried, incredulously.

"Why don't you ask my soldiers who have been wounded by roadside bombs, hit by landmines, or ambushed by RPGs?" I countered. "No such warnings were afforded my men. We are clearly within the laws of land warfare."

While a bit annoyed by her stance, I was happy for the chance to answer those kinds of questions. We didn't get that opportunity from everyone, though. Not waiting for the details, the French AFP media went to the hospital where they found two Iraqi boys from a village about 30 kilometers across the river who had been injured by an unexploded shell of some kind in an unrelated incident. Assuming the boys were somehow connected to our actions against the enemy, they flashed pictures around the world stating Americans had wounded the boys by gunning them down and throwing grenades at the market. I was furious. Our soldiers had incredible discipline and were doing the tough work of separating insurgents from the innocent population. They clearly knew the difference between schoolboys and armed insurgents.

Fortunately, the rest of the media reported it accurately. Our actions sent shock waves through the town and effectively curtailed illegal arms trade in the city. The Governor thanked us, as did the mayor. General Mezher, the Salah ad Din police chief, informed us that the two men we killed from the red car were known thugs who smuggled weapons from a major military complex on the outskirts of Baghdad. They would show samples, fill orders, and arrange deliveries. He was very happy to see them removed. It was certain we would see no more weapons traded openly in Tikrit.

5. TARGETS

RAIDS AND ROCKET GRENADES

Unable to take us on directly, the enemy began to focus more on explosive apparatuses in his attempt to strike at us. Each week we discovered some of these devices before they could be used and foiled some new attempt before it struck. I could feel the prayers of many back home making that possible.

Still, all it would take was one incident to give the appearance of enemy vitality to people not directly involved with our operations. West of Tikrit, an unfortunate soldier driving a truck lost his leg when he and a fellow soldier supporting Mark Huron's 299th Engineer Battalion ran over an anti-tank mine positioned along the edge of a road. To the south of us, one of Dom Pompelia's 4-42nd artillerymen lost his life in a similar episode.

We worked feverishly to counter such activity, operating on the premise that the best way to prevent an exploding bomb was to kill the guy trying to plant it. Short of that, we looked for anything unusual and took immediate action against it. Our snipers and combat patrols continued to shoot at suspected devices while locals helped intercept several others. We remained vigilant because it was in our best interest to do so. The enemy was beginning to use more indirect means to hit us, having mostly failed with direct contact. Obstinately, he did not entirely abandon his direct attacks.

Brad Boyd's men scrapped with an insurgent cell south of the Birthday Palace on August 11 when insurgents ambushed his patrol with three RPGs. The assailants fled in one white and one black Mercedes when Brad deployed his men and began to engage them. Saddam's loyalists were not going to surrender until we had either killed more of them or forced them into submission.

On August 12, we successfully raided three more objectives in large block sections of Saddam's birth village, Auja. I reinforced Mark Stouffer's A Company with First Lieutenant Jason Lojka's platoon from C Company. Scouts and my command elements worked with Jack's SOF team. We combined both family network targets with mid-level targets for a giant surprise daylight raid. It paid some key dividends. Two former Republican Guard officers were captured: General Kareem Jasim Nafous al-Majid, a "Five Family" network man who had been a division commander, and the other, a corps-level chief of staff. They were both on several wanted lists. The third objective netted a leader and payment officer of the Fedayeen militia. Also among the detainees was Nafit Ali Hussein al-Heremos, another "Five Family" network man. It was a very good day.

By August 13, we had seen small enemy attempts to harass or strike back at us. On a secondary market street, Captain Boyd's convoy once again narrowly escaped harm as assailants rolled a volley of RPGs down the street like a game of ten pins. The enemy attackers had fired from several hundred meters away in the middle of a street and then fled. The rockets whooshed, skipped, and scraped along the pavement but did not explode. One rocket was discovered with the safety pin still in the nose—rocket grenades are far more effective with the pin removed. There were no complaints from us.

Our actions continued to gain momentum. By mid-month, two men wanted by our forces turned themselves in. One of them worked for Saddam's wife. On the same day, we received weapons from helpful Tikriti merchants with keen eyes. That evening, Jack's SOF men, with support from our scouts, netted another "Five Family" network man named Rashid Abdullah al-Heremos. We were penetrating the inner circle of Saddam's bodyguard network.

Even so, the young and the stupid continued to step forward as this network attempted to recruit for the insurgency. In a suburb to our south, attackers launched a volley of RPGs at A Company soldiers in yet another classic "miss and run" attack. Our "Gators" responded so quickly that the enemy was forced to flee for his life and abandoned his rocket launchers in the street. The attackers blended into the local population before they could be apprehended. Hence, we continued to work with the locals and the sheiks and planned more raids.

Planning raids against the Saddam network, continuing street battles to subdue the city, and working on local governance and Iraqi security to fill the gap characterized our operations at this point. We continued to work with the Governor and invested a great deal of time establishing a municipal government in the city that had never existed before. Much effort was also invested in dialogue with the major tribal sheiks.

One benefit of that dialogue was the recruitment of reliable Iraqi men to train for the militia. Tapping into some previous experience I had forming executable plans for the Afghan National Army, we launched a modest training program that began to produce small but good-quality elements to assist the local government and the American forces. In Afghanistan, there was a concern about "vetting" soldiers to ensure that we did not hire Taliban or al-Qaeda. We asked each of Afghanistan's thirty-two provincial chiefs to provide us with their own recruits. If they sent troublemakers, we could turn back to the provincial chief and play to his honor.

Our situation in Tikrit was on a much smaller scale, but I would introduce the same concept. Although there were plans to establish a national army, we would create local platoon-sized troops ultimately able to evolve into functional battalions under Iraqi command. Leaders in Baghdad called these "Civil Defense" troops to distinguish them from the new army troops being formed. Their deployment would be local. Although there was some discussion that they might be absorbed into the new Iraqi army in the future, the immediate plan was to train local levies for hometown security. Recruitment would be tricky because of widespread anti-American sentiment in Tikrit and latent support for Saddam.

I had been meeting for weeks with the tribal leadership in the area. Tikrit was far more tribal than other cities because it was nearly all Sunni, and though renowned throughout Iraq, was a small city given its wide range of influence. I recognized the need to engage tribal leadership in the process, but finding the "real" sheiks of major tribes would take some effort. I had an idea in mind.

I announced the plan to form a "Tribal Council of Sheiks" and used Governor Hussein's assistance to broadcast the message. At the first meeting, I intentionally orchestrated a twenty-minute delay on a hunch about Arab culture. Watching the small auditorium fill with men in their robed finery soon confirmed the hunch. The men sat wherever they wished but seemed to sit in a pecking order. Some, who initially imagined themselves to be more important, would rise and surrender their seat at the entry of another whom they felt was more important. By the end of the twenty minutes, the front row appeared to be filled with the key players.

I presented some basic information about progress and the desire to create dialogue. I thanked everyone for coming but asked those on the front row to remain for additional information. These were the men I needed and now had a chance to identify. At the follow-up meeting, I recorded their names and tribes and expressed the desire to meet with them regularly. Thus was born the Tribal Council of Sheiks. It would serve us well.

The council paid benefits in recruits for the new Iraqi troops we wished to train. I told the sheiks that we could offer their best men good jobs as local security troops for $110 a month (about $10 above the average monthly wage at that time). This piqued their interest. Appealing to their status and power, I explained to the tribal leaders the impossibility of recruiting soldiers without their help because only they could identify their best men.

To make it fair, I asked them to sort out among themselves the number of recruits each tribe should provide according to their own populations. I did not wish to involve myself in that process as they could execute it more fairly. I firmly stipulated that I would not accept a single recruit without a signed letter of endorsement from their tribal sheik—not local but tribal sheik. No paper, no head sheik signature, no recruitment. No exceptions.

The idea appealed to their sense of power and influence and created quite a murmur among them. While removing us from accusations of favoritism, it secured the recruits to us as they did not have to be so much loyal to us as to their own tribe. Further, it bonded the tribes in our area to one another, as they joined together on task for the new Iraq.

Soon, we had far more "vetted" recruits than openings for them. I promised that the loyal men would be placed on the recruiting roster for the next training class. The quality of men we received was generally very good. Only once did we have a soldier disappear for an extended period. I took his name to his sheik, and soon the man reappeared. He was barely able to walk and some-what bruised, but we never had another problem with him again.

Through the exceptional work of First Lieutenant Jason Deel and Sergeant Major Cesar Castro, and with the assistance of several former drill sergeants from each of my companies, we moved forward to train Iraqis in martial and civil arts to help stabilize their own town. They were initially called the "Iraqi Civil Defense Corps" (ICDC). Our effort was merely one of many across Iraq, but we were the first to mobilize so quickly and efficiently. In doing so, we gained the attention of Secretary of Defense Donald Rumsfeld and Assistant Secretary Paul Wolfowitz.

We trained the recruits on a palace island we occupied in the middle of the Tigris River. The site was ideal for training as it was isolated, heavily vegetated for concealment, and had large, beautiful buildings for training and billeting. We were even able to construct a firing range on the island. Colonel Hickey, impressed with our work, nicknamed it the "James Bond Island."

To further meld our new Iraqi brothers to our soldiers, we lived and trained with them. We also designed a shoulder patch that incorporated the crest of our regiment and solicited a local vendor to produce them. This was a point of pride for all of us, and it eventually marked our trained recruits. Changes would transpire as the troops became more and more integrated into the new security forces of Iraq, but for our immediate needs, these men served and fought alongside us as auxiliaries of the Regulars. Just four months earlier, we had been fighting each other.

In addition, Tim Morrow continued to sift through some great tips from Iraqi civilians willing to inform us about a cell leader and bomb maker known as Thamer Mahdi Salah Hamoudi. He soon became known as "Thamer the Bomber." We raided his house on August 17 as a part of a wider operation. Though we missed netting him, we did find plastic explosives, electronic switches and devices, fragmentation pellets, blasting caps, and a few weapons. While raiding this house, alert soldiers outside began to root around the fields across the street and found three grenades and a complete 60mm mortar system with seven rounds of ammunition. All in all it was a very productive week.

The enemy continued to adapt his tactics to counter ours. He attacked bravely but hid immorally among the population and legitimate emergency services, placing civilians in great danger. It was despicable. This strategy violated every law of land warfare.

For example, on the night of August 18 at a temporary checkpoint, our soldiers searched an ambulance transporting an older man home from the hospital. Exploiting these circumstances, some men in a white car placed an explosive on a side street and ignited the fuse. A Company soldiers reacted to the blast west of their location. The ambulance drove north to escape danger. As it did, the white car pulled alongside the Red Crescent vehicle to mask its own movement as the enemy in it sent a burst of gunfire toward another unit's outpost. The outpost responded, seeing the fire come from what appeared to be the ambulance.

Observing the fire exchanged between the outpost and the ambulance, our snipers engaged the emergency vehicle as it sped north, the victim of a cruel crossfire. The white car, fully masked in its movements, veered down a dark alley and made its escape. The ambulance shuddered to a stop. The driver, fearing for his life, abandoned the vehicle to escape the bullet exchange. He nearly made it but for one round that hit his ankle. Another aide was cut by glass from the windshield. The patient took a round to the shoulder and the thigh. The police and our forces quickly arrived along the dark street. The police took the seriously wounded victim back to the hospital where he was stabilized, and he ultimately survived.

The ambulance then began its journey northward toward a checkpoint where it was met by both police and our scouts. The driver's ankle wound was treated, and he was transferred to better care for professional removal of the bullet. We also returned the ambulance to the emergency workers, and the Iraqis helped us piece together the confusing puzzle of the preceding events. While frightened and initially angered, they became more incensed when they learned that the attackers had once again used innocent people as shields.

Such immoral incidents infuriated me. The insurgents callously placed men, women, and children at risk to launch their attacks and promote their agenda. They continued to use the protected status of hospitals, ambulances, mosques, and the like to find safe harbor. Many decent Iraqis would die as a result.

This inhumane behavior incited such rage in the Iraqi people that they would surrender significant information leading to the apprehension of the perpetrators. Such was the case with the Hadooshi farm we had raided before. It was where we uncovered eight and a half million U.S. dollars and Sajida Hussein's papers and jewelry on 17 June. Locals told us that the enemy persisted in planning and funding attacks from that location.

We acted quickly on local intelligence about an alleged planning meeting at the farm. Confirmed sightings of two particular individuals on our hit list energized us to charge in quickly with guns bristling. Our source indicated that a portion of the Musslit family would be present and that perhaps even Saddam himself would be there. Jack's SOF team had a great interest in the intelligence and wanted to join us. They were always most welcome. I did not want a repeat of the last raid where we had even odds at the gate with armed men. I did want to send the message that we were on to them.

We surrounded the farm with reconnaissance troops to set the cordon and then A Company rolled up to the capacious compound gate and flattened it with a Bradley Fighting Vehicle. The

Bradley continued forward as residents of the two large farm complexes scrambled in every direction. Jack's SOF guys rolled up in their specialized vehicles, darted to the farmhouse, and cleared it with their usual precision.

Our soldiers poured through the gap in the wall, and more soldiers spilled from the back of the Bradley. Fingers of light from flashlights mounted on soldiers' rifles danced around each corner and flashed around each window and room. Back alleys were cleared, aqueducts were jumped, and orchards were searched. Activity seemed to slacken at the farm.

Joe Filmore and a SOF man went to work interrogating the farmhands and women detained. We learned that Rudman and Mohammed Ibrihim Omar al-Musslit had left about three hours earlier. We also found evidence that Saddam might have been there. More questioning revealed a secondary farm location across the Tigris about 20 kilometers east toward Al Allum. It belonged to a man known as al-Asawi. Disappointingly, nothing was found at that farm either. After an exhausting night, we had narrowly missed Saddam's key henchmen. They fled knowing that they were hunted men who must live like the rats they were. We wanted them to know that no rat hole would be safe.

The next day, on August 20, we got an emergency request for help from a Special Forces unit working in our area on Cross Street in downtown Tikrit. While they coordinated information with a local vendor on a market street, armed attackers blending in with the general population opened up a deadly burst of gunfire. The soldiers' translator fell dead, shot through the torso. Another soldier collapsed with a serious thigh wound, and yet another was severely wounded in his extremities. The soldiers returned fire as best they could, but they had been horribly surprised. The enemy's damage done, he fled, unchallenged by this small wounded band of Green Berets.

147

Men from our C Company rushed to the scene. Brad's troops lifted shocked and bloodied men into vehicles, accompanied by their angry and equally shocked peers. Our soldiers cordoned the area and conducted a wide search but gathered little information from the locals. Most shuttered their shops in typical fear and went home. Those who remained claimed to have seen nothing. The soldiers' lives were saved by a medical evacuation, but the translator, an American citizen, would speak no more.

These guys had made a fatal mistake. Their team sergeant chose to reject our counsel even though we had warned him of the area's volatility. He saw us as mechanized infantry toads who lacked the skill and grasp that they possessed. As further evidence of this superior attitude, the Special Forces soldiers in this clash had not even worn their body armor or helmets and had been talking to a vendor about plastic chairs in a busy market, seen by all for some length of time. It had been an ambush waiting to happen.

While certainly not characteristic of the competent Special Forces soldiers I had served with and fought alongside in Kosovo and Afghanistan, it was, nevertheless, a costly mistake made by what I viewed as a "too cool for school" team sergeant who chose to ignore our warnings and intelligence. We knew our city. His rejection of that knowledge resulted in a combat-ineffective team soon to be replaced by another. What was worse, a gallant Muslim-American citizen faithfully serving his country was dead.

Vigilance, vigilance, vigilance. My daily burden was for all of my soldiers to go home alive and with all of their limbs. God had spared us from much in the midst of battles, and we usually caused more damage than we received, but many more battles awaited us.

One such sparring occurred on the 22nd of August. A tip from a distraught Iraqi warned us of a plan to attack the Tigris Bridge. The assault was to take place within an hour with RPGs, small arms, and mortars. A water-services truck would conceal the movement. Our response was immediate. I ordered Jon Cecalupo to send a section of M1 Abrams tanks to change the scenery of the bridge and our checkpoint there. The enemy did materialize at a distance and pathetically launched two 82mm mortar rounds at us, impacting just across the west bank of the river at dusk. It was another miss and run.

An hour later, our Scout Platoon headed south along the main highway. Chris Morris led his men in four scout trucks and approached a decorative gate incongruently guarding a wadi that funnels waste by-products from Tikrit into the Tigris River. Our men affectionately referred to this depression as the "Stink Wadi." That night it exuded more than just a foul odor. Explosions erupted near the gun trucks, followed by small arms retorts from a squad-sized insurgency cell.

Caught by surprise in the ambush but quick to react, Corporal Andrew Brokish and Specialist Steven Bournazian each ripped a burst from their .50 caliber machine guns at the muzzle flashes spotted in the wadi. More scout weapons erupted in a converging arc as the scout drivers slowed to stabilize the platforms for firing. As the gunfire stitched the suspected enemy location concealed in the wadi's bulrushes, there was a large explosion. It was not clear what was hit, but all enemy fire stopped abruptly.

The soldiers' disciplined posture and alertness made the enemy pay, with no loss to our men. Unable to get to the scene quickly because of distance and rough terrain, the scouts could not determine the extent of damage inflicted, but they definitely blew up something. When searched later, the area was vacant, revealing little information.

Information, whether given to us or deduced from combat actions, was the oil upon which our operations flowed. Without the cooperation of the Iraqi people, we would not have been as far advanced as we were to this date. Still, there was much fear afoot as the locals watched to see who would prevail.

The revelation of information took a different form in Tikrit the following morning. Our C Company posted security along the main street of the city near the telephone exchange offices. Bradley Fighting Vehicles and tough soldiers blended with the squat, dilapidated structures of the city dotted with civilians. A small crowd gathered at a new café in town—an Internet café. Words were exchanged, cameras rolled and snapped, and a pair of scissors was lifted from a pillow as the owner and I cut a ribbon at the entrance.

While thrilled to participate in this mundane community activity, it all seemed so foreign given the context of the previous days. For a brief moment, these exercises in civility awakened much inside me. As I left the café, an old woman was nearly struck by a car and a bicycle as she attempted to cross the busy street. Our soldiers stepped into the four lanes to block traffic. Joe Filmore called out to her in Arabic, "Come, Mother, let me help you," and escorted her across the thoroughfare.

Pulling away in our vehicles, we cradled our weapons, fixed our eyes on the rooftops, studied every trash pile, and checked every alley. We quickly scanned a sea of people. What do they hold in their arms? What do their facial expressions reveal? Do they make unusual movements? Fading away from civility, we reentered our world.

DUCK, DUCK, GOOSE

The farmlands along the Tigris River lay rich with vegetation. Palm trees stood like sentinels, row upon row, in alignment with and supported by murky irrigation ditches. Fields adjacent to the palm groves produced wheat. Varieties of trees sagged under the weight of pomegranates, apples, and citrus fruits. An occasional farm surfaced amid the boundless orchards and fields. The farm occupants, subsistence farmers who worked for middle-aged men with girths expanded by too much lamb, tended the crops. Some of them also planted "underground" crops. Hidden between irrigation ditches lay pits concealing mortars, rocket-propelled grenades, artillery rockets, grenades, and machine guns. As imperative as it was to uncover and confiscate illicit weaponry, finding the "arms farmers" was the real objective.

We targeted two such "sowers of discord" south of the village of Auja, the birthplace of Saddam Hussein. They were siblings from one of the "Five Family" networks, with the now familiar string of tongue-tying names conveying ancestry, tribe, and birthplace. Our soldiers had worked hard to disclose these brothers because they were among a group of five al-Hasan spawns who had attacked our forces with RPGs. They were also believed to be part of the inner circle of Saddam's security network. We arrested the first brother, Yada Adham Ibrahim al-Hasan, in Auja. We had now pinpointed the exact location of their family farm along the Tigris.

Our forces moved in and quickly cut off egress routes in coordination with Jack's SOF elements and attack aviation. By dusk, we had surrounded the brothers' farm. The remaining brother, Omar Adham Ibrahim al-Hasan, sought refuge in the darkness of nearby fields, but helicopters spotted him easily with thermal vision technology. We closed in on him and found him hunkered down in a field, his war now over. Two more were tracked down on the hunt for Saddam and his henchmen.

Others continued in their belligerence, however. On the 26th of August, an informant advised us of a farm southwest of Auja harboring weapons and surviving Fedayeen fighters. We had experienced attacks along the main highway nearby, making this information seem credible. I dispatched Chris Morris to scout the area to see what they could uncover. They took Joe Filmore along should a translator be required.

Two sections of scouts approached the farm just after dusk. They turned off the main highway and were soon greeted with a hail of gunfire from the AK-47 "Welcome Committee." The scouts immediately returned fire, forcing the retreating assailants deep into their own farmhouse. Rifles popped, .50 caliber machine guns barked, and 40mm Mark-19 grenade launchers thumped in a warlike cacophony of gunfire. Joe hunkered down in the Hummer as hot metal links and brass trickled down around him. The projectiles smacked the modest farm, chipping the block and plaster walls. Two individuals were briefly spotted running out the back and into an irrigation ditch directly behind the structure.

Chris Morris reported the fight, requesting additional force to effect a proper cordon. He still had visual contact with the enemy. Captain Mark Stouffer's A Company responded with a quick reaction force. Soon the area was cordoned with Bradleys, infantry, and scout Hummers. The four attackers were captured in the primary farmhouse and the structure connected by the irrigation ditch behind it. I was amazed that none of the enemy had been seriously injured as I surveyed the damaged farm. They were detained, and all of their weapons were captured, while not a single one of our men was wounded.

As this drama played out south of Tikrit, another unfolded on center stage. Repetitive roadside bomb attacks along 40th Street and 60th Street plagued the modest homes and businesses there. For three months we had fought battles along these alleys. While most of the attackers had been ambushed or subdued, the explosives threat continued.

Just the night before, my command convoy had turned onto 60th Street when an Iraqi youth dressed in black suddenly jumped up from a curb and bolted for a side street. Alerted by this, we gave chase for two blocks, but he had disappeared over the many-walled housing compounds. He appeared unarmed but could have been a scout or a bomb initiator. We queried the locals but none claimed to know him—convenient, but quite possibly not true.

One night later and not far from the same area, C Company had a rifle squad from its 2nd Platoon led by Sergeant Kermet Ross patrolling the side streets between 40th and 60th Streets. About three o'clock in the morning, well after curfew, the distinct sound of AK-47 fire shattered the night air. The soldiers took cover along the edge of the street and alerted toward the gunfire. Suddenly, an Iraqi man ran at full gallop around the corner as more gunfire erupted.

Private William Haines, on point but under cover behind a trash can, raised his M-249 and fired at the man. Several others opened up on him as well. A round caught the Iraqi squarely in the head, carrying away a portion of his face. The sprinter stumbled to the ground, losing his sandals before he fell.

Diverting our patrol to the scene, I saw the man lying facedown in a pool of blood with one of our rifle squads pulling security. He was dressed in dark clothing, like so many of the Fedayeen we fought. I immediately recognized him as the same man we encountered the night before. I asked the men what had happened. They were somewhat shocked by the ordeal, not because he was dead or because they shot him, but because they could see no weapon.

"Has anyone searched him?" I asked.

"Not yet, sir." they replied.

A few men were somewhat taken aback as First Sergeant Evans, Captain Boyd and I rolled his lifeless form over in his own fluids so we could search him. Some had still not witnessed death personally at close range and were probably afraid to touch him. While unpleasant, it needed to be done. As we rifled through his pockets, we found batteries of the type used to initiate roadside bombs.

Brad explained what happened. Apparently, both our troops and local Iraqi citizens fired at the man. No one knew who he was. His body lay for days unclaimed in the morgue, perhaps a recruit from Baghdad, or even a foreign fighter. We would never know as he carried no identification.

"Haines," I called out.

"Yes, sir," he replied.

"Good job. Do you know what these are?" I queried as I held out the batteries for initiating improvised bombs confiscated from the dead man's pockets.

"No, sir," he replied.

"These are the same batteries used to detonate explosive devices, and this is also the same man we tried to capture last night. You got him tonight. Good work," I assured him.

I was always concerned any time my men took human life. Soldiers take these actions very seriously. It is they who squint through the rifle sights and make the call to kill or not. It is they who must live with their decisions and they who will see those images the rest of their lives. Young Haines did the right thing that night. He didn't hesitate. He killed an enemy who purposed to annihilate us. It was important to validate his decision, to affirm that, while the weapon the enemy possessed was not visible, he was still a combatant with the intent to set a bomb against one of our patrols.

As August closed, information came to us by way of our well-established network of sheiks. The weekly "Council of Sheiks" was already proving its worth for the time invested. Developing this network had been no small task. Sheiks, by custom, could be appointed to represent several families or could represent thousands. How does one determine which sheik represents 40 people and which sheik represents 40,000?

When we arrived in May, every man claimed he was the sheik that the Americans should deal with, and as such, he was entitled to special privileges, badges, weapons, cars, and even women should we have them—whatever we could provide. They, in turn, would "guarantee" everything from security to support with the coalition, promises of uranium, "vital" information, and even Saddam himself—should they see him, of course.

Our challenge was to separate the men of grandiose self-esteem from the real sheiks who commanded the respect of the locals. By the end of August, we had solidified a genuine council with ten tribal heads from the controlling tribes who represented a populace of about 200,000 in our region.

One of the ten sheiks had been very cooperative with us already. Although secretive (Iraqi Arabs revel in the thrill of private liaisons, with theatrics), he provided information that would bring important breakthroughs regarding those resisting our efforts. Now he wanted a private dinner meeting east of the Tigris River on one of his more modest tenant farms for secrecy. I had come to call these dinner liaisons "lamb grabs" because the custom was to pull the meat of a slaughtered goat or lamb from the bone with bare hands. While the information provided that late evening in August was noteworthy, I will remember the dinner for another reason.

The tenant farmers had a solitary mud house in which they accommodated four families and twenty children. Unlike other lamb grabs we attended, here the wives and children were necessarily present. This allowed for some unexpected but welcome interaction among our soldiers. The laughter of the young ones, as they chased the laser lights on our weapons like playful kittens, was uplifting. Soon, the soldiers were teaching them some American games.

The best instructor of games that night was Specialist Holly McGeogh. She accompanied the convoy that night with permission (not her normal modus operandi). I had scolded my operations sergeant, Gil Nail, about Holly sneaking onto combat patrols. More than once, while on patrol, I had discovered her pulling security when we dismounted our Hummers. I was naturally concerned for her safety, both as a woman and as one of only three wheeled mechanics assigned to the entire battalion. She was a fine soldier, but combat patrolling was not her mission. Nor was it the mission of the other seventeen women in my support company.

Having women on the front lines was a dilemma I had not had to deal with before. I did not question their service or sacrifice, but I had to make sure that their special skills, like a mechanic's, were not put in jeopardy.

On this night, though, the likelihood for contact was minimal, and she was allowed to join us. Holly and my driver, Cody Hoefer, kept all twenty children entertained. The most enjoyable game they taught that night was the American favorite wherein a child is tapped on the head in a circle and dubbed a certain waterfowl. Being hailed as one type of bird causes the child to run after the name caller. "Duck, Duck, Goose" had come to Iraq.

Laughter filled the open desert all around us as the bonfire silhouetted the giggling children. Sheik Kanaan Hawas Sadeed of the Shumer tribe, our secretive host, smiled broadly while the other sheiks present nodded in approval. Women peered sheepishly from their doorways with warm smiles. As I absorbed it all from a short distance, it was hard to hold back the tears and the longing to be with my own children.

BOMBS AND BOMBAST

While we enjoyed this out-of-place respite near the foothills of the Jabal Hamrin Ridge east of the Tigris, our C Company soldiers on patrol spotted a white, bullet-ridden car driving in downtown Tikrit. They immediately stopped the suspicious carpool and subdued four insurgents with three AK-47 rifles. No one ever said insurgents were always smart.

To the north of the city, near the village of Mazhem, Jon Cecalupo's tankers began the opening round of what became the "battle for the ammunition supply points." On the night of August 28, the "Cougars" found fourteen looters living inside a bunker bloated with munitions. The bunkers were roughly the size of gymnasiums with double outer walls that formed a catacomb around the structure, allowing the looters to hide in nooks and crannies in complete darkness. Our men would have to clear them, much as they would a tunnel and with the same associated risks.

Looters, hired for about two dollars a day, were brought in from Samarra. They had an entire operation in process, salvaging 57mm anti-aircraft shells. They removed the rounds from the wooden crates and then cracked the seals from the brass case with a hammer—a definitive indicator of their intelligence. It was like some 1940s Looney Tunes animation of gremlins whacking bombs and munitions with sledgehammers.

Naturally, the looters worked best while smoking during all this hammering of live shells and pouring of powder. After cracking the seals, they emptied the powder pellets into bags, stacked the brass, and then bagged the warheads to be vended to a local bomb maker. The warheads were the type often used in roadside improvised explosives. The fast-burning propellant was used to make other types of bombs as well. To ensure that nothing was wasted, the brass was melted down into ingots and sold to teapot and plate makers. The proceeds supported local terrorists.

The enemy knew that we had insufficient manpower to cover the vast ammunition depots and bunkers. Consequently, the IED war manifested itself significantly in our area. Because we were killing the enemy in direct firefights in the city, they were forced to find other means of attack. They could salvage munitions north of the city with minimal risk of encountering our patrols.

I assigned the task of ending this operation to Captain Cecalupo's C Company, 3-66 Armor. Although not a tank mission, we needed the manpower, and this was his area of operations. Jon, the son and brother of infantrymen, aggressively put his talents into the task and established a series of ambushes with his dismounted tank crews.

Each night for a month, a "cat and mouse" war developed. The insurgent-paid looters would come into the perimeter, most of the time armed, to set up shop for the night. Business was brisk. In about thirty days, Captain Cecalupo's men had engaged literally scores of the enemy. They had killed five, wounded sixty-five, and captured more than one hundred. For every night of bloodshed, a new day of replenished looters awaited them. It seemed like we were just shoveling fleas.

Concerned, I met individually with the tank men performing the grisly work of separating the stupid and lawless from the living and breathing. What I found was yet another example of how professional and dedicated our soldiers were. The men assured me that they fully understood the mission. For every bomb material supplier they killed or maimed, one less bomb would be on the road. They were exactly right. At the end of a month's hard fighting, the battle of the ammunition supply point appeared to be won in the region north of Tikrit. Nevertheless, the bomb war continued to be waged in the streets and supply routes of Tikrit and its surrounding villages.

On August 29, we patrolled the streets of Tikrit, much like any other night. Long shadows stretched beyond the pale streetlight while wild dogs roamed about in packs, eager to begin patrols of their own. About 11:30 p.m., as we turned onto 40th Street, a pack of dogs assaulted us in an impressive wedge formation, all barking in support as they pressed to within five feet of our vehicles. While we were admiring their aggressiveness and disciplined formation, a violent brown explosion silenced their barks and our thoughts as a concussive blast washed over us. What was that? I thought. An acrid stench filled the hazy air. I could only vaguely make out the canines as they made hasty retreats.

Attempting to assess the situation, I swiveled to catch a glimpse of the trail vehicles. They appeared to be unscathed. In fact, we all seemed to be unharmed. Instantly we turned the vehicles around, covered both double lanes of traffic, and headed south back toward the enemy. Reaching the approximate point of attack, we bailed from the vehicles and sought to engage him. Once again, we shouted taunts at the enemy and attested with oaths and epitaphs to their incompetence. This time, none answered our challenge.

On the west corner curb, the precise location on which I had been attacked in July when Phillips was wounded, was evidence of the explosion. A vegetable oil tin, packed with what we determined to be ten blocks of TNT and a hand grenade thrown in for good measure, was the basis of the bomb. Clearly legible on a piece of the ruptured metal were the ironic words "A Gift from Sweden."

A gift indeed! Due to poor wiring of the explosives, the bomb did not have the force it should have. I was not complaining. The grenade and two blocks of TNT detonated, but the other eight blocks lay scattered around us like playtime at a nursery. Our dispersion and tactics had lessened the effects, as the timing of the blast occurred between my vehicle and the one behind me.

A curious man, unrelated to the incident, observed us with amusement from the balcony above his well-lit restaurant. He seemed to be mocking us. Not knowing his intentions, red rifle lasers lined up on his man dress and he, like the dogs, beat a hasty retreat to safety. The attacker could be any one of several thousand people concealed in nearby houses and apartments on 40th Street. There was nothing to do but resume our patrol. I thanked God yet again for sparing our lives.

August 30 dawned with yet another bomb on the streets. Infantry from C Company discovered this one constructed of two sticks of C-4 hooked to batteries and tied to a bottle of diesel fuel. Our soldiers called the explosives experts to detonate it. Later that afternoon, not far from the bomb locale, a C Company patrol dodged a volley of RPGs that missed widely. One crashed into an Iraqi house, horribly wounding a two-year-old child. Our soldiers immediately responded and saved the life of the terrified girl. She was stabilized and transported to the local hospital. It was a scene of heartbreak and suffering, enough to kindle the desire to slaughter every insurgent and terrorist in Iraq with the same insensitivity.

Even as this drama unfolded, we received a tip regarding a weapons cache of RPG launchers on yet another farm. We made haste to the residence of the alleged farm owner. He was not home, but a relative answered the door. On gut instinct, we advised him that there would be no trouble if he led us to the farm and disclosed the weapons. He complied. His brother was already in jail, and this man wanted no trouble with us. He pledged to help. He did.

After a ten-minute countryside journey, the man escorted us to a deep irrigation ditch and pointed to a pile of cut hay at the bottom. As we extracted six sacks of weapons, we realized that we stood little chance of ever finding these weapons without informants. We returned to headquarters with no fewer than twenty-six RPG launchers. It was one of the single largest RPG hauls we had ever seen.

The enemy attempted to keep up the pressure. Over the next few days, our soldiers handled an attack on the Governor's building and more roadside bombs. September 2 was particularly noteworthy. It started with a chilling discovery on the northern highway bypass. Several large caliber artillery shells were "daisy-chained" together behind the guardrail. Each had been mounted and concealed from passing drivers. Connecting each heavy artillery shell was detonation cord, allowing every shell to explode instantly and simultaneously at eye level upon detonation of a single device. It was a macabre and deadly ambush-in-waiting. We disarmed the shells immediately, thankful once again for having been spared from disaster.

We soon tore down every guardrail in the city but new innovations took their place with increasing frequency. I assessed the situation my command was facing and did not like the conclusion I reached. The enemy was clearly on the offensive now in a lethal roadside bomb war. While we had gained the initiative in direct fights, we struggled with the indirect nature of roadside bomb attacks. Even worse, these attacks were camouflaged in broad daylight by innocent civilians.

With the guardrail ambush effectively thwarted, C Company patrols discovered two additional bombs in northern Tikrit and detonated them both. At the southern highway bypass, a patrol from Mark Huron's 299th Engineers discovered yet another. We were thankful. As long shadows signaled day's end, a convoy from our support company carrying both supplies and soldiers returning from emergency leave would most certainly have traveled directly into the path of this bomb. No matter. Another one awaited it.

First Lieutenant Chris Eagling led the convoy in Hummer A44. He had already survived one ambush when his Hummer was blasted in the CMIC attack in June when Halling was killed. On this day, the enemy would get a second chance. Positioned behind the driver, Eagling saw an object in the road. That object was a tire concealing a 152mm heavy artillery shell packed into a sack of ball bearings and connected to a blasting cap with a cell phone to dial up the explosion.

The Hummer and its occupants were suddenly consumed in a brownish cloud of sand, flame, and shrapnel. In the right front seat, Second Lieutenant Ali Adnan felt a sharp pain in his right knee and arm as he was blown horizontally into the center console. Adnan was a brand-new officer only recently assigned to our support company. It was a rude welcome to the unit. The soldier seated behind him fared no better. Thumbing a ride on our battalion's support convoy for his return trip from leave, Sergeant First Class Charles Chenault from A Company was thrown laterally into the middle of the Humvee. Shrapnel lacerated his neck and fragmentation peppered his body. Welcome back to Iraq.

The Hummer was not the only victim. The concussive mixture of brownish cloud, flame, blast, shell fragmentation, and flying ball bearings lashed into cargo truck A181A as it trailed them, cutting tires, metal, and flesh. Seated and on guard in the back of the truck's cargo area, Specialist Michael Regehr from our support company felt a deadening pain to his face, head, and shoulder. Blood poured from his gums where several of his teeth had once been. Another soldier, Specialist William McBroom, facing the back, felt fragments slice through his left foot and suffered abrasions to his face. Amazingly, no one was critically injured.

Sergeant Chenault staggered from the vehicle. Lieutenant Eagling joined him as they made their way forward of the blast site. They waved down an approaching MP patrol from Dave Poirier's 720th MP Battalion to warn them of danger ahead. The MPs radioed to our battalion and aided the wounded. Our soldiers gathered their wounded comrades and rushed them to an aid station a few kilometers up the highway. It was located at a small Iraqi auxiliary airfield dubbed "FOB Packhorse" in honor of the 4th Support Battalion's moniker.

We raced south upon hearing the blast to assist in securing the area, equipment, and damaged vehicles. As I walked a length of Highway 1, I found chicken breast-sized chunks of the artillery shell embedded in the asphalt. The tire that concealed the bomb was a willowing array of belted cords, while loose rubber had bounced in every direction. We were able to recover cell phone parts and other key items that would help us find the bomb's signature.

With casualties and equipment secure, we quickly recovered everything from the scene. My men knew I wanted no damaged vehicles to linger after an attack. Insurgents would never dance on American equipment. Ever. We would kill anyone who tried. I would not tolerate a burning hulk from my command being on display before a gloating enemy or illustrating some disingenuous concerned commentary from an evening news reporter.

I had clearly endured enough. We had some leads and were fairly successful in stopping the bombs, but one always seemed to elude us. Acting on our first solid intelligence on September 3, we struck back. An Iraqi informant tipped our soldiers about suspected bomb makers in Tikrit named Ibrahim and Raid Kasim Muhammed Muhammed. We hastily planned a 1:00 a.m. raid on the house located on the western outskirts of the city. As we prepared for the raid, a half dozen mortar rounds slammed into the ground near the Tigris bridge access road, riveting both thoughts and bodies. All fell harmlessly into an empty lot.

Reports from lookouts crackled over the radio identifying the location of the attackers to a field east of the river. Counter-artillery radar confirmed the same location. We alerted the Brigade Reconnaissance Troop, commanded by Captain Dez Bailey, whose troops owned that sector. I could see on the FBCB2 that they were several kilometers north of the activity at that moment. With our troops being a good bit closer to the activity, I resolved to cross the river to prevent the slippery insurgents from escaping before Dez's troops could get there. Of our troops currently out on patrol, my own command element was the closest thing to the suspected area.

As both Dez's element and mine closed on the suspected location, I could see from my FBCB2 "fishfinder" that Dez would not make the intersection before me. We had only small arms on the convoy, and while I would not hesitate to fight, it was as if all the hackles on the back of my neck rose to the danger.

"Hold up a sec," I shouted to Hoefer. "Let's let the BRT catch up. We're too far ahead, and I don't want to blunder into something."

To this day I still wonder what caused me to sense the danger on that stretch of road. Just a minute later, as we watched the BRT vehicles come into view, a violent firefight erupted. Their convoy came under heavy RPG and small arms fire about 400 meters to our front. Tracers shot across the sky, washed out by brilliant explosions from crashing rockets.

Unlike us, Dez was well armed with crew-served weapons. The haste of the insurgents shifting their focus from our little band of merry men to his well-armed combat vehicles gave him an edge. Bailey and his men returned a vicious fire with .50 cal. machine guns, 40mm Mk 19 grenade launchers, and rifle fire. After radioing a hasty call for Brad Boyd to bring up his Tikrit Quick Reaction Force, I put foot to pavement and ran toward the fight with a few of my men.

The brush caught fire with the second outburst. The insurgents were using an aqueduct as cover, and the flames of the surrounding grass fire had washed out our night vision as the din of machine guns mixed with the thumps of Mk 19 grenades and rifle fire. I conferred briefly with Dez on the ground to let him know that we had some support on the way with Bradleys and infantry.

Soon Brad and his men joined forces with Dez as they moved into the farmland along the aqueduct. Flames licked at the night sky, but the shooting had completely stopped. Determined soldiers and company commanders joined together to search the area. As the flames and floating sparks swirled into the air, violent eruptions suddenly showered sparks and debris over the area. Something was cooking off in the brush. It could have been abandoned RPG grenades or mortar ammunition. We may never know.

The next morning, soldiers found a bloody sandal in a concrete aqueduct. The charred area around the attackers' launch point attested to the one-sidedness of the fight. The mortar launch point was confirmed, but there were no detectable blood trails to track due to the blaze. Still, it was clear that the insurgents had paid dearly for their attack while none of our soldiers had been wounded in either scrap. While proud of our soldiers' ability to react quickly and work cohesively with adjacent units, I was acutely aware of the narrow margin by which I missed leading my little convoy head-on into disaster. I felt that God had once again preserved our lives.

Returning to my Hummer after that fight, I found an excited reporter who had recorded much of it on video. I had forgotten that Andrew Cawthorne of Reuters was with us. By this point in the war, I nearly always had a rider or two from the media. We made an effort to accommodate reporters and photographers as expediency allowed. Andrew had asked to accompany us that night, as it was his last night with us before heading to Baghdad and ultimately home. His peers from other bureaus had been less interested and had chosen a respite versus what might have been a tedious and uneventful patrol. However, when Andrew came back with incredible footage of the fight, the other news agencies were scrambling to get his story. By the time the evening news aired back in the States, the footage of our fight had been flashed around the world.

With the conclusion of that fight, we continued preparations for the raid on the bomb maker house later in the evening. Moving swiftly, we completely surprised the occupants at that hour. We netted C-4 plastic explosives, five types of propellant, sealants, clocks, timers made in China, switches, wire, grenades, and rifles. Both bomb makers were captured in that raid. If the local demand for bombs was not down, at least the supply of bombs and bomb makers would be.

On September 5, we found ourselves guarding Tikrit and its environs in a most unusual way. Our instructions were to ensure a four-hour window free of attack. No bangs, no booms, no fuss. It was a tall order but one that we clearly understood. No doubt, gunfire and bomb blasts were not the backdrop that Secretary of Defense Donald Rumsfeld would be expecting upon his arrival in Tikrit to announce the success of Iraqi security forces and clearly visible signs of progress.

To maximize the effort, patrols were increased and made more visible. I ordered Jon Cecalupo to bring a platoon of M1 Abrams tanks downtown. It was also the perfect opportunity to introduce the Tikriti people to our Iraqi Civil Defense forces. The effect was total.

The appearance of Iraqi soldiers on patrol in the city made quite an impact on the local psyche, even more so than our tanks. While the Iraqi native levies were not quite ready for prime time, they were more than able to make a show of force by walking alongside our soldiers, accompanied by tanks and Bradleys. The people were amazed at the sight. Only days from graduation, these young Iraqi men walked proudly on the streets of their countrymen. Bystanders gazed in amazement. One woman clutched her heart and shouted words toward the soldiers. Joe Filmore turned to translate her words: "Our army! It has returned!"

Our training efforts had been very successful in the Iraqi Civil Defense Corps. Learning from my experience with the Afghan National Army project in the spring of 2002, I had assembled a program smaller in scale but equally important given our geography and world attention at that moment. From the cadres of trainers precariously pulled from our frontline troops to the vetting we had by recruiting from the tribal sheiks, the result was greater than I had hoped. We had no problems with enemy infiltration or Iraqis learning the basics of soldiering and security.

The initial crop of Iraqi soldiers had proven worthy of the new government and was not afraid to take risks in our area of operations. While others may have experienced problems, we did not because we invested up front. A tight relationship had been established among former army soldiers, government leaders, and tribal sheiks. We backed them fully and conducted operations with them side by side. From this day forward, we would fight and bleed together.

Although we could not fully realize it at the time, this cadre of Iraqis would eventually form the foundation for the force that would be among the first in the country to completely relieve a major American base—ours. It would be one of the first to assume responsibility for keeping peace in the city that had once been so volatile. That would be in the future, but today, the day Defense Secretary Donald Rumsfeld came to speak of security and progress, his safety would be assured. There would be no big booms or gunfire report to heckle his remarks. His claims would be irrefutably truthful.

As much as we enjoyed visible signs of progress, it was no substitute for success. Our battle for the streets of Tikrit continued. A sniper team placed near 40th Street to safeguard that troubled area reminded us that, like the arcade game "Whac-A-Mole," we had to keep swinging at the devious and elusive enemy.

On September 6, Specialist Juan Cantu and his sniper team traversed from a rooftop hideout along a wall to cover a different location. As they did, three Iraqis engaged them with gunfire and fled. Not satisfied with this outcome and undaunted by the terrain, Cantu bounced his team across catwalks and rooftops in the direction he believed the assailants had disappeared. Approaching a corner, he saw the men congratulating each other, flushed with their imagined heroics. Their victory party was soon shattered by gunfire from our soldiers. Cantu and his team ripped into the men, killing two and wounding the third. This enemy paid a heavy price for his bombast.

That same day, Jon Cecalupo's "Cougars" continued the battle of the bunkers, killing one and wounding another. There seemed to be an endless supply of idiots with hammers, cigarettes, and AK-47s. They continued to stack up like the 57mm casings they came to loot.

My chief concerns during this time were defeating bomb makers, combating street fighters, and hunting for Saddam Hussein and his henchmen. It was an intense balancing act stretching and reaching in every direction that intelligence led us or instinct urged us. While Colonel Hickey's focus was decidedly fixed on the trail of Saddam, we could not ignore the day-to-day fights that necessarily deterred us from our main effort.

Once he realized that we were looking for Musslits, the Governor's security chief, Colonel Mohammed Jassim Hussein, provided some unexpected but much-needed support. Jassim's men nabbed two Musslits within a two-week period. Although cousins to the main family we were tracking, the brothers, Nasir and Ahmed Yaseen Omar al-Musslit, helped connect the dots from the insurgency network that protected Saddam to those who inspired and recruited insurgents, to those who planned ambushes on Americans.

In many ways, these were all symbiotic. The insurgency was struggling to take the initiative, inspired by money and weapons provided by leaders of the former regime. To what extent Saddam was influencing events was not clear at the time. We now know that he was attempting a loose insurgent campaign to be executed by the party faithful, namely his inner circle of bodyguards. Our strategy seemed to be giving us the advantage.

Regardless, street fights had become a priority again. We began to position more outposts and ambushes in the most likely areas of enemy activity. In doing so, we continued to uncover an odd relationship of active cells having direct ties to Saddam's old networks. Their locations varied from downtown shops to residential suburbs or to quiet villages. On the night of September 6, we raided three suspected locations based on tips and detained seven insurgents and their weapons. The information we gained further validated our interpretation of events.

One of the newly placed outposts provided surveillance of Thamer Hamoudi's house in hopes of being able to eradicate the bombing and insurgent network we had deciphered. Hamoudi's house was in close proximity to Abid Mahmood's house in Cadaseeyah, where the Ace of Diamonds had been captured in June. Like Auja, the area was full of trouble. Jon's tankers were still too busy with the bunkers farther north to cover Cadaseeyah, so I ordered Brad Boyd's troops to expand a bit north and take up observation in the area with Chris Morris' scouts in mutual support. Mark Stouffer would assist with his "Gators" by assuming some city patrols and taking up the battalion reserve.

We had come far in our ability to emplace sustained outposts since July. Brad was able to infiltrate an eight-man outpost of line infantry led by his 3rd Platoon Leader, First Lieutenant Mike

Isbell. They landed silently in a 74th Engineer Company V-hulled boat on the west bank of the Tigris River and stealthily moved up a wadi in search of suitable locations for their surveillance. They avoided any insurgent lookouts observing the main roads to the west. The outpost was composed of several sturdy unfinished houses in a setting that afforded them excellent observation of Thamer's house without being in the direct line of any traffic. After some promising signs of activity on the first night, Isbell consolidated his team on a single house that offered the best observation. Little did we know it was also a meeting place for an insurgent cell operating in the area.

At sunset on September 7, Isbell led a three-man team to gain a closer view of Thamer's house. He believed he saw Thamer's car and wanted to confirm his presence. Scanning with a command launch unit (CLU), a thermal device that attached to the Javelin anti-tank rocket, Isbell's eyes diverted to Specialist Jacob Lynn who was flailing wildly and acting quite erratic.

"What's wrong with you?" an irritated Isbell whispered.

"Hornets, sir!" Lynn rasped as he battled the nasty little pests.

Confirming what he believed to be Thamer's car, he made his way back to the outpost. About an hour after twilight, Isbell and his men heard the crunching sound of tire rubber on the dusty hard-packed ground. He spied a blue Toyota heading straight for their location, apparently unaware of their presence, yet arriving without headlights to conceal their movement. Isbell craned up to see the car and ordered Specialist Lynn to alert the others downstairs. Sergeant Matthew Rose had already taken a position by the entrance. Staff Sergeant Joe Williams motioned to Specialist Radhames Camilo, Sergeant John Garza, and Lynn to stay low and still.

Two Iraqis exited the car. The first one entered the doorway and walked right into Sergeant Rose. "Grab him!" shouted Williams.

Then he, Lynn, Camilo, and Garza took off after the second Iraqi who was attempting to flee. Both Iraqis, now subdued, were brought into the outpost. Sergeant Rose ordered Private First Class Justin Brog, a medic, to switch off the Toyota's ignition. As he did, he thought he saw men armed with AK-47s off in the distance.

Meanwhile, from his second floor vantage, Isbell noticed the same armed men drifting out of Thamer's compound. He could distinguish two for certain. One appeared to speak to the other before running back into Thamer's house.

"I need the CLU," Isbell called to the men downstairs.

Grabbing Sergeant Christopher Wright's PVS-7b night vision goggles, Isbell adjusted them in an effort to see the men in the distance. Although the residential lights washed out the night vision, he could see one of the armed men take a knee. Private First Class Brog spotted another man moving about 150 meters from the kneeling man. They were attempting to flank the outpost.

A thousand thoughts raced through Isbell's mind. He had two Iraqis detained, his position was compromised, armed men were assembling at Thamer's house, and others were arriving from different locations. He radioed to Captain Boyd, gave a brief contact report, and asked for backup. Then, without hesitation, Lieutenant Isbell made the decision to move on the armed men before they could act.

"I need three men!" Isbell called out in a hushed tone as he flew down the stairs, leaving Wright alone on the roof. As he exited the doorway, he heard the familiar sound of a charging weapon. Gunfire reverberated in the bare outpost as Sergeant Wright opened up with his rifle. Specialist Camilo ripped a burst from his squad automatic weapon just as Isbell came up. Seeing the tracer rounds climb into the air, Isbell instinctively placed a hand on the barrel to push the rounds lower, flinching with the searing heat of the barrel. Camilo understood and adjusted his aim in the darkness as Isbell raised his own rifle to join in. They thought they saw the kneeling man fall to the ground.

"Cease fire!" ordered Isbell. Suddenly, the man leapt up and rushed over to some bushes nearby.

"He's up!" shouted Specialist Lynn, who had followed Isbell outside.

"Shoot the m_____ f_____!" screamed Isbell as he fired his weapon, watching the man tumble near the bushes.

As Isbell's men began to secure the area, Brad Boyd moved to the location with his reinforcements. Chris Morris moved his scouts from their location in the Cadaseeyah area as well. I nosed my convoy toward the sound of the guns and authorized release of the battalion Quick Reaction Force platoon from Mark Stouffer's A Company. I gave instructions for them to take orders from C Company.

As Brad moved his troops toward the area, Lieutenant Isbell captured six suspected insurgents. Making his way to the wounded Iraqi who had been shot through the legs, he evaluated his surroundings and noted that things had grown eerily silent. All activity at Thamer's house had ceased. Isbell kicked the chrome-plated AK-47 from the groaning Iraqi's reach as blood continued to pour from his wounds.

"We need to get him some help, but he won't be able to walk," Isbell said to Lynn.

"Why don't we use the Iraqi car?" suggested Lynn, pointing toward the recently acquired Toyota parked at the outpost in the distance.

"Go get it," ordered Isbell as he instructed Specialist Camilo to cover the wounded man. Specialist Lynn ran to retrieve the car in which they would move him to the outpost.

Once there, Private First Class Brog treated the wounded Iraqi's gunshot wounds and administered an IV. Meanwhile, Brad's troops struggled to find Isbell's location in the darkness. The residential lights hampered the night vision, and the infrared chem lights could not be seen at all. Finally, Brad told Isbell to flash a red lens flashlight to assist them with linkup. Picking up the signal, Brad moved swiftly to Isbell's location.

Bryan Luke and I arrived at about the same time as Captain Boyd. Brad and I conferred briefly. We both felt that the opportunity for catching Thamer that night had probably dissipated but decided to raid his house anyway to see what we could find. The raid yielded some useful material though Thamer reportedly fled when our outpost was compromised by the chance encounter with the blue Toyota.

There would be another encounter with a Toyota the next day. This one would be white. Staff Sergeant German Sanchez was leading his foot patrol along 40th Street when they found themselves under fire from a white Toyota Crown driving by a connecting alley. The enemy fired RPGs and rifles whereupon the patrol immediately returned fire and blasted the car. They forced the enemy to flee but were unable to flush them out. Sanchez's troops complained that, unlike in the movies, you can hit a car with a supernatural amount of fire without obliterating it.

While all this action failed to net Thamer, we were connecting more dots on the bombing network. Acting on a tip the night of September 10, we cordoned three businesses along 40th Street and raided them. Among the goods in the stores were TNT and C-4 explosives, clocks, mercury for detonators, mortar ammunition, AK-47s, and shotguns—a diverse assortment for the discriminating shopper.

Most intriguing were several radio-controlled cars that were being converted into bombs. The cars themselves would be discarded, but the bombers stripped the electronic components to attach them to blasting caps. They were then wrapped in plastic explosives and placed inside various containers for camouflage. The "hobbyists" would then use the handheld R/C steering device to detonate the bomb as a convoy passed. The range on these devices was about 100 meters. In a built-up urban environment, that distance could provide endless possibilities for an attacker to strike and hide.

As we sifted through the material captured in this raid, my soldiers inadvertently made a noteworthy discovery. Unable to resist the temptation of the confiscated toys, the unaltered cars were soon zipping all around the marble floor of our palace headquarters. Watching in amusement, I noticed that when one soldier attempted to steer his toy car, it interfered with all the others. Never ones to concern themselves with FCC regulations, apparently the Chinese had built them all to operate on the same frequency.

Intrigued, we tested our observations and found that all of the cars were, indeed, on the same frequency. If the insurgents in our area purchased the cars in bulk, then we could also assume that their bombs detonated on the same frequency as well. To counter some of that threat, I taped down the levers on one of the R/C controllers. Resting on the dashboard of our Humvee in the "on" position during patrols, it served us well as a poor man's anti-explosive device. It was risky, perhaps, but far superior to bombs striking us through discovery learning.

The ever-increasing improvised bomb threat challenged military minds everywhere. While we battled them, politicians and reporters seemed especially excited to find a cause célèbre to grab headlines and show genuine concern for soldier safety while never missing an opportunity to castigate our defense leaders or their political enemies. Never mind that most of them could not identify a bomb four out of five times in a display of only bombs.

Consequently, we began to receive all manner of ingenious ideas and implements of intelligence to counter the bomb threats.

Unfortunately, most of these devices were long on promise and short on delivery. Rushing each new solution to the front lines, we answered the well-wishers' queries via burdensome field reports that their contraptions didn't work or worked on the wrong things. "High speed" jamming equipment in their "high speed" vehicles also jammed all of our "low speed" radios—not the best strategy for preserving our troops in life-and-death situations.

Other items of note sent to us included a massive white Chevy Suburban with enormous NASA-like black antennae protruding from the top. We might as well have painted a bull's-eye on each side as an added touch. It was like going to war in a Winnebago—hilarious for the movie *Stripes* but utterly inept in Tikrit. Powered up, not only would it jam all of our communications, but it seemed to have the potential to pull down orbiting satellites, invert black holes, and tear irreparable gaps in the universe.

Next came advocates of armoring everything and everyone. Once accomplished, we were to hunker down and retreat into consolidated bases to reduce the number of options for effective placement of bombs. Never mind the enemy's delight to have been presented with fresh targets on limited access points requiring minimum effort on their part. Why didn't we just hand them a treasure map with X marking the spots—"Plant bombs for Americans here." If a bomb was discovered, heaven forbid we should deal with it ourselves. After all, what could infantry possibly know about things that explode or go bump in the night? No, the bomb experts could rush to the scene. They were guaranteed to arrive posthaste within at least twelve hours. The entire plan from concept to execution was utter nonsense.

The best way to manage the early bomb threats was to regard the bombs as obstacles. The best tactic for defeating them was the employment of ambushes and informant networks. If bombs were detected, they could be cleared like obstacles. The procedure was much the same as removing a landmine—isolate and detonate. The theory seemed rational to us, but we found it impossible to convince anyone apart from our field commanders. Thankfully, they gave us the freedom to tackle the bombs with low-tech tactics.

Such tactics were extremely effective in countering explosives. Over seventy percent of the bombs in our area were preempted before they could discharge. Of those that did, fewer still caused major harm because of our proficient tactical dispersion and formations. While affording no protection in case of impact, our unarmored, stripped, and open vehicles yielded excellent visibility for all eyes on board and facilitated instant reaction. We had not deployed with armored Hummers or trucks. We creatively used what we had in the best way possible.

We rendered the full measure of respect these bombs commanded and would continue to take casualties from them. I reasoned, however, that we must never adopt a defensive posture to counter them. To do so would surrender the initiative to the enemy on a silver platter. That would never happen if I could prevent it. Fortunately, General Odierno and Colonel Hickey held the same view concerning these early improvised bombs.

A FREE AND DEMOCRATIC IRAQ

After the street fighting early in the month, mid-September arrived with promise. The heat remained insufferable, but the soldiers handled each task magnificently—whether ambushes, patrols, training native levies, or engaging local officials in democratic processes. The first class of Iraqi Civil Defense soldiers graduated, and training of the second class began. The "Council of Sheiks" was formalized. Making the head tribal leaders authorized representatives precluded the need to hear every individual with a complaint.

This allowed us to focus on the most pressing issues. Our mayor, Ibrahim Waal, drawing from his vast diplomatic experience abroad, established an effective system to improve public works. We worked closely with the provincial police chief, General Mezher, who had hired the third Tikrit municipal police chief—the first was fired, and the second was transferred. Our relationship with the Salah ad Din provincial government continued to gel.

Against this backdrop, Major General Ray Odierno charged each of his units to select delegates for each city and province to form representative councils. Their task would be to aid the governors of the three provinces under the umbrella of the 4th Infantry Division. Having long before engaged many of the sheiks and leaders, we assembled an able group composed of ten sheiks and five professionals from which to choose the representatives from Tikrit. Other cities did the same. We convened at Colonel Hickey's 1st Brigade headquarters for the representative election of 34 delegates to serve on the Salah ad Din Provincial Governing Council.

The big day arrived on September 13. I met with our Tikritis in a private room after all were gathered in a general assembly. Iraqi judges were present for each selection to administer the ballot count alongside each battalion commander. I gave each prospective councilman the floor. The qualifications they voiced were varied. One touted his ninth grade education and character. Others spoke of their law or engineering degrees or their achievements as medical doctors. Some had previously held political offices. But my absolute favorite was the Nasiri tribal head sheik who stated confidently, as he adjusted his robe lapels and delicately opened his palms toward the assembly, "I am Sheik Mahmood." That was the summation of his qualifications as he yielded the floor to the next individual with a sweeping gesture of his hand. He was not elected, but he did get several votes.

Two very prominent sheiks were elected, however. Sheik Kanaan Hawas Sadeed and Sheik Najii Hussein Jabori were both head sheiks of sizeable tribes that we had come to know well already. Additionally, Ali Ghalib Ibrahim Ali, a lawyer, and Khatan Habadi Salah, a civil engineer, joined them to represent Salah ad Din in the larger government now forming in provinces all across Iraq. It was exciting to witness a new and free Iraq emerging if even in these representative, elected appointments. Perhaps this new Iraq would finally win a respite after decades of suffering.

We would get a miniscule reprieve of our own during that period. Following the tremendous intensity of previous weeks, mid-September was eerily still. To be sure, we had whacked the insurgency with the big stick at every level in the days leading up to the calm. Jon Cecalupo's men had killed five insurgents, wounded 27, and captured 65 in a single month of bunker operations farther north of the city. His men were acquitting themselves brilliantly. Jack's SOF men secured important information about portable surface-to-air missiles that might be employed against our helicopters in the area. We collaborated diligently to find their location. Our informant network was becoming first-rate. Our intelligence was even better as a result. Whatever the reasons, we enjoyed three consecutive days without a single direct attack on our soldiers.

Finding release from the conflict, I used the time to stress the urgency of leadership in the sustained daily fight to my squad leaders and staff sergeants. It was crucial to understand that they were the key to the success or failure of this campaign. I communicated that our troops and team leaders were doing well but that I felt the team leaders had more grit than the squad leaders, who needed to step up to the plate. I recounted a sequence of minor incidents across the battalion that indicated to Command Sergeant Major Martinez and me that these small unit leaders were neglecting some battlefield basics and diligence in discipline. My style was to address issues head-on but to allow the squad leaders a voice in support of their stance. The session went well.

On the afternoon of September 18, we were returning from a visit to Scott Thomas' B Company in Bayjii. It had been my honor to hang the Combat Infantry Streamer on the "Bear" company guidon that morning. On the way back, I was concerned with the power line area that paralleled Highway 1 at a distance of several kilometers. Looters had ransacked the electrical lines before the Coalition Provisional Authority entered into agreement with sheiks to control certain sections of the service road, for minor compensation.

We traveled the power line road for about 35 kilometers to see how things were progressing. It was actually great fun, and my men seemed to enjoy traveling cross-country over desert sands, through mud farms, and across irrigation berms. As we endeavored to get out of one enclosed embankment, we confirmed the theory that Humvees will actually catch some air if the angle of the berm and the speed of the vehicle are just right.

Our journey ended south of Tikrit, near Auja. Not far to the south, two Humvees and a wheeled ambulance were transporting a sick soldier north along Highway 1 to the military hospital. Little did they know that they would add war wounded to their casualty list before arriving.

At about 4:00 p.m., as the lead vehicle neared the spiral arches on Highway 1 south of Auja, a violent blast shattered the vehicle's windshield, front tires, and side. The Humvee belonged to a First Sergeant from 1-66 Armor who was leading the convoy. We heard the distant whump followed by a radio transmission requesting assistance. The driver lay bleeding but conscious when we arrived. The other soldiers were understandably shaken by the event. Coming face-to-face with trauma, the mind reels as it attempts to process information at supersonic speed.

I went to the young driver laid out on the ground. His leg was mauled but not seriously damaged. There may have been fractures but no major bone crushing. His mouth and face were covered in blood. He seemed worried and was obviously in pain. Soon, the armored battalion's sergeant major arrived, and we both reassured the soldier and told him to take a deep breath and relax. He was going to be okay. He calmed a bit and then expressed the need to spit. Blood had collected in his mouth through gaps where he once had teeth.

The unit collected their casualties and equipment and put their convoy back together. Fortunately for the wounded soldier, he was traveling with an ambulance and medics. He was going to be fine. I assured their men that we would recover the impaired vehicle and remaining gear and return them at the brigade aid station.

A hasty examination of the area uncovered the remnants of a Motorola radio bomb. These were not your average bombs. The range of these deadly devices was several kilometers. As we were in an open expanse of desert along the highway, anyone within a wide radius could have initiated the apparatus. Several non-military vehicles had also been damaged by the blast. We never learned if any Iraqis had sustained injuries.

We returned to our command post to eat and then resumed patrols. I was in the villages to the north of the city that night when I heard some disturbing radio calls from across the river. A section of Hummers from Dez Bailey's Brigade Reconnaissance Troop had been surprised in a nasty ambush similar to the one Dez and I fought our way out of just two weeks earlier. This, too, was a night ambush, but it was played out on the precarious dike roads dividing the flooded farm fields. The situation made maneuvering nearly impossible.

Bailey's soldiers were responding to reports of an RPG being fired in the area. A two-vehicle scout section moved into the hamlet and flooded area. At approximately 9:30 p.m., both vehicles were caught in a murderous fire of RPGs, small arms, and grenades. Two soldiers lay dead, and three others were severely wounded in the initial strike. The remainder of the men fought off the attackers and maintained contact with the enemy. Dez brought in the rest of the troop to reinforce them and requested immediate medical evacuation support. He said that air evac was out of the question due to terrain. If I could pick them up at the Tigris bridge, he would appreciate it.

We immediately responded from our side of the river. I sent C Company with Bradleys and infantry to support G Troop. The wounded and dead were brought to our aid station, and though we reacted instantly, another of the wounded died. Three soldiers had now been slain in the initial ambush.

Captain Brad Boyd supported the cordon of several farms in the area with C Company until late afternoon the next day. It was exhausting and tedious work. Colonel Hickey used whatever assets he could muster to throw up a cordon around the area to net the attackers.

It was not in vain. Three of the six attackers were captured outright. A total of forty were eventually hauled in, and from these the other three attackers were brought to account. Even so, the outcome could scarcely remove the pain of such loss. All the dead and wounded belonged to the artillery battalion supporting our brigade and the troop. Our best comfort lay in taking it back to the enemy.

Very late that night I made my way to the aid station to get Doc Marzullo's report on the wounded. He believed the two critically wounded would survive. He tried everything within his power to revive the soldier who died enroute, but the blood loss was just too extensive. Two others had been killed before reaching our aid station.

The still air was cooler now as I stepped out of the aid station and made my way to the palace porch overlooking the Tigris River. There, encased in body bags on surgical stretchers with neatly dressed American flags draped over them, lay the broken bodies of Sergeant Anthony O. Thompson, Specialist James C. Wright, and Specialist Richard Arriaga. All three were artillerists from Lieutenant Colonel Dom Pompelia's 4-42 Field Artillery Battalion that occupied Ad Dawr. They were from his Headquarters Battery but were attached to Dez Bailey's Recon Troop. Command Sergeant Major Martinez posted a guard to stand vigil with our brothers that night until they could be brought gently home to the country they had died to protect.

The next evening I mounted my Bradley and led a fair portion of my battalion across the river. Mark Stouffer's A Company and Jon Cecalupo's tank company joined Bryan Luke and me to patrol the entire swath of land with Bradleys, M1 tanks, and infantry from our task force. Brad Boyd got a breather. He stayed behind because he had been on duty for 24 hours solid, and I needed some force in Tikrit should trouble brew up.

We continued to support Dez Bailey's G Troop with a section of Bradleys and some mortars for some time afterward. In the coming weeks, the locals begged us to stop operations in the area. Captain Bailey treated them as fairly as they deserved—and captured or killed those who were undeserving.

TAPS

As the units belonging to Lieutenant Colonel Pompelia and Captain Bailey recovered from their losses, we prepared to pay our respects to the fallen. We were able to strike back at the enemy for the ambush that robbed the lives of three more soldiers, but it did not diminish our grief for our fallen brothers. On the eve of the memorial service in their honor (the 20th of September and my mother's birthday), Colonel James Hickey called me. He had received a Red Cross message. I did not think this unusual as many of my soldiers had received these unfortunate messages. I, in fact, had received one when my grandfather, Ed Porter, died in July. I missed him sorely, but he went out in a style the rest of us could only wish for—active to the last in his late eighties, loading a new lawn mower in the trunk of his car.

I was not prepared for the news Colonel Hickey delivered. My stepfather had died only hours earlier, and my family had requested my presence. I was stunned. I was accustomed to death on the battlefront but not on the home front. I immediately missed him.

Just days before, I had received one of his letters. In it he wrote,

I know it seems as though the heat and the enemy will never cool down, but they will and the temperature will get to its winter mode soon. . . . I want you to be vigilant and tell all your men to do the same. Remember, he who shoots first shoots last! Remember what we studied in church today, 'if God is with us, who can be against us?' We pray you and your men will all be well.

Colonel Hickey would support whatever decision I needed to make. After calling home, I knew my place was with my family. My mother had found him in bed, dead from a coronary, on her birthday. They had just moved into a new house not a week or two before. It was all so very tragic. I needed to be certain that things were in hand and he would be buried with the military honors he deserved from his Korean War service with the 5th Cavalry of 1st Cavalry Division.

I called Colonel Hickey with my decision. I needed to go home for the funeral. He understood and supported me fully. The battalion would be in good hands with my executive officer, Major Mike Rauhut. I had an ample roster of talent ensuring the upcoming raids would be well executed. I left the next day.

The rotor blades began their wide inertial swings as the high-pitched whine of the engine announced their movement. I climbed aboard Brigadier General Mike Barbero's helicopter flight en route to Balad, Iraq, on September 21. Always mindful of danger, I scrutinized my surroundings vigilantly the whole way. My hands reflexively searched for my M4 carbine, even though I had reluctantly left my weapons behind in order to fly home.

Privately, I was happy to be flying. No roadside bombs to worry about. Plus it was faster. I traveled with Sergeant Jesse Sample of my Scout Platoon who had also been called home on emergency leave. We formed a buddy team for the trip. Once we landed in Balad, we walked straight to the ramp of a C-130 cargo plane revving up for takeoff to Kuwait. At that moment, I began to relax. Months of combat tension and weight of responsibility lifted from my shoulders as the plane lifted from the ground. Moments before, I had been in charge of a thousand men. Now I was in charge of one.

I was saddened by the circumstances taking me home but could not help feeling a measure of release to have escaped Iraq, if only for a moment. A wash of guilt immediately flooded over me. I should remain with my men as long as they were in harm's way. This was the defense I had used with my Command Sergeant Major and my executive officer before leaving. They had given me a sound scolding, insisting that I needed to go home. They would not hear my argument. Later, my wife told me that when she heard that I was coming home for the funeral, she felt that I still considered our family more important than my career. To stay would have been so easy and the reasons all too justifiable. But how could I do that to my family? My absence during this critical time would have merely added to the hurt.

After landing in Kuwait, we burned off about six hours waiting for tickets home. Sample and I washed away the dust of Iraq and changed into the rumpled, pathetic-looking civilian clothing each of us had deployed with for such emergencies as these. We looked as though we had slept in our duffle bags. Our hands and faces were gaunt, tan, and weathered; everything else blaze-white. What imposing figures we must have looked in our soft clothes! It felt bizarre to be wearing blue jeans, to have nothing strapped on my leg, nothing in my hands. Absent was the lung-pinching, collarbone-crushing body armor capped with a cumbersome helmet to oscillate on my head.

Stretched between two worlds and two lives, Sample and I sipped little drinks on the commercial airline. We perused civilian pursuits in the newspaper trying to comprehend a world that cared for such things. I mostly slept on the plane, waking to eat at every offering in a hazy dream where airline food tasted good. After each catnap, I woke up in Iraq, blinking slowly to gather my senses.

From Amsterdam to the States, I had a pleasant conversation with doctors from Kansas City, Missouri, who were returning from medical missionary work in Romania. How diametrically opposed our objectives had been. They had spent the summer repairing lives while we spent it destroying them. How completely converse our callings had been.

We landed in Dallas, eventually, and reentered civilization. It all seemed so very unfamiliar—civilian clothes, clean streets, serene activity, and nice people walking around making no demands. I had forgotten that this world existed. There my five children and my beautiful wife greeted me. Feelings I had not permitted for months suddenly washed over me. I was sad to be home for the interment of my stepfather but so very happy to see my wife and children. Mixed emotions would not escape me a single day of the trip.

On the drive from Dallas to Ft. Hood, I saw no white taxis with orange fenders. I saw no men sporting dresses. People had different colors of hair and eyes. Roofs were angled and had shingles. Curbs were not yellow and white candy-striped. The signs and billboards were penned with letters rather than incomprehensible squiggles. There were no palm trees. There was grass. And there was peace. Glorious peace.

About the time I made my trek from Dallas, Mike Rauhut led the battalion on a raid we had been working from a tip. It led to the capture of Saad Abdul al-Hasan, another of the "Five Family" targets who would prove invaluable on the twisted trail to Saddam.

At home, my body completely shut down. Months without rest coupled with the weight of responsibility for other lives gave way to sleep—deep sleep. We decided to go to Oklahoma the next day, or I should say my wife decided. I would not have known if I had been thrown in a bag and carted there. I slept for a very long time.

I woke up in Iraq. Where did it go? What is the current status of such and such? Where is the latest enemy activity? Why am I sleeping on sheets? Who painted the walls? Where am I?

We loaded up the kids and headed north on Interstate 35. For the first time in five months, I was driving a car. I drove the 300 miles to Oklahoma City looking for tires and trash on the road and successfully dodged them all, feeling foolish each time for thinking that they were bombs. Once we arrived at my mother's house, I quickly realized which world I was in and readjusted to different responsibilities. I was now truly home.

On Friday, September 26, we laid Garland Dean Skidgel to rest in Del City, Oklahoma. The day was pleasant as a somber crowd of relatives gathered around the cemetery plot marked with cheap green AstroTurf and folding chairs set on uneven ground near the freshly dug grave. Relatives and friends struggled through the mixed emotions of reuniting and grieving.

A funeral detail from Ft. Sill, Oklahoma, stood in attendance. They noticed my weathered look and dress uniform ribboned and badged and knew that I had seen battle. They stood a little taller with our family. Matt Nichols, a Coast Guardsman and my sister's middle son who also returned home for the funeral, joined their flag detail with me. Words were spoken in a feeble but sincere attempt by a church minister who did not know him as we did. It was hard to sum up all that the man was, but we were brightened by the hope of his faith in Christ. The detail stood as sentinels around the casket. They lifted the national colors, expertly stretching and folding it. Taps wailed in mournful tones from a bugler in the distance. A tear rolled down my face as my mother received the flag, feeling for it but not seeing it for her pain.

A world away, my men on night patrols clashed with insurgents in the industrial area of the city. The Iraqi Police were also attacked at their main police station. The enemy strikes were anemic, and the attackers seemed content to miss and run, as if making their presence known was enough. We suffered no casualties.

The next day, Major Mike Rauhut led the battalion on a magnificent raid into the farmlands south of Auja that once again received broad press coverage. Based on an informant's tip, the "Gators" of Mark Stouffer's A Company cordoned the lush, densely vegetated farm. A bountiful harvest of weapons awaited—23 shoulder-fired SA-7 anti-aircraft missiles, four RPG launchers with 115 rocket-propelled grenades, 400 hand grenades, one mortar with 39 rounds of ammunition, 51 smoke pots, and more than 1,000 pounds of C-4 explosives with 1,300 blasting caps. This deadly crop was carried away in our trucks for eventual destruction. While a great haul, it clearly indicated that the enemy continued to be well supplied and able to replenish his strength.

After the funeral, I enjoyed a few days in Oklahoma. I hurt for my mother and prayed her pain would ease soon. My sister and brother would be a big help to her. I was grateful for that because I had to return to the war. We enjoyed each other's company for the very short time we had. Cindy, the kids, Jack (our Jack Russell terrier), and I returned to Texas before the scheduled date of my return. These few days were wonderful for me, but they were deadly for my soldiers in Iraq.

The "Cobras" of C Company had their palace rattled by RPG fire on September 29. The next day, an informant led our operations officer, Major Bryan Luke, to a cache of 60 more rocket-propelled grenades. After weeks of successful raiding, the enemy was being severely disrupted. The fresh quantities of advanced and deadly weapons that our men were finding in the area still concerned me. The enemy was clearly stockpiling for more strikes. This, coupled with Jack's SOF intelligence about SA-7 missiles, caused us all great concern as these projectiles could quickly knock our helicopters out of the sky. We were thrilled to have found 23 of them, but we feared that there might be many more of them in our area. Even a single missile could spell disaster.

While we had successfully stopped a potential disaster with anti-aircraft missiles, the enemy continued to gather strength from the old Saddam networks and reorganize his efforts. Saddam's cousin and a member of the Hasan family, Jeliu Abdul Hasan, had been a general for Saddam. Mike Rauhut led the raid that had just captured his brother, Saad, and our troops were hunting his other brother, Raad.

Unknown to us then, Jeliu's son, Mohammed Jeliu Abdul Hasan, was set on vengeance for when we captured his uncle Saad a few days before. He was teamed up with the Khatab family—the same family that produced Abid Hamid Mahmood al-Khatab, aka the Ace of Diamonds, whom we captured in June. Amer Kalid Abdullah al-Khatab's family had successfully smuggled in some powerful explosives, and he and fellow insurgents had been busy building explosive devices in Cadaseeyah. Now, he and Moham-med Hasan decided it was time to test them, but not in the Ca-daseeyah area. They would employ one of the new devices farther south in the city of Tikrit.

Amer al-Khatab and Mohammed Hasan selected a spot along Highway 1 near the soccer stadium, using the cover of a cement factory owned by a man named Thamir al-Asi, an insurgent leader connected to Mohammed al-Musslit. Once the device was deto-nated, they could make their escape west and slip unnoticed into the city.

On October 1, as I awakened to a new morning in Killeen, Texas, with early preparations to return to Iraq, my support com-pany commander, Captain Curt Kuetemeyer, was conducting a mission supporting our battalion half a world away where the afternoon steadily approached dusk. The "Aggressors" of A Com-pany, 4th Forward Support Battalion were a permanent part of our task force since the invasion began. Curt and his command element were returning from the parent forward support battalion near Auja to head back to his company, which was collocated with Brad Boyd's C Company. Traveling north in downtown Tikrit where Highway 1 morphs into the main city street, they passed the soccer stadium, a few hundred meters shy of the Tuz-Tikrit highway turnoff.

Curt suddenly went completely deaf amidst a bright flash as the Hummer rose sharply. The air immediately turned a thick dusty brown with a sickening sulfur smell. Something was terribly wrong. The Hummer seemed to be drifting, as though pilotless, at about 40 miles per hour.

HIT THE BRAKES, he thought. *Maybe they're damaged.* His mind raced as he braced for impact.

The unguided vehicle continued to travel several hundred me-ters more, smashed into and bounced over the curb, flattened a road sign, and scraped to a halt. Everything seemed to be on fire, and Curt felt an intense heat at his lap and to his left. Though not hearing much at all, he could make out a scream and immediately took stock of his soldiers. They were in bad shape. His driver, Private First Class Analaura Esparza, was still behind the wheel and in terrible pain. Specialist Aldolfo Lopez, also visibly and audibly in pain behind her, seemed to be pinned among the flames.

Flash-burned, pelted, and stunned, Curt stumbled from what was left of his stripped, open-top Hummer and grabbed Private Edward Stephenson sitting behind him, who seemed to be faring somewhat better. Despite the shock of the concussion, Curt seemed intact and able to move.

First Sergeant Ronald Davis and Specialist Karen Guckert, following close behind, watched their company commander's vehicle disappear in the blast with stunned disbelief. They braced themselves as they entered the brown flaming fog and pulled up to the blazing vehicle.

"Pull security!" yelled First Sergeant Davis to the other soldiers as he ran toward the flaming Hummer.

Davis, seeing Kuetemeyer was on his feet and assisting Stephenson, went to help Esparza. She was not responding much at all. He couldn't seem to get her out. The vehicle was burning intensely, and she was stuck. Seconds mattered. Kuetemeyer, seeing Davis, joined him to help extract her. They managed to free her broken body and carried her to the median.

"Talk to me!" demanded Davis as he kneeled over Esparza. "Talk to me, Esparza! Breathe!"

Esparza had been hit from head to toe on her left side. Her uniform was tattered and scorched, her left leg at an impossible angle.

"Talk to me, Esparza!" insisted Davis.

"Bemak, pull security!" ordered Specialist Guckert to Specialist Jason Bemak, a gunner on the convoy. "Regular Mike, this is

Aggressor Seven Delta, over," she voiced as she placed a call to our battalion headquarters.

"Regular Mike, over," the calm voice on the radio answered.

"An IED hit our convoy. Three casualties, request Medivac ASAP, over," Guckert matter-of-factly intoned.

The battalion responded immediately after Guckert, calm and in charge, made this radio transmission for help. In the midst of this pandemonium, gunfire began to pop. The soldiers looked around for the source but, dazed as they were, could not recognize that ammunition from the burning Hummer had begun to "cook off." During this bedlam, an unruffled Guckert described the incident and guided lifesaving assistance to the scene, fully aware of her dangerous surroundings.

Lopez was in agony, semi-conscious, and on fire. Davis, hearing his cries of agony, ran to free him. Captain Kuetemeyer saw Stephenson slapping his own legs, attempting to extinguish his burning shins. While Davis worked Lopez free, Curt grabbed a bottle of water from the floor of the burning Hummer and emptied the contents on Stephenson's legs. Working in concert, they managed to free all three wounded soldiers from the blazing hulk.

As Davis and Kuetemeyer busied themselves with the wounded, Guckert spotted a convoy from 3-66 Armor nearing the scene from the south. She informed a captain of the situation. The convoy immediately pulled security around the vehicles. Guckert then joined Kuetemeyer and Davis, who encouraged the wounded to hang on as they rendered aid. Guckert grabbed her aid bag and attempted to help Esparza. Karen tried to comfort her good friend, Analaura, but she was not responding. Esparza's entire left side was bloodied, tattered, and burned.

Captain Brad Boyd from C Company raced up and provided immediate help with his men. The wounded soldiers were loaded onto First Sergeant Davis's Hummer and taken to our battalion aid station. There, Major Bill Marzullo, our surgeon, along with physician's assistants Captain Alex Morales and Second Lieutenant Armando Buergette, struggled to save Esparza. She died of multiple puncture wounds, trauma, and extreme blood loss. The other soldiers were treated for serious burns, concussions, lacerations, and broken bones.

Brad Boyd assumed command of the situation on the ground and doused the partially charred Hummer that was listing to starboard, sagging, and fusing to the ground from the intense heat. Highway 1 returned to normal after C Company recovered the vehicle. The men were accustomed to the drill. They knew well my standing orders to recover all evidence of battle: No opportunities for Iraqis to dance on our equipment or gloat in some Internet propaganda video. Not in this town. Not in any town we owned. We would kill anyone on sight if they attempted to touch our damaged equipment.

As word and details became available to Major Mike Rauhut, who was in temporary command of my battalion, he relayed them to Captain Matt Weber, our rear detachment commander. Weber had been sent back from Iraq for just such contingencies. I was leaving a store with my kids in Killeen, Texas, when I received a cell phone call from Matt.

"Sir, there's been an attack, and we have some casualties. Major Rauhut is trying to contact you," informed Captain Weber.

"Understood, Matt. I'll stand by for his call," I said with a sinking feeling washing over me as I stood in the peace and safety of a Killeen parking lot. The phone rang a short time later.

"Sir, I have some terrible news," uttered Mike Rauhut, my exec. I listened intently as Mike described what he knew of the event at the moment. The full details described above were as yet unknown. I only knew that I had lost a soldier and that more were wounded. It pained me deeply. At the heart of the situation and in need of encouragement was Major Rauhut, feeling he had some-how failed me.

"Mike, nothing could have been done any differently had I been there. There is no need to blame yourself," I encouraged, knowing all too well the guilt a commander feels with every loss suffered in command. Still, I needed to talk him through it.

The battalion continued to work the area. The street fight waned somewhat, but the locals became emboldened by our recent casualties. The Iraqi police showed genuine resolution as General Mezher aligned with our forces to put down some demonstrations near the ambush site a couple of days later.

I spent the next two days mentally preparing for the transition to Iraq, trying to keep as current as possible on all issues. My mind had never really left there. It was wonderful seeing my family even under these circumstances. Yet I would have traded every precious moment to have my stepdad back.

On October 3, I boarded a plane in Dallas. Cindy and I had been through the goodbyes before: Kosovo, Kuwait, Afghanistan, and Iraq. Now we parted once again. I watched with a lump in my throat as our van full of kids eased through the airport departure lane and faded from view.

Half a world away in Tikrit, the soldiers of the 1st Battalion, 22nd Infantry and the 4th Forward Support Battalion gathered at Saddam's Birthday Palace. The Aggressors of A Company, 4th FSB stood on the asphalt still marked with lines for Saddam's military parades. A chaplain stepped forward and prayed. A Purple Heart and Bronze Star medal for making the ultimate sacrifice were laid on a pair of boots overshadowed by a lone rifle with a Kevlar helmet planted on top. At a podium, commanders and friends struggled to find words that the English language failed to provide. Soldiers stood at attention. Private First Class Analaura Esparza-Gutierrez's name rang out for roll call. She did not answer. Taps resonated mournfully from a bugler nearby. Tears rolled down soldiers' faces as they remembered her life.

AS LONG AS WE HAVE BREATH

Forty-eight hours later, I was back in Tikrit. The situation had become much more intense. Our successful raiding on members of Saddam's supporting cast would have to be secondary until we could gain control of the trigger pullers, even though I felt that many of these bodyguards were behind the attacks. The media pressed us for the status of the Saddam hunt. We replied that, while Saddam continued to be a focus, we could not ignore the boiling security situation we faced. The enemy seemed a bit more organized now and was attempting to regain the initiative. We could have none of that.

Mike Rauhut and Bryan Luke updated me on our operations and gave me their own assessments. The roadside bombs were taking their toll. We were finding a great many of them, but the sheer volume of ordnance was a challenge. To counter the dangers, our rifle companies were patrolling in Bradleys and conducting bomb sweeps along the main routes. Foot patrols had been almost entirely eliminated. Their update continued, and I didn't like what I was hearing. Not wanting to be insensitive, I expressed the need to put our infantry back out on the ground.

"Sir, these mounted Bradley patrols were directed by Colonel Hickey," Mike explained in an effort to clarify that neither he nor Bryan had invented or endorsed the shift in tactics.

"Well, I'll have a talk with him," I said, still angry at the turn of events. "While a certain number of patrols and changes are good, I think it is insane not having our infantry out on the ground. Patrolling in Bradleys is an ambush waiting to happen without our troops on the streets."

Colonel Hickey's reasoning was sound enough. He believed that armored patrols would lessen the effects of the bombs. While it seemed to make sense on the surface, I did not agree. I felt it could create new problems we didn't want. Certainly, the effects of the bombs would be lessened, but our chances of being ambushed and bombed would be magnified. Armored patrols, noisier and far more visible, would announce our arrival at every turn.

It was my firm belief, based on years of infantry experience, that soldiers walking on the ground and patrolling in open vehicles afforded the greatest opportunity of surprising the enemy. They were better able to spot bombs with a 360-degree field of view. Hearing was not impeded by enclosed crew helmets, internal radios, and the steady drone and vibration of a Bradley. Walking was personal and kept the senses alive and attuned to movement on the city streets at a pace permitting full assessment of the surroundings. Bradleys are tremendous infantry support vehicles mounted with powerful weapons, but they were not designed to withstand anti-tank rockets, and they are vulnerable to mines, which they were likely to encounter. We had already suffered these types of casualties to Bradleys earlier in the mission.

I was always respectful to Colonel Hickey, a stern disciplinarian, when challenging his decisions, but I felt strongly about this issue. It was my duty as his only infantry battalion commander to make such recommendations; it was an even greater duty to my men. The risk of confronting him was great. As an old cavalryman, he knew as much about Bradleys as any master gunner or tactician. But scouts were different from infantry, and infantry fighting was my training and expertise. I knew it well. I felt compelled to make a case against a modification of tactics that could jeopardize our momentum and the safety of our soldiers.

Colonel Hickey graciously allowed a hearing of my dissension. He recognized that changes were made in my absence but made it quite clear that his decision would stand. To be fair, Colonel Hickey was as brave a senior commander as I had ever served with, constantly on patrol with a rifle in his Hummer and himself a survivor of enemy ambush. He knew the environment beyond the headquarters and the map because he was constantly out with us.

When I protested that a lack of infantry patrols would create manifest problems and would essentially end our successful "Salt Lick" operations, he did allow for a compromise. Rather than riding in the Bradleys, the rifle squads on the ground could be loosely coordinated with the mounted patrols. This helped tremendously but would decrease the number of our outposts and ambushes because the only mounted Bradleys at our disposal were for the ready reserves and quick reaction forces in the companies and battalions. They had served well in that role but now would be constantly on the move, and the crews, once able to take on other infantry tasks when not in action, would no longer be available. We would just have to make the best of it.

In addition to roadside bombs, a different kind of threat was generating. Demonstrations were breaking out in several Iraqi cities. Quick responses by our men had prevented the October 3rd demonstration from taking hold, and the protest was rapidly diffused. I believed that demonstrations should be quashed before being given the opportunity to develop. They might be tolerable in a country with a stable government where people generally respected the law, but such was not the case in Iraq. Seared in my memory was the summer of 1999 in Kosovo when an angry crowd of 5,000 surrounded a dozen and a half of us following a raid. I never wanted to experience that again.

On October 9 and 10, we received intelligence about some prospective demonstrations. I ordered our forces to flood the suspected area of the city with soldiers, tanks, and Bradleys to discourage the activists with a demonstration of our own. It was successful. The protestors never materialized.

Meanwhile, our scouts continued the surreptitious observation of Thamer the Bomber's house from an outpost in Cadaseeyah. In the evening, Staff Sergeant Sean Shoffner repositioned this outpost and received fire from a distance while doing so. Shoffner's group was not hit but returned fire and continued its mission. We then raided several houses in downtown Tikrit tied to bomb makers and bomb layers. Four insurgents were captured, but no Thamer. Clearly, his influence and the network of insurgents were growing.

The next night, several mortar rounds slammed into our training compound for the Iraqi Civil Defense forces on our little resort island in the Tigris River. A few rounds crashed into the main building but caused no appreciable damage. Perhaps the casualty most grieved was the hot water tank that fed the trainers' building. The soldiers were incensed. C Company, along with our scouts and the Iraqi soldiers under our command, immediately set out in pursuit, heading toward muzzle flashes reported in the area of likely attack. They found and captured three more insurgents in the distant fields.

October 12 dawned with the threat of sweltering heat. The weather had eased slightly in the previous week but not on this day. We were more than ready for the transition to cooler weather. Other transitions were already under way. Jack's SOF team was rotating out of Iraq. I was sorely disappointed to see them go. I did not know if the new team would continue the close cooperation we enjoyed with Jack's team. Our joint efforts had netted so much along the trail to Saddam.

By this stage, we had a clear enough picture of Saddam's network to sustain pressure on the families within it, but we did not have the same access or direct intelligence priority outside of our area as the SOF guys. While my own network of Iraqis had relinquished crucial leads and netted some very key players, we had little influence outside Tikrit. Maintaining the same caliber of cooperation with the new special operations task force would be vital to the hunt, considering that the principle players were still likely to be within my area.

To this juncture, we had worked in concert to thin out substantial numbers of Saddam's closest supporters, with a focus on the Ibrihim Omar al-Musslit family line. Two of the ten Musslit brothers had already been netted, but the one we wanted most desperately was Rudman Ibrihim Omar al-Musslit. Since our first raid on May 27, he had successfully eluded us no fewer than three times, often escaping with just moments to spare. We had captured quality photographs of him and several of his brothers during the July 7 farm raid of Omar al-Musslit, the granddaddy of all Musslits. An additional picture captured on September 25 even revealed specific tattoos that would aid in identification. With an excellent idea of his appearance and tips about his family being fed to us steadily, I believed that it was simply a matter of time until he was found.

We also believed that Rudman was the key to finding Saddam Hussein. Whatever power his former Presidential Secretary and the Ace of Diamonds, Abid Mahmood al-Khatab, once held, it seemed to be dispersed within the Musslit family after we captured Mahmood in June. The Musslit family also had strong connections to the other families of the network, many of whom were a part of "The Forty" and "The Twenty-Five" groups of bodyguards known as the "Himaya." We had thinned out a great many of those as well, from the Hasans to the Hadooshis to the Heremoses and the Majids. Supporting families like the Rashids, the Khatabs, and the Ghanis were also in our sights. We wanted to keep them there.

By early October, I felt that we had successfully raised the edge of the carpet on Saddam's inner network and were slowly rolling it back. There was no way of knowing the full measure of it or how long it would take to expose all concealed beneath it. The inner circle of bodyguards continued to coordinate resistance with Saddam's inspiration and funding. Their recruitment activity had greatly increased the number of street fighters. They easily acquired and delivered large quantities of dangerous weapons. The inner network continued to effectively protect Saddam. While the hunt was a high priority, we could not neglect the street fight for even a moment. We could lose the upper hand in the blink of an eye if we blinked an eye. It was not only possible for the initiative to pass to our enemies; it could even spread beyond to Sunni Baathist holdouts throughout Iraq.

So as Jack's SOF team prepared for departure, I was concerned that any shift in attitude toward our joint operations between the unconventional black ops teams like his and conventional forces like mine would be a major blow to us and perhaps the whole manhunt. My fears were completely unfounded. When Jack brought the new team to Tikrit for introductions, we had a long and encouraging first meeting. It was a beneficial exchange of information, ideas, and possibilities from both viewpoints. We clearly needed each other and had the same goal of following the trail until it led us to Saddam.

John was the new SOF team's leader. He was shorter than Jack and not quite the cut physical specimen. He was equally broad-shouldered, slightly more compact and, no doubt, as powerful. If it were possible, he seemed even more laid-back than Jack. Back home he might be mistaken for a hunting buddy or any good ole boy you'd want to have around in a scrap. His sidekick sergeant major and ops man, Kelly, appeared to be as extraordinary as Matt had been. I clearly liked this team and its leader. While I would get to know the entire team, it was John and Kelly (like Jack and Matt) with whom I would become best acquainted.

Relieved and optimistic that we might not skip a beat in our mutual cooperation, I focused the battalion on the rising insurgent activity among street fighters for the next few days. I told my staff to use every tool available, including propaganda, recordings, radio, bulletin boards, and the like to separate the common Iraqi trying to survive tough times from the insurgent hiding among them. We used every means to prevent the insurgents from convincing the people that we would not prevail if only they resisted.

We even began a counter "red ops" program built around a fictitious resistance group. We had already encountered leaflet drops in Arabic from the "Army of Mohammed" inciting locals to rise up against the infidel and the new government. Perpetuating the theme, we named our faux group "Mohammed's Faithful." The brainchild of my intelligence officer, Captain Tim Morrow, this insurgent "group" advocated resistance only toward the occupation and not toward brother Iraqis and the new leaders of government who were working under the most stressful of circumstances. In this way, we hoped to divide resisting sentiments.

We countered the genuine "Army of Mohammed" leaflets with a message tempering the hatred while being cautious not to advocate any type of surrender. The message was cleverly crafted to appeal to their sense of order and desire for peace. It also discouraged retribution among the local population. If successful, we could keep the neutrals off the field and locate the bad guys more quickly.

To accomplish this, we produced leaflets handwritten in Arabic and photocopied to emulate the locally produced propaganda already seen in circulation. Joe Filmore, with his inimitable background and understanding of the Iraqi mind, wrote the messages periodically to counter the real threats we faced. Joe made a strong, poetic, and convincing message for non-violence against local civilians, citing Koranic verses for added emphasis. We knew that we had scored when we began intercepting insurgent messages that called "Mohammed's Faithful" a bunch of traitors who did not believe the true message of jihad and offered reward for their identification. We were already beginning to segregate the insurrectionists from the people while causing division of the enemy within their own minds.

To strengthen and assist the fledgling government in our area, we used recordings of Iraqi officials as a means to broadcast to the "Arab Street." I told my staff that the number one cause of stress was lack of information. We could reduce the anxiety of the people by communicating with them using their own traditions and their own people. The key was to transmit the message by bulletin, leaflet, and loudspeaker from their countrymen. The result, I predicted, would translate into morning tea shop talk. That is where the real communication needed to occur.

Staff Sergeant Charles Darrah of our attached 362nd Psyops Detachment did a tremendous job aiding these efforts. His Hummers were equipped with loudspeakers and a recording machine. Prerecorded messages by the governor or chief of police could be broadcast to the city while driving through town.

On the morning of October 12, Darrah and his team left to coordinate the recording of messages. They had traveled no more than 500 meters beyond our compound when a tree exploded on the right side of the road. They were enveloped in a downpour of splinters, leaves, twigs, concrete, brown dust, and debris. Darrah was out cold momentarily, suffering a concussion. Sergeant Antonio Carrizales sustained a concussion and lacerations. Specialist Malcolm Mosley was not as fortunate. He received some nasty leg and arm wounds on one side. Doc Marzullo, Alex Morales, and our medical crew were able to treat them all swiftly as the aid station was in close proximity to the scene of the impact. Marzullo coordinated Mosley's evacuation for more intensive medical care whereupon he was ultimately transported to Germany.

As Darrah's men were being evacuated to our aid station, I examined the blast effects of the contact site. The tree that so cunningly concealed the bomb also shielded the soldiers to some degree. The insurgents had positioned the bomb between the tree and a wall to obscure it. Consequently, the blast ricocheted between the tree and the wall before lashing back into the direction of the street. We were fortunate that morning.

On the heels of this attack, we detected another bomb at a gas station in Cadaseeyah. An Iraqi local fingered two men plotting their evil deeds and alerted the police and our soldiers. We were able to locate and capture one of the bomb layers. The attack was averted solely as a result of the goodwill of a local Iraqi citizen. Perhaps we were beginning to win the battle for trust in the city.

Such was not the case in the city north of Tikrit where my B Company conducted combat operations. Captain Scott Thomas and his "Bears" patrolled an area on the outskirts of Bayjii known by our soldiers as "The Projects." Only the day before, they had received a cool reception that turned colder still when locals began to hurl rocks and shake their fists.

Captain Thomas, never one to concede ground to the enemy, decided to revisit this troubled spot that evening. Scott typically organized patrols with two Bradleys carrying a rifle squad and one M1 Abrams tank. It was a patrol of this configuration led by Second Lieutenant Erik Aadland from B Company, 3-66 Armor with a squad of "Bears" and their two Bradleys that approached "The Projects" in the early evening hours. Thomas informed Aadland that the neighborhood had been relatively quiet all day.

As Aadland's patrol rumbled up a trail intersecting a "hardball" road, the soldiers noticed an absence of people. Specialist James Powell pulled the lead Brad up tight with the tank, but it was necessary to keep some security as well. Powell was piloting yet another B14, a replacement Bradley of the same name lost in July.

Staff Sergeant Donald Smith ordered Powell to follow the tank closely in echelon to the right. Smith was in charge of the platoon in the absence of Sergeant First Class Joseph Walden, on medical leave from wounds sustained in the July attack that destroyed the original B14. The trail Bradley, B13, led by Specialist Jason Duncan, also followed in echelon manner to the left of B14.

The security was good, the patrol confident. As they moved toward the dense residential area in town, they readied themselves for confrontation with locals and possible demonstrations. What they encountered was far more vicious. The ground unexpectedly erupted into a violent explosion. Smoke and flame shot through the driver and engine compartment of B14 as a concussion of dust encompassed the three vehicles. Staff Sergeant Donald Smith's night vision goggles, once tethered around his neck, vanished in the blast, lost in a fog of acrid smoke and dust. Specialist Leonard Johnson, the gunner, was wounded above his right eye but was otherwise intact as he and Staff Sergeant Smith began to grope around the turret.

The vehicle stopped abruptly as a result of a shattered engine and final drive, a missing sprocket, and several missing road wheels. The track sections lay like a broken snake behind them. Specialist Powell had not yet dropped the ramp, so the soldiers scrambled to escape from the crew compartment hatch on top of the vehicle.

"Red 1, this is Gold 3. Gold 4 just struck a mine, over!" radioed Specialist Jason Duncan from his trail Bradley to Aadland's tank, using the call signs of B Company 3-66 Armor.

"Roger, break," replied Lieutenant Aadland. "Blacknight 5, this is Red 1, contact over."

"Drop the ramp!" shouted Specialist Duncan in the trail Bradley, as Aadland radioed requests for assistance from nearby units.

Staff Sergeant Paul Marler, the squad leader, and his team raced from the back of B13. Still struggling to breathe inside B14, Staff Sergeant Smith began to take account of his men. He observed his guys bailing out the top hatch in the back. Glancing down to his gunner, he identified a cut on Johnson's head, though he appeared to be moving without difficulty. The vehicle was smoldering from the instant blast of the halon fire extinguishers, but did not seem to be on fire.

Assessing his surroundings immediately, Staff Sergeant Marler ordered his squad to pull security before dashing from B13 to the incapacitated Bradley. It was a ghastly sight. The track on the left side was blown off. Three of the six road wheels and the entire sprocket were missing. Consequently, the Brad was listing heavily to port, as though kneeling on its left knee and crouching forward. The turret and gun were permanently immobilized in a left-facing position.

Jason Duncan also dismounted B13 and ran to his stricken wingman. The M1 tank could take care of anything that might threaten the infantry vehicles. He climbed atop the driver's hatch and shouted, "Powell! Powell! Are you all right?"

"You guys all right?" called a concerned Staff Sergeant Marler to his men who had escaped through the top hatch of the troop compartment.

"Yeah, we're okay, but not sure about the others," his soldiers responded.

"Powell! Can you hear me?" asked Duncan, still on the top of the stricken Brad. There was no response. Lifting up the hatch, he continued to shout to Powell. Inside, Powell appeared to be unconscious or worse. He was in dreadful shape.

"Sergeant, we gotta get him out of there to help him!" suggested Specialist William Evans, the medic.

"Roger, okay, I'll go down inside," answered Duncan.

As Duncan entered the Bradley through the hatch, he wiggled

his way around the turret mount space that connects the troop compartment with the driver, affectionately known as the "Hell Hole." Evans and another soldier reached down into the driver's hatch from above. As the men struggled to get him out, they noticed a four-foot gaping hole in the bottom of the Brad. Blood, fuel, and hydraulic fluid soaked the cratered ground below. The men tried to ease Powell from his cramped station, but his broken and shattered limbs precluded an easy extraction. There was still no response from him.

Those not directly involved with extracting Powell pulled security as Lieutenant Aadland called for a medevac helicopter. Once the men eased Powell to the ground, Staff Sergeant Marler applied tourniquets to his limbs, and Evans administered CPR procedures.

The troops, though stunned by it all, reacted quickly and bravely. First Lieutenant Matt Fahey, the Executive Officer of B Company, 3-66 Armor, who was leading the evening's patrol, quickly called for medevac support and recovery assets. Sergeant First Class Christopher Koski, already skilled in recovering decimated B Company Bradleys, loaded up his noisy M88 recovery vehicle and thundered out of the B Company compound. Fahey's men, as well as others who heard the blast, began moving toward the scene.

Captain Thomas knew the situation would be dismal when he arrived. As men began clearing the area, the Blackhawk medical chopper fluttered into view. It landed near the devastated Bradley just twenty minutes after receiving the emergency call. The men bore Powell's bloodied and broken body to the bird that would initiate his long journey home. Powell was transported to the field hospital for immediate care, but it was likely that he had died instantly in the explosion.

Sergeant First Class Koski's recovery assets continued to inch forward. Upon arrival, his men began recovery of debris from the vehicle and surrounding area. The mechanics lashed the inoperative vehicle with cables in an effort to tow it back to the compound. As always, nothing would be left behind for enemy souvenirs.

The deafening M88 lurched ahead, dragging its crippled cousin awkwardly along the asphalt. Sparks from the grinding metal of exposed road wheel arms appeared to ignite pools of fuel inside the vehicle. The Bradley caught fire. Its halon fire extinguishers already blown, the Bradley erupted into flames.

As the vehicle was being towed at a safe distance from the M88, Captain Thomas decided to proceed. The Bradley was obviously a total loss anyway. If left to the enemy, it would be worse still. Koski ordered his mechanics to continue marching with the flaming wreck in tandem. Once on the compound, it would be extinguished. As the peculiar procession pressed on, the ammunition inside the blazing Bradley began to cook off. Because it was armored, no harm came to those outside it, but if the vehicle was not already a total loss, it was now.

I received the report of this action as I always received such news—like a knife in my chest. Another Regular was dead, and more were wounded. I was at once angry and sad. October was exacting a high price. The enemy was becoming more lethal. Our successes were diffusing in the shadow of mounting defeats. I wanted to lash out at someone or something, but I had to keep my composure. I had to be patient and resolute because my men would mirror my response. I had to remain confident and assure them that we were on the path to success, that good would prevail over evil. As another painful day ended, I had to remind myself that a new day would dawn. But new days are not always better days.

Operations continued in Tikrit the next day. We conducted bomb patrols along main thoroughfares and secondary crossroads.

Brad's troops were primarily responsible for the urbanized area of the city while Mark and Jon's companies covered south and north of the city.

The early morning had already yielded high adventure. One of C Company's Bradleys had been ambushed by a roadside bomb. Fortunately, the timing had been miscalculated, and the Bradley escaped injury. Jon's tank company had been attacked in a drive-by with insurgents firing from two gray vans. They sped away and disappeared into alleyways before our troops could follow in pursuit. The assailants were never found, but they also inflicted no damage.

The enemy was up for the game that day. That had already been proven. It was speculated that Thamer Mahdi Salah Hamoudi, aka "Thamer the Bomber," was likely behind some of the morning's activities. He continued to be an elusive thorn in the side. Unknown to us, he had recently acquired assistance in the form of an associate, possibly even a relative, named Abbas Mahdi. Much of our recent contact had been related to Thamer, but Abbas was new. He was a member of the expanding and emerging "Third Tier" guys, the "Trigger Pullers" hired by Saddam's mid-level organizers. They were financed and motivated by the upper tier we so desperately wanted to resume hunting.

With our guard already up that afternoon, Brad Boyd's 1st Platoon from C Company patrolled with Bradleys and infantry in the part of the city we called the "Chevron." On the map, the area forms a giant inverted V-shaped symbol capping the northern third of the city. First Lieutenant Jason Price was leading the two-vehicle section along the street parallel to the mosque near the soccer field. He was to deliver his squad to the market area and pick them up after the tracks made a loop around the surrounding area. The tactics were sound, and the Bradley would never be very far from the infantry squad should they meet trouble.

We did not know then that Abbas Mahdi had begun to organize a small cell that had worked closely with Thamer around the
"Chevron." Mahdi, at a friend's house discussing the situation,
heard the high-pitched whine and rumble of American tracked
vehicles. Peering outside, he spotted a pair of them approaching from the Tikrit market area. He rushed back inside to grab a
weapon.

Like most patrols, our soldiers scanned every window, every
corner, and every alley. A calm moment could change in the blink
of an eye. Lieutenant Price's Bradleys turned right, heading east
toward Highway 1 near the "Lucky Panda" ice cream shop. They
were looking for curbside bombs or the formation of demonstrations that were reportedly possible that day.

Abbas and his friend were prepared to fight should the Americans be coming for them. He grabbed the RPG. The troops might
simply be on patrol or they might be specifically stalking them.
Either way, he was prepared.

Staff Sergeant Michael Bordes, in the trail Bradley, had his
turret positioned to the rear to provide 360-degree security while
Price's Bradley covered the front. He looked forward to guide his
driver, Specialist Nathan Hebert. Covering the rear was the turret's
gunner, Specialist Donald "DJ" Wheeler. Their view was obscured
by residential walls as they rounded the corner toward Highway 1.
Wheeler stood up for a better view and leaned on the Integrated
Sight Unit (ISU) as he scanned behind them with the turret.

RPG in hand, Abbas left the house and narrowly peered
through the gate that hid him from view. The Americans were
indeed coming but appeared to be on patrol as they didn't seem
to be focused on his friend's house. The first vehicle turned to his
left, heading toward the Bayjii-Tikrit Highway. The trail vehicle
was making the turn; the front vehicle had just passed. Sensing
an opportunity to attack in the blind spot, Abbas and his friend

opened the gate and kneeled up to the corner with a shouldered and loaded RPG launcher. Abbas aimed at the turret and pulled the trigger. Then they ran as fast as they could to disappear into the residential neighborhood of the "Chevron."

A short distance after the Bradleys made the turn, Staff Sergeant Bordes blacked out. He came to in a daze, realizing something was horribly wrong. He determined that Hebert was okay after talking to him, and Wheeler was standing next to him. Rising to his feet to make certain he, too, was okay, he noticed that Wheeler was not actually standing. He was lying back against the hatch, his helmet blown off his head. The shoebox-sized ISU in front of him was blown apart and impressed against his chest.

"Are you guys all right?" Lieutenant Price asked his crew through the vehicle intercom after hearing and feeling the explosion. Both gunner and driver responded, "Roger."

"Cobra 6, Red 1, over," Price radioed.

"Cobra 6, over," Boyd responded.

"Roger, we have an IED contact, over," informed Price, not yet fully aware of what happened.

As Price looked behind, he could see Staff Sergeant Bordes motioning and pointing to Wheeler. Jason could tell something was wrong. Wheeler was lying on his back. His helmet was gone, his face disfigured. He informed Captain Boyd of a possible casualty and called for a medevac. His men did what they could for Wheeler while simultaneously pulling security.

There wasn't much to be done for the unresponsive Wheeler. Bordes moved the shattered ISU away from his chest as Specialist Willie Ewing, the medic, and Corporal William Velez from Price's Bradley made their way to the scene. Price called on the platoon internal radio for the squad to assist.

As Bordes lifted the ISU from Wheeler's chest, he saw a gaping hole just below his sternum where the RPG blast passed completely through him. Bordes and Ewing tried to bandage Wheeler. As they did, he fell to the floor of the turret. Velez, Ewing, and Bordes gently carried him out the back of the Bradley.

Captain Boyd rushed to the scene and began to clear the area, searching for the attackers. Captain Jason Deel, now leading the American-trained Iraqi troops, also arrived with an Iraqi pickup and several ICDC soldiers. First Sergeant Mike Evans, Staff Sergeant Felipe Madrid, and Staff Sergeant Bordes eased the lifeless gunner onto a stretcher. Captain Deel and the civil defense troops transported Wheeler to our battalion aid station.

I had just concluded a meeting with tribal sheiks and local officials when Brad radioed the news. I raced to the area, but there was nothing I could do to change what had happened. Brad brought in another platoon to thoroughly search the neighborhood, and I ordered all my elements to be on the lookout for anyone or anything that might be related.

Apart from its gun sight, the Bradley was not damaged. Brad's men drove it to the Birthday Palace. I called for a city fire truck to wash the blood from the streets. I wanted no visible evidence over which the enemy could gloat. We took our losses then cracked down on the city in search of the perpetrators. Iraqi police assisted us with the help of General Mezher. Locals provided some useful information, and a manhunt netted partial results over the next few days. The most important revelation was the name and information of Abbas Mahdi. It would not be the last time we encountered him.

On October 15, the soldiers of the 1st Battalion, 22nd Infantry and some from 3rd Battalion, 66th Armor gathered at Saddam's Birthday Palace. The "Bears" of B Company and the "Cobras" of C Company stood on that same asphalt used for Saddam's military parades. A chaplain stepped forward and prayed. Purple Hearts and Bronze Star medals for making the ultimate sacrifice were laid on pairs of boots overshadowed by bayoneted rifles stuck in the ground with Kevlar helmets planted on top. At a podium, commanders and friends struggled to find words.

I, too, stepped to the podium, but to make a pledge. "We mourn their loss; we honor their sacrifice," I said. "We will finish their mission. As long as Regulars draw breath, we shall not forget them."

Soldiers stood at attention. First Sergeant Louis Holzworth began the roll call of B Company soldiers. Specialist James Edward Powell's name rang out. He did not answer. Neither did Specialist Donald Laverne Wheeler, Jr., of C Company when called by First Sergeant Mike Evans. Silence filled the parade ground until rifle shots cracked in three sharp volleys from a line of soldiers on the balcony once used by Saddam to shoot his rifle in arrogant displays of defiance to the world. The live rounds from the volley interrupted soldier reflections, a startling reminder of the price of freedom. Taps resonated in mournful tones. Tears rolled down faces as we remembered the lives of our brothers. As long as we have breath . . .

DJ Wheeler, twenty-three, of Concord, Michigan, left behind his parents and 11 siblings, never knowing the joys of marriage or children. James Powell, twenty-six, of Mark Center, Ohio, would leave behind his wife, Ruby, and his two-year-old daughter, Lauren. He was scheduled to leave the next day to rotate back to the States, his term of enlistment being complete. He couldn't wait to see his family and begin his new after-Army life.

RAIDS AND ROTOR BLADES

Twelve-year-old Zenab and her seven-year-old sister, Chenar, played in front of their house located near one of the city laundry shops in Tikrit. An Egyptian named Adel, a Coptic Christian who felt his fortune would be better working in Iraq, had established the shop years before. The locals admired his hard work and honesty. Abas Omran Ali, the girls' father, had become friends with Adel and they often had tea while the girls played.

Two women and a man walked along the street in front of the laundry about mid-morning on the 16th of October. One of the ladies carried a flimsy, black plastic sack, the kind commonly furnished by local shops and food stands. She paused, conversed casually with her companions, and then walked away.

Chenar noticed that the lady forgot her grocery sack. She and Zenab picked up the bag intending to carry it to the lady in the distance who left it behind. Chenar advanced only a few steps before she was ripped apart by a powerful blast. Zenab, mangled and bloodied, could not walk or see. She struggled to crawl to her house, marking her progress with a trail of bloody handprints to the gate. The gutless attackers blended into the daily bustle of the city.

The locals were frantic. Abas and his wife wailed in horror and disbelief at the sight of their girls, not knowing what to do. Our soldiers arrived very quickly. The only recourse for Chenar was burial. Jon Cecalupo's men rushed the barely breathing Zenab to the hospital. She survived but would be permanently blinded. If only the images of the morning could be blinded from the memories of our men as well. Even as highbrowed discussions regarding the need for our mission roiled at home, the setbacks of the last two weeks provided little doubt as to why we were there.

It was clear, during this "holy month of Ramadan" that the insurgency was spreading and striking on multiple fronts. Not only were the weapons and tactics used against us more sophisticated, the assaults on local Iraqis had multiplied. It was one thing for soldiers to fight elusive insurgents in street battles. It was quite another to defend every civilian, especially when those afforded protection could be the very ones trying to kill the protectors. It was time to exhibit our ability to remove the offenders from the picture as we had demonstrated so successfully in prior months.

I had to get our minds off the casualties that we had suffered in the last three days. Two more of our men were dead, and a half dozen more had been wounded. Those who were not injured were dealing with scenes of children ripped apart by bombs. I continued to focus my men on only a few objectives. Any more would dilute the effort. We would fight the "Trigger Pullers" and ambush them. We would raid the middle tier "Bodyguards" to disrupt organization of the insurgency. We would pursue the "Big Guys" protected by that middle tier, shattering their leadership and funding and, hopefully, follow that trail right to Saddam. All indications were that Saddam's inner circle was connected to all of this activity. We had to keep after them.

It would not be an easy task, but if we wavered from this strategy, everything won to date would be lost, and we would be visionless for the future. No amount of political progress or goodwill projects for the people would matter if we could not secure them. This was no time to be passing out lollipops. It was time to bring down the hammer on the bad guys. We had to prove ourselves to be strong and win the trust of the locals.

Colonel Hickey and our brigade, John and his SOF team, and the commanders in my task force felt that the path we were pursuing would continue to bear fruit if we stayed on it. Reassuring key leaders above us would be the challenge. Fortunately, Major General Odierno believed the operations in our area were succeeding and needed to be replicated across the spectrum. I was grateful for this and believed that it saved lives in our area and brought stability sooner. Peers, pundits, politicians, and popular writers already choosing to shape the history of the war to suit their own agenda even at this early stage would criticize his decision. From their armchairs, they opted for a more "velvet gloved" approach that I believe would only prolong the human suffering.

Lieutenant General Tom Metz, an equally tough-minded commander of III Corps paid us a visit on October 17 along with many of the old friends I once worked with at Ft. Hood on the Corps staff. I briefed General Metz on our operations whereupon he expressed appreciation for our efforts. Our division fell under the command of this man of great repute at Ft. Hood. By spring, he would be the senior ground commander in Iraq, going on to show once more why he was so respected. Major Tim Karcher was among the general's group. It was good to see an old friend. Our paths had crossed on various occasions since Tim was a lieutenant and I was a captain. Seeing some familiar faces triggered reflection on happier times and places where people had not utterly lost their minds. The visit also afforded an opportunity to reiterate past operational successes and reaffirm current tactics with senior commanders.

The next few days were fairly calm. We found more roadside bombs and rendered them harmless, typically by shooting them. We captured more 60mm mortar ammunition and some RPGs, along with some trigger pullers. We were able to nab another upstanding citizen of Auja, Saddam's birthplace, in a joint raid with John's SOF team. Although this raid merely produced a minor player, it would be the first of many raids with the new team. On the day we lost Powell, Mark Stouffer's Gators netted Ahmer Abdullah al-Hadooshi, a member of the "Five Family" network, after launching a hasty checkpoint. It was good to be back on the hunt again.

The enemy seemed equally determined to counter us on all fronts as we struggled to keep the initiative. On the evening of October 20, the mortar attacks returned, this time falling near our C Company, 3-66 Armor's compound. Jon Cecalupo's "Cougars" endured several of these attacks, and although most of the shells dropped into the open desert around them, one was slightly more accurate.

Private Antonio Hernandez, manning a .50 caliber machine gun atop a storage building at their front gate, felt the concussion of shells and heard the cracking rounds "walking" their way closer. Hernandez spun around and dove for cover behind some sand bags. As he did, a round landed in the nook between the gate and the building, exploding in dirty flame. Large chunks of fragmentation caught Hernandez in the armpit and leg. Fortunately, his body armor prevented serious injury. He recovered and returned to duty shortly afterward.

Our intelligence reports indicated that several of these mortar attacks were being organized in a farm village north of the old Republican Guard military complex. The complex was rife with weapons, many of which made their way into private hands when the Iraqi army collapsed. We believed that Saddam's supporting cast of thugs orchestrated these attacks as they attempted to cultivate the insurgency. Too many incidents of late seemed to be well coordinated, having the mark of Fedayeen tactics, Republican Guard expertise, and Saddam inspiration. Timed bombings, rocket attacks, RPGs, mortars, attacks on our helicopters—these were not the signs of unrelated activity, but rather highly evolved, creative organization.

On a tip from our expanding informant network, we raided a series of houses on October 22, netting explosives, grenades, an RPG launcher, a heavy machine gun, and a host of other ordnance. My soldiers with mine detectors discovered the deadliest of these weapons beneath some dairy cattle in a stable. The owners, not realizing we would use such devices, had confidently pled innocence prior to this discovery. Their attitude quickly changed. While not the mortarmen we were seeking, they certainly intended to do us harm. Now they would be doing time.

On the night of October 23, the mortar attacks returned to the "Cougars." This time, Jon Cecalupo's men were ready. Seeing the mortar flash in the far distance through their tank gun sights, they engaged a car with two men. The men attempted to escape at a high speed with a mortar tube in the trunk. Amazingly, the car continued on even after several hundred machine gun bullets ripped into it. The car veered around a corner and escaped from immediate view. We discovered later that the tankers had killed one of the insurgent occupants. It couldn't have happened to a nicer guy.

I ordered increased outposts in an effort to ambush these escalating mortar attacks north of the city. They were hard to prevent because the insurgents, like the duo that Jon's men engaged with the tank, could roll up, toss a few rounds in a 60mm mortar tube, and flee even before they impacted. Still, "hard" is not "impossible." The enemy was using short-range mortars with predictable launch points in the open area of Cadaseeyah in the northern part of the city. I firmly believed that taking them by surprise with ambushes on likely routes was the best tactic.

Ever mindful of the shortage of men for the task at hand, I added to the observation posts the next night with one of my own. I set up observation with my command group and maintained control of the battalion with radio contact. That allowed Jon's men and Brad's men to lay at least one extra ambush in the northern suburb where all the mortar activity had been taking place.

My men and I infiltrated a nearly completed three-story house overlooking Highway 1 leading to Bayjii. The ground floor was locked tightly. We could have forced our way in, but that would have created unwanted attention, so we elected another option. The bottom rung of an assault ladder unhooked from a Hummer was tenuously balanced on the top of an eight-foot wall to enable an acrobatic access to a third-story balcony. As I forced my forty-year-old body up the ladder, I wished to be twenty-something like all the young men around me. What was I thinking?

I managed to scale the ladder and pull myself over the balcony without incident (or accident) and we set up the observation post. Hours passed as night fell on Tikrit. The locals were oblivious to our presence. A family next door carried out their evening routine of cooking, playing, and conversing while sitting in their ubiquitous white plastic chairs in a patch of green courtyard. While watching the highway and surrounding residential area, I thought about how tough it must be to raise a family in the midst of war.

We continued to spy, noting peculiar characters and unusual traffic until curfew took effect. The night proved to be relatively quiet, undoubtedly due to the machine gun marksmanship of our tank company on the previous evening. We crept out of our third-story hideout in the early morning darkness. I returned to headquarters before dawn and hit the sack for what little sleep I could snatch.

Later in the morning we would host an important visitor. He came to investigate the potential of our fledgling Iraqi troop training effort firsthand. I was impressed when Deputy Defense Secretary Paul Wolfowitz got out on the ground with us and spent several hours with my men to grasp the full scope of the program. Impressed with our efforts, he asked about the various plans for training Iraqi soldiers. He also discussed with me at length the situation in Iraq. Of particular concern back home was the widespread debate as to whether the national leadership had erred by invading Iraq with an insufficient number of troops.

"Do you have enough troops, Colonel?" Wolfowitz queried.

"Sir, I'm not going to lie by telling you what I think you and others might like to hear," I offered, knowing such questions might typically be answered with "Oh, we're fine, sir," or "We're making do, and we'll get the job done," as high officials were accustomed to hearing.

"It's not a question of having enough troops to accomplish our mission, sir. It is a question of choosing which missions not to accomplish for lack of adequate troops. We're getting the job done, but there is a lot more job out there. I'll tell you straight, sir, that I need more troops.

"This program you see here is a classic example of why," I continued. "Every soldier training these Iraqis was pulled off the line to do it. Even if they were not, we still cannot see what is beyond us on the periphery in villages and farms, as we do not have sufficient troops to patrol there. I could accomplish so much more if I had even the troops I am normally assigned back home."

"Interesting," he commented. "I appreciate your candor, Colonel. I am going to make a note of the reasons you gave me."

I felt certain I would hear about it later. The most likely outcome would be the very senior leaders asserting condescendingly, "Oh well, of course, the battalions say they need more troops. Wouldn't they all like to have more troops?" Still, I wondered what would happen if every colonel and general in the trenches spoke out with the truth. Would our military and political leaders listen and respond, or would we be told to drive on? Would we gain the momentum to roll forward or watch the wheels fall off the cart?

I felt confident that Secretary Wolfowitz had listened. I appreciated his coming to the front lines to see the situation firsthand. That was far more than some of our very senior generals in Baghdad had done. I took some satisfaction from at least being able to say, "Yes, we need more troops."

As if to illustrate the example from our conversation, an Iraqi man sputtered around on a red motorcycle through the fields along the banks of the river, easily visible from the Tigris resort island where Secretary Wolfowitz and I were conversing. Because of prior insurgent activity carried out with them, I had issued orders for the local government in Tikrit to seize all motorcycles on the road during the summer. This one, being across the river, had escaped notice. The area of operation for Dez Bailey's G Troop was so vast that it could only be patrolled, not fully covered. This lush farmland along the Tigris harbored rebels and resistance.

The Secretary's departure was followed by an influx of other airborne visitors, though not from our division. Shortly after lunch, rotor blades snapped at the air about 300 feet off the deck as a pair of Blackhawk helicopters with an Apache escort hugged the surface of the Tigris River. They cruised down the watercourse carrying a special group of officers visiting a special group of troops.

Meanwhile, on the rim of a verdant orchard adjoining the fields along the Tigris River just opposite Tikrit and our headquarters, that same motorcyclist took a weapon to his shoulder, aimed it toward the sky, and squeezed the trigger. A white smoke trail traced a short line from ground to helicopter.

The soldiers flying on the trail Blackhawk heard a loud bang as fragments sprayed the engine compartment. Alarms on the bird began to sound. Flames instantly fused with smoke as the blades whirled kaleidoscopic circles in the sky. The helicopter started to plummet, the spinning rotors offering just a modicum of balance. Only a few hundred feet from the ground to begin with, the pilots pointed the craft as best they could to a field off the bank of the river, hoping to avoid the water. There was no time to think, only react.

The aircraft was hopelessly sluggish as fire leapt out the engine exhausts. The pilots squeezed the last bit of control from the bird and somehow manged to land it roughly and fully intact. Only the extreme skillfulness of these men prevented complete disaster. The passengers dashed from the blazing craft, including an adrenaline-pumped soldier wounded in the calf when the missile struck.

The lead helicopter pilots, hearing the distress, banked their craft and watched in disbelief the scene playing out before them. The escorting Apache continued to fly wide. The lead Blackhawk also swooped a wide circle and then leveled, attempting to rescue some of the survivors. Miraculously, there appeared to be no serious casualties.

The fleeing enemy, throttling away on his Chinese motorbike, had no idea whom he had nearly killed. We never disclosed the identity of those passengers. I have often wondered whether the target was Secretary Wolfowitz on the earlier flight or the very senior special operations general on this flight. Either would have been a grand prize and perhaps could have altered the course of history.

This attack happened in full view of our headquarters on the bluff overlooking the Tigris River, so our soldiers witnessed the aircraft go down. Rushing across the river to the craft, we beheld what was becoming a red-hot mass of burning aluminum. Mark Stouffer and Brad Boyd were both in the area with their command convoys and headed to the site upon hearing the radio traffic. The functioning Blackhawk was just lifting off as we approached the scene. I ordered Brad Boyd to take his men north of the crash site to cut off the attackers. Mark Stouffer and his men linked up with the battalion quick reaction force I had released back to his unit. I ordered him to cordon the eastern road bisecting the farmland. If we acted quickly enough, we could possibly seal the main exit roads.

Captain Troy Parrish, the S4 Supply Officer serving on my staff while waiting for an infantry command, immediately brought his Hummers and medical support across the river from our headquarters. He assisted in the evacuation of the wounded soldier. The stricken chopper was fully gutted by this time, a mere 15 minutes after the crash. I radioed command headquarters with orders to have the local fire department bring a truck to extinguish the flames.

At the time, we speculated that an RPG could have knocked down the helicopter, but it was difficult to be certain. A surface-to-air missile was equally plausible. That was a frightening thought. We later learned that it was indeed a surface-to-air missile. We had captured twenty-three of them in a September raid led by Mike Rauhut. While a setback to the enemy at that moment, more of the projectiles had obviously been amassed. That was cause for grave concern for all helicopters throughout Iraq in the days ahead.

Colonel Hickey brought his Brigade Reconnaissance Troop, under Captain Dez Bailey, to reinforce our unit and help secure the ravaged site. Mark and Brad's men searched roughly 100 vehicles along the roads leading into the villages. Nothing was found, though a few weeks later informant tips would prove to be invaluable. The wreckage was recovered from the farm field and towed to the 4th Aviation Brigade's airfield just north of Tikrit at Camp Speicher. We were once again diligent to our dictum that no enemy would ever dance on American equipment on our watch. It was startling to lose a helicopter so close to us. I was thankful no one had died.

GOOD MISSION, BAD TIMING

We hosted another visitor on October 26. The stamina of this seventy-year-old man afflicted with Parkinson's disease amazed me. Robin Moore, author of *The Green Berets* and *The French Connection*, visited to gather interviews and information for a new book he was writing about the manhunt for Saddam. What a delight to meet with and listen to him. We corresponded a great deal following his visit. My hopes were that, whatever became of our efforts, the story of our great soldiers and their sacrifices would be preserved for posterity.

In addition, the relationship I developed with our embedded press continued to bear fruit as correspondents recounted the labor of our impressive soldiers. We had learned a tremendous amount about how the press operated since we had been spotlighted in the hunt for Saddam and his henchmen. They were professional for the most part, fearless to a fault, and inclined to file fairly accurate stories. Even cases of inaccuracy appeared to be just a result of erroneous information and not speculation on their part.

Many that I got to know well, like Brian Bennett, Greg Palkot, and Kim Dozier, were great fact finders and took personal risks beyond measure. They truly were craftsmen, seeking to separate the emotion of mission felt by the soldier from the skepticism of critics back home and attempting to find the truth of it all on the ground.

While the reporters accurately conveyed the stories of events from our unit, we learned that editors of various news organizations might never pick up the many positive accounts they would file. Some of the copy they did use was often edited to portray a different meaning altogether. A sense of frustration developed even among field reporters and photographers when a story they risked their lives to get was bumped for the splash headline of "Another Soldier Killed in Iraq Today" or "Celebrity X Enters Rehab."

While acknowledging the public's right to be informed of casualties, the reporters felt a focus on losses did not portray the truth when clear signs of progress were being made. Consequently, our raids continued to be well covered but were often misconstrued by those back home as exacerbating the situation. Only later would our tactics and results be examined and appreciated for their impact.

By October 26, we had gathered enough information from

informants to raid a troubling little village named Hamra, on the bluffs of the Tigris at the northern end of the old Republican Guard military complex. We conducted a joint raid with John's SOF team, as they were also interested in what we might uncover. We detained one of Saddam's physicists and about eight others who added more information about Saddam's closest circle of friends for later raids. The most important of those captured was one of Saddam's cousins from the Hasan family. We found large caches of ammunition and heavy weapons in the farm fields nearby, including ground-launched, unguided rockets. These were quickly becoming an enemy favorite for long-range but insignificant attacks on airfields and outlying compounds.

The city of Tikrit was becoming somewhat more civil with our increased efforts. Our raids seemed to cause the enemy to retreat, if only for a moment. Consequently, Colonel Hickey pressed us to persevere with raids based on intelligence and informant tips. There were still roadside bombs and sporadic mortar fire to contend with, but fewer rebels seemed willing to go toe to toe with us in street battle. Our patrols, ambushes, observation posts, and raids appeared to tighten security while relaxing the local population.

We attempted to further gain the confidence of locals by increasing the visibility of the Iraqi soldiers we trained. We also expanded our propaganda war with plans to place pro-Iraqi posters on lampposts across town and continue our "Mohammed's Faithful" campaign. My brilliant intelligence officer, Captain Tim Morrow, had prepared another leaflet and was eager to plan another mission to drop it.

The evening of October 28 marked an increase in enemy activity. Mark Stouffer's men narrowly missed an ill-timed roadside bomb. As Mark and his men began to investigate, a white Toyota approached them. Spotting the soldiers, the driver wheeled around. Mark's troops fired warning shots to stop it. The truck did not stop, and the passengers fired back. A brief gunfight ensued. The Toyota escaped, but none of our men were hit.

Captain Stouffer reported the event and alerted all units to be on lookout for a white Toyota transporting armed men. Even though half of Iraq drove white Toyotas, Major Bryan Luke sent out the call to be watchful. The enemy was out tonight. So were we. Jon Cecalupo had troops across the river and tanks to patrol the area of the mortars. Brad Boyd had troops in the central and northernmost parts of the city. The Tigris bridge was well secured on both ends. Mark's evening had already been eventful in the southern part of the city.

Approximately one hour before the 10:00 p.m. curfew, Captain Morrow, Specialist Jason Werts from battalion intelligence, and Specialist Gersain Garcia from my command element began their strategic leaflet drop. As in previous missions, they drove a light gray Iraqi civilian Toyota SUV previously captured from insurgents. Their plan was to cruise around the periphery of our troops with a faux "patrol" nearby pretending to attempt apprehension of the littering activists. Similar drops had been executed in like manner on previous occasions. They were always risky, however, and required meticulous coordination. Command Sergeant Major Martinez would act as the decoy patrol.

Specialist Ryan Steckler was on the bridge with the Iraqi Civil Defense Corps troops led by our trainers. The proximity to the frequent mortar attacks and the recent helicopter attack made this point a vital place to secure. It was also the only standing bridge on the Tigris River between Bayjii and Samarra. Having additional force to cover it, even if only with native levies led by our men, was a great relief to me. In fact, having Iraqis at the bridge offered one unique advantage. They could communicate with the steady stream of civilian drivers entering and exiting the city. They were on alert for the Toyota reported earlier.

Tim's leaflet mission had been well implemented. With just ten minutes left before curfew, it was time to wrap things up. Pete Martinez patrolled parallel to Tim on the main highway in northern Tikrit while the light gray Toyota traveled toward an entry ramp under the Tigris River bridge. That move would conceal them long enough to arrive at headquarters without suspicion.

As the traffic waned and curfew neared, Steckler noticed another car approaching. It was a light-colored Toyota. Not overly alarmed as there were still ten minutes until curfew, the soldiers readied themselves to inspect the car as it drew closer to their checkpoint. Their position was situated to avoid exposure to the streetlamp. All appeared in order as the occupants of the car acknowledged them by switching off their headlights.

Pete Martinez continued his patrol along Highway 1, conducting spot checkpoints in the city to delay traffic briefly, while Tim Morrow, according to plan, stealthily moved along a side street to make the river bridge turnoff to our compound. Tim cut his lights to escape the notice of any lingering civilians. In the dark, he inadvertently missed the turn. Traveling but a short distance before realizing his mistake, he stopped, put the Toyota in reverse and backed up to the turnoff point.

Specialist Steckler recognized the Toyota as the one encountered only minutes before. When the driver threw the car in reverse gear and started for the exit ramp, Steckler ran toward it shouting, but it disappeared down the ramp that curved under the bridge where he was standing. The Iraqi soldiers on the bridge heard his shouting and drew alongside him in support.

Tim Morrow drove down the ramp and under the bridge, completely oblivious to the scene playing out above him. He guided the car along the side road leading toward our headquarters some distance away.

"Stop!" Steckler shouted from the bridge above. Loud whistles ensued. "Hey! Stop!!"

Realizing that the suspicious Iraqi Toyota could be heading toward our headquarters, Ryan Steckler had but moments to react. A gunshot cracked through the air. He had fired the warning shot hoping it would be heard above the yelling and whistles, which had not been effective. The Iraqi soldiers with him, misunderstanding the meaning of a warning shot, aimed their AK-47 rifles at the car and fired enthusiastically, eager to be of assistance to Steckler.

Captain Morrow heard loud reports as rifle fire began to rip through his Toyota. Specialist Garcia, sitting behind Morrow, readied his weapon and tried to locate the source of fire. He leaned out the back door precariously and fired a burst in the general direction of the sound of gunfire. Specialist Werts looked behind from the passenger side but could not determine where the fire was coming from either. They were able to clearly determine that they were the target. Glass shards exploded from the rear windshield. Morrow tromped on the accelerator. Their only hope was to speed through the ambush.

Above on the bridge, Steckler saw the car begin to race forward as one of the occupants leaned out and fired. This was similar to what Captain Stouffer had reported earlier following the roadside bomb, and the car fit the same general description. Now he and two Iraqis began to pour fire into the car as it sped away. The other soldiers ran across the bridge to Steckler's aid.

In the distance, Pete Martinez began to hear M-16 and AK-47 gunfire. He ordered his patrol to move in the direction of the battle. Those already on the ground began running toward the sound of the guns. Specialist Michael Bressette and a couple of soldiers from Martinez's patrol could see a car racing toward them in the distance.

Captain Morrow struggled. He slumped forward at the wheel as the vehicle slowed. "I'm hit. I'm hit in the chest," he managed as he summoned all his strength to keep moving the Toyota forward. Rounds slammed into the backseat and the driver's seat, and two found their way into Tim's upper back. He grasped the wheel to hold himself upright as he nosed the vehicle around the curve ahead. Finally clear of the shooting, he saw Command Sergeant Major Martinez's patrol ahead.

"Captain Morrow's been shot!" yelled Jason Werts to Michael Bressette and the other soldiers running up. "We need a medic, NOW!"

Pete's patrol rushed to the stricken Toyota and pulled Captain Morrow to safety. The men grabbed a stretcher for him from one of their vehicles. Like all battle scenarios, the situation was confusing. Pete struggled to sort out the details. Bressette and Werts ripped the sterile packaging from bandages in their first-aid pouches and pressed them onto Captain Morrow's back and chest. Pete took charge, pulled the patrol in, and rushed Morrow to the aid station.

My staff and I were organizing plans for operations the next day when the radio calls started coming in. Reports filtered through our Headquarters Company as Specialist Steckler reported the contact at the bridge when they tried to stop armed men fleeing in a Toyota. On the battalion net, calls were coming in from Command Sergeant Major Martinez about contact and casualties.

"Sir, there is contact by the Tigris bridge," informed Major Bryan Luke. "Tim Morrow's been shot," he said in measured sadness.

"What?" I queried, stunned at the news. As I grabbed my gear and rifle, Bryan further informed that they were en route to the aid station.

I ran to our combat aid station praying along the way. God,

don't let him die. Please, God. Give Tim strength and save him. I arrived just as Tim was being brought into the compound. Staff Sergeant Sean Bach and the other medics grabbed the stretcher supporting him and lifted him gingerly from the Hummer-turned-ambulance.

"Aaahhhh. Aaaaaahhhhhh," Tim moaned. "Ohhh, it . . . hurts."

Doc Bill Marzullo sprang into action. His surgical scissors sliced deftly through Captain Morrow's uniform, exposing two AK-47 bullet holes in his chest. Needles, morphine, IVs, blood, pain. Looking at the exit holes in Tim's chest, even I knew it didn't look good. A thousand questions were racing through my mind. Why were his wounds there? How did the rounds get through his body armor? The answers would have to wait.

I prayed as I prayed each time I was near any of my guys who went down. I begged God to intervene. Doc Marzullo was the best, and nothing was too hard for God. I had to let Doc work his magic and God work His miracles because there was absolutely nothing I could do. I felt utterly helpless, and in that operating room, I was. Now it was time to find out how this happened—and why.

"Werts!" I called as I motioned for Specialist Jason Werts outside the aid station. "What happened?"

"I don't know, sir. We were coming in under the bridge when they opened up on us. We never saw them. I couldn't make out where it was coming from."

"What were you doing?" I continued.

"We had just finished a leaflet drop," he explained, "and were on our way in. They just opened up on us."

After checking a little further and talking to my sergeant major, I started putting the pieces together. I still did not understand the earlier reports of insurgents in a Toyota, but with Steckler's report and the location of Tim's wounds, it was becoming obvious that a terrible, terrible tragedy had taken place. Good men. Good mission. Tragic timing.

Armed with more anger than information, I examined the situation. Tim had not been wearing his body armor in order to facilitate his disguise while driving. He had positioned it behind himself in the seat and leaned back against it. The unworn body armor absorbed two hits, but it might have prevented the ones that penetrated his chest had he been wearing it.

Back at headquarters I ordered Bryan Luke to my hooch. I was furious. I blasted into him as I never had before or since. I demanded to know who authorized the mission on this night.

"Sir, he went out on his own." Bryan tried to respond. He was more than a little shaken to see a side of me he had never witnessed. "He coordinated with the sergeant major while we were out."

"All right," I said, still worked up. "All right, I got it." Then recovering somewhat I offered, "Sorry, Bryan. Let's sort this out."

I ordered an immediate commander's inquiry as it looked like a possible—no, probable—fratricide. Even if that was not the case, we needed to ferret out the truth. I called Colonel Hickey and gave him the few details I had. He informed General Odierno. We were able to piece it all together, and while communication with the native levies could have been improved slightly, it was just one of the catastrophic consequences that occurs when men try to manage violence against an enemy that hides among the civilian population. Ryan Steckler did nothing wrong. Tim Morrow did nothing wrong except make a foolish and costly decision about wearing his body armor. The situation was complicated when the leaflet droppers unwittingly and coincidentally replicated the enemy's earlier actions of the evening in a vehicle very similar. Sadly, it was what it was.

I was devastated. Captain Morrow was an intelligence officer of the finest order, the kind not likely to be replaced. While my prayer was that he would recover fully, I now had a gaping hole in my team when we were making so much progress on the enemy insurgency, Saddam's network, and the association linking them.

Captain Mitch Carlisle called in a nine-line medevac procedure that resulted in fluttering Blackhawk blades whirring near our aid station. Tim was encased on the stretcher in a heat blanket, accompanied by IVs and medics. The high pitch of the Blackhawk engine announced his departure as he was rushed to emergency surgery at the 28th Combat Surgical Hospital on Camp Speicher, located north of Tikrit.

"I got him stabilized, sir," reported Doc Marzullo as he peeled off the garments of his trade. "He's lucky they got him here when they did. He's still got a chance."

"Thanks, Doc. Thanks. Thanks for all you do. Now we can only pray he makes it," I offered. "Keep me posted on his condition as you get news through the medical channels."

"Roger, sir," Bill replied. "Sir, he's a very tough guy. He'll pull through."

Walking in the stale night air outside my headquarters, I looked up at the stars, always so bright and cheerful, even in this desolate place. I thought of Tim's wife and kids. I thought of the calls she would get. Half a world away, she was probably having a good day. It was mid-morning in Killeen, Texas. Maybe she was with her kids. Perhaps she was shopping. She could be with friends. By the time dusk descended on Texas, her whole world would be forever changed. If only time could be frozen.

JAGGED FENCE, CROOKED TOWN

As Halloween approached, it was nearly time to implement the plan we had labored over for weeks. Prior to my emergency leave in September, my staff knew I wanted to resolve the problem with Auja, Saddam Hussein's birthplace. This town of about 3,500 people continued to be a thorn in our side. Even the town's name decreed its heritage. Translated literally from Arabic, Auja means "crooked." Every defeated regime cell or captured insurgency funder or planner seemed to have ties to this town. Ultimately, we hoped that those making clandestine appearances in Auja would still have ties to Saddam. Catching them was the challenge.

I analyzed the dilemma of how to thwart insurgents from "swimming" in the population at large and finding a safe harbor in which to plot their evil deeds. If there were only some way to pool them in a "fishbowl" to monitor them more efficiently, we could make them vulnerable. For the bodyguards and inner circle group, Auja certainly had that potential.

I remembered studying Napoléon's directives to expose insurgents in the Rhineland by means of a census. I took note of particular techniques used by the French in Algiers to expose insurgents veiled in the teeming masses of the Kasbahs. While not a perfect fit, there were parallels to be drawn from both campaigns.

I first broached the subject with my majors. "How much barbed wire would it take to fence the entire village of Auja?"

"Ha, that's a good one, sir. That would be something," they replied.

"I'm serious. How much would it take?" I then told my staff that I wanted to fence the entire town and conduct a census as Napoléon had done. They clearly thought I had taken leave of my senses, but I knew that without a comprehensive cordon, only honest people would voluntarily appear for registration. With the town locked down, the only way out would be to register. It was a monumental undertaking but one I felt we could synchronize with our routine tasks and missions.

There would be a multitude of benefits to be reaped from this effort. Should criminal elements attempt to hide within Auja, their movements would be disclosed or severely hampered. If they took flight, they would relinquish their base of support, number one wife, most extravagant house and all the amenities of the good life. They would be far more conspicuous and vulnerable to exposure, living in the primitive mud huts on their farms. If they opted to settle openly in town and amend their ways, well, that would result in an equally desirable conclusion.

Mike Rauhut and Bryan Luke listened as I itemized practical ways to accomplish our objective:

- Surround the town
- Register every male over the age of fifteen at the police station
- Issue photo identification cards
- Control the single entry point
- Utilize local police and sheiks to assist in implementation of the plan
- Give them no alternative

I pitched the plan to Colonel Jim Hickey. Not surprisingly, he liked it. Still, such an endeavor was bound to create a major concern. Colonel Hickey would arrange for me to brief Major General Ray Odierno, our division commander.

Both officers appreciated the merits of the plan. It was risky, but the payoff promised to be enormous. General Odierno knew that there would be major press interest, which would likely be interpreted by them as typical heavy-handedness. While I pathetically offered that I would be the one charging forward with a plan of my own making, he just smiled and said, "I wish it were that easy, Steve."

Both commanders understood what was at stake. They also recognized how much ground had been gained in tracking Saddam's henchmen and impairing the former Baathist insurgency. Taken

together with the Ramadan attacks, the recent helicopter downings, and the surge of violence, this strategy had the potential to
put the enemy off guard.

"Approved," General Odierno declared. "I want you to keep me
informed at each step. You handle the operations, keep the place secure, let me know what you need, and I will deal with the fallout."

I was grateful to have such open-minded commanders as Colonel Hickey and General Odierno. Without Jim Hickey, I would
never have gained an audience with the General on the matter.
Hickey's grasp of the enemy and of history was such that he was
able to envision the plan immediately. He customarily approved
strategy that he believed would put us on an aggressive footing
as long as it synchronized with his overall operations. As we conferred daily, it was not difficult to deduce his intentions.

General Odierno had been monitoring our tactics for some
time and advocated many of our successful methods on a wider
scale, urging other units to examine them with an eye for application in their own areas. Pundits and armchair warriors at home
criticized him for a "mishandling" of the region that resulted in
violence. Later, however, they realized that his head-on approach
to defeating the insurgency in Iraq was innovative and forward-
thinking. The lid would blow off other areas after the first year of
the war, but much of Ray Odierno's area had a rock-solid foundation that put it on a path to stability.

Given the green light, we initiated the fencing effort at midnight on October 30. Rolling into Auja and up the path to a
sprawling mansion, I roused tribal head sheik Mahmood Neda al-
Nasiri from his sleep. He welcomed me as always but was shaken
by the hour of the call. I conveyed to him our objective and its re-
quirements. All males over the age of fifteen must register and receive a photo badge in order to enter or leave town. To secure the
badge, it would be necessary to complete an information form in

person at the police station. Once badged, they could move about as before but would be subject to search at a single entry point. All other exits into and out of town would be obstructed. I tried to paint him a picture of what Auja would look like by morning. He was shocked but fully compliant.

I knew this would place the sheik in a tough spot, as the Nasiris were fellow tribesmen of Saddam Hussein. I also knew any appearance of collaboration with us would not bode well for him. In this way, he could claim forced compliance. Afterward, he could serve as the liaison empowered to represent the town's complaints and negotiate for the removal of the fence. If, when confronted, our purpose was fulfilled, we could release the town and he, in all his sheik glory, would be the hero.

As morning approached and an orange, distorted sun began its lazy ascent, rolls and rolls of concertina wire lay scattered along the boundaries of Auja like tossed rings. Soldiers unraveled wire and pulled security. Bradley Fighting Vehicles and a few M1 Abrams tanks scanned the corners of the town and the spaces between them. The scratch of serrated steel on pavement signaled the end of life the townspeople once knew. Pounding sledgehammers drove reinforcing pickets into the earth to form the prickly fence. From the sky, it looked as if three giant, saw-toothed Slinkys had been unrolled and stacked into a pyramid. Auja was now entirely encompassed by them. The Iraqi troops trained by U.S. forces assisted the effort with fifty additional Iraqi laborers garnered from the local "rent-a-worker" pool in town, complete with a paid contractor. Stimulating the local economy turned out to be an added bonus.

Simultaneously, the intelligence and signal staff readied their computers with camera databases and began issuing badges. Hundreds of Aujite men arrived at the police station by 9:00 o'clock in the morning. They waited as badges were churned out and, once they had their badge, were allowed to leave through the single remaining exit leading to Highway 1. By November 3, we had badged twelve hundred men. Approximately three-dozen of those were immediately detained when their names matched our wanted list. Others were a Who's Who of Saddam's distant relatives and associates.

To discover the less obvious, I followed Napoléon's example during his Rhineland campaign. I instructed our men to ask each head of household to identify all those living in his house, as well as the houses to his left and to his right. If any registration form was later discovered to have omitted a resident listed by a neighbor, that homeowner and resident immediately became a person of interest.

The operation amazed not only the Aujites but the international press as well. *Time, Newsweek,* Associated Press, Reuters, and the major dailies all seemed to be fascinated by the audacity of the move. An already active press in our area now added even more visitors. Many of them drew comparisons to the partitioning of Gaza or Jerusalem, but in reality, that had never entered our minds. Nor was it a fair comparison. For one, we had an entire rifle company (my A Company commanded by Captain Mark Stouffer) inside the wire with them. Second, we were not trying to separate one culture from another. Third, the town was not sealed—just controlled. They could still come and go at will, provided they had identification and submitted to a search.

The impact of the fencing of Auja proved invaluable. We disrupted the enemy's command and control structure, confirmed by numerous signal intelligence intercepts. For those away from home at the time of the operation, we were able to expose them either in other villages or as they attempted to enter Auja. We were content to just watch other suspects. By leaving them undisturbed, they could potentially lead us to yet other suspects.

The immediate result of the operation was the accumulation of intelligence on targets we had been seeking since June and July. A sense of excitement and mounting momentum restored our belief that we could indeed knock the supports from under Saddam's protective circle. While we did not know the full scope the cordon would have on the terrorist infrastructure or Saddam himself, we knew it had to have some kind of impact.

While the fence was being erected on the night of October 30, Brad Boyd's "Cobras" and Jon Cecalupo's "Cougars" were keeping Tikrit proper under control. Brad's men found yet another roadside bomb and dismantled it before it could be discharged. Later that evening, several insurgents in the northern suburbs fired a 60mm mortar toward the "Cougars'" compound. Nothing was hit, but our snipers observed the muzzle flash and were able to acquire the enemy at long range. They managed to get off enough rounds to wound two of the perpetrators.

Meanwhile, in a village in the northernmost part of our sector, a reconnaissance platoon observed several men firing AK-47s into the air. Captain Cecalupo's men closed on the house and engaged the rooftops with small arms. Supporting Apache helicopters on patrol joined in and lit up the house with 30mm cannon fire. It turned out that several off-duty police were smoking hash on the roof of an empty house and were having a jolly time. They dove into the basement when our fire began to hit the roof and were found by our soldiers. Miraculously, they were not killed. They were reported to the police chief, General Mezher, who subsequently made them wish they had been killed.

November 2003 opened with a combination of raids and patrols that netted some important local insurgent cell leaders and intercepted an outbreak of roadside bombs, including new varieties of explosive devices. Doorbell switches to initiate the explosives became a favorite, followed by keyless locks, toy cars, and in one case, a bomb with a pressure switch. Our sweeps continued to net the majority of bombs before they could be detonated, but the types of bombs and their increasing numbers betrayed the enemy's desperation. From a signal intercept of a cell phone, we learned that the enemy admitted, "We are losing Tikrit and must reorganize."

For Finar Khatab Omar al-Musslit, the situation was becoming desperate. He was now the ranking leader of the insurgency in the Tikrit area and was brought in to deal with the recent setbacks. The Americans were aware of his family's involvement and were hunting his cousins, Rudman and Mohammed. His networks in the Cadaseeyah area of northern Tikrit were being thinned. To the south of Tikrit, Auja was fenced and cut off. Finar needed to find a way to retaliate to ease the pressure. He would make this point in one of his regular meetings with his cousin, Mohammed Ibrahim Omar al-Musslit, Saddam's closest confidant. They met to coordinate efforts in a cement factory owned by Mohammed's friend, Thamir al-Asi, on the main drag of Highway 1 on the south edge of the city. He needed Asi's money and support from his cousin, Birhan, another of Mohammed al-Musslit's brothers.

He also needed more foot soldiers. His friends and their families were certainly doing their part, but he was losing hope. He needed better weapons to strike at longer distances. The roadside bombs were having some impact, but the Americans were discovering and destroying them most of the time. It didn't help that those traitorous cowards in the sham police force or on the street would betray them by pointing them out to the Americans. He needed weaponry like rockets and mortars as well as anti-aircraft and anti-tank missiles. If only he had these, the Americans could be put on their heels.

In Auja, the enemy attempted to break our siege with harassing fire and mortars. They were cheap shots—both without effect. We had anticipated as much, and an elusive hide-and-seek game developed with our men initiating or returning fire in every case. In the city proper, a black Opel or Toyota sped by and lobbed an RPG at a C Company patrol. The men returned fire, but as they did, a large Mercedes truck inadvertently pulled into our line of fire and the attackers escaped down a back alley. Other patrols netted eight mortar tubes with ammunition while my scouts, led by John's SOF team, again raided the northern suburbs in Cadaseeyah. We nabbed the last of the Ghani brothers after having pursued them for some time. Mahmood Abdul Ghani was the brother-in-law of Saddam Hussein.

At this stage, we were thrashing Saddam's network in Cadaseeyah. John and the SOF guys wanted to keep the pressure on them as well. With Auja effectively isolated, we were able to strike at points north and west. There was no doubt that we were close to penetrating the last shell of protection surrounding Saddam. Colonel Hickey was obviously pleased with the targets we were snaring. We needed to continue raiding as much as possible. To that end, my new intelligence officer, Captain Clay Bell, and one of John's SOF guys, discovered a remarkable connection between the Khatabs, the Ghanis, and the Musslits. Their connect-the-dots game was bringing us closer to the prize. Clay Bell was a godsend. I had been devastated when Tim Morrow was wounded and evacuated, and I was certain that our momentum would be lost or decelerated, but Clay was one of the fastest studies I had ever seen. With a fresh set of eyes, he even picked up on things we had missed earlier.

Now Clay, with his able intel NCO, Staff Sergeant John Ferguson, together with Kelly from John's team, deciphered the connections with some interconnected data gathered by Major Stan Murphy and Chief Bryan Gray from Colonel Hickey's staff. It was becoming clear that the Ghanis and Khatabs were tied together along with the Rashid family in a greater resistance effort in Cadaseeyah and villages north. The Khatabs were related to Saddam by Ghalib Mahmood al-Khatab's marriage to Saddam's half sister, Bissan Ibrahim al-Hasan. The Ghanis were also related to Saddam by the marriage of Mahmood Abdul Ghani to another of Saddam's half sisters.

We had been pursuing portions of these families since June, when Abid Hamid Mahmood al-Khatab, former Saddam Presidential Secretary and the Ace of Diamonds, had been captured. What we did not know in mid-summer was the degree of interconnectivity. In retrospect, we realized that Abid Mahmood was living next door to one of the Ghanis and one of the Rashids when he was captured.

The Maher Abdul Rashid family was bad news in every respect. He was a former member of the Himaya, the select bodyguard of Saddam Hussein, and a former Republican Guard commander whom the locals had sighted with Saddam since the invasion. He was also related to Saddam by marriage. His daughter, May, was married to Saddam's son, Qusay. I killed his son, Ali, in a violent engagement in July when his cell ambushed my men.

We had now been able to isolate and hamper the insurgent network to a great degree. In Cadaseeyah, the Khatabs, Rashids, and Ghanis were the foremost network of street fighters and mid-level organizers. In Tikrit proper, the Musslits, Hasans, and Hadooshis were active but more upper tier. In Auja, the Khatabs, Majids, Heremoses, and Hasans were isolated. We still believed that the Musslits were at the center of it all, inspired by Saddam Hussein. Events of the next week only confirmed this belief.

By November 4, the Aujites in the south seemed resigned to their new fenced-in routine. I met with Sheik Mahmood and the town elders. They initiated a series of frank and honest discussions about the need for the Bayjat tribe, including the Nasiris, to reconcile with the rest of Iraq. Without some degree of reconciliation, they would have no future. They would be forced to fight or die. I told them that one would surely lead to the other and that reconciliation should be pursued.

The topic of reconciliation provided for some lively discussion at the Monday morning sheik council meeting. The other tribesmen and elders admitted that a resolution was needed, but they refused to welcome the Bayjat tribe back without blood compensation. They required revenge killings or at least ransom for wrongs. As I listened to the sheiks weave their tribal and feudalistic tales, I was thankful to be an American.

Their discussions did not seem to deter the enemy element that engaged Mark Stouffer and his "Gators" of A Company that evening. Firing from the vicinity of an abandoned air defense bunker, the enemy launched an RPG at one of our patrols and followed it with rifle fire. Undaunted, the "Gators" gave back in spades. The thump-thump-thump of a Bradley chain gun preceded the crack-crack-crack of 25mm shells exploding on the bunker. The soldiers cordoned the area, but the attackers were able to beat a hasty retreat from a defiladed position before the cordon was set.

The following night, the cat-and-mouse game continued in Auja. Our soldiers were alert as usual when, suddenly, the power was lost, and the village became black. A clattering of small arms fire was coming from within the wired village. The town was searched, but the devious attackers blended into the village population and were never found. At daybreak, Captain Stouffer locked the only gate into and out of town. We used it as a bargaining chip to compel the sensible Aujites to make their brethren knock off the attacks.

On November 6 on the "Chevron" in the northwest part of Tikrit, a C Company ambush led by Staff Sergeant John Gilbert observed a man setting up what appeared to be a roadside bomb.

Within Saddam's security groups, he also had personal bodyguards in two subgroups known as the "Forty" and the "Twenty-Five." To Saddam's right is his number one personal bodyguard, Adnan Abid Al-Musslit. *Hussein family photos captured by 1-22 Infantry*

Saddam with his close confidant Mohammed Al-Musslit. Musslit, a relative unknown to Western intelligence, would prove to be the key to finding Saddam. *Hussein family photos captured by 1-22 Infantry*

Although Saddam's residence took three JDAM Missile hits, it was amazingly strong. While gutted and charred, the building was largely intact and stable and was used as an observation post by our troops for its great view of the area. Here I am with Efrem Lukatsky, an award-winning AP photographer who spent many months with us, and Capt. Mark Stouffer, commander of my A Company.   *Author*

Although we missed Saddam at the Hadooshi Farm, he had definitely been there with his wife. We captured the Hussein family photo albums, important family papers, $2 million worth of Sajida Hussein's jewelry, and this stash of $9 million in cash.   *Photo by CSM Pete Martinez*

Saddam in earlier days with Presidential Secretary Abid Hamid Mahmood Al Khatab (L) and Yasir Arafat. In a huge breakthrough, Jack's SOF team and our troops captured Mahmood on June 16, 2003. He was the Ace of Diamonds in the deck of cards. Saddam's bodyguard, Adnan Abid Al-Musslit, is seen in the background on the right staring at the camera.
Hussein family photos captured by 1-22 Infantry

An unexpected consequence of the Mahmood raid was Saddam's sons, Uday and Qusay Hussein, fleeing from Tikrit to Mosul. Jack's SOF men with Baghdad reinforcements and Capt. Dan Miller's D Company, 3rd Battalion, 327th Infantry, 101st Airborne Division would kill Uday, Qusay, and Mustafa Hussein. Shortly afterward, they were buried in my area in Auja in the crude graves above.
Author

"Gators" from my A Company, 1st Battalion, 22nd Infantry commanded by Capt. Mark Stouffer, prepare for an extended patrol. Mark's troops led many of my raids.
AP photo by Efrem Lukatsky

"Cobras" from my C Company. It was the tough, young soldiers in this company who patrolled the heart of the city of Tikrit. *AP photo by Efrem Lukatsky*

Capt. Jon Cecalupo radios instructions to his company team of "Cougars" of C Company, 3-66 Armor. Jon's tanks were permanently attached to my task force and controlled the northern suburban areas of Tikrit called Cadaseeyah. He also fought heavy actions on the ground in the old Republican Guard Corps base north of the city.   *AP photo by Efrem Lukatsky*

Working every possible lead was crucial. Iraqis knew the people we were hunting. Getting them to tell us what they knew was a constant effort. Here, Joe Fillmore translates for Bryan Luke, Cesar Castro, and me some information about boat traffic this lady saw on the Tigris River not far from where we would find Saddam a week later.   *AP photo by Efrem Lukatsky*

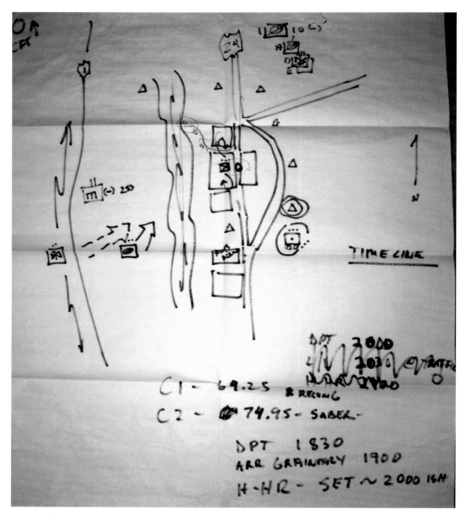

During the huddle between Col. Hickey and John, Brian Reed and Kelly tore off a sheet from a butcher tablet to make a planning sketch. The simple concept for what would become Operation Red Dawn started on this sheet of paper. The strikethrough on the timeline was due to Hickey's concerns of being just a tad late as had happened to us previously. Hickey believed the sooner the better. John concurred but had many reinforcing assets from Baghdad that would join him and time was needed to get them together. The result was an H-Hour of "2000-ish."
Provided by Jim Hickey

The farm where Saddam was captured in relation to Tikrit and Auja. One could literally look from the bluff of the site where Saddam was found and see his old mansion and the Hadooshi Farm. *Graphic by Author*

The two farms that became Wolverine 1 and Wolverine 2 during Operation Red Dawn. Saddam was captured at the farm at the top center of the photo that looks to the south. Ad Dawr is in the background. The Tigris is at the right of the orchard and Auja would be across the river. *AP photo by Efrem Lukatsky*

John's team gathers around a subdued Saddam as John's translator, Samir, poses with the former Iraqi dictator. This photo is the only known picture of Saddam at the hole.
Photo provided to Author

Col. Jim Hickey at the hole on December 13, 2003. *Left to Right:* Chief Warrant Officer Bryan Gray, Command Sergeant Major Larry Wilson, Col. Hickey, and Specialist Joe Ghamdi. Ghamdi is holding a chest belonging to Saddam containing $750K in US currency.
Photo provided by Jim Hickey

Saddam was shuttled in a Little Bird helicopter from the hole to the Water Palace in Tikrit until he could be transferred to Baghdad in great secrecy. *Photo provided to Author*

Saddam would be transferred late that night on a helicopter flight coordinated to send him to Baghdad with an Air Force escort. *Photos provided to Author*

At midnight on December 13, 2003, my command group assembled in front of the colors for this picture. The world would discover the news the next day. *Left to right:* Sergeant Major Cesar Castro, Command Sergeant Major Salvador M. "Pete" Martinez, me, Major Mike Rauhut, Major Bryan Luke. *Author*

A tired Capt. Dez Bailey, commander of G Troop, 10th Cavalry, guards the Saddam site on the morning of December 14, 2003. Dez had been up for several nights at the time of this picture. In addition to often being attached to my task force, Dez would later command one of my rifle companies. *Photo provided by Dez Bailey*

The opening was very narrow. I could not get inside the hole without removing my gear. *US Army photo*

Inside the hole, there was barely enough room to sit. It was like sitting underneath a 6-foot folding table. *US Army photo*

Saddam Hussein was captured with a Glock 18C, Serial Number BZG970. This weapon was full auto capable and was presented to President Bush in the spring of 2004.
Photo from National Archives

The only other item that Saddam had in the hole with him was this pair of medium "Khoshpa Shoe" sandals. These cheap vacuum-formed, rubber, simulated-buckle sandals complemented the rest of Saddam's appearance at capture. *Photo provided by CSM Larry Wilson*

The Presidential Suite where Saddam slept. This room had many books to read for leisure. Note the can of Raid. *US Army photo*

The Presidential Kitchen. It was here that Qais Namaq Jassim prepared Saddam's meals. All the rooms were disheveled from extensive searches. Photos were taken December 14, 2003. *US Army photo*

A small trail from the hut through a plush fruit orchard led to the nearby Tigris riverbank. Here is the Presidential Yacht used by Saddam for his liaisons across the river at places like the Hadooshi Farm. *US Army photo*

Capt. Mark Stouffer, Commander of A Company and Capt. Brad Boyd, Commander of C Company pay a visit to the hole. Before it was destroyed, the hole became a favorite photo spot for soldiers. *Photo provided by Brad Boyd*

Major General Ray Odierno, Commander of the 4th Infantry Division, briefs the world on the details of his troops' raid that netted Saddam. *AP photo by Efrem Lukatsky*

Brigadier General Mike Barbero, Assistant Division Commander of the 4th Infantry Division, listens to Col. Jim Hickey as he provides the details at the site of the raid.
AP photo by Efrem Lukatsky

The commanders and top sergeants of Task Force 1-22 Infantry. *Back row, L to R:* Capt. Curt Kuetemeyer, A Co, 4th FSB; Capt. Chris Fallon, Headquarters Co, 1-22 IN; First Sergeant Ron Davis, A Co, 4th FSB; First Sergeant William Matlock, C Co, 3-66 AR; Capt. Mike Wagner, A Co, 1-22 IN; Capt. Brad Boyd, C Co, 1-22 IN; First Sergeant Mike Evans, C Co, 1-22 IN; Capt. Jon Cecalupo, C Co, 3-66 AR; Front row, L to R: First Sergeant Jaime Garza, A Co, 1-22 IN; Command Sergeant Major Pete Martinez, 1-22 IN; me; First Sergeant Louis Holzworth, B Co and Headquarters Co, 1-22 IN; Capt. Mark Stouffer, A Co, 1-22 IN. *Not pictured:* Capt. Scott Thomas, B Co, 1-22 IN; Capt. Mitch Carlisle, C Co, 1-22 IN; and First Sergeant Delionel Meadows, Headquarters Co, 1-22 IN. *Author*

With the incomparable gentleman, the late Peter Jennings. Bryan Luke is in the background. *Author*

He began by tying wire to a lamppost before running it to a location across the road. He did not accomplish this immediately because each time he saw military vehicles in the distance, he would back off and sit down passively like one of so many Iraqi men who squat on the side of the road. He was oblivious to our men observing him, waiting in ambush. Watching the pattern, Sergeant Ramon Esparza-Reyes, Private First Class Kevin Kammer, and Private Tyler Hood clearly viewed the bomber's activities and confirmed that he was emplacing a roadside bomb. What followed next was a given. The soldiers placed him in their sights and hit him with a round each. The man dropped on his own trap— another Fedayeen foot soldier dead.

FIRE ISLAND

November 7th dawned with somewhat cooler weather but by mid-morning evolved into a very pleasant day. General John Abizaid, the commander of the entire Central Command (CENTCOM), arrived for an update from the leadership of the 4th Infantry Division. He and Major General Odierno came to the 1st Brigade at approximately 9:00 a.m. to meet with all the battalion commanders and our own commander, Colonel Jim Hickey. I had served with General Abizaid in Kosovo and Germany when he commanded the 1st Infantry Division.

Colonel Hickey's headquarters was in its usual immaculate state. God help the soldier who screwed that up. Colonel Hickey could be calm and reserved and was as brave as any soldier in his command, but he was well known for his ability to strike fear in members of his staff. We even joked amongst ourselves about which member of his staff was serving as the "human piñata" on a particular day! Today he seemed quite satisfied. In addition to the impressive array of easy-to-read maps and charts posted on partitions around the commanders' briefing area was a display of a different kind—a feathered one.

Some weeks before, our friend Brigadier General Abdullah Hussein Mohammed had presented Colonel Hickey with a falcon. As a skilled falconer, General Abdullah felt that a warrior such as Colonel Hickey should have a bird of prey. The falcon, now dubbed "Skyraider" as a nod to the 1st "Raider" Brigade, was indeed impressive. The predator had his own perch and a litany of soldiers rostered to tend to his every need. Most of the time he sat motionless but for an occasional blink or head shift, always scanning, and ready to strike.

It was only fitting that Skyraider found a place at this important brief among insurgent predators. At a moment of serious discussion between Colonel Hickey and General Abizaid about the motivations of the insurgency, Skyraider went bonkers. Tethered as he was by the foot, he became helplessly enmeshed in his own line. His claws and wings were dramatically splayed across the partition, and down and feathers drifted through the air. The amusing scene reached a crescendo with the bird's shrieking calls for help.

"Is that thing OK?" asked the U.S. commander of all forces from Africa to Central Asia.

As if on cue, a pair of gloved hands appeared from behind the partition, first bracing and then whisking the entangled creature up and over the partition. Skyraider's contribution to the briefing added little to solving the complexities of guerilla warfare but certainly furnished a memorable and entertaining break in the gravity of war.

Colonel Hickey's pre-Skyraider update resumed and actually went very well. We had frank and open discussions with General Abizaid about the best method for gathering intelligence. The general was impressed with our observations and later passed them on to other units. He confirmed that our leads on Saddam and his network were good and encouraged us to operate in the confidence that everyone develops patterns. Saddam would be no different, he assured us. He closed with some guidance to all the commanders and offered his vision on the future of the war.

Even as Skyraider was having his convulsions and we were deep in discussion with General Abizaid, Selwan Adnan Hamdi al-Nafat and his brother Sofian gathered in the northern suburb of Cadaseeyah in Tikrit at a friend's house to have a discussion of their own. They were now ready to execute a plot received from the area insurgent commander, a member of the Musslit family named Finar Khatab Omar al-Musslit. Saddam, they were advised, had conceived this new strategem himself.

Selwan and Sofian, in possession of a long, tube-like object known locally as a "Hatashi" missile, took up a position near the riverbank of the Tigris. They were alive with anticipation. These new Russian-made SA-16 anti-aircraft missiles had just been smuggled in from Syria. A mole working for the Coalition Provisional Authority in Tikrit had alerted them to another flight of American helicopters skimming south along the Tigris River from Mosul.

First Lieutenant Phil Thompson, from our tank company, was patrolling with two M1 tanks and his gun Hummer along Highway 1 in the northern Tikriti suburb of Cadaseeyah in search of bombs. Saqr Ghani, a local resident of the Cadaseeyah district, observed Thompson's patrol as he sat with several other men going through their morning ritual of small talk and tea. He cursed under his breath, still stinging that relatives of his had been captured by the evil Americans a few days before for insurgent activity. To the north, he could hear helicopters. He wondered what the Americans were up to and where they would strike next. He was relieved when Thompson's patrol passed by without stopping.

A pair of Blackhawk helicopters clipped south along the Tigris River aiming toward the helipad at the 4th Infantry Division headquarters just a few kilometers distant. The birds flew just above ground level but perhaps three hundred feet above the water.

Chief Warrant Officer Kyran Kennedy had flown this route dozens of times, but he and his co-pilot, Captain Ben Smith, were particularly vigilant that day, as they were transporting some especially important visitors. With several of the highest-ranking Staff Judge Advocate (SJA) personnel on this mission, the passenger load was split between the two birds making the flight. Smith and Kennedy would fly trail carrying Command Sergeant Major Cornell Gilmore, the Army's senior SJA enlisted soldier. Staff Sergeant Paul Neff and Sergeant Scott Rose, the crew chief and engineer, trained their machine guns on the bluffs and rooftops of houses dotting the bank's edge.

Kennedy looked forward to a little downtime in Tikrit. His wife had just sent him a beautiful case lined with red flannel for his handmade dulcimer. It arrived in time for his 43rd birthday the week before. He had crafted the hammered dulcimer himself on their farm in Hopkinsville, Kentucky, near Ft. Campbell where they were stationed. Now it would be protected as he carted it around.

Flying the rich farmland along the Tigris reminded Kennedy a little of home. He liked the simple life even though he was actually a Boston native. Clearly, the Kentucky farm he and his wife, Kathy, and their three children lived on was far better-looking than anything over here.

In the back sat Chief Warrant Officer Sharon Swartworth, accompanying her commanding general on her last assignment with the SJA office. She had already sold her house in the DC area and would retire after this brief interlude to visit the troops in Iraq. She had been excited about this opportunity to see things firsthand, capping a great career. Tomorrow would be her 44th birthday; she never imagined she would celebrate it in Tikrit! She looked forward to returning home to "live in paradise" as she put it, as her naval captain husband had just received orders to Hawaii.

Major General Thomas J. Romig, the Staff Judge Advocate of the Army (the Army's highest-ranking lawyer), sat in the lead bird. As the chopper began to ease up and prepare for landing on the helipad just ahead, he felt relieved to have made it to Tikrit without incident. He had important work on this trip concerning the testimony and allegations of Iraqis held in custody by American forces. One thing was certain: he wanted to ensure that his soldiers had the best support possible and encourage them to operate with full confidence to protect U.S. soldiers from undue criminal allegations as they attempted to sort out the enemy in this difficult insurgent war.

After passing Saqr Ghani and his tea-drinking cronies at approximately 9:40 a.m., First Lieutenant Phil Thompson patrolled south close to the riverbank with his tank men. He caught a flash out of the corner of his eye. A flaming rooster tail spewed from a Blackhawk helicopter as another one flew ahead. The trail bird was obviously in serious trouble as it struggled for altitude. The nose began to pitch forward.

Saqr Ghani, seeing virtually the same thing from his location, began to jump and shout, "Allah Akbar! Allah Akbar!" as he and the other tea-drinkers shared in the jubilation.

"Regular Mike, Regular Mike, this is Cougar Five, over!" called Thompson.

"Regular Mike, over," came the reply.

"I just saw a Blackhawk go down near my location! I'm heading there now with my patrol," announced Lieutenant Thompson as he switched radio handsets to contact his own company.

Chief Kennedy and Captain Smith felt a violent bang and immediately lost control of their craft, affectionately known as "The Goat." This was bad. Very bad. Where to land? Blackhawk #92-26431 was going down. No time. The pilots used what little control they had to aim for a sandbar island to avoid the river. The tail section gave way completely as the craft began a violent summersault. Debris, weapons, and soldiers fell from the stricken craft before it completely disappeared below the river bluff.

Phil Thompson quickly gathered a small force of three tanks and three gun Hummers and raced to the bluff. What he saw below did not look good. As he secured the bank and checked for enemy activity, Staff Sergeant David McClean and Sergeant Joseph Jago scrambled on foot down the tenuous cliff trail to the island land bridge below. A grisly, flaming scene rose before them.

Our battalion headquarters could track Phil's location with his digital tracking system. Headquarters Company security outposts could also see fire on the sandbar island north of their location. They called in the approximate grid.

Within minutes, our task force spurred into action. Major Mike Rauhut radioed my driver, Cody Hoefer, and then dispatched forces to the location in my absence. Captain Brad Boyd darted a patrol north from his downtown location, while Captain Mark Stouffer alerted his quick reaction force already on standby in the city. Command Sergeant Major Pete Martinez was holding a promotion board with several of the company first sergeants when the word came. Suddenly, soldiers from every one of our companies burst into action.

Staff Sergeant McClean and Sergeant Jago continued to thread their way down the tenuous trail to the island. What they saw was traumatic. The helicopter lay scattered along a straight pattern, perhaps a hundred yards long. The lighter the pieces, the less distance they traveled. The main body of the aircraft tumbled into a ball and burned profusely. McClean and Jago raced to the disconnected parts of wreckage looking for American soldiers.

Phil Thompson met Captain Brad Boyd at the top of the bluff. Brad took charge of the site as Phil's "Cougars" and Brad's "Cobras" worked together to do what they could. Mike Rauhut began feeding everything to Brad, who was now the senior commander on site. Sergeant Major Cesar Castro, who had been out checking up on the "Cobras," followed after them. We now had a very able force to work the grisly task at hand.

The sandbar was covered with bulrushes and monkey grass about eight to ten feet high. About a quarter of the island was on fire, and the flames were spreading. Aluminum, magnesium, and steel morphed from aerodynamic marvel to molten mass as the wreckage burned intensely. Brad and our soldiers hastily searched for survivors in the wreckage.

I emerged from the meeting with General Abizaid shortly before 10:00 a.m. My driver and operations sergeant reported the news to me. We sped north to Cadaseeyah, arriving about ten minutes later. The island was belching smoke and flames. My first priority was to extinguish the fire so recovery of remains and aircraft could begin. As I took in the scene before me, I could not imagine any human surviving this inferno. We drove down to the island. I called Mike Rauhut for fire trucks, Army or city—it didn't matter. We needed serious help to contain the flames. Until they arrived, there was little that we could do. I ordered Brad Boyd and Mark Stouffer to make sure security was tight. The enemy was active, and we could be vulnerable to mortar or sniper attack.

"Look, a couple of things need to happen," I told my two company commanders on site. "First, we need to recover the bodies and all the equipment. These Blackhawks are usually armed with waist guns. We need to find those and any personal weapons and gear that may have been scattered over the area. Second, we need to sanitize this site once we secure it and the aircraft is properly recovered. I want nothing for the Iraqis to gloat over. I want it to look as if this had never happened. We're gonna be here awhile until we get all this cleaned up. There will be no dancing Iraqis on any helicopters."

"Roger, sir," they acknowledged.

"Sir, we've consolidated the remains in Charlie 7 and can take them wherever they need to go," informed Brad.

"Let's make sure we have everybody," I answered. "I'll try to get GREGS (graves registration and mortuary affairs personnel) out here to recover them properly. Investigators will want to know exactly what happened here, so we need to make a sketch and note what we find and where."

As we conferred, flames began to spread. While not yet critical, we had to douse the flames before they spread to the dense monkey grass and burned whatever might be scattered in it—whether survivors, bodies, or wreckage. Sergeant First Class Gilbert Nail, Cody Hoefer, and I began to stamp out the flames to try to clear the trail running down to the island. First Sergeant Mike Evans and some of his "Cobras" spotted us and came to help. We whacked the grass, stomped the ground, and tried to contain it to the areas already burned. Captain Jason Deel and the Iraqi Civil Defense soldiers arrived and began to assist. Soon, we were making a little headway.

"Jason, take your men to the north end of the island and look for wreckage or remains," I called out.

"Roger, sir," Captain Deel replied as he moved with his sergeants and Iraqi soldiers up the trail.

With the flames contained, we focused on the wreckage at the south end of the island.

"Sir, we've found some equipment back over there and one of the machine guns," updated Major Bryan Luke, who had gone with Jason's men.

"Sir, we only have four and a half bodies," reported Captain Boyd.

"Four and a half?" I replied.

"Yes sir. When we first came down, Sergeant Madrid, Venegas, and I found a leg that doesn't belong to any of the bodies we've found so far."

"Well, we need to find the rest of him and consolidate them all over there," I instructed, pointing to a clearing near the path that climbed back up the bluff. "Bryan, we gotta know how many we're talking about here. We need to know the manifest."

"Roger, sir. We know more than anyone at brigade right now, but maybe we can get them to ping higher," he replied.

Pete Martinez and Captain Alex Morales arrived with an ambulance from battalion headquarters to help in casualty aid. Brad informed them that only bodies had been recovered so far. Without hesitation, they began placing the corpses into body bags.

As the search continued, Bryan Luke pulled me aside. "Sir, look at this," he said softly as he showed me a smoldered desert camo top. On it were two stars of a major general. The name tag said Romig. My heart sank.

"Roger, I'll call it up," I muttered in dismay. "Was he in it?"

"That's the thing, sir. We only found the uniform," Bryan explained.

"Let's pray he was on the other bird," I offered.

I walked to my Hummer and called brigade on the point-to-point tactical satellite phone for privacy. I briefed the brigade staff on our findings. They stated that Romig was not on board the downed bird and had landed safely. I asked about the manifest. Brigade confirmed a crew of four and two passengers, one was the JAG sergeant major and one was a female warrant. I validated the body count so far and hung up the receiver.

"Brad, are any of the bodies women?"

"No, sir."

"Well, we're missing one and half people then. One is a female warrant."

Staff Sergeant Matthew Rose from C Company had split off from Brad's group to stamp out a fire he saw flaring up by the main wreckage. The fire was on the side of the chopper leaning toward the ground. He started pouring water from his canteen to put out the flames that he could not stamp out because of the wreckage. As he did, he noticed something inside the helicopter.

"Sir, we got a body!" called out Rose.

Brad, Mike Evans, Medic Staff Sergeant Felipe Madrid, and I advanced to the crushed compartment of the aircraft. Slumped over and still buckled in was the female soldier. Her hair was still pulled back in a bun, her head was tilted downward, and wisps of smoke still rose from her charred body and clothing. Out of respect to her memory, I will not describe the remainder of the scene. We unbuckled her seat belt and tried to extricate her, but it was impossible. Her lower torso was pinned by the wreckage.

"We're going to need recovery assets to remove her," I commented. "Let's get her tags."

As we lifted her head, Staff Sergeant Rose grabbed the dog tags and removed them with care and dignity. He handed them to me. I put the bloody, smoldered identification in my pocket. There was nothing more we could do.

Shortly afterward, Bryan Luke and a group of men to the north found the dismembered soldier. We also recovered what appeared to be all the aircraft armament and personal weapons. With everything accounted for, the gruesome task of recovery began.

As we worked, several leaders from our division and other units arrived. Brigadier General Mike Barbero was first on the scene. Recovery was delayed due to concerns about the aircraft investigation. I gave him a rundown and showed him an initial sketch of what had been found. Once he grasped the situation, he thanked us and allowed the recovery to press forward. Soon, the fallen soldiers' battalion commander, Lieutenant Colonel Laura Richardson, arrived with Colonel Mike Moody from our division's aviation brigade and thanked us for responding so quickly. We assured them that we would secure the site and recover the human remains and the wreckage. By nightfall, all this had been accomplished. We carried the wreckage to the same spot we deposited the helicopter from the October 25 crash. Nearly all of it had been saved from the grass fires, allowing for a more thorough investigation. It was an exhausting, tragic day.

I had left the scene by late afternoon to confer with Colonel Hickey at my headquarters. We were determined to shake up the town. This would not stand. While we had inflicted great loss upon the enemy recently and were ripping into his networks, it was clear that he still had the resources to strike back. The insurgents and the local population that continued to harbor them had to understand that the American Army was more than just Humvees. We were tougher and more determined, and we would sap the motivation right out of them.

That night I reflected on the abominable events of the previous twelve hours. The next few days produced many reports on these soldiers in the news. Learning about their lives made the manner of their deaths even more repugnant to me. That was the strange part. Unlike wars in the past, news of military deaths was being broadcast worldwide before the bodies and wreckage turned cold. In fact, reporters were trying to film our recovery efforts from the bluff even as we sifted through the ruins and remains below. In the next few days, I would try to couple the horrific scenes of the soldiers' demise with the bereaved comments of their loved ones. As I studied on the Internet smiling photos of them in happier times, I was thankful that their relatives didn't see the carnage we witnessed. Soldiers carry such memories for life. Thankfully, their families could remember them the way they were.

The brutal deaths of more fellow American soldiers angered me. They died in my town on my watch, and I failed to prevent it. My head knew that the enemy was fully accountable for these grievous crimes, but my heart could not help but wonder if we could have done something more. It is an unfortunate reality of war that the enemy also gets a vote on the battlefield. When men endeavor to kill one another, both sides can succeed. It is who is left standing that matters.

THE BEER HALL FAITHFUL

Back at my headquarters, Colonel Hickey and I contemplated the situation. We both knew it was imperative to strike back hard. At the same time, we could not afford to lose any momentum in the search for Saddam Hussein and his insurgent networks. Clay Bell hypothesized a likely correlation between the trigger pullers and the family networks. Pursuing one would be equivalent to pursuing the other. The weapons, we speculated, were too sophisticated. While it was possible that a mere RPG had downed the latest Blackhawk, we all sensed that it was a surface-to-air missile. This was the third helicopter downed in as many weeks.

"I want you to work your informant networks, Steve," ordered Colonel Hickey. "This is a different situation now. They have sophisticated weapons, and we must maintain the initiative. It is essential to be relentless and aggressive. Time matters."

"Roger, sir, I'll work them," I responded. "Maybe Colonel Jassim and the Governor can help as well."

"We have to act quickly," affirmed Colonel Hickey. "They have to react to us. Only our forward momentum will insure that. We have too few troops to hold everything down. If they ever discover that, things will only get worse."

I asked Joe Filmore to contact the Governor's office for an immediate meeting. We rolled down Highway 1 to the Salah ad Din governmental offices and conferred with Governor Hussein and Colonel Jassim. I conveyed our need for immediate information. There would be major consequences in the city, I explained. Any information that they could glean would help minimize the escalation. Colonel Jassim agreed to extract what information he could for us. He had several updates for us as well. We agreed to meet again the following morning.

That night, Colonel Hickey and I discussed our options. We both felt that it was time to strike the areas we had been watching. Though these sites were not always occupied, they were significant as meeting places, insurgent transit points, and weapons supply sites. We typically observed them for the opportunity to kill insurgents or uncover leads to their cell networks. From this moment forward, those locations would be regarded as legitimate military targets.

A series of strikes was organized to destroy these points on a massive scale. The strikes would be synchronized to maximize the shock effect. Our objective was to unmistakably convey this straightforward message to the public: It is more dangerous to cooperate with the insurgents than to cooperate with us. While we always took care to shield the innocent, we would boldly demonstrate the willingness to destroy whoever or whatever was aiding and abetting the insurgency.

Such tactics bore some risk, but the risk of no response is always greater than that of swift response on a legitimate line of attack. We would hit legitimate military targets to disrupt enemy activity, slow their resupply, and shake their confidence to the core. This would illustrate to civilians the consequences of abetting the insurgency or aligning with Saddam's henchmen. Saddam was a master of motivation by fear. That's how he inspired the Tikritis to serve his former cronies. We aspired to exchange their fear of Saddam for a greater desire of self-preservation. It was time to abandon Uncle Saddam.

Colonel Hickey arranged big support in the form of airpower and artillery for the coming strikes. We would be allowed to use any of the weapons at our disposal on targets that we would define ourselves, and he wanted to review those proposed targets as soon as possible.

Mike Rauhut, Bryan Luke, Clay Bell, and I combed every possible target in our area. My guidelines were to choose locations known to have been weapons caches and locations from which attacks had frequently been launched. In that way, we would be hitting legitimate military targets. Should we destroy a building used for such purposes, it would also have a military impact. We selected several choice targets at points around the city and in surrounding villages. On the evening of November 8, we would array our forces to hit them simultaneously.

As the day dawned, Bryan Luke, Clay Bell, and I called on the Governor. The information he offered was consistent with what we were tracking, but we also left with some important new information. We learned that the insurgency in Tikrit was currently being led by Finar Khatab Omar al-Musslit. Finar, who had earlier fled to Kirkuk and Hawija, had been recalled to take over the area. It fit. With his cousins Rudman and Mohammed Ibrahim Omar al-Musslit already in our sights, Finar was one more link to pursue who could lead us directly into Saddam's inner circle. It also cemented our belief that we were narrowing the gap between us. We also learned of a son-in-law of Rudman named Hussein Ahmed Mohammed Hazaa who, with several of his relatives, was behind all the recent activity. How nice of them to keep it all in the family.

While we would later secure information on the helicopter shooters themselves, the information that Colonel Jassim had given us was of greater worth and would prove invaluable in the weeks to come. It was a shattered and shaken insurgency that hit back, but we were decimating their cause significantly. Now they were trying to counter by coercing former Himaya and Special Security Organization officers closely connected to Saddam into the breach. We immediately shared this new intelligence with John and his SOF team and found it paralleled some new information that they were tracking. Between us, we were exposing enough targets for a massive roundup.

Colonel Jassim's new feedback fit a pattern regarding those on our wanted list. The difference now was that Saddam's shrinking circle appeared to be more directly involved due to a dwindling supply of foot soldiers. We were given a lead pertaining to the Tikrit cell principals directly connected to the families that we believed harbored Saddam. It further validated that our "Three Tier" strategy was working and that the lower tiers would lead us to the higher ones and, hopefully, to Saddam himself.

That evening, we proceeded with our plans to raze several military targets where insurgents were known to have found safe harbor. One was near the site of the Blackhawk crash, perhaps even the very position from which the missile had been launched. It was an unfinished house atop the bluffs north of the location where the helicopter went down. Locals reported spotters using a cell phone to signal the attackers from there.

At curfew, Phil Thompson rolled a tank platoon and his own headquarters tanks from the "Cougars'" compound across the highway to Cadaseeyah to target this house. Jon Cecalupo was still on leave, so Phil would lead the tank company. Brad Boyd's "Cobras" maneuvered Infantry and Bradleys to a building in south-central Tikrit where we had been attacked on several occasions. Mark Stouffer's "Gators" deployed south of Auja toward a bunker where we had also been engaged in several fights. Within an hour, tank rounds, TOW missiles, AT-4s, and machine guns leveled these buildings. Air Force jets screamed overhead. Bombs glided along laser beams across the river at targets designated by Colonel Hickey, based on information provided by Captain Dez Bailey. Our mortars and artillery cracked in support.

By morning's light, the locals were utterly terrified. They told us that they had not been this frightened since the previous April. Good, I thought. Tell that to your Fedayeen-supporting, Saddam-loving neighbors. Don't you realize we have the might and resolve of the United States of America at our disposal? Did you honestly think we were merely an Army of Humvees?

Capitalizing on the momentum, we rolled a large number of combat vehicles into the city on November 9. We brought in tanks, Bradleys, and about 300 Infantry. We did it at the height of the business day for maximum visual effect. By amassing our own forces, we gave the appearance that reinforcements had been brought into Tikrit to crack down on the city. Tikrit became somewhat more subdued, but more importantly, we saw an increase of information flowing from locals willing to help us.

While we were busy tightening down Tikrit, Kaied Ghalib Mahmood al-Khatab was preparing for some action of his own. Although we had already thinned out a few of the Khatab family, all we really knew at this point was what we had observed from the receiving end of their attacks. Now we began to put the puzzle pieces together.

Kaied's father was at the center of the resistance in Cadaseeyah. Kaied was a first cousin to Abid Mahmood, the Ace of Diamonds, whom we had captured in June. The Khatab family collected sophisticated bomb-making material and manufactured scores of roadside bombs that they employed against us. Our previous connection to them was their good friend, "Thamer the Bomber," who carried the devices from their house and employed them. It was also a Khatab who had killed Esparza and wounded several of my soldiers in October.

Now lacking in foot soldiers, Kaied desperately decided to strike us himself, hoping to catch our forces by surprise. While we were concentrated in large numbers flooding the city with troops, he and Ossam Ali Hussein al-Sumadie transported their powerful bomb in a small white taxi, easily blending into Tikriti traffic. What they had not counted on was hitting a deep hole in the road on the way out of Cadaseeyah that somehow connected the electrical circuit to the blasting cap of the bomb. The taxi was instantly transformed into a volcanic, flaming convertible. When the car eventually smoldered out, our soldiers saw that it was still occupied by the remnants of two evil men frozen in their charred poses. To me, it was a perfect portrayal of the 64th Psalm in the Bible. We would henceforth refer to these two insurgents as "Crispy One" and "Crispy Two."

That night we blasted at previous insurgent mortar locations with our own harassment and interdiction fires. One enemy mortar location that had been prepped with a cache of rounds for their next attack yielded a massive secondary explosion when our rounds hit it. In the days that followed, the town became even more subdued and quiet. We resumed our patrols. Our informant network grew as people began to cooperate with us. Whatever the correlation, one thing was certain—we were making irreversible progress in holding the initiative.

Militarily, we were pleased. Public relations weren't perfect but they were moving in the right direction. We were satisfied despite second-guessing from pundits back home. We knew that we could not win over the people of Tikrit while Saddam remained at large. We continued to be kind and compassionate to those who cooperated with us, but the general Tikrit population detested us for the most part. Power, however, they respected.

Some reporters continued to question our forcefulness and were mystified at the value of shows of force. Even so, I knew we could not win the favor of the locals by handing out lollipops—not in Tikrit. Too many of my bloodied soldiers bore witness to this. I likened this hometown group of Saddam-lovers to the "Beer Hall" crowd of Munich in 1945. Having given birth to National Socialism and benefiting greatly from it in its heyday, they just could not believe it was all gone. That was Munich. This was Tikrit. Like Hitler's faithful, I believed Saddam's loyalists would have to have power and privilege forcefully wrested from their grasp.

DRAINING THE SWAMP

Reporters asked many times about the status of the hunt for Saddam. He was always a priority, I responded, but our mission would be accomplished whether or not he was captured. I shared how close we were getting and asserted that it was merely a matter of time before he was snared. Frequently they would ask whether I supposed he was in the area. I told them that I believed he could be as his support base was clearly in Tikrit.

There were many clues leading to Saddam. While we saw a few obvious road signs that confirmed the path, we would later see detailed signs that reinforced just how straight our course was. Even so, we would rarely receive a sighting that was timely. Usually it would come as third- or fifth-hand information and almost always: "He was here four days ago." Thanks, buddy. That helps a lot.

Rumors depicted Saddam as a sheepherder, a taxi driver, or a street fighter in the heart of Tikrit with an RPG. He was everywhere, yet nowhere. We called these ruminations "Elvis" sightings. Like the rock-and-roll king who continued to live in the hearts and the tabloids of his faithful followers, it seemed for every good Saddam tip we pursued, there were at least twenty such "Elvis" sightings. We often joked that he was probably pumping gas in Auja.

While the Saddam rumors were routinely discounted, we took seriously the cascade of information allowing us to track those who actually knew his location and were likely concealing him. We had a pretty clear picture of that elusive network. For months we believed that the network revolved around the Musslit family in particular. The problem was getting to them and, once that was accomplished, how to move in on Saddam swiftly enough before the information decayed. We had been so close yet always a step or two behind.

The trickle of information began to leak into a watershed that drained out a swamp of ugly characters. As snout, eyes, and tail were exposed, we began to see months of effort pay off. We had some incredibly good fortune with a series of raids over the next three weeks. Part of our ability to connect the dots between the Khatabs, Ghanis, and Rashids and further tie them to the Musslits, Hasans, and Majids was due to an act of kindness that would pay huge dividends.

One day, while visiting General Mezher, the Salah ad Din Police Chief, I was approached by a kindly police officer not much younger than myself. He had issued several invitations to visit him at his home. On a whim, I decided to go. He lived in a critical section of town not far from 40th Street where there had been much heavy fighting. A set of ears and eyes in that neighborhood would be good even if only to expose the street fighters.

One day, my translator, Joe Filmore, and I visited the policeman and engaged in pleasantries. He introduced me to his elderly father and stated that he was the Mukhtar for that district of Tikrit. The old gentleman looked terrible. His face was ashen, and he had a peculiar smell, rather like raw hamburger and Limburger cheese. Looking down at his feet, I could see why. The man's big toe on one foot was decayed to the bone. It was like looking at an x-ray. The next toe was halfway into becoming its big brother. Clearly, diabetes was taking its toll.

The policeman asked if we could help his father, so I left to retrieve my field surgeon, Doc Marzullo, who immediately went to work. He arranged to have the old man operated on at the Tikrit hospital by Iraqi doctors to avoid any suspicion. He made a full recovery after having the two decayed toes amputated. By our next visit, he was flush, full of life, and ever afterward grateful. I was happy to have helped. As we visited, the man's son said, "Wait here, I want to show you something."

He returned shortly. "Look at this," he offered, holding open a page from an oversized, hardbound Iraqi Army registry. Each page was handwritten with a photograph adhered beside each soldier's entry. Even though I could not read Arabic, I knew that the page I was looking at displayed an 18-year-old Saddam Hussein.

"Holy cow!" I said, not sure how Joe would translate that. "Where did you get this?"

"I was the personnel officer for the Republican Guard Corps near here. When your forces came, I secured all the records," he divulged with the confident assertion of fulfilling his military duties in the face of extreme circumstance.

"Are they secure?" I asked.

"Yes, I have them all." He said flatly.

"Holy cow!" I said again, instantly recognizing the significance of his words. He had thousands of records. Every soldier ever conscripted in Tikrit had been chronicled, complete with a period photograph. Further, the man's father had been a Mukhtar for decades in the city. In Arabic culture, the Mukhtar is paid a small fee to record all the births, marriages, and deaths of his neighborhood. It is a position of great respect and honor. In this case, it also meant a gold mine of additional family records had just been made available to us.

Over a brief time, these men helped us in a true spirit of gratitude. I was ever careful about being seen anywhere near them. Occasionally, on patrol, our soldiers would stop at a Pepsi stand with a back door connecting to a courtyard. I believe the policeman's brother owned it. From that walled compound, I could hop another wall and be at the back door of the Mukhtar's house. Our soldiers would leave, giving the appearance that we had all moved on. Then Joe Filmore, Clay Bell, and I would have time to sift through the latest family connections.

There was a bit of concern from Bryan Luke among others about our safety on these collection missions, but I felt it was worth the risk. It was in the heart of bad country where many former SSO and Himaya bodyguards lived and where I had personally been involved in several vicious fights. Even so, we obviously could not enter this man's home with a large number of soldiers or have them posting sentry around his house. He and his father would become dead men. Still, being in the heart of that neighborhood, I felt secure. It wasn't likely that they would bomb us on that dense neighborhood street, as they would be unable to shield their own families, houses, and property. The trick was to get in and out invisibly without compromising the Mukhtar and his son.

These men were a source I categorically refused to share with anyone. While Colonel Hickey was aware of the prized connection and John's SOF team and I often discussed the finer points of targets we were trying to crack, I never disclosed the name, the location, or any of the details of this covert source. I only said that it could be completely trusted. Added to HUMINT (Human Intelligence) and SIGINT (Signal Intelligence), we now had MUKHINT (Mukhtar Intelligence). This was just one more payoff in the next three weeks as we pursued Saddam.

With this windfall of connecting information, Clay Bell and I updated John and Kelly from the SOF team about the Khatabs, Rashids, and Ghanis and sifted through the networks of the Musslits. Meanwhile, Lieutenant Colonel Dave Poirier of the 720th Military Police Battalion had come upon some critical information of his own. Dave had been working with the police and passing information from his perspective to John and his SOF guys as well. This time, he was certain he knew where to nab one of the Musslit brothers. Faris Yaseen Omar al-Musslit, a first cousin of Rudman and Mohammed, was one of the most wanted men we had all been tracking.

On November 8, Dave's MPs and General Mezher's police captured Faris when an informant, whom few wanted to believe, came forward. Dave decided to take the risk and carry out the raid even if no one else joined them. We were not permitted to pursue the target as the location, beyond the Jabal-Hamrin Ridge, was miles outside our sector. John and his SOF team could have gone but decided to pass because several things just didn't quite add up. Dave, however, felt it was worth the effort if there was even a small chance that Faris could be there. Fortune smiled on the 720th, and we were all grateful that Dave pursued this lead. One more nefarious creature had been snagged from the swamp.

While we were unraveling the Khatabs, Rashids, and Ghanis and the 720th was following their lead on Faris al-Musslit, John's SOF guys had been more interested in a tip on Rudman Ibrahim Omar al-Musslit. The tip led them to a sparse mud-brick farm near Rawa in the Haditha area west of us in Al Anbar province. John's team hastily organized a raid using other SOF elements from Baghdad for support. It was a huge success but had one unfortunate outcome.

When I learned that John's SOF team had scored Rudman, I was ecstatic. We had been pursuing this man since May as we were convinced that he would surely know Saddam's location. When John appeared on November 9 to hash out more information, I congratulated him on the successful raid. In the last 48 hours, two Musslits had been captured, and details of the major insurgent network had been uncovered as we linked the street-fighting families with the Musslits and Hasans.

"There was a little problem," John said with his typical understatement. "After we nabbed him, I guess he couldn't take the stress. He keeled over with a heart attack."

"That sucks," I said. "What happened?"

"I don't know," John said in all seriousness. "It wasn't anything we did. When we found him, he was totally surprised and just kind of dropped his head in resignation. We needed his information more than him. I guess his ticker just couldn't take it."

It was a devastating blow to the good news of Rudman's capture. We kept his detainment and death a secret, hoping to gain some time. As we discussed the fallout of events, we were more certain than ever that the Musslits were the key to finding Saddam. Only Mohammed, Rudman's brother, could possibly hold that key now. While we felt that he may have been the missing link all along, we also felt that Rudman would have known Saddam's location as well. With Rudman dead, the critical question was one we had also been asking for six months: Where was Mohammed Ibrahim Omar al-Musslit?

To answer that question, we pulled out all the stops. John's team, my battalion, and indeed the entire 1st Brigade focused on this issue while we tore into the insurgent networks. We scrutinized every miniscule bit of information, every link and photo until they surrendered enough information to lead us to a substantial number of revolutionaries. As John and I conferred with our respective staffs, we felt perhaps a massive roundup raid might be a worthy option. The timing would be critical.

We were once again hot on the trail to Saddam. We had orbited widely around it in September and October but had to fight back the street fighters protecting the network. With that accomplished, we now had a clear blood trail to Saddam's inner circle. The excitement began to escalate. If we could shatter the inner circle, we felt, the entire network would rapidly collapse. It did.

On November 13, John's SOF team and my battalion conducted another small raid to get at Mohammed al-Musslit. There was some dubious and sketchy information implying that certain targets might be linked to the recent helicopter downings. I was doubtful as the informant reported that the helicopters had been shot down with RPGs. I knew that they were taken down with SA-16 anti-aircraft missiles smuggled from Syria. Even so, we all agreed that the raid might be worth the effort.

While Mohammed was not the objective of the raid, we believed the targets to be his drivers and business associates. Among the nine men detained were the four targets we were specifically seeking. Four more creatures were fished from the swamp. Although lesser players, an elderly guy named General Hamer "Abu" Dries and his two sons possessed critical information. Dries was a former Director of General Security and a close friend of Mohammed al-Musslit. This small raid would initiate a string of connections to groups encountered in Tikrit and Cadaseeyah, linking Mohammed al-Musslit to them all.

Each raid was becoming crucial at this point, revealing vital information that unfortunately had to be acted upon without delay. With Rudman dead, our focus on Mohammed was a given, but we quickly realized that it was Mohammed who had been in charge all along. Rudman had a huge responsibility in Baghdad and Tikrit and the area west of the Tigris, but even he apparently answered to his brother, Mohammed.

With shows of force and the subsequent heavy raiding, the

majority of locals reached a peak of discontent, not that they had ever been fond of us anyway. Reporters filed stories parading this discontent, charging that our "big stick" approach was creating more problems than solutions. The press had often criticized our seeming lack of effort to win hearts and minds. But how can you win a black heart and a closed mind? Some members of the press failed to understand that the people we dealt with could not be swayed. Passing out lollipops meant nothing to them. They understood and respected power. Anything less posed an opportunity to strike back at us.

I sensed we were at a tipping point. We all did. I could have cared less what newspapers in Los Angeles, Washington, DC, or New York had to say about what I should do in Tikrit. Now was not the time to take counsel of fears or be given to hand wringing or worry about how it would hurt my chances to become the next field marshal of the army. This was about defeating enemies. Nothing silences critics like success. If we could put the street fighters off balance, we just might be able to get at the protecting families of Saddam. To do that, we had to continue to show ourselves strong. I did not wish to lose the momentum in a repeat of tough fights like those of September and October that had resulted in more killed and wounded soldiers. We had them on the ropes, and it was time to start slugging.

FAITHFUL EFFORTS

We continued to face numerous roadside bomb attacks, but providentially, we had been spared casualties or found the bombs before they could be detonated. We retaliated with a powerful display of weaponry. General Odierno had given orders across the 4th Infantry Division to seek out targets and hit them in a coordinated effort. This had followed our earlier operations in our own brigade that had hit enemy supply sites and displayed shows of force. On the 17th of November, our battalion once again rolled tanks, Bradleys, infantry, scouts, and Iraqi civil defense soldiers into town.

There were reporters on the streets from all the major agencies and networks watching the surge of activity. "Colonel, what is this all about?" they asked.

"It is not a display so much as responding to enemy operations as they occur," I explained. "We are taking a very offensive stance to take the enemy out whenever we can."

"By rolling tanks through the city?" asked one, not fully understanding the power that shows of force can wield to disrupt enemy activity.

"Our raids are devised to remove enemy threats," I allowed. "We want to eliminate those threats and bare our fangs and claws."

"What message will that send?" asked another.

"The message is this: Give up. It's over. Get on with the future of Iraq. Support the new government," I replied.

Part of the renewed effort to find military targets included the use of mortars in harassment and interdiction fires. I was thankful that Colonel Hickey had won this freedom of action for us. In every war, H&I fires were effective in disrupting and deterring the enemy while protecting friendly forces. We used the missions to great effect by targeting the very fields on which the enemy had launched mortar attacks on us. From the outset, the result was no more enemy mortar attacks from those areas.

As we continued employing every means to cause Saddam's faithful to lose hope, we, on the other hand, had to maintain a hope of our own. We knew we were on the right track. We knew we could prevail. We knew we had the means. Still, at times, the prize seemed so elusive. It took a certain measure of faith to pursue what was so improbable. Colonel Hickey was adept at keeping us patient and focused. Each new day could yield the very things we pursued if we did not lose faith in our strategy.

Faith. Perhaps best defined as the evidence of things hoped for and not seen, it still drove us forward. It was fueled by a deep conviction that we were participants in something bigger than ourselves. That is not to say that we did not have our doubts and setbacks. We did. Faith would erase the doubts and, coupled with the encouragement of fellow warriors, it allowed us to build more confidence in our mission.

Reporters took note of my faith because I would often play the guitar while our battalion adjutant, Captain Craig Childs, would lead singing at the chaplain's services to our headquarters troops. They found faith in the field intriguing, amusing, or perhaps even foolhardy. Saul Hudson from Associated Press did a feature story in September 2003 that took the foolhardy approach. Rory Mulholland wrote a book called *Camp Britney* about his brief stint with my task force. He struggled to interpret what he regarded as the incongruity of my faith with the greater whole of combat soldiering. My soldiers had less difficulty with it. They knew two things about me: I would ensure that they had everything needed in battle and I would personally lead them from the front lines. I was honored to have their respect as both soldier and man of faith.

My executive officer, Mike Rauhut, also a man of great faith, encouraged me often. We had even met each other months before I took command at a Bible study at Ft. Hood. We prayed often for God's guidance, wisdom and protection in our capacity as leaders of a thousand soldiers.

Truthfully, most of my soldiers knew of my faith. I never tried to hide it. For me, freedom of expression and religion are among the fundamental aspects of liberty for every American. While some might imagine the military culture to be an imperfect environment in which to exercise faith, I wholly disagree.

Some might argue that such expression of faith might be better suited for the unit chaplain. We each had our roles. Mine was as a leader and combat infantryman. Showing a sense of faith and character was never a deterrent to my soldiers or our mission. Most would argue it enhanced it. For me personally, I know it did. I determined to be a good soldier first and then my faith would speak for itself.

The Army chaplains fought an interesting war of their own. While we fought for streets and cities, they fought for hearts and peace of mind. We took life, and they proclaimed new life. Our relationship with them was good, and in times of duress, soldiers rarely turned them away.

My battalion chaplain was Xuan Tran, a living testimony of endurance, patience, and new life. When Xuan was a boy in South Vietnam, he endured the horrors of war as a civilian, something few Americans can fathom. When South Vietnam fell, Xuan's parents mustered together their best attempt at escape and literally drifted in the ocean for days until picked up by a passing vessel.

They were taken to the Philippines, and eventually, Xuan's father was able to come to the United States where they started life from scratch in California. Xuan was an atheist, but while in college, he encountered a faith in Christ that changed his life forever. After schooling, he applied to become a U.S. Army chaplain. Our battalion was his first posting.

The banter between soldiers and this good-hearted man was relentless. Xuan gave it back in spades with his thick Vietnamese accent. Of particular annoyance to the soldiers was Tran's musical talent. His singing certainly qualified as "joyful noise" but little else. He often turned to his accordion, which made the soldiers long for his singing. When the two were combined, soldiers were sent howling.

The good-natured friction reached a critical mass when some

young headquarters officers took the chaplain's accordion hostage. First Lieutenant Colin Crow and Captain Chris Morris, who led my Mortar and Scout platoons, respectively, were the prime suspects. Periodic ransom notes made from cut-up newsprint stated that if Xuan did not stop playing at all hours, the accordion would be gutted. Mike Rauhut was eventually able to negotiate the accordion's release without injury.

What Xuan lacked in musical talent, he compensated for in ministry to the men. He baptized scores of soldiers in one of Saddam's swimming pools near the Water Palace. I was grateful for all the assistance we could rally in our efforts in Iraq. Chaplain Tran supplied weaponry of a different kind for battles of a different kind.

That is the ironic thing about war. Soldiers become very connected to their mortality. In a war zone, where death and human suffering are constant companions, soldiers cling to the very things scoffed at by the highbrowed university professor amid the comforts of protection and peace.

I often told my soldiers that if God intended for me to die in Iraq, then nothing could prevent it. If not, there was nothing the enemy could do to make it so. I took comfort, like millions of Americans, in my Christian faith. I could lead from the front because I believed that my life was in God's hands. It didn't eliminate my fear of death, but it eliminated my anxiety about death.

Because our task force received continual press coverage, my personal faith was public knowledge, resulting in scores of encouraging notes and pledges of prayer support pouring in for our soldiers from Americans back home. Among the most remarkable of these was a message from a man who lived in Harker Heights, Texas, that I believe became one more part in the capturing of Saddam Hussein.

In late November, Dick Dwinnell, like many Americans, had

been following the war, wishing for an opportunity to do something to encourage our troops. During personal times of reflection and prayer, he asked God for success in our efforts and victory for our troops. He had an epiphany, a sudden intuitive leap of understanding: God knew the precise location of Saddam Hussein. If the soldiers would petition God asking Him to expose Saddam's hiding place, they could capture him.

With this in mind, Dick researched press reports of our task force with regard to the hunt for Saddam. He found my name, looked it up in the phone book for the city in which my unit was stationed before deployment, and dialed the number. My wife, Cindy, answered the phone.

"Hi, you don't know me, but my name is Dick Dwinnell. Are you the wife of Lieutenant Colonel Steve Russell?" he queried.

"Yes, I am," replied my wife apprehensively, not sure where the call might be going.

"Is he the commander of 1st Battalion, 22nd Infantry?" he continued.

"Yes, he is," Cindy treaded cautiously.

"I understand he is a man of God and has a deep faith . . . "

"Yes, he is . . . " Cindy interrupted.

" . . . and I just felt like I should call you," Dick explained as he offered his motivation for calling. He asked her to forward a message of encouragement to me. "The next time you talk to him, please tell him that God knows where Saddam is. It is just a matter of leading soldiers to that location. If he and his men will pray and seek God's wisdom, I believe God can lead them to that location."

"I will," Cindy assured him. After a short conversation of pleasantries, Dick had delivered his message. Cindy relayed it to me just a few days later. It was certainly a message to ponder. I felt that Dick was right; God knew the location of Saddam Hussein, and it could not hurt to further seek His guidance.

With Chaplain Tran out for some medical tests, I called on Major Oscar Arauco, Colonel Hickey's chaplain for the brigade. I asked Oscar if he would come to lead us in prayer. Staff, soldiers, and anyone else were all welcome to participate. I would never force anyone to join us, but I knew that many would choose to do so. For the next several weeks, the chaplain led us in prayer asking God to expose the evil man to the light of day. The flood of information that broke loose in the next three weeks was simply astounding.

A SENSE OF MORTALITY

On November 19, joined by John's SOF men, I led a very successful raid in pursuit of those plotting to shoot down our helicopters. The raid evolved from a tip we received on some insurgents who had reportedly acquired SA-7 anti-aircraft missiles and were said to be planning an attack for November 20.

With little time to prepare, we had to move quickly. I wanted to take no chances. As far as I was concerned, I had lifted the last charred American from a melted helicopter. I never wanted to experience that again. I located with Brad Boyd's "Cobras" who seized two targets in close proximity while John's SOF men and my scouts under Chris Morris took two others.

The raid resulted in the capture of some key figures, some we believed to have information about the helicopter attacks. The most important of these was Munther Mohammed Ahmed. He was a leader of trigger-pulling cells and had occupied a prominent position on our wish list for some time. More information would surely generate more raids. As the swamp continued to abate, a shadowy image of the alligator began to appear below the murky surface.

While developing more information, we continued an indirect

271

war with the trigger-pulling group of insurgents. Mortar rounds slammed into Auja, narrowly missing the "Gators" of A Company. A powerful SS-30 rocket missed the "Cobras" of C Company as it fell short of its intended mark. The rocket left a bomb-sized crater in town, blew gates from walled compounds, and destroyed a car. Reacting quickly to the rocket's launch trajectory picked up on Dom Pompelia's artillery radars, Reg Allen's 10th Cavalry Squadron found the launch area on the east side of the Tigris River and engaged several of the rocket-slinging enemy, killing five. We learned that they were from Fallujah.

I was glad to work with Lieutenant Colonel Reggie Allen's 10th Cavalry Squadron who had now been attached to our brigade. The 10th Cav was General's Odierno's divisional reconnaissance battalion. They were equipped with tanks, Bradleys, and their own attack helicopters in a fine display of flexibility and power. For months, Colonel Hickey had been pleading for help in order to hold the areas that Dez Bailey and I had cleared on the east side of the Tigris. Now, with Reg's troops, we could focus our efforts and find even more troublemakers in a greater area. I had known Reg since we were captains in school at Ft. Knox. It was reassuring to know that I could now call on a fellow battalion commander for helicopter support should the need arise.

Indirect attacks were but one of the perils we faced. Roadside bombs continued to be the enemy's favorite. On November 24, Captain Jon Cecalupo, back from leave and in command of the "Cougars," was leaving the battalion command post when he made a right turn onto Highway 1. As he did, a powerful blast showered the convoy with dust, chipped concrete, and smoke. Strangely, the blast made less impact than might have been expected. The bomb, detonated by a wireless doorbell, had been placed in the opposite lanes. Consequently, it discharged away from Jon rather than toward him. We were thankful not to have another commander in his command convoy face the fate of Captain Curt Kuetemeyer the previous month.

Shortly afterward, I repositioned my convoy to the site of the attack, always studying the enemy's techniques as we encountered them. As I stepped into the street, Sergeant First Class Gil Nail informed me that the on-board jammer, known as a "Warlock," was activated. It would disrupt any signal sent to a bomb but would also routinely jam our radios. Bryan Luke had advised headquarters prior to switching on the device.

The crater and blast on the street bore the marks of a clean-burning bomb, probably pure C-4 plastic explosives in a container of some type. I couldn't understand why they would detonate a device set to blast in the wrong direction. It made no sense unless they had noticed that we would often drive in the wrong lane to avoid bombs.

When we saw some locals venture out, Joe Filmore and I approached a local shop owner.

"Salam Aleykum!" I called.

"Alaykum a Salam," he slurred. Thayir Faisal and his buddies were tanked on a local licorice drink called Araq. They were having a good old time sitting in the back of their shop after closing. "The lights went out," he proclaimed with hand gestures for emphasis. "Then BOOM! If I had been up here, you would not see me anymore."

As I looked around the shop, I tried to determine the angle of the device to establish the probable origin of detonation. Sensing this, Faisal stood and began to assert his innocence. "We are sick and tired of people putting these bombs here," he overdramatized. "If I see anyone doing this, I won't tell you, I will kill him myself!" he boasted, pointing to his chest while getting a little too close to me.

"You have had a little bit to drink. I can smell it on your breath." I assured him, "We don't suspect you."

Only a fool would detonate a bomb that would jeopardize

his own life and livelihood. I could tell Faisal was not involved because all of his shop windows were smashed, and his own late-model BMW was peppered with concrete fragmentation, proving him either outright innocent or downright stupid. While both seemed viable, we were satisfied that he did not know the perpe-trator. Iraqis cared deeply about their cars.

"If you see something, take action. Get an Iraqi policeman or a soldier, and we will help you," I pledged.

Faisal and friends locked their shop door—probably out of habit because the holes in their shattered store windows were large enough for grown men to crawl through. Walking back to my Hummer, I was talking with Betsy Hiel from the *Pittsburgh Tribune-Review* and Kevin Sites from NBC News, visiting report-ers who accompanied us on patrol. As we discussed the incident next to my Hummer, Specialist Mike Bressette interrupted us. "Sir, we are standing next to a bomb."

At my feet was a cinder block, its cavities packed with plastic explosives and capped with cement. Protruding from the holes were red pigtailed wires connecting the two halves for sympathetic detonation. We called them "Allah Akhbar" bombs, an allusion to the handwritten phrase "Allah is powerful" scrawled into the concrete of the cinder block hole caps. They were enormously po-tent, capable of shredding a Humvee and all those in it. A sense of mortality washed over me, sending chills through me from head to foot. "Yes, we are!" I said, gingerly stepping backward as I was standing less than two feet from the device.

Now it made sense. Two bombs had been set to snare us on both sides of the road simultaneously. The effect of that sympa-thetic blast would almost certainly have been fatal. For some rea-son, the bomb on this side of the road had not detonated. With the jammer engaged in my vehicle, any new attempt to detonate it would be somewhat more difficult.

We backed off and set a cordon on Highway 1 to protect innocent passersby. Bryan Luke told our headquarters what to expect as we decided to discharge the bomb. Gil Nail took a position at what we calculated to be a safe distance. We stood a little farther behind him. Nail's rifle was an odd mixture of personal add-ons and Okie ingenuity. It was a standard M-16A4 with 20-inch barrel, camouflaged tan with an added retractable butt stock. Mounted on its flat top rail was an apparatus that roughly resembled the Hubble Space Telescope. Gil was affectionately known as "Mr. Gadget" for the multitude of devices, trinkets, and modifications he ever seemed to possess. On this night, the normal taunting of "Mr. Gadget" was swiftly replaced with admiration.

Sergeant First Class Nail shot one round of tracer into the cinder block and hit it squarely. Immediately it began to burn. Soon, a white-hot jet of flame shot up from the block like a magnesium flare. That was followed by a medium-sized "pop" of the blasting cap. Thinking it would continue to burn after the blasting cap failure, we kept the area clear and waited for it to burn out.

Suddenly, a violent explosion split the night air. Nervous laughter and banter ensued as a shower of flying concrete, spalls, and sparks flew up and over us. It was a brilliant light show, reminiscent of a Fourth of July fireworks show.

"I think it's burned out now, sir," Nail chimed in with his hilarious staccato laugh. My earlier sense of shock and mortality had been replaced with nervous laughter and overwhelmingly welcome relief. The reporters watched in amazement as the bizarre scene played out, but it was not an uncommon experience for our soldiers. We frequently cleared bombs to prevent the enemy from having freedom of action or to make us vulnerable to subsequent ambush. Kevin Sites caught it all on film, and as a sleepy America rose that morning, they watched the drama unfold on the television screen. We resumed our evening patrol.

I couldn't help feeling a bit angry with myself for being caught unawares. I always had my guard up. Always. Even if surprised, I made it a point to be alert and react quickly. What if that bomb had fulfilled its purpose and killed the men for whom I was responsible? I was reminded once again of my mortality. Life, my life, could be snuffed out as easily as a candle. I had been in wars and firefights, and would be again, but standing toe to toe with a bomb that could have obliterated us gave me great pause. I was thankful that our lives had been spared again.

HOLY MONTHS AND MILK MONITORS

As the Muslim holiday of Ramadan approached at the end of November, Iraqi leaders urged us to lift curfews in the cities on the condition that they be reinstated if there was even a single outbreak of violence. We gave it a shot. It was a nice gesture. Our goodwill lasted approximately five minutes. Shortly after what would have been curfew, automatic weapons fire erupted near the main gate of the 4th Infantry Division. No one was hurt, and we were never able to determine exactly what had transpired there. In Tikrit at least, the holy month of Ramadan would also have a holy curfew.

The holy month of Ramadan—it even sounded out of place in Tikrit. I knew the significance of Ramadan as I had served in other garden spots in the world, but I had never been given a comprehensive explanation of Ramadan until Sheik Mahmood al-Neda al-Nasiri enlightened me in Auja.

"During Ramadan, we don't eat," he asserted, omitting the exception about eating after sundown. "We don't smoke," he explained as he brandished the Marlboro cigarette in his right hand for emphasis. "We don't drink," he lied, as everyone knew Mahmood had some of the finest blue label whiskey in the province of Salah ad Din. "We don't . . . "—then rotating his downturned palm from side to side, he finished the sentence—"with the women." Finally, with a straight face to declare something he actually observed, he asserted, "And we don't lie . . . as much." It was the most honest assessment of reality in Iraq I had heard regarding the holy month.

On November 25, we located more roadside bombs. A large one made up of an 82mm mortar round packed with plastic explosives around it had been set in the median of the main highway downtown. We discharged it without incident. That evening, some insurgents crept along the palace wall on "Excellency Street" in front of our battalion headquarters to fire an RPG that skipped down the road near one of our guard towers. It failed to explode, and no one was harmed. The insurgents, in their haste, forgot to pull the safety pin from the nose of the rocket.

In contrast to the events of previous weeks, the next several days were calm. The press tried to make something of the Thanksgiving we celebrated, but in reality, it was just another day for a fighting soldier. The big spreads, the hype, and the lofty "care about the troops" speeches rarely affected the soldier on patrol. He ate his usual fare or got his choice of the pickings after all the rear echelon troops had their fill. There were nice mess halls, but they were not readily available to troops on patrol or soldiers waiting patiently in position for forty-eight hours to ambush insurgents.

I tried to explain this to the head mess sergeant and chief at the contract dining hall who promised great things for Thanksgiving. He just could not understand why I wanted food sent to the troops' locations. In his view, the troops should all feed at his facility. When I explained that I had troops scattered in seven different locations, the learning light began to come on. It was the continuation of a rocky relationship that never improved. I had been personally banned from the mess hall just weeks after it opened.

It started out innocently enough. Sometimes, returning from a patrol, our soldiers wanted a cold drink. There's nothing like an ice-cold can of Coca-Cola to remind a soldier of home. We rarely saw them. Troops on the line routinely got generic brands of disgusting grape drink or odd-flavored sodas that no one wanted or recognized. The "good stuff" was in the mess hall at the division headquarters. So, when patrols came in from the streets, they would often stop for a cold drink and maybe a decent meal.

One day on patrol, my guys pressed me for a diversion to the "cattle trough," as I affectionately called it. The morning had been successful, and the guys were laden with some enemy plunder for the battalion weapons holding area. It was unbearably hot outside. I did not want even one of my soldiers to stand guard over the weapons while others ate comfortably inside. So, stinky, sweaty, and bristling with our own weapons plus some grenades and enemy AK-47s wedged in the tops of our assault packs, we casually dropped in.

You might have thought we were exhibits at a zoo. Soldiers in clean, even pressed uniforms stared unbelievingly as though we were hideous bog creatures rising from the vapor, reeking with the stench of salt and sourness. Last in line behind a dozen of my men, I blended in with everyone else. My kit was the same and I fought with a rifle, the commander's pistol merely a backup. Suddenly, some spoon starts ripping into my soldiers.

"You guys can't be in here," declared Sergeant Spoon.

"What's the matter, Sergeant?" asked Specialist Jeff Barnaby, one of my troops.

"No crew served weapons, no grenades, no AT4s, and no enemy weapons!" he itemized. He might as well have added, "No dogs and no infantrymen."

"We didn't know, Sergeant . . . " Barnaby explained.

"You do now!" he interrupted.

That was enough. "What's the problem, Sergeant?" I asked, stepping up the line.

"Who are you?" He smirked. He didn't see my rank under the body armor and fighting kit or the one covered by burlap strips on my helmet. He also missed the black oak leaf I had pinned on the center of my camouflaged, armored vest.

"I'm the commander of 1-22 Infantry, and these are my soldiers."

"Sorry, sir, I thought you were one of the men," he stumbled, paying me a great compliment. "Sir, we can't have hand grenades and such in here."

"Sergeant, my men just want something cold to drink," I reasoned. "There are no signs or rules that I can see, and I do believe my men know the difference between the enemy and you. You need not worry about them employing their weapons in a mess hall."

He tried to come back with something lame, but I cut him off. I told him that I would supervise my soldiers and we would soon be on our way. Thinking the worst was over, we navigated the line and sat down for a quick lunch. I started for the coolers to get a drink, when I was intercepted by a female sergeant first class.

"Sir, you need to clear your weapon," she demanded.

"My weapons are clear," I answered flatly with some irritation.

"Not your pistol." She pointed in a game of "gotcha."

"Sergeant, the pistol is clear." I contained myself.

"Sir, there is a magazine in the weapon," she continued with the confidence of a smart-ass.

"That doesn't mean the weapon is not clear," I answered, as I pulled the magazine out to avert more conflict. My soldiers had orders to keep magazines in their weapons at all times to counter any infiltrators who might slip into camp. I would never allow our guys to be shot up with no weapon or ammo at hand because of some stupid peacetime mentality.

"You need to go outside to clear it," she said, overstepping.

"And you need to get lost," I quipped. "I told you that the weapon is clear, and that means the weapon is clear. In all of my years, I never thought I would see the day a Sergeant First Class would deploy to war to serve as a milk monitor."

The sergeant stamped off, no doubt to find her boss. I took a cold drink from the cooler and had sat down to my plate when out came the head spoon, a warrant officer, to set me straight. I ambushed him before he could open his mouth.

Standing up, I said, "Chief, don't even start. You and I will just say things we will both regret. I'm sure you're a fine man and just trying to do your job. We are combat soldiers just looking to eat in peace and then we'll go. Now, please, leave us alone."

"All right, sir," he replied calmly and professionally, and then walked away.

We finished our meal, but the incident was far from over. That evening, the division Chief of Staff and my former brigade commander, Don Campbell, called me. "Steve, what happened at the mess hall today?"

I explained what happened, expecting to get flamed. Instead, Colonel Campbell simply said, "Stay away from the mess hall. You are too important out on the streets to have something like this slow you down. Keep away from it."

"Yes, sir," I acknowledged. "Does that apply to my men?"

"No. Just to you," he said calmly, only half concealing his amusement.

"Roger, sir." I acknowledged again.

"OK. I've made my call. I am sure we won't have any more trouble at the mess hall. You are doing great work out there. Keep it up."

The next day, signs with bold lettering appeared at the mess hall entry: NO CREW SERVED WEAPONS. NO HAND

GRENADES. NO AT4s, etc. They might as well have added, NO REGULARS. My soldiers asked me if I had seen the signs. Not thinking, I said, "Yes, how ridiculous. Those things just need to go away." A commander always has to be careful about what he says.

About 2:00 a.m. a few days later, I came in from patrol and availed myself of the facilities in the latrine connected to my private hooch. Behind the toilet rested the sign from the mess hall. I burst into laughter. When I went into ops center for an update, the soldiers all looked at me sheepishly as if they had no idea how it got there.

I did not set foot in the mess hall again until Thanksgiving morning. I had been invited to sing at General Odierno's prayer breakfast where he and Chaplain Gil Richardson encouraged us and articulated the many blessings for which we had to be thankful. In order to obey the contradictory orders to attend the prayer breakfast and to stay away from the mess hall, I had only coffee.

6. TYRANT

THE RACE

We took advantage of the Thanksgiving lull to further refine some of our intelligence with observation outposts and informants. During this time, we found evidence of weapons caches being brought in for future use. On November 28, we found another SA-7 anti-aircraft missile as well as 35 boxes of mortar fuses. We swept the same locations the following day and found more than five hundred 120mm mortar rounds still in their packing crates. This many mortar rounds would have been sufficient to level much of Tikrit. These munitions had been cleverly hidden in the municipal trash dump on the west side of the city.

December 2003 arrived with gentle rains that, no matter how they tried, failed to wash away the dust and filth of the land. The nasty weather reduced the number of attacks on our forces, but the attacks did not stop altogether. A roadside bomb planted on the main street in downtown Tikrit heralded the first of December. An alert but unarmed security guard observed as a man pulled up in a sedan and waddled to the median cradling a heavy five-liter vegetable oil tin in his arms. The car sped away, and the man ran into a back alley. The guard called the police who, in turn, called our forces. They also flagged down Captain Brad Boyd of C Company who was on patrol.

Brad and his men detonated the bomb. It exploded powerfully in the center of town. No one was harmed, and no major damage was done except to the brickwork on the median. Thank God for Tikrit's wide city streets and the alert security man who potentially saved the lives of both troops and civilians. I rewarded him with a new 9mm Glock 17 pistol for his efforts.

It was December 2, and information continued to flow. A hot tip produced some HOT missiles manufactured jointly by the French and Germans. They were wire-guided and similar to our TOW anti-tank missiles. The cache contained 20 of these powerful weapons. It was a relief to find them before they found us. The influx of anti-aircraft and anti-tank missiles unmistakably validated Saddam Hussein's ability to garner steady support and impressive weaponry.

We were now beginning to break through the street fighters and hit the big guys again. Our earlier pressure had caused them to strike back, but now we were inside their group. As we set about our tasks on December 3, John, Doug, and Kelly from the SOF team paid us a visit to discuss cell networks and a raid proposal. There was no doubt that we were winning the connect-the-dots game when we discovered the correlation between the Musslits and the Ghanis, Rashids, and Khatabs. John had intelligence that could possibly net Mohammed if he was being harbored by these friends and associates. As I listened to his proposition, Clay Bell chimed in with some interesting connections to various key players.

The scope of the raid we were planning was more massive than any attack we had ever attempted. It had to be. Mohammed could find refuge among a multitude of drivers, business associates, and brothers who were only too eager to hide him. We knew several of these players lived in Tikrit and its suburbs. The big question was this: Could we snare them all in a single massive raid?

I felt we could. John felt we could. The assets were available, and as long as there were no more than three or four groupings of targets, it would be possible to hit multiple structures in close proximity. Surprise would be crucial to success, but the very scope of the assault was bound to create some momentum. It would be a race against time to act on the information before the enemy's network could adjust and react. If we moved swiftly and remained alert, we could very possibly catch Mohammed al-Musslit firmly ensconced in some place of refuge with a false sense of security.

Our targets for the immediate raid would center on Mohammed's business partner who owned the cement store on Highway 1. His name was Thamir al-Asi. Mohammed, we learned, would frequently meet Thamir at his place of business to coordinate attacks, provide funds, and focus the insurgent effort. They also played cards and dominoes there.

"We also want to hit Musslit's brother, Birhan," revealed John. "We have a fix on his location. We don't know how much he is directly involved, but he is the money guy. He lives behind the government offices south of the hospital."

"Do you think Mohammed is there?" I asked John.

"I don't think so, but it's hard to say," he speculated. "I think he stays with friends in Tikrit. His wife and kids are here. Our informant, Bassam, who is the cousin of the Director of Justice, thinks he might be in Samarra."

"Wasn't Bassam Musslit's driver?" asked Clay Bell.

"That's the guy," confirmed John. "He's singing pretty good right now. We don't know where all of this is heading, but with what you've picked up on the networks in Cadaseeyah and with what we are getting, it is all starting to come together on finding Musslit. And speaking of drivers, we got a lead on his new one, a guy named Wa'ad Abdullah Haras. He lives here." John pointed as Doug oriented the satellite imagery of Tikrit that we used. "If we can grab him, we think we can find Musslit. That's why we want to hit all these targets at once."

"OK." I reviewed aloud. "So we've got al-Asi in the 40th Street neighborhood, Wa'ad's house is by the Birthday Palace, and Birhan's house is between the Fruit Loop Apartments and the hospital."

"That's pretty much it," John answered. "We're also trying to run down a location of Musslit's hooker. Nothing yet—but we do know Wa'ad has a sister in Cadaseeyah. We might go after that, too. Your information on the Rashids makes sense. It's in the exact same area," John continued. "Or we might do a follow-on raid based on what we get tonight."

"Maybe we hit even more, John." I added. "If we are going to go after Wa'ad's house in Rashid's neighborhood, let's take out the Khader targets as well. They're right there. We've been tracking them since October, and they're connected to the same people." Clay Bell and Bryan Luke showed him where Abdel Khader, Kamil al-Awayes, Ayman Hameed Bardee, and Thamer Jasim's houses were.

"Sounds good to me, but we may need to get confirmation on Wa'ad's sister's house and other possible locations first. We'll take Thamir al-Asi and the driver but could use some of your guys to help secure the area," John informed. "You got the Cadaseeyah targets, and if you could take Birhan that would be great. And any targets that spring up we'll just regroup as needed."

"'Comanche' goes with you, John," I informed. "I'll put 'Gator' on Birhan. 'Cobra' will hit the Cadaseeyah targets with 'Cougar.'" We set the time for late evening on the 3rd, and the raiding would continue into the early morning of the 4th.

What unfolded that night was a mixed success in our minds

but later proved to be so much more. We couldn't find Musslit's driver, Wa'ad, who was the main objective of the raid, though we did nab his father and son. Maybe that would help. Still, we did get Birhan Ibrahim Omar al-Musslit, the third Musslit brother of Mohammed in as many weeks. We found him at home with his wife and daughter. We also found an interesting diary kept by his daughter detailing some of Birhan's activity since the invasion.

In the north, Brad's "Cobras" and Jon's "Cougars" searched a possible Wa'ad house but found nothing. The same could not be said of Thamir al-Asi. John's men and my scouts under Chris Morris caught Thamer along with his two sons, Amir and Ahmed.

After hours of searching these targets, a spinoff developed. John now wanted to search Asi's cement business on Highway 1. No one had been there since curfew the night before, and it was all locked up. I called Mark Stouffer's men to cordon the area while John and I set up shop in the parking lot. My men pulled security as his went in with crowbars and a tactical rotary saw to use on a safe they had spotted. Since al-Asi and Birhan were financiers, we could only guess what might be secured inside.

An ancient security guard was found in the building. John had an interrogator on his team named Eric who began to question the old man. His connection with Mohammed al-Musslit was readily apparent. Inside, crowbars smashed, doors popped open, and saw blades whirled. Out came one of John's SOF guys cradling a small safe. As quickly as we had ransacked the cement store, we tore down the operation and left. Now it was time to connect the dots to the targets we had captured.

We were exhausted. While the raids had lasted nearly nine hours, our men had been patrolling and raiding for more than twenty-four consecutive hours. Yet, we pressed forward. As the day unfolded, we were inundated with an abundance of information. Our teams regrouped and refit, firm in our conviction that hours mattered. Our response and alertness to details mattered. Our ability to quickly reach exposed targets mattered. The excitement fueled us, driving us to what we had been pursuing for six months.

As the SOF guys worked through the new captives, Colonel Hickey and I reviewed the bidding ourselves. Hickey was pleased with the scope of the night's raid, which he had dubbed "Raider Forest." Hickey joined us on the Birhan capture and was taking in all of the intel that we were, using his battalions to assist John's SOF team with potential follow on raids in Bayjii and Samarra. Thamir al-Asi and his cement store certainly filled in a lot of blanks for us: the ties to the money, the roadside bombs, and the rendezvous point for covert conspiracy. It made perfect sense in retrospect but left me with a deep sense of frustration. Why hadn't we seen it earlier? The enemy had been meeting right under our noses, hiding in plain sight.

As the swamp continued to recede, there was an escalation of unusual events while we focused intently on Mohammed al-Musslit and his driver, Wa'ad. Captain Mitch Carlisle, one of our battle captains, expressed it most succinctly: "Every day in Iraq is the strangest day of my life." December 4 most assuredly fell into that category. We received a call from our higher headquarters that a soldier's mother was at the division gate of the massive palace compound. We were told she had traveled from the States representing an anti-war group and had demanded to speak to her daughter. It was being covered by a number of reporters. I said, "You've got to be kidding!" They were not.

The soldier was from one of the divisional support units. We were instructed to ignore her mother and the reporters should we happen upon them in town. As the mother and cohort were not demonstrating, we did. I began to imagine a weird exchange between soldier and mother: "Mom, would you please go home? You are embarrassing me in front of my friends!" I never cease to be amazed at human interaction. It was one of the most bizarre episodes in Iraq I can remember.

Even as we went about routine combat patrols and raid preparations and dealt with an occasional off-the-wall distraction, we were primed to go to the next level. Wa'ad Abdullah Haras had dodged the net we cast the night before and might still be in the Tikrit area. John's team was following leads to Samarra. I received a note from John on December 5, 2003, as we were unable to meet face-to-face. In it, he laid out some information gleaned from Thamir al-Asi and especially his son, Amir, who was apparently working hand in hand with Bassam:

Gents,

Here is the latest on the interrogations . . . on Thamir Al Asi (and sons), Birhan Ibrahim Omar Al Muslit, and Bassam Latif: Bassam and Thamir's oldest son, Amir, are now cooperating fully as they now have realized that if they do not help us capture Mohammed, then they will never get out of prison. Amir ran the bulk of his father's businesses for Mohammed and is aware of all of Mohammed's business and Fedayeen operational contacts.

Birhan, John explained, would be sent to Baghdad because he would not cooperate. He confirmed what we already knew about Mohammed Ibrahim Omar al-Musslit's brothers and cousins being in charge of various parts of the country and organizing insurgent efforts. After Rudman's death, we had assumed that Mohammed was in charge, but we now knew that he had been in charge all along. Rudman had, in fact, worked for him. It seemed likely, with the ring closing around Tikrit, that Mohammed might have taken flight to Samarra. John's note continued:

Mohammed's partner/confidant is a guy named Sabah (last name unknown) aka "Abu Ayman." Allegedly, Sabah is in charge of the Fedayeen in Samarra. Amir and Bassam are both certain that Mohammed Ibrahim is now staying at Sabah's house in Samarra. They also stated, however, that Mohammed rented a house in Samarra in Sabah's name, for an unknown purpose and neither Amir nor Bassam know the location of the rental home.

John wanted to find Sabah and the house believed to be rented by Mohammed's brother, Sulwan, where Mohammed was purportedly staying. They would have to do a reconnaissance on the houses, which would take some time. John also wanted to keep the pressure on Wa'ad who, most likely, was somewhere in Tikrit.

If we end up with a dry hole tomorrow night, we want to assault every known location of Wa'ad Abdullah Haras. We will do the [recon] of all of the locations in Tikrit/Cadaseeyah during the day on 8 Dec and hit them that night at 082400 Local. . . . We plan on hitting Wa'ad's sister's house in Cadaseeyah and would like 1-22 to hit the aunt's house in Tikrit. Amir and Bassam believe they can convince Wa'ad to give up the info on Mohammed within an hour of his capture.

There was much at stake and much to accomplish in a short amount of time. Bryan Luke, Clay Bell, and I set about looking over the Wa'ad targets to make sure that we were ready. We also had some leads of our own that we would pursue on the Khader and Rashid families to help get at Wa'ad and we acted on a tip that Munther Idham Ibrahim al-Hasan was in Cadaseeyah. He was Saddam's cousin, and we had already captured three of his brothers. We raided several more houses the night of December 6 with some success but did not catch Munther.

That same night, John's team was partially successful in Samarra. They did not find Sabah's house, but they did nab his brother, Luay. They also found Mohammed's rental house, but Mohammed was not there. Still, they did not come up completely empty-handed. They found Mohammed's son, Musslit Mohammed Ibrahim al-Musslit, which was exciting news. They also found a stash of cash totaling $1.9 million. We were definitely on Mohammed's trail. He had fewer and fewer places in which to move about freely.

THE BOY

December 7 dawned with more combat patrols and more raid planning. The night before, Command Sergeant Major Martinez and I paused long enough to light a Christmas tree in our headquarters. The tree was graciously provided by the Iraqi governor's staff and was presented to us by the Governor, General Abdullah, and the Governor's security chief, Colonel Jassim. We were deeply moved; the gesture flew in the face of the concept that Iraqis would never accept our friendship. We sang carols and had a generally good time. We ended the lighting ceremony by singing "Feliz Navidad" as more than one third of our battalion was Hispanic. With only a moment's reprieve from the demands of war, it was back to the grind and the evening raids.

Even so, it was nice to think about Christmas, even if briefly. There were still parts of the world that cared about holidays and delighted in the details of what to buy and cook and wear. My prayer was that we would soon have a special Christmas gift of our own.

As the day unfolded, we began getting tips on the Khatab family, the one from which the Ace of Diamonds, Abid Mahmood came. Despite having scattered Mohammed al-Musslit's network and the upper tier leaders, it had made minimal impact on the trigger pullers if the day's activity was any indication. A policeman, a relative of Bassam Latif, was on patrol when a hand grenade was tossed into the back of his police pickup. Fortunately, he was not hurt. Our own patrols found and eliminated three more roadside bombs. The bomb stuffed in a wheat sack on Highway 1 had two 120mm mortar rounds capped with plastic explosives. It was powerful enough to have killed anything within a 250-foot radius. Bomb sweeps were dangerous work, and I was thankful that we continued to find so many of them before the enemy was able to bring their evil plans to fruition.

Jon Cecalupo's "Cougars" in Mazhem and Cadaseeyah reported seeing the remnants of the volcanic car that blew up a Khatab and a Hussein on November 9. When the car hit a bump in the road, the bomb they were transporting detonated prematurely (or on cue, depending on one's perspective). I decided to pursue the leads and ordered Chris Morris' scouts to run two targets to ground to find the connections to the Crispy Khatab. While yielding little, the enemy could not miss the clear message sent to them: we could be everywhere all the time.

The success of recent raids loosened the lips of many locals. Seeing known Saddam sympathizers thinned out, they became quick to distance themselves from their erstwhile neighbors. John and his special ops team, as well my battalion of Regulars, began to receive a flood of information on Mohammed al-Hadooshi. While Hadooshi had taken a backseat in priority in recent months, we were always interested in him because of his pre-war position as Saddam's personal secretary. Most of the information turned out to be useless, but we did get some critical information tying together a family whose last name was Ali.

The Alis were not strangers to us. Early in the war they skirted along the periphery, making contact with Americans through their in-laws. The most prominent of the in-laws was a former decorated general named Thamar Sultan. There had been many meetings with General Sultan and fish bakes at his palatial home in Mazhem on the west bank of the Tigris. A raid on his home once produced more than 250 AK-47s from an outbuilding and six tons of plastic explosives from his front yard.

Sultan claimed that he had been working covertly with an undercover organization and was to serve as a link between Sunnis and Kurds for an uprising against Saddam in the north as our troops came in from Turkey. He claimed that the weapons had been stockpiled for that purpose. He knew too many details to be a total liar, even supplying names and descriptions of individuals with whom he professed to work. When we cross-referenced his association to various organizations, we were told to leave him alone. We declined, however, to return the AK-47s or the explosives.

Sultan and a man named Dr. Sami Sharif Shehab Ahmad, a former Deputy Minister of Oil under Saddam Hussein who had been educated in Houston, Texas, had become well known to Mark Woempner when he first led our battalion north of Tikrit in April and early May of 2003. "Dr. Sam" and General Sultan were among the first Iraqis with whom I had conversations upon arriving in May. Though the relationships I maintained with them were by no means close, Sultan and Sharif were quite well known to us. What was not well known to us then, we were about to discover in a few days.

After pooling our leads and coordinating them with the flow of intelligence coming from the SOF team, we had another breakthrough on December 8 regarding the trigger pullers. We compared our information with John's special ops info on Wa'ad via e-mail and went after the Khader targets discussed earlier. We raided four targets in Cadaseeyah as Brad's "Cobras" and Jon's

"Cougars" nabbed Kamil al-Awayes, Ayman Hameed Bardee, and Thamer Jasim Mohammed Ali. Abdel Khader and Wa'ad Abdullah Haras were not found, but we detained eight insurgents and unearthed vast quantities of explosive-making materials, including several radio-controlled cars used for their electronic parts.

The next day we gained a critical lead in the race to find Mohammed al-Musslit. A teenaged boy presented himself at the front gate of Colonel Hickey's headquarters between Tikrit and Auja on the west bank of the Tigris. The soldiers on guard were alert enough to grab an interpreter rather than just shoo the boy away. It was not long before Colonel Hickey decided to talk to this young man himself.

The boy claimed to know where some important people were hiding. His information was specific enough that Hickey decided to believe him—not only because he was a boy but also because he claimed to know where people were right now. Following our dictum "If you do nothing, you get nothing," Colonel Hickey promptly radioed me with orders to raid the farm in question.

Since the farm was to the south and west of Tikrit proper, I called on Mark Stouffer's "Gators." We hashed out the details, and Mark set out for the farm with Joe Filmore in tow to translate. The raid was enormously successful and set in motion some very surprising links.

By evening, we had captured Thaier Amin Ali and some of his other cronies at the farm. As Joe Filmore pored over the information and questioned them, it was obvious that something was up. In the search, we found pictures of the captives with persons of interest whom we had been hunting for six months. The ties went so much deeper than snapshots.

Thaier's father, known as Haji Amin Ali because of his trek to Mecca, had once owned a farm on the east bank of the Tigris River, near the village of Ad Dawr and across the river from Auja.

Apparently, Thaier's father had helped Saddam escape following his failed attempt to kill Iraqi Prime Minister Abdul Karim Qassim in 1959. As a young Saddam was in hiding, Iraqi forces closed around that farm near Ad Dawr to arrest him, but he swam the river and was given a horse on which he rode off into the sunset to become the future tyrant of Iraq. Each year, Saddam would re-enact the swim with his peers. Little could we know in just a few days the significance of that very location.

Saddam had always treated the Ali family with favor out of gratitude for the help that Haji Ali had given him in 1959. That simple good deed catapulted the Ali family into the inner circle of trustees. Thaier Amin Ali and his brother, Mahsin, were also very close to Mohammed al-Musslit. So close, in fact, was their association that Thaier and Mohammed co-owned a gravel business. Mohammed had hidden five of his automobiles on Thaier's farm when the war erupted. Further, Thaier's sisters were married to Mohammed al-Hadooshi, General Thamar Sultan and Dr. Sami Sharif's brother. Thaier's oldest brother, Khalid, had inherited the mantle of his father's namesake as "Haji Amin Ali" and was living in Mazhem, home to another brother, General Sultan, and Sami Sharif.

As if the Ali family reach were not long enough already, we learned that Gazwan Nazhem Sharif Shehab Ahmed, the son of Sami Sharif's brother, worked as a translator at the local office of the Coalition Provisional Authority in Tikrit. We immediately notified the CPA as we suspected Gazwan of tipping off the insurgency to the recent inbound VIP helicopter flights. I was taken aback by the information we were drilling through. Still, every new vein seemed to be connected to the same families. Once again, the enemy was hidden in plain sight until we could unravel the big "ball of yarn," as Colonel Hickey once put it.

The result of Colonel Hickey's intuition to raid the farm on

December 9, based on the boy's tip, would prove critical. John and his SOF men were already on the hunt for Thaier's brother, Mahsin. They believed that Mohammed al-Musslit might now be in Baghdad. The information Thaier and Mohammed's son, Musslit, were able to provide pointed to a very narrow group of targets among which Mohammed al-Musslit could be hiding. John updated Colonel Hickey and the rest of us on a follow-on raid by other special ops men in Baghdad:

> *Gents,*
>
> *Our guys in B-dad caught two . . . who are still undergoing inter-rogations . . .*
>
> *Nasar Farhan Jasim: This name is an alias, another detainee says his real name is Mahsin Amin Ali . . . he is a good friend of Moham-med Ibrahim Omar Al Musslit's . . . is from Mazhem village. Mah-sin's brother ended up giving up two additional target locations, one about 20 km SSE of Tikrit where Mohammed Ibrahim's brother uses a farm as a safehouse and another location in Samarra where Mo-hammed Ibrahim's girlfriend, a hooker, lives. 1-22 IN just rolled up Mahsin's brother, Thaier, in a raid last night and we are questioning him now.*
>
> *Qusay Shehab Ahmed: some fisherman at the wrong place at the wrong time.*
>
> *Will keep you advised when we get something actionable. John*

At the time, John believed the first guy was Thaier's brother when, in fact, he was Nasar Farhan Jasim, a cousin of Mohammed Khader. Apparently, he was related to Thamer Jasim whom we rolled up trying to find a Khader in Cadaseeyah on the same night of the Baghdad raid. The second captive of the Baghdad raid, the fisherman, was actually connected to the Shehab Ahmed family information we were deciphering from Thaier's raid. Even he was part of the network.

By December 10, we had plowed through almost more information than we could handle. It was like getting a crate of Cracker Jacks; it was more than enough to feed you and nice to have, but you really just wanted the prize. We had probed every Mohammed al-Musslit enabler in the Tikrit area. Unless we developed new leads from recent raids, we would have to pursue Tier 2 targets. Clay Bell and Bryan Luke had put a couple of these targets on hold while we were chasing Mohammed al-Musslit. Now, there were no more places in Tikrit to search for Mohammed. We had connected as many dots as we could to try to find him. It would be up to John's SOF men to focus on the Baghdad leads with information garnered from the combined raids of the last few days.

I deemed it best to keep the momentum building and ordered the Tier 2 raids to proceed anyway. Even if I had not, Colonel Hickey would have done nothing less. It was not uncommon for trigger-puller raids to net important links to the big guy networks. If nothing else, it would discourage the enemy from throwing a counterpunch while we were closing in on them. Consequently, we hit Mohammed Abdul Karim Waheeb and his brother, Mahmood, in south-central Tikrit that night. We found a small amount of potentially explosive material in their house in a residential neighborhood, and I was prompted to call in the mine detectors to thoroughly search the yards and garden.

Reporters at the scene were astonished at the raid because it initially appeared to be yet another example of Americans raiding homes in the middle of the night, hauling innocents from their beds while their women and children huddled weeping in the corner. When the house search produced nothing other than large quantities of cash, you could see the sympathetic looks given to the two brothers and their families. When we started digging out vast amounts of explosives, weapons, and ammunition from the yards and garden, their outlook changed.

"Colonel, what do you make of this?" asked Robin Pomeroy from Reuters.

"Well, it is not very often we get the middle guys, the guys that supply the street fighters," I explained. "These are the guys that are connected to the top tier but supply weapons to cells," I continued. "We are draining the swamp at both the high end and the low. It is starting to get pretty good . . . as good as it was in July and August."

"What do you make of the types of things you have pulled out of the ground?" reporters continued.

"It is a wide variety of items. It is like a Fedayeen candy shop, where you could find almost anything you were looking for," I tried to illustrate. One reporter estimated there was enough weaponry to launch fifty attacks. The candy shop quotes went around the world that night. I was just content to pull the stuff from our little corner of it.

Any type of attack could have been planned with the variety of weapons we found buried in the front yard of that filthy little house on the outskirts of Tikrit. We seized roadside bombs, Pepsi can bombs, RPG launchers with rockets, two different and complete mortar systems (one in the outhouse), small arms, ammunition, grenades, explosives, and radio-controlled devices for bombs. The Waheeb brothers denied all knowledge of the find, claiming that the Iraqi Army must have planted it all there. Oh, I did not think of that! Of course, our own Army issues the Mark 1 Pepsi Can Bomb. And I would never have noticed a large caliber mortar system in my own outhouse. My disgust for the enemy was reaching a peak. The sooner we could knock them out, the sooner Iraq could find its true potential.

FAT MAN, FIREFIGHTS, AND FIREFIGHTING

The key to Iraq's true potential was to sever its ties to Saddam Hussein forever. With sons Uday and Qusay (and even 14-year-old grandson Mustafa) dead, Saddam remained the only direct link to the past. In him was little hope for the future. Even so, every day he remained at large bolstered the Iraqi belief that his power and regime still existed. To find him was to offer Iraq a clean break with that sordid past. After months of analyzing intelligence, pursuing leads, and looking under rocks, it appeared that there was only one man who could lead us to him—The Fat Man.

Apart from Saddam himself, Mohammed al-Musslit had been the primary focus of our efforts, though little of it was known to the outside world, including most Coalition military leaders and intelligence chiefs inside Iraq. At the ground level, ours had been a strategy of striking at Saddam's support, chipping away at the base of his pedestal by hitting the Special Security Officers and Fedayeen leaders in the group of followers closest to Saddam. We had targeted the Musslit family as early as May 2003. By June, we were tracking named individuals with sets of photos.

We knew the tiered strategy was working when important gains were made in June and July. Yet, with the exception of Saddam's personal bodyguard, Adnan Abdullah Abid al-Musslit, and a few Ibrahims and Khatabs in the lineage of al-Musslits collected along the way, there was little to show for it in the following months. Nearly all of our captures had been enablers. Most of the enablers had been disabled by this time. Only the primary players were left on the field. We were certain that Mohammed would be found in a matter of time. It is impossible to explain how we all sensed and felt it. Still, even with high expectations, we realized that time was against us.

Mohammed Ibrahim Omar al-Musslit was an elusive figure.

Little was known about how this man came to be so trusted by Saddam. In retrospect, it should have been obvious that he was a close confidant of Saddam. A review of the last public footage of Saddam in Baghdad on 9 April 2003 revealed some clues. Playing to the cheering crowd, "the benevolent dictator" perched himself defiantly atop a white Oldsmobile in which he would later flee. The man that jumped up beside him with a pistol to protect him was none other than Mohammed al-Musslit. His trustworthiness was total, and his connections were immense.

As John's team of special operators focused their efforts on the lead to locate Mohammed Khader in Baghdad, thereby hoping to grab Mohammed al-Musslit, we received a tip about an emergency Fedayeen organizational meeting south of Auja in the town of Oynot. The tip had copious details, too many to ignore. I sent Mark Stouffer's "Gators" to carry out the raid. Six men belonging to a cell operating between Samarra and Tikrit led by one Mohammed Jabar Mahai were captured. He was a trigger puller with connections not entirely clear but loosely connected to Saddam. In addition to the cell leader, his two brothers, Abdul and Sofian, and three of their insurgent peers were captured. One of those peers, Arkan Hardin Ali, was the son of the bodyguard of Saddam's half-brother, Sabawi.

Also confiscated in the raid was a bounty of small arms, grenades, ammunition, and papers. One case of submachine gun ammunition had been concealed under the bedding of a baby crib—complete with baby! Our soldiers left the baby with its mother but seized the ammunition and the very nice PPSH-41 Russian submachine gun to which it belonged. The weapon, dated 1943, was in museum-quality condition. Later we took it for a spin, much to the pleasure of all who got to fire it.

John's SOF men were closing in on Khader after dragging information from his cousin, Nasar Farhan Jasim. They planned a coordinated raid focusing on a house in Bagdad belonging to one of Khader's uncles. We awaited word of the raid and continued our combat patrols. Still nothing.

Faris Sahim Shehab and his cousin, Sami Muhad Shehab, were enraged. The Americans had been far too active, and nothing, it seemed, was being done. The strategy of standoff attacks and roadside bombs was not working. Perhaps the older men had lost their courage. True, there had been some setbacks in the summer when they tried to fight the Americans toe-to-toe, but surely, they were not invincible. After all, it appeared that the occupiers were becoming overly confident. They were all over the streets day after day just walking about as if they owned them. The soldiers would be easy targets if surprised.

After seeing their countrymen and even their own family members struck down at the hands of the Americans, they decided to mete out a measure of justice for Iraq. Full of anger and Tuborg lager and armed with AK-47s, Faris and Sami hit the streets in their late-model, black Toyota, waiting for an opportunity to materialize. They would strike quickly, race away undetected, and arrive safely home before curfew.

On the evening of December 12, Tikrit was still fairly active. Our soldiers discovered another roadside bomb on Highway 1 and blew it up with gunfire. Raids in the last 48 hours had yielded a harvest of cell leaders and weapons from the city proper, down to Auja, Oynot, and Samarra. The trigger pullers were in disarray, desperately trying to reorganize after losing their chain of command.

It seemed to me that the insurgents, in their desperation, were taking more risks so I ordered increased patrols in the city. Even the engineers were patrolling the Tigris River in their bridge boats. Our mortars were still conducting harassment and interdiction fires to keep enemy mortar fire and rocketeers at bay. Brad and Mark had their company patrols out, and Jon had tank observation posts and ambushes out in Cadaseeyah. I circulated among all these points.

In the heart of Tikrit, near the upscale 40th Street district where so much action had been seen, Staff Sergeant German Sanchez led his 2nd Squad of "Cobras" from 2nd Platoon, C Company, 1-22 Infantry on an evening patrol just before curfew. Zigzagging his soldiers on both sides of the road like the points of a lazy letter "W," Sanchez posted Sergeant Michael Trujillo's A-Team at the nose of the formation and Specialist Jaime Garza's B-Team behind him. They were heading south from the Birthday Palace into the neighborhood immediately to the south of what we called the "Evil Mosque," otherwise known as the Saddam Mosque.

As the last soldiers of B-Team made the turn, a black car was spotted moving slowly in the distance with its lights out. Sergeant Trujillo watched with surprise as it suddenly began to speed toward them. Instinctively, he locked his eyes onto the driver's side of the car to determine what was happening. As he did, gunfire sailed toward the squad from the window of the car.

Faris Sahim Shehab saw the first of the American soldiers walking down the dark alley. He and Sami sat quietly observing their actions. They seemed to just saunter along casually down the street, hardly an imposing threat. The opportunity that they had been waiting for had just presented itself. If they maneuvered up the street inconspicuously, they could race past the Americans, spray them with fire, and be down the street and around the corner before they could react. Faris also had the advantage of surprise. He was on the left side, but his cousin, Sami, was actually driving in the right-hand-drive vehicle. The soldiers would not know what hit them.

Advancing at normal speed, they passed the first few soldiers.

This was it! Faris leveled his AK-47 on the edge of the left window and blasted away as Sami drove at full throttle down the street.

Sergeant Trujillo couldn't believe his eyes. The guy had brazenly propped up an AK-47 and fired at his team! Instinctively, he spun around and squeezed off six shots at the driver. He might be shooting, but that guy was not going to get away if he could help it.

When Sami Shehab saw Faris shoot at the Americans, he was filled with adrenaline and completely focused on the end of the street when glass and ricochets began to fly around him. The crack of Faris's AK-47 was replaced with the sharp crack of enemy fire. Something was terribly wrong. Faris jerked violently and slumped against the dash, his head shattered and bleeding. His rifle dropped inside the car. Terrified, Sami stopped the car, shoved the door open and put up his hands.

With weapon raised and aimed, Sergeant Trujillo fixed his attention on the stopped car and the occupants. That our soldiers didn't shoot the driver is a testament to their discipline. "Standish, Arispe, check 'em out!" ordered Trujillo.

"Roger, Sergeant!" replied Private First Class Jason Standish as he approached what they believed to be the driver's side of the car. Private Brian Sorrels went toward the guy on the other side.

"Sorrels, pull security at twelve o'clock," ordered Trujillo.

"Roger, Sergeant," acknowledged Private Brian Sorrels, one of the newest members of the platoon.

Staff Sergeant Sanchez then ordered Specialist Garza's team to pull perimeter security. Specialists William Gilstrap, Jason Klepacz, and Private Joseph Morris rounded out the perimeter as Standish dragged the bloody Faris from the car about twelve feet into the street, kicking his AK-47 aside. Private Abel Arispe moved on Sami and ordered him facedown as the soldiers searched and cuffed him.

"Red 6, this is Red 2, over," radioed Staff Sergeant Sanchez.

"Red 6, over," replied First Lieutenant Jason Lojka.

"Contact, on Kansas, one enemy wounded, one detained, over," reported Sanchez.

"This is Cobra 6, monitored and en route," intercepted Captain Brad Boyd. After getting the details, Boyd then switched radios and called me. "Regular 6, Cobra 6, over."

"Regular 6, over," I answered.

"Roger, sir, we got contact near 40th Street, one street to the east. One enemy WIA and one detained, over," Brad informed. He relayed the details and then requested media support. We both felt it would be enlightening for the press to see that the enemy was still intent on destruction and that our troops were up to the task. After grabbing a few interested reporters from the press pool, my command group soldiers, Bryan Luke, and I headed for the site.

On arrival, I was amazed at the outcome. Sergeant Trujillo's marksmanship in the dark, at a moving target, and under fire was exemplary. Of the six shots fired, four hit their mark—the head of the enemy who fired at the squad. Not a single one of our soldiers was hurt. They were all pulling security.

In the street lay the enemy, flat on his back in a pool of his own bodily fluids, most of them oozing from his head. The soldiers had attempted first aid, but with four shots to the head, it didn't take a doctor to know he was a dead man. Faintly breathing, he lay splayed in his underwear on the cold street. In moments, he exhaled his last breath.

His driver, his own cousin, Sami, lay facedown on the sidewalk with Private Arispe pulling guard. The driver's legs were shaking violently with fear. We pulled him to his feet, and Joe Filmore questioned him. He claimed they were just celebrating from a wedding party. Yeah, right. Perhaps a marriage with death, I thought. As we would soon decipher, these enemy were a part of the Shehab family. Their rashness had cost them dearly.

"Colonel, why is the man lying naked in the street?" asked Robin Pomeroy from Reuters.

"The soldiers attempted first aid, but there was nothing they could do."

"The driver stated they were coming from a wedding party. What do you make of that?" the reporters asked.

"We know the difference between a wedding party and this," I answered. "Driving through the streets firing an AK-47 isn't a wedding, it's a funeral."

We secured the area as the Iraqi police arrived to collect the body and a wrecker arrived to collect the vehicle. The fire department washed the blood and fluids from the streets. With the ordeal concluded, Brad's men resumed their patrols.

While Brad Boyd's men were taking life in the city center, Mark Stouffer's men would save it in the south part of town. A man hoping to make it home before curfew was driving a bit too fast to negotiate a curve and lost control of his car. His car jumped the curb, spun, and hit a light pole, which fell and crushed the top of the car. The driver had been ejected and was pinned beneath the back of the car.

Captain Stouffer's command convoy and the battalion snipers were making their way northward on Highway 1 toward the center of the city when they observed the crushed car centered high on the median. Flames were leaping from the engine. Uncertain of the cause of the commotion, the soldiers deployed for action. One of several Iraqi bystanders reported in broken English that a man was trapped inside. He directed their attention to a man they had pulled from the car and then to a pair of legs protruding from the back of the car, pinned by the fuel tank. Determining it to be a car accident, Mark ordered his men to barricade the highway and grab the fire extinguishers.

"Hey, Sergeant Owens, there might be someone in the car!" called out Specialist Matt Summers to Staff Sergeant Brad Owens of the Sniper Squad. After talking to the bystander, Summers ran to the car and checked the man for a pulse. He was still alive. Fuel appeared to be leaking from the engine and gravity was slowly drawing it toward the rear of the car. With flames spreading to the interior, there was little time to effect a rescue. Summers could see the man laboring to breathe, but the car was crushing the life from him.

"Hey, guys, give us a hand!" called out Owens. Staff Sergeant Cesar Tenorio, Sergeant Ronald Wycoff, and Specialist Barrye Saylor raced to the car. What they saw was bad.

"We gotta get this pole off the top or we will never get him out," pointed out Specialist Summers. "I tried to lift him, but he won't budge."

The heat was searing. With no regard for his own safety, Summers returned to the man as Wycoff, Owens, and Saylor worked to raise the car. The heat was unbearable. While Sergeant Tenorio ran for his aid bag, the other soldiers decided to use the broken portion of the pole as a lever to hoist the back of the car.

Flames had entirely engulfed the interior of the car by that time and fuel dripped toward the pinned man. With superhuman exertion and ignoring the pain of the heat, the soldiers managed to budge the car just enough for Summers to extract the victim. They all immediately cleared the car.

"Keep going, this thing is going to blow!" warned Owens as the car popped and hissed. Mark and the others were already trying to extinguish the fire, but the heat was too severe to contain. After Owens and his group dragged the man to safety about forty feet away, the car exploded and was completely consumed.

We sent an alert to the Iraqi police and the fire department. Brad Boyd's other patrols joined Mark's men to assist with security as the police and an ambulance recovered the injured. The fire department, already actively washing the streets from the C Company firefight, doused the fire. Our men left the scene in the capable hands of the Iraqis who had the debris cleared by morning.

For their bravery, Owens, Tenorio, Wycoff, Summers, and Saylor would later be awarded the Soldiers Medal for disregarding their own lives to save another. In the two hours before midnight, our soldiers in Tikrit had taken life and saved it. Concurrently, to the south in Baghdad, John's special operations troops were executing a raid to apprehend Mohammed Khader and, hopefully, the Fat Man.

PHONE CALLS

While our evening would be fraught with action, it would not be so for Colonel Jim Hickey, who was restless. Something was troubling him. In a rare move, he did not go out on his normal patrols but instead told his Command Sergeant Major, Larry Wilson, to stand down the command group. Wilson knew that the colonel was definitely preoccupied with something.

Hickey's mind turned over and over. He scrutinized all the information unearthed in the last two weeks, but he could not put his finger on the missing puzzle piece. He knew that Mohammed al-Musslit's apprehension was imminent, but he also knew that, at the moment, it was out of our hands and he could do nothing more to make it happen. Musslit was the key. Perhaps there was one other person who knew Saddam's location, but he, Izzat al-Duri, remained at large. Hickey decided to get some rest that would surely be needed in the coming days.

On the morning of December 13, Hickey awoke surprisingly

refreshed. Keeping to his back office rather than the command post, he tended to a multitude of little things for which a commander of several thousand troops is responsible. At approximately ten o'clock that morning, his private phone line rang. It was John.

"Hey, sir. Did you get my e-mail?" asked John.

"No, I haven't been where I could check it," Colonel Hickey answered, as the message would have been on a secure network in his command post.

"We got him," John said abruptly.

"Who?" queried Colonel Hickey, discerning it could be Musslit or maybe someone even better.

"Musslit," John clarified. "Last night in Baghdad," he said matter-of-factly. "He was with Mohammed Khader. We didn't know we had him at first, but one of our interrogators broke him and was able to figure out it was him. He puts Saddam somewhere in Tikrit."

"You know what this means?" urged Colonel Hickey. "It means we are doing a raid tonight to capture HVT#1."

"You think so, sir?" asked John.

"How much information do we have, and how much chance is there we can get what we need?" followed Colonel Hickey.

"I don't know, sir . . . maybe twenty percent," speculated John.

"We've got to get him up here ASAP." Hickey's mind began to race. "We've got to get forces prepared for action now. He's got to know where Saddam is. We don't have much time."

"Roger, sir," John agreed. "We can move him to Tikrit right away."

Immediately after talking with John, Colonel Hickey began to alert his units. I received a phone call on the secure and point-to-point digital tactical satellite phone. This information was not for the radio.

"Steve, John's guys got the Fat Man last night," informed Hickey when I answered.

"Holy cow!" I replied. "That's great news!"

"I want to get all your forces ready," instructed Hickey. "Pull out everything you have and have it standing by."

"Roger, sir," I acknowledged as I continued to listen.

"I will request some additional force from the CG to replace your troops in the city later, maybe Dave Poirier's MPs," he explained, intending to request this support from General Odierno. "But I want everything available."

"Roger, sir," I replied.

"Keep the lid on this," cautioned Hickey. "We've got to proceed quickly, but we must keep this very quiet. I've got a meeting with the Governor and Sheik Mahmood that I intend to still go to, to give the appearance that everything is normal. Alert your commanders, but keep this close hold."

"Roger, sir. We'll be ready for whatever you need," I answered.

"John says Musslit gave Saddam's whereabouts somewhere in Tikrit," Hickey continued. "We're going to get him up here and try to pinpoint that location. I've sent Brian Reed over to John's compound to do the initial coordination. I am also bringing Dez Bailey down from the desert west of Bayjii. It will take him a couple of hours to make that trip, but I don't think we'll have anything before then. In the meantime, get everything ready and I'll get back to you."

"Wilco, sir," I answered, and with that, Colonel Hickey began a myriad of preparations. I hung up the receiver and grabbed Mike Rauhut and Bryan Luke. I then called my company commanders together to relay the situation. We had been through this so many times before but never with Mohammed al-Musslit providing the information. The sense of excitement mounting cannot be fully expressed as we set our own task force in motion.

By noon, Mohammed al-Musslit was seated in a back room of the small Water Palace complex where John's SOF team was headquartered. He had been flown from Baghdad, under heavy guard. An intense interrogation began to extract Saddam's exact location from him. Major Stan Murphy, Chief Bryan Gray, and First Lieutenant Angela Santana of Colonel Hickey's intelligence staff observed the special operations interrogation team. They listened for subtle clues and links as they were intimately familiar with the upper tier family networks. An hour passed.

At John's Water Palace compound, Brian Reed and John conferred about the facts known to date. Musslit established Saddam on a farm near Tikrit. It was still unclear whether the farm was on the east or west side of the river, but they believed it to be south of Tikrit. Expecting Saddam to be well guarded, Brian and John worked out the force needed to strike, cordon, and, if necessary, fight. It was certainly going to require more forces than a typical raid.

If perhaps 20 or 30 men guarded Saddam, it could be assumed that they would be armed with RPGs and automatic weapons. Armored vehicles would be needed. Colonel Hickey's entire brigade was either tanks or my mechanized infantry, so that would not be a problem. John's SOF team had special armored vehicles available and their own air support as well. The basic troop plan was taking shape. But how vast an area would we need to cordon?

John understood that the key would be finding the exact location. Even cooperative Iraqis were inept at reading aerial and satellite photographs or maps. They were just not accustomed to visualizing things from that perspective. Close tactical reconnaissance was the only way to pinpoint the farm and that meant Musslit would have to accompany the reconnaissance. The plan held a certain amount of risk, but one way or another they would compel Musslit to surrender Saddam's location. We had come too far and too close to fail now.

My men had quietly pulled back from the city and points around Auja. We were coiled and ready to go. Without betraying the details to their soldiers, my commanders readied their troops who, in turn, prepared and maintained their weapons, ready for any contingency.

By mid-afternoon, Musslit was being contradictory, revealing just enough of the truth to appease the Americans while obscuring the real truth to protect Saddam. As the interrogators stepped up the pressure, several other events were set into motion. Other SOF teams from their parent task force in Baghdad would reinforce John's SOF team. Dez Bailey arrived from Bayjii and was quickly refitting his unit after two weeks in the desert. Colonel Hickey had concluded his meeting with the Governor and headed directly for General Odierno's headquarters. It was time to fully brief him, not on the radio or satellite phone, but in person.

In the Ironhorse Division headquarters, Colonel Hickey sat down in Major General Odierno's office. He began to update Odierno, beginning with the capture of Mohammed al-Musslit.

"Sir, we've got him right now undergoing interrogation," explained Hickey. "I intend to conduct a raid to kill or capture Saddam as soon as we get the information on his location."

General Odierno had also been through this same scenario before. Colonel Hickey's soldiers had participated in no fewer than a dozen specific raids with special operations forces to find Saddam.

"What do you think the chances of success are?" he asked.

"Sir, I think they are as good, if not better, than any previous mission we've conducted so far," he offered.

General Odierno felt the momentum as well. Only a week before he had advised Secretary of Defense Donald Rumsfeld that he believed it was only a matter of time until they got Saddam. In that meeting, Rumsfeld had asked what more could he do, what more was needed. He told the Secretary that he believed that they had the resources they needed and were on the verge of success. Now, here he was face-to-face with his one field commander who had the best prospect of making it happen.

"Sir, we have as good a chance as we will ever get." Hickey continued, "Only one other man may possibly know as much as Musslit, and he is still at large. I'm confident that we can get him. Our troops are at their peak of effectiveness and have been pursuing this with special operations forces for months."

"Let me know what you need," offered Odierno. "Keep me informed if anything new breaks."

"Yes, sir," answered Hickey. "Once we get the location, I should have the details of our plan pretty quick."

As General Odierno and Colonel Hickey were conferring, Musslit was vacillating. He tried to insist that Saddam was on this side of the river or that side and kept the location ambiguous and generic. He spoke of an "underground facility." He even suggested that Saddam had not been to this farm for four months. Game time was over. With pressure brought to bear on him, he yielded the location of a farm to which he had alluded earlier during an interrogation in Baghdad. It was near Ad Dawr on the east side of the river near the bank of the Tigris.

Special operations interrogators and Major Murphy's intelligence shop pieced together the emerging information. It could be one of only a few farms north of Ad Dawr and just east-southeast of Auja. This would affect the force structure substantially. Unlike the western desert raids that produced Musslit's brother, Rudman, and his business partner, Thaier Amin Ali, the terrain on the riverbank was densely vegetated with palm groves, orchards, and farm fields. A much tighter cordon and adjustments for armored vehicles would be required.

John's men were ready to proceed, accompanied by Musslit and the information at hand. They conducted a stealthy reconnaissance of the area that Musslit had referenced and were able to narrow it down to an area of two farms with a possible third as a secondary target. The two farms were in an orchard on the east bank of the Tigris River a few kilometers north of Ad Dawr. From the Hadooshi farm bluff on the other side of the river, it was a mere three-kilometer straight line from bluff to bluff. Had Saddam been here all along?

After leaving General Odierno's headquarters, Colonel Hickey went to the Water Palace to meet with John, who had just returned from the recon. They began to discuss the options. It was now about 4:00 p.m. and would be dark in three hours. Outside, two flights of Little Bird helicopters had arrived. Odd-looking armored vehicles had collected on-site along with other teams from the SOF task force brought up from Baghdad.

Inside, Colonel Hickey, John, Brian Reed, team leaders, and their ops men began to structure the initial plan, based on the recon. Someone ripped a piece of butcher paper from an easel pad and laid it on the table. John proposed a timeline based on a hit time of 9:00 p.m. Units would move out by 8:00 p.m. and link up at a corn granary on the other side of the Tigris north of the farms by 8:30 p.m. Colonel Hickey wanted to change the time frame. He remembered at least two occasions on which he felt we had narrowly missed Saddam. An earlier raid might have netted him. He knew the information we had was good. The sooner we struck, the better.

John agreed but still had moving parts arriving from Baghdad. They reconfigured the timeline with a departure of 6:30 p.m. Scrawled on the butcher paper were the military times of 1830 for departure, 1900 for granary linkup, and 2000 for the hit time known as "H-Hour." John added "ish" to 2000 to allow some flexibility. Therefore, "2000-ish" became the planned time.

So it was. One of the most important military raids in all of history was planned with Magic Markers on a piece of butcher paper with a "2000-ish" hit time. In reality, nothing more was needed for the operation. Our forces had worked together for more than six months. Colonel Hickey was right. We were at peak efficiency. Our relationship and trust with one another was complete. We knew that we could rely on each other to quickly assemble for any action.

The force would raid two farms. Dez Bailey's G Troop would provide close inner cordon support to John's men working the orchard and outbuildings with the other teams from his unit brought up from Baghdad. John's men would be under the overall command of "Bill," the higher-level special operations commander recently arrived for this raid.

To supplement the two farm targets, Colonel Jim Hickey and "Bill" the special operations commander, would bring their own forces to bear. An outer cordon was vital. Farm targets in a dense orchard on the bank of a river increased the prospect for the raid's failure in a variety of ways. Saddam had eluded his would-be captors by swimming away once before from this exact location in 1959. A repeat performance was entirely possible. He could slip out again by swimming or rowing a small fishing boat across the river.

To cordon the objective, Colonel Hickey needed a tight noose around the area. Major Steve Pitt and the 4th Battalion, 42nd Field Artillery (normally under Lieutenant Colonel Dom Pompelia who was presently on leave in the States) would be responsible for the overall portion east of the river. Two howitzers would be prepped to support the assault force if things went badly.

Colonel Hickey ordered Lieutenant Colonel Mark Huron's 299th Engineer Battalion to place forces on the west bank of the river. An additional screen on the west side would be flown by A Company, 1st Battalion, 4th Aviation in Apaches to prevent any situation from developing on the west side. My own forces under

Mark Stouffer's A Company would tie in south of Auja on the west bank of the river with those that Mark Huron would bring up from the south. Lieutenant Colonel Reg Allen from the 10th Cavalry Squadron would provide his A Troop as an armored reserve for the overall mission.

"Bill's" SOF forces were more specialized than the conventional forces of Jim Hickey. The flights of Little Birds would provide both special operator transport and attack air support to the ground teams. If Saddam Hussein were captured, they would whisk him out as well. An MH-53 with a special ops surgeon would provide emergency medical support. Specialized armored vehicles would also support the ground teams. Combined with Jim Hickey's forces, the total for the mission would number approximately eight hundred soldiers.

With the basic plan now established, both conventional and unconventional forces went to work. Colonel Hickey updated his commanders. He informed me that Saddam's location had been pinpointed near Ad Dawr on the east side of the river. The artillery would handle the outer cordon on that side, and he wanted to bring up Mark Huron's troops to handle any potential water-crossing issues on the west bank in my area. While I would tie in my A Company with that cordon, his main orders to me were to have a ready reserve to send troops to either side of the river.

I assigned Brad Boyd the mission to prepare for an east side reinforcement. Mark Stouffer was already in position with the cordon just south of Auja. While we were all excited, I was also a little bummed. Cordons were nice, but instinct told me that this was the raid for which we had all been waiting. Every one of us wanted to be raiding that small farm objective. Even so, we had all worked very hard to get here. Hopefully, the cordon would never be tested, and my standby forces would never be needed. We now all waited for the move out.

RED DAWN

Colonel Hickey made a last coordination with his executive officer, Major Troy Smith. Troy had the operations center set and ready to go. Captains Mike Wagner and Geoff McMurray had been assisting Major Brian Reed and knew the plan. Colonel Hickey had dubbed the objectives WOLVERINE 1 and WOLVERINE 2. There was no particular explanation for this, just names that bubbled up to Colonel Hickey's mind, as often happens when commanders and operations officers need a moniker for a particular operation.

It seemed only fitting to McMurray then, as they worked on the fragmentary order with the simple sketches and imagery provided, that the operation should be named "Red Dawn" in a nod to John Milius's 1984 classic movie *Red Dawn* starring Patrick Swayze. In the movie, communist forces invade, catching a small American town in Colorado unawares. A group of high school students led by Swayze decide to resist, using their school mascot name, the Wolverines, as the name of their group. The operation name stuck.

While Major Reed would accompany Colonel Hickey, Captain Mark Paine was ready as the battle captain supporting Troy Smith. Major Stan Murphy would also remain to coordinate the intelligence. Chief Bryan Gray would dispatch with Colonel Hickey.

The question on everyone's mind was whether Musslit had stalled so long that Saddam might suspect that he had been compromised. We would soon find out. Colonel Hickey and Command Sergeant Major Wilson moved toward the linkup point.

John's SOF team and the other teams were on the move as well. All units began to migrate toward the assault position. By 6:45 p.m., the assembly was complete at the granary near Highway 21, the north-south road running parallel to the Tigris River's east bank. Jim Hickey and "Bill" deliberated while the assault leaders and commanders briefly rehearsed the sequence of attack. Dez Bailey's men had already consulted with John's SOF team and the other SOF task force teams. The sun was setting.

It seemed almost providential when the power went out suddenly in Ad Dawr at 7:45 p.m. This was about the same time that all the assault elements were departing the granary for that "2000-ish" hit time. With the aid of night vision and thermal vision, our forces would have a decided advantage.

The air was brisk on that December night. Soldiers wore gear for protection against the elements. They manned their weapons or readied themselves for the ground assault. Radios were silent. Vehicles were totally blacked out. In the far distance, Little Bird and Apache helicopters nosed toward the objective.

The two farms were dark. The orchards covering them were a mix of brown wintered vegetation mixed with green palms and bushes. Citrus fruit hung from trees interlacing the date palms. Hemming the orchard on the east side was a chain-link fence adorned with thousands of narrow palm fronds latticed into the diamond-shaped links, effectively concealing what lay behind it.

Extending out from the fence was a wheat field with several small storage barns, some sheathed in opaque plastic sheeting. A dirt road separated the fence from the wheat field while another road, not much better, led out toward Highway 24 in the distance. To the south lay the blacked-out city of Ad Dawr. To the northwest and just across the river lay Auja, Saddam's birthplace, illuminated by the many generators still in the hands of Saddam's privileged loyalists living within our ring of barbed wire. Between Auja and the orchard curved a rich farmland, cut mostly on the east side by the wide Tigris River.

The SOF soldiers forming the ground assault element swooped into place at 8:00 p.m., joined by assaulting elements in Little Birds. Dez Bailey's platoon from G Troop pushed tight on them to form the inner cordon. Colonel Hickey and "Bill" rolled up behind them and co-located their command vehicles in the wheat field adjacent to the orchard. Major Brian Reed with the 1st Brigade command group Bradleys set up in overwatch nearby. Apaches patrolled the west bank of the Tigris, while below, Mark Huron's Engineers and Mark Stouffer's "Gators" from my battalion scanned the east bank where so much activity was now taking place.

Hearing the commotion, Qais Namaq Jassim and his brother spurred into a flurry of activity of their own. How could the Americans be here? There was no warning. Hoping to divert the soldiers, they quickly went into their concealment drill and then ran north into the orchard away from the farm now designated WOLVERINE 1.

Whirring above them leading his flight of Little Birds, "DB" spotted movement in the orchard. The assault team saw them, too. After a brief chase, Sergeant John Iversen with Dez Bailey's men apprehended the fugitives. They turned out to be Saddam's cook and the cook's brother. An intense search was now on as men wove through the orchard. To "DB," "Pat" and "Brian" observing from their birds, the scene took on a concert-like appearance as the soldiers snooped around with their rifle lights.

After stumbling around a bit, Musslit, brought along on the raid for just this purpose, was able to pinpoint the area in which they should search. He was perched in the back of a Humvee, looking exceedingly unhappy.

Dez and his men joined the SOF ground effort, acting on scant info about an "underground facility." The soldiers searched in earnest through the palm groves and even the garbage pit that serviced the two farms. During the search, Dez and John tried to assess the situation.

"Well, Dez," commented John, "looks like it might be another dry hole."

"Let's check it one more time," replied Dez. They agreed that Saddam had to be there.

A handful of SOF soldiers began to interrogate the captured men back at the southern farm they had tried to flee. The cook and his brother were not being very cooperative. Iraqis generally feared American working dogs, but even the presence of the sniffer dog did not compel them to capitulate. They offered misleading information in an attempt to draw the assault element away from the southern farm. John knew that they must be in the right location. Where was this "bunker" or this "underground facility" that Musslit mentioned? Did it even exist?

Enough was enough. John decided to grab Mohammed al-Musslit. The special ops men confronted him, saying, "You said he was here," and saying some other colorful things as well. "Where is he? Where is the bunker?"

"He's there. Trust me. Keep looking," replied Musslit through the translator.

Instead, they again grabbed Musslit and brought him through the farm gate opening in the latticed fence. The farmhouse itself was not very big. Three disjointed, rectangular rooms formed a small "L" around a small concrete patio area. The rooms bore a kitchen, bedroom, and living area. A hasty search had already netted two AK-47s and a chest of American money.

JACKPOT

Mohammed al-Musslit was terrified. He spotted Saddam's cook, Qais. A look passed between them, each hoping the other would expose Saddam. Musslit did not want to be seen or heard, but the soldiers continued to pepper him with demands to show them the location. The game, he knew, was already over. Telling them quietly and walking a few steps across the small patio, he began to gesture toward a foot mat. He tapped it with his foot. It looked quite normal positioned adjacent to the patio's west edge.

Drawing it aside, the special ops soldiers noticed soft earth beneath the mat. Two of them kicked to brush away the dirt, exposing a bit of rope. After more digging, a soldier exposed what appeared to be handles. Musslit was taken away, along with the other two detainees.

"Sir, we may have a potential jackpot," alerted John to Colonel Hickey.

"Roger," answered Colonel Hickey, waiting patiently. Fifteen minutes had already passed. The two apprehended men were acting abnormally. Something, he sensed, was about to give. Even if it were not, Colonel Hickey was satisfied that he had a force sufficiently large to search every square inch of the area for as long as it took. Saddam had to be here. For now, he simply let the soldiers execute in the manner they knew best.

A small group of special ops soldiers gathered around as one began to brush the dirt away. A door or hatch of some kind began to take shape. The edges appeared to be Styrofoam. One of the men readied a flash-bang grenade while another lifted the handles. The others covered with their weapons.

A thick two-foot square of Styrofoam began to work its way from what now appeared to be a brickwork entrance to whatever was below. As the top was tossed away, a haggard man in a charcoal-colored dishdasha began to move. Lights and muzzles bore down on the man, illuminating him inside the darkness. Seeing no immediate weapon, the SOF men kept the flash-bang grenade at bay.

"Samir," a soldier shouted, calling out to an Iraqi-American refugee working with the special ops team, "come and talk to him. Tell him to come out before he gets killed."

"Who are you?!" demanded the soldiers through the translator.

"I am Saddam Hussein, the duly elected president of Iraq," the startled man replied. "I am willing to negotiate."

"Well, President Bush sends his regards," answered one of the men. Then, turning to Samir he said, "Tell him to put his hands up and come out."

Saddam either could not or did not clearly understand Samir's order to put his hands up. He raised one. When ordered again, he raised the other but not both. Finally, he raised both and stood directly below the opening with enough of his person exposed to grab him.

Hands extended from every direction into the opening and snatched Saddam literally by the scruff of his neck, hair, beard and clothes. John's men promptly went to work. A Glock 18C fully automatic pistol was found inside the hole. The Hussein Hilton was not much larger than the tyrant himself. Dimensionally, it was similar to a six-foot folding table one might crawl under with barely enough room to sit in a slumped position. There was a rug covering the dirt floor and a small switch that controlled an electric fan that drew in air from outside. The only other item in the hole was a pair of brown flip-flops.

There was much cursing and bantering between the translator and Saddam. Tempers flared. Finding nothing on Saddam, John's men began to inspect him for known physical marks. Angry, he attempted to shove the soldiers away. That was a stupid thing to do. He was immediately "encouraged" to cooperate. With his mouth bleeding and a cut above his eye, he became much more cooperative. The men examined him for the sunburst tattoo on the back of his right hand. It was there. They checked the back of the left hand between the thumb and forefinger for the "Three Dot" tattoo, which represented "God, Country, Leader" and the national motto. That, too, was there.

"Sir, we got him. Jackpot! We got him!" radioed John to Colonel Hickey as the men zip-tied his hands behind him.

"That's great," replied Colonel Hickey in a relieved voice.

Jim Hickey turned to "Bill." Broad grins formed on their faces and like athletes on a sports field after a game-changing play, they spontaneously hugged and slapped each other on the backs. The time was 8:26 p.m.

While word spread to the immediate commanders in the wheat field, Samir and the ex-president continued their hateful exchange in Arabic. John's men pulled Samir back, trying to calm him. As they prepared to escort Saddam to his awaiting flight, Samir convinced one of the men to photograph him with Saddam. It was the only known picture taken of Saddam at the hole.

John had called for extraction. Up above, "Brian" peeled off in his Little Bird and landed in the wheat field near the farm. Years of rewarding special ops flying had been capped with this extraordinary moment. The bird fluttered in, its rapid whirring sound slackening as it touched the ground. Many soldiers in the cordon, unaware of recent developments inside the farm area, merely witnessed a man being ushered out with a sandbag over his head and zip-tied hands. His appearance was identical to that of thousands of other insurgents captured and detained.

Dez Bailey was back at his command vehicle now. That "one more check" had certainly paid off. As he was taking it all in, his driver became curious.

"Sir, what did he just say on the radio?" he probed.

"Troop, you just keep watching your sector and keep your head in the game," Bailey cut him off, knowing that they had to keep it all under wraps. In the short distance, Dez saw the bag-covered Saddam being steered to "Brian's" Little Bird. The blades picked up the dust around the bird and the high-pitched whir of the sleek little helicopter signaled liftoff. Dez watched through his night vision goggles as it proceeded toward Tikrit.

Colonel Hickey made his way across the stretch of wheat field to the farm. He spotted John. The two engaged in another congratulatory hug.

"Congratulations, John," offered Colonel Hickey.

"Right back at you, sir," acknowledged John, reflecting the embodiment of teamwork that had brought all of us to this point.

"Sir, I've got about a million bucks for you," he informed through a big smile. "We found it in a green chest."

Colonel Hickey, Chief Gray, Command Sergeant Major Wilson, and John made their way to the farm. There it was, the green chest containing seven hundred and fifty thousand U.S. dollars. Colonel Hickey had seen more than ten times that amount in the first big breakthrough raid that narrowly missed Saddam at the Hadooshi Farm, but this one was sweet indeed. Less money—far greater prize.

Colonel Hickey conferred briefly with John and "Bill" and then ordered Dez Bailey to secure the site and seal it off. He also ordered Dez to keep the information close hold.

There was a brief pause to record the moment. Gathering up the money, Colonel Hickey, Command Sergeant Major Wilson, Chief Gray, and Colonel Hickey's translator, Specialist Joe Gamdi, who held the money chest on his shoulder, posed for a picture.

Hickey took a last look around before walking to his vehicle. Lifting the receiver on his commander's tactical satellite phone, he called General Odierno.

"Sir, this is Jim Hickey," he stated.

"Yes, Jim," answered General Odierno with some curiosity.

"We've captured Number One, and I have about a million dollars in the back of my Humvee to give you."

General Odierno was stunned and elated. After confirming the Colonel's news, he whispered to his main staff sitting with him. A roar went up, and he realized that they must lock down the information. It had to be controlled until national leaders had been notified.

"I'll be at your headquarters in twenty to thirty minutes to go over it with you," informed Hickey.

CESAR ROMERO

At divisional headquarters, General Odierno ordered his signal officer to lock down all Internet and cell phones. Everything had to be shut off. He then began to notify his own chain of command in Baghdad.

Major Troy Smith had been monitoring the entire operation from Colonel Hickey's headquarters. Stan Murphy was on pins and needles. Smith received a phone call from Hickey. After several "Roger, sirs" and "Yes, sirs," he hung up the satellite phone. Troy Smith would launch the first in a string of announcements echoing John's initial radio call to Colonel Hickey. It would reach all the way to Ambassador Paul Bremer by morning.

"Attention in the TOC," Smith alerted the staff in the ops center. "Ladies and gentlemen, we got him!"

Cheers went up inside the brigade headquarters, after which Troy followed with the same sets of shutdown instructions. He then called Colonel Don Campbell to give him the same news. The words "We got him" just seemed to be the most appropriate way to phrase it.

On the other side of the river, I received a call on the commander's tactical satellite phone as well. The radio would not be appropriate for the information I was about to receive. I lifted the receiver to hear Colonel Hickey's voice. He broke the news to me a bit more creatively.

"Cesar Romero!" announced Colonel Hickey with a subdued chuckle. In the summer, images had been released by the Department of Defense showing what Saddam might look like in disguise—with a beard, without a beard, bald, with hair, etc. One of the altered images looked amazingly like the actor Cesar Romero, best known as the "Joker" in the 1960s *Batman* television series. From that point forward, we used it as a comical code name for Saddam.

"Oh my God," I said under my breath, stunned. I began to thank God for answering countless prayers. I didn't know what to say. I listened speechlessly as Colonel Hickey paused.

"Not a word," Hickey ordered. "The announcement must be official. The president has to be notified, and this will take some time."

"Roger, sir," I answered. "I understand the importance of it."

"Tell none of your soldiers what has just happened," he reinforced. "I want you to quietly ensure you cut off Internet and cell communications."

"Wilco, sir," I acknowledged, still stunned.

After a few more details, Colonel Hickey was on to the next call to his field commanders. Putting on my best straight face, I hung up the receiver. I could show no emotion even though I was bursting at the seams. We did it. It really happened. I had to go find a place to be alone.

Once there, I could not help but reflect on all the months of fighting, raiding, and hard work; the blood, sweat, and tears that our soldiers had shed; the family networks; the "three tiers" strategy and the network of bodyguards; the scores of joint raids and the cemented relationship we had with Jack and John's unconventional teams. The results of that were: the Ace of Diamonds, the Queen of Hearts, the Two of Diamonds, over sixty percent of the enablers from the five family networks, and now this—Saddam himself, captured. I thanked God for giving us the victory that night. To have participated in the hunt and capture of Saddam Hussein would become one of the proudest achievements of my life.

Saddam had been flown by "Brian's" Little Bird to the Water Palace compound. There, John and the combined special operations force from Baghdad eventually congregated in Saddam's old digs to gape at the tyrant who had defied the world. His shabby appearance was all the more disheveled against the stark contrast of the opulent palace from which he once ruled. His hair was long and matted, his beard was unkempt, and his eyes were angry. He looked remarkably similar to John Brown of Civil War days. The SOF men kept close watch on him until the coordination could be made to transfer him to Baghdad under a veil of secrecy. A special ops helicopter would take him on board with an escort of attack helicopters and Air Force jets. It would be impossible for him to slip through their fingers.

That night, "Mark," the special ops flight surgeon who covered the raid from above, would spend the first night with Saddam. The dictator was very chatty. "Mark" was able to quiz him on a number of subjects. Retiring to his hooch, the surgeon celebrated the raid by drinking two Heinekens and reflected on the evening's experience. That night he wrote in his journal a detailed entry about his conversation with the man who shook his fist in defiance of the world.

Now, back in my own headquarters, it was difficult to refrain from telling my men that they had participated in the historic capture of Saddam Hussein. Just before midnight, even as "Mark" was conversing with Saddam in Baghdad, I assembled Mike Rauhut,

Bryan Luke, Pete Martinez, and Cesar Castro, my two majors and two sergeants major.

"Meet me at the battalion colors," I said to Bryan and Pete.

"What's up, sir?" they queried.

"Meet me at the battalion colors," I reiterated. "I'm going to find Mike."

Mike had already bedded down after having been up for hours. He needed the rest but not as much as he needed to hear this news. I woke him.

"Mike," I called out. "Get up and meet us at the battalion colors."

Once we were gathered, I whispered the news. "Tonight's raid was successful. We captured Saddam Hussein. Years from now, you will want a picture of us together on this day." We snapped the photo and sat tight on the information until the next morning.

When Colonel Hickey returned to his headquarters, he gathered his command group elements together. He delivered the news with a word of warning.

"I don't want any of you to talk about this," he cautioned. He attempted to convey that, while enormously proud of their success, the proper protocol of official notification to our highest-ranking leaders would have to be observed.

Seeing the soldiers return, a reporter from CNN climbed onto an upper balcony near the place Colonel Hickey was speaking to his men. He flipped his camera on and began recording Hickey's conversation. He pieced together the essence of the day's events. Perhaps taking the Colonel's own words to heart himself, he withheld release of the tape that would have surely insured instant fame or, possibly, notoriety. Later, his recording would document this historic moment for posterity.

Some of Colonel Hickey's immediate troops had yet to return to headquarters. Dez Bailey was still at the site of the hole. His men had been on the move for days, having driven from the desert west of Bayjii just to get to this raid. Even so, with all the recent events, you could have plugged them in an outlet and illuminated all of Ad Dawr. Bailey's men guarded the area while the special ops troops departed and another group raked through it for any useful evidence. They arrived at approximately 3:00 a.m. on December 14 and tore the place apart.

The three rooms of the stark farmhouse had an odd story of their own to tell. In the kitchen, "Happy Brand" tuna, an open box of Belgian chocolates, cartons of eggs, American-made chips and snacks revealed an interesting side of the dictator. In his "presidential suite," Saddam's ratty bedroom wall was decorated with carpets bearing the image of a large buck on one and a sailing ship on the other. Most interesting of all was the Noah's Ark calendar tacked on the wall. Stacks of novels lay littered about with a can of "Raid" nearby to ward away pests. The guard and the cook had probably occupied the remaining, more sparse room. At the bank of the river, a small fishing boat lay ready to ferry him across to safety.

By first light, the guys poring over every square inch of the farm had departed. In a matter of hours, the world would learn what a small number of us had known for some time. The world's reaction was much as ours had been. Standing before a throng of reporters who had been alerted of the special news conference, Ambassador Paul Bremer repeated Troy Smith's exact words to the world from the Coalition headquarters in Baghdad: "Ladies and gentlemen, we got him!"

7. TUMULT

FALLOUT

On December 14, the world was abuzz with rumors. The rumblings instantly gave way to official confirmation with the electrifying announcement from Baghdad. At last, we had the liberty to speak openly of recent events and their worldwide ramifications. That evening as we patrolled, the city was quiet as a mosque mouse. There was no more activity at 9:30 p.m. than one might expect at 3:00 a.m. Across the city, in each flophouse, apartment, and home, the outlines of the residents were faintly illuminated by the glow of the television. The threat of Saddam's power had come to an end.

We braced ourselves for the resistance sure to follow, especially in Tikrit. I remembered vividly the spike in violence after Saddam's spawns were eliminated in Mosul in July. Once the shock of his capture wore off, the local Tikritis would, no doubt, channel that energy into revenge. The wait was a short one. Activity was low on December 14, though a C Company patrol found itself under fire just short of the "Chevron" in the north part of the city. Although none of our men were injured, the alleyways and distance facilitated a clean escape for the attackers.

As we braced ourselves for more gunfights, a new type of resistance emerged on December 15. We had dealt with a few attempts at demonstrations in late September and early October but disbanded them quickly as they tried to assemble. Our strategy now would be no different. I had waded through the preliminaries of the tribal council of sheiks meeting at the government building that morning at about ten o'clock when Sergeant First Class Gil Nail, my operations sergeant, interrupted our meeting.

"Sir, we received a report of several hundred students forming at the tip of the 'Chevron' and a separate group downtown on the main street," he whispered.

"OK, thanks," I replied, trying to process the information. I closed the meeting with apologies to the sheiks, merely saying that something needed my immediate attention. We mounted up our Humvees and sped in the direction of the demonstrations.

Captain Brad Boyd had already moved to the "Chevron" to contain about 500 male students. They were marching south along Highway 1 and appeared to be traveling toward the second group that was moving north. Captain Mark Stouffer heard the chatter on the net and readied some of A Company to support us. I would be grateful for his anticipation of the forces I would soon need.

There were about nine soldiers, including myself, in our command convoy speeding north along Highway 1 where it morphed into the main street. In the distance we could see a group of about 250 people, most of whom were women. Brad reported that he had forces closing on the northern group and approximated the size of the crowd. Looking ahead, I told Sergeant First Class Nail to ready the bullhorn. I had learned in Kosovo that a bullhorn could double as siren and loudspeaker.

Hundreds of women, led by men, many carrying large signs of Saddam's likeness, were blocking the highway as the procession made its way north, presumably to merge with the student group. With cars blocking the intersection, it was clear that we would have a tough time closing in on them. Cody Hoefer very shrewdly bounced the Hummer up sidewalks, making it possible to bypass the cars blocking the intersection.

"Close up on them," I ordered.

We pulled up behind them, hardly slowing down at all, and activated the blaring siren. The ensuing development was reminiscent of that Blues Brothers scene in which they drive the big car into the Nazi demonstration on the bridge. These, however, weren't Nazis. They were Saddam Baathist loyalists. Startled women in their flowing black robes scattered in every direction. Cowardly men, once shouting bravely in the lead, suddenly melted imperceptibly into the population at large. Our soldiers grabbed the posters of Saddam while Joe Filmore shouted through the siren-turned-loudspeaker for all to clear out or be arrested. Gaining the element of surprise with my small force bought a modicum of time. I needed Mark Stouffer to assume traffic control and keep the main highway open. He was already moving our direction with a platoon of soldiers.

The women, initially alarmed, regained their courage. We had scattered them to the sidewalks, mostly on the market side of what we called Cross Street. My soldiers formed a picket while Joe Filmore and I advanced toward the most agitated group to advise them to keep off the street. As I began to speak, a woman near me stepped forward and spewed no small amount of spit into my face. Most of it hit my eye protection then gradually slid down the lens to my cheek. It was not a pleasant experience. Wiping it off with my gloved left hand, I could see it was only the nine of us restraining them from the street. After the spit greeting, I took a step backward and scanned the area to ensure that we were not being set up for an insurgent ambush or targeted by an angry Saddam loyalist. I could hear Mark Stouffer's Bradleys in the distance coming to reinforce us.

Up north, Brad Boyd and his soldiers encircled the large student group attempting to join the "ladies." By carefully maneuvering his men and machines, he herded them into a dead end. Soon, the scratch of concertina wire could be heard surrounding the trapped troublemakers as Brad's soldiers uncoiled the wire stowed on the front of every Bradley. His men had already gained moral dominance by heading directly toward the angry-faced ringleader and proceeding to subdue him soundly with a couple of axe handles. Once this was accomplished, the crowd became benign but, encircled as they were by the wire, had no place to go.

Handing the downtown situation over to the "Gators," we headed toward the "Cobras." Brad had the situation well in hand and the police chief, General Mezher, arrived to support us. We were able to resolve the situation and agreed to relinquish the student leaders to the Iraqi police. The remainder were searched, given a reprieve, and sent on their way. Both groups had one thing in common—local educators had organized the demonstrations. I found that very unsettling because the action had clearly been conceived in defiance of the new government. I intended to reinforce this with the governor the next day.

That evening we reviewed our procedures for crowd handling. Under Saddam, no demonstrations of protest were ever allowed and, under the new government, they still were not allowed. No matter. I refused to have our supply routes cut off by demonstrators and emphatically advised my men that demonstrations would absolutely not be tolerated. When a peaceful democratic country was established, Iraq could worry about the democratic rights of peaceful demonstrators.

After reviewing our actions and plans for heightened violence, I traveled to report the situation face-to-face with Colonel Hickey, who had returned from Baghdad. He had gone there to brief Lieutenant General Ricardo Sanchez and dozens of others prior to the capture announcement. After informing him of the new demonstration activity and the expectation of violence to follow, we took a needed pause and just relaxed awhile. I took the liberty to reflect a bit about the past six months.

We had both come so far since that first meeting over steaks at the Texas Roadhouse in Killeen, Texas. After the ambushes and street fights, the raids and the successes, we experienced dark days wondering where all this would lead. Colonel Hickey had remained resolute about Saddam. Although I had the same resolve, even I had moments of doubt wondering if we would ever see the result that had just happened.

"Sir, you remember last August when we were trying to assess the enemy insurgency and our impact on Saddam's inner circle?" I asked. "You said at that time that you thought we would have him by Christmas."

"I said that?" Colonel Hickey responded.

"Yes, sir, you did." I affirmed. "I know we all believed in different outcomes as we pressed forward, but I just want to say thanks for keeping us focused. When we took a number of casualties in October, it was hard not to be overly focused on the street fight and miss the bigger picture, but you kept us on track. I appreciate that. If I never get the chance again, I just want to say thanks now, sir."

"Steve, the world will likely never know what we achieved," he reflected. "You and the Regulars have been at the front of this fight, and our entire brigade has done remarkably well. Our work with John and Jack's men will also probably escape notice. But we are accomplishing our missions, and I knew that if we kept up the momentum, we could make an impact."

"Well, we've certainly done that, sir." I replied.

"We still have work to do," he reminded. "We have hurt the Baathist-led insurgency severely. It remains to be seen what direction the resistance will go now. We have to be on our guard and stay on the offensive."

With the dawning of December 16, we anticipated more demonstrations and actually expected to find even larger crowds. At about 10:00 a.m., we received reports of a protest forming north of town. Captain Boyd loaded up his Hummers, proceeded toward the reported location, and called forward one of his platoons to follow him. Traveling north along the "Birthday Palace" boulevard known as "Saddam Boulevard," he spotted a white Mercedes near one of the drains alongside the road. The Mercedes masked the drain and then accelerated sharply. Sensing instant danger, Captain Boyd turned to his driver, Specialist Miguel Romero, and yelled instructions that were never heard or followed.

A deafening roar accompanied concrete, smoke, shards of glass, and a concussive blast. First Sergeant Mike Evans, in the second of the three vehicles, witnessed a billowing smoke cloud engulf the view to his company commander's Humvee. The smoke expanded until it reached the other side of the four-lane road. The sound of small arms cracked in the midst. Specialist Romero could not tell if Captain Boyd was firing, receiving fire, or both.

Evans hoped that the lead vehicle had passed before the bomb detonated, but he soon discovered that was not the case. He pulled his Hummer off to the side, and they immediately dismounted. Hearing the gunfire, he noted a few insurgents near a dump truck. Evans and his men opened up with their rifles to suppress the enemy in the distance. In the haze, he could see that Boyd's vehicle had drifted into the next lane, stricken and punctured. He thought he could hear rifle fire stemming from it.

Staff Sergeant Patrick McDermott, sitting uninjured behind Romero in the stricken Hummer, was already at Boyd's side assessing his condition. He ordered Romero to nurse the vehicle out of the kill zone area across to the other lanes, which he did.

First Sergeant Evans and the other soldiers continued to fire in support of their commander, in the direction of the Mercedes and at the source of enemy fire. Insurgents taking cover behind the dump truck fired shots at Evans and the other soldiers but broke contact when Sergeant First Class Stephen Yslas spotted them from his trail Hummer and suppressed them with his M-16. The white Mercedes, racing away, faded into the more urban part of the city. Suddenly, the firing stopped.

As the smoke began to diminish, Boyd's Hummer was seen listing to one side, mangled, perforated, and sporting a flat tire. There were obviously casualties. Evans ran to Boyd, as Staff Sergeant McDermott tended to his wounds.

"Sir, are you all right?" asked First Sergeant Evans.

"My legs are . . . burning . . . I think I'm OK." He grimaced. He was not. Blood flowed from his face. His right bicep was hanging out of his skin and the arm was covered in blood. Both legs were bloody tatters as his shredded uniform blended with his singed wounds. But he was alive. Groaning behind him was Staff Sergeant Felipe Madrid. McDermont had pulled him clear and behind the Hummer. He appeared to have sustained the worst of the injuries. A nasty hole in his face was coursing blood. His arms and legs were also bleeding.

Private First Class Rodrigo Vargas had been manning the .50 caliber machine gun in Boyd's truck when the bomb detonated. He was still manning it despite some light fragmentation wounds to the hands, arms, and legs. McDermont inquired of his condition, and he said he was okay but needed help with his hands. They were bleeding, as were slighter wounds to his legs and arms. McDermott bandaged his hands and Vargas stayed on the gun.

First Sergeant Evans quickly directed his men to pull out the stretchers and called to alert our aid station. The C Company quick reaction force under First Lieutenant Mike Isbell arrived within minutes, pulled security, and recovered the battered Humvee. They also brought medics since the company doc, Staff Sergeant Madrid, had been seriously wounded.

Specialist Brian Serba and Specialist Justin Brog had already stuck IVs, applied bandages, and administered 5mg of morphine to Captain Boyd and "Doc" Madrid. Mike Evans loaded his company commander into his Hummer, along with Madrid and Vargas, and raced the casualties to our battalion surgeon.

Handling some coordination on operations with Bryan Luke that morning, I received the news from my XO, Major Mike Rauhut. This one hit me like a sledgehammer to the head. Only moments before, Brad and I had been talking and coordinating battalion actions with the morning patrols. I threw on my gear and bolted to the aid station, praying to God that these men would be OK. God, please spare them. Please spare their lives. Not Brad, Lord. Please, not Brad. We had gone seven weeks without a single casualty, and now this morning we had three.

At the aid station, Bill Marzullo was already in action, prepped and ready to receive them. Down the hill you could hear the roaring engine of a Hummer as it approached the aid station. I stood aside, taking it in and letting my surgeon and his assistants do their job. As a fighter, I could do nothing but watch and pray.

The scene was familiar. We had been through it so many times before. Wounded soldiers were transported into the converted kitchen on battle stretchers as their company field medics held IVs steady. Doc Marzullo, Alex Morales, and Armando Burguete shifted into autopilot, making a hundred quick assessments and giving orders in rapid succession to the medical specialists in attendance. The medical assistants seemed to retrieve everything asked for and handed it to them.

In a twist of cruelty, Doc Madrid was brought in and laid on the table knowing what to do. Unconsciously, he was giving instructions to the other medics. This time, he was the patient and had to allow them do their job. He was in excruciating pain. I walked up to comfort him.

"Doc, let them take over," I encouraged. "Take a deep breath . . . you're gonna be fine." I held his head, trying to calm him as I spoke. Noticing that they were bringing in Brad Boyd, I withdrew my hand from Madrid's head to go to Boyd and could feel Doc's wet blood on it. Why couldn't I prevent this? What more could I have done? These were my men, and I felt responsible for them. I could fight, I could kill, and I could lead them from the front lines, but now I could do nothing except comfort them and pray.

Captain Boyd was just as tough on the stretcher as he was on the street. He was struggling through the pain and trying to report to me what happened.

"Brad, relax! Let them take care of you," I ordered. His six-foot-one-inch muscular frame lay splayed on the table as Doc Marzullo and the medics' scissors slashed off his gear and clothing. Although his arms and legs were bloody, his torso, thank God, was untouched where the body armor had protected him. Now he shivered with cold. He tried to keep talking, moving around on the table attempting to be in charge, all the while suffering from shock and delirium. His wounds needed to be dressed.

"Brad, settle down," I assured him. "Let the docs help you. These aren't your medics. They're mine. Listen to them! They have to dress your wounds."

"Roger, sir." He smiled through a blood-smeared face. He began to grow calm. It is difficult for a commander at any level to relinquish control of any given situation. Brad began to let go. We even found a few moments of humor together there in an awkward sort of way as only soldiers can understand.

It was hard to hold back my emotion, but I did out of sheer ne-cessity. Specialist Vargas was in the corner getting his hand wounds dressed as orderlies cleaned the superficial fragmentation from his legs and arms. I could distinguish the nature of their wounds and knew that they were going to be fine. I breathed a sigh of relief while every side of our little aid station was overwhelmed with purpose and activity.

As the docs continued to work, one of the special operations soldiers entered the aid station. He said nothing. He simply walked in, snapped on some rubber gloves, and quietly began to work. I don't think any of us even knew his name, just that he was one of us.

Mike Rauhut had already prepped a ground medevac to trans-port our wounded to the 28th Combat Surgical Hospital located at Camp Speicher, north of Tikrit. The surgeons there were the best. Unfortunately, they knew too many of us far too well. First Sergeant Evans conveyed his commander out with the others and began to place them in the ambulance.

"Sir, don't take me out of command." Brad struggled, lifting his head to speak.

"Brad, put your head down," I ordered. "They have to get your stretcher into the slots in the ambulance."

"Sir, don't take me out of command," he repeated, pleading.

"Don't worry about your command," I replied. "The 'Cobras' will be fine."

"Sir, don't give the company to the XO," he continued. "He's learning, but he is not ready yet."

"Brad, listen!" I ordered, looking directly into his eyes. "Don't worry about the company. Get healed. Mitch Carlisle will take the 'Cobras' until you get back on your feet."

With that, Brad seemed to completely relax. He laid his head on the stretcher as they locked it into place. The medics closed the ambulance doors and slapped them with their hands, signaling to the driver that they were ready. The vehicle sped away to the hospital.

Emotionally, I was torn apart inside but could not display it to the men. It was then I realized that the media had been nearby all along. The expressions on their faces were similar to those on ours. I was not angry with them nor did I feel that they were intruding. They were not the enemy. Having been on many patrols with us, they also knew the men lying on the stretchers and were deeply affected by the reality of the moment. They did the only thing they knew to do. They began to record it. To their credit, they did so in a dignified manner so as not to show the faces of our men on the stretchers.

Concerned about how the loss of their dynamic leader would affect the "Cobras'" morale, I called Mike Evans over and asked him to assemble the soldiers from Brad's convoy. I explained the need to channel their emotion and cautioned them to use it to their advantage and to take it to the enemy but not to view all Iraqis as the enemy. I had seen that same reaction so many times before in various combat locations, and it never boded well. There was still much work to do, and these wounded would return to us. I did not want to lose more soldiers due to rash behavior.

The men seemed fine. They had already recouped their equipment as they remounted their Hummers in preparation for the remainder of the day. It was not yet noon. I readied my command group as well. Seeing the Governor was my immediate priority. If we were to regain control of the city immediately, we had to counter the people behind these senseless demonstrations. As we readied, a report crackled over the net of a demonstration gathering in the city center. We sped to the location.

As we arrived, we noticed two "Cobra" Bradleys had just arrived in a herringbone formation on the northbound lanes of the main street. The men started spilling out the back as several sergeants began pointing to a side street east. Suddenly, a rifle cracked off just as I stepped out of my vehicle. It was immediately followed by another. The rifle fire was completely drowned out by a substantial burst from one of our 240B machine guns.

Running to the machine gunner, I asked why they were shooting.

"Sir, someone in the crowd threw a pipe bomb at our vehicles and took off into this back lot," replied Sergeant Jeffrey Loehr, a tough, Ranger-qualified soldier from C Company. I could see several alleged insurgents scaling a wall in the distance, unfortunately into a densely crowded area of the city.

"Sergeant Minzer, get control of your guys. Watch for baiting tactics," I cautioned. "Be careful about being drawn into something."

"Roger, sir," replied Staff Sergeant John Minzer, who had served with me in the 26th Infantry "Blue Spaders" in Kosovo in 1999. I knew he could handle the situation.

The pipe bomb had failed to explode. Although the crowd had already scattered, Joe Filmore, our translator from San Diego, questioned several students nearby. We advised them to disperse immediately or be arrested. They wasted no time leaving the area. It was time to move on toward the Governor's building. I could see Mike Evans's patrol coming to reinforce Minzer's, and I knew at that moment that C Company would be able to perform its duties without skipping a beat—at least for today.

UPPITY

We remounted our Hummers and headed toward the Salah ad Din government building. As we passed the shops along the streets, the locals sent us dagger-like glares. Men spat and narrowed their eyes in sideward glances. Uppity. They were getting uppity. Fine. I would solve this right now. I already had three casualties that day and did not want more. I put out a net call on the battalion radio for all my commanders to assemble at the Birthday Palace. I told them to assemble every piece of equipment that could roll and all the infantry they could spare.

I then called Lieutenant Colonel Reg Allen at 1-10 Cavalry to ask for attack aviation support for 2:00 p.m. I explained my intent to level a heavy-handed patrol against the city to implant fear and clear the streets. I had known Reg since he was a First Lieutenant in the advanced course that we attended together. We knew each other well. He offered to supply anything I needed. Reg was a good man.

I assembled my commanders at the Birthday Palace, and we readied a large force. I unfolded a satellite image of Tikrit across the hood of my Humvee and pulled some little lead tanks and plastic toy soldiers from an Altoids tin kept in the butt pack on my gear. The toys were for hasty "sand tables" and visual planning such as this. We talked through a quick concept using the figurines on the map and executed the plan just twenty minutes later.

Captain Jon Cecalupo brought the "Cougars'" M1 Abrams tanks down the main street of the city. The "Cobras" followed directly behind in a herringbone formation with about eight Bradleys in the main intersection of downtown. The ramps fell, and our infantry rushed at the sidewalks, immediately clearing the crowds. Reg's aviators swooped their attack helicopters overhead at intimidating heights in perfect timing with us. Captain Mark Stouffer followed with "Gators'" infantry and Bradleys. Captain Darryl Carter followed with the Iraqi Civil Defense troops we had trained.

The town immediately became calm. People scattered, shops closed, and streets emptied. Tikrit was firmly in our hands once again. We patrolled in this way for the next several hours, looking for trouble. No one wanted to give it.

Satisfied that we had regained control, I called for the Psyops truck from Staff Sergeant Charles Darrah's 362nd Psyops Detachment. We entreated Governor Hussein for his assistance in making a recording to play for the people throughout the city. The recording would be broadcast from vehicles on the streets and would be about demonstrations and general unrest. He drafted a tough message for his own people. He then asked permission to accompany us as we played the soundtrack around town. I readily accepted his excellent idea. We were further escorted by his personal security detachment of a half dozen Iraqis armed with MP5 submachine guns.

As I readied the new effort, the Governor boarded my Humvee, loaded Glock pistol in hand, and off we went. This was my kind of Governor. We drove at idle speed around the city as his recorded message blared into the alleys, shops, and residences of Tikrit. His bodyguard flanked him on each side. Our soldiers watched the shock on the locals' faces as their own governor instructed them to cease and desist lest the Iraqi government use lethal force to break up demonstrations. They warned that they would imprison surviving demonstrators. With no wind left in their sails, the demonstrations came to an end, and by sunset the town became eerily quiet.

FOR ANOTHER DAY

Using the respite to refocus, Mike Rauhut and I traveled to the field hospital that evening to see the guys. Brad's gunner, Rodrigo Vargas, had already been released back to his unit. He would need time to recover but could do it there. Doc Felipe Madrid had been evacuated to Baghdad to be shipped stateside for a lengthy recovery.

I found Brad lying on a hospital bed in the inflated rubber tent hospital. He was stable and awake. He looked pretty good and seemed to be in decent spirits for what he had just come through. We chatted a bit before the talk turned to the "Cobras" of C Company.

"Brad, I am sending Captain Mitch Carlisle to fill in for you until you heal," I reminded, unsure if he recalled the conversation from the aid station earlier that day.

"Thank you, sir. Mitch is a great guy," he offered. "Sir, I have another request."

"What is it?" I asked, not sure where this was leading.

"Sir, they told me they are evacuating me," he informed. "I don't want to leave."

"Brad, you have to heal," I tried to reason. "You were hit pretty bad."

"Sir, you and I both know that if they evacuate me, I will likely not be able to come back, and I don't want to leave my men," he countered.

"Well, you are probably right about that," I concluded. "It wouldn't be my doing, but if you are out of the net, they may force the change. I'll do what I can."

As we were talking, a chaplain entered and drew me aside.

"Sir, aren't you the commander of 1-22 Infantry?" he whispered.

"Yes," I replied apprehensively.

"Sir, they just brought in another one of your men," he revealed.

A sickening feeling filled the pit of my stomach. "Thanks, chaplain, where is he?" I asked grimly.

While Mike and I were traveling to the hospital and visiting with Brad, Second Lieutenant Warren Litherland was leading an element of the "Bears" from 3rd Platoon of our B Company, under Captain Scott Thomas, cross-attached to the 3-66 Armor battalion in Bayjii. They were conducting a standard combat patrol as they looked for roadside bombs along Highway 1. Warren had prior enlisted service as a sergeant. He was older and more mature than the typical new lieutenant, and the men of his platoon were glad to have him.

The patrol employed a pair of Bradleys with an infantry squad on board. The lead vehicle, B32, under Sergeant Michael McGrath with his gunner, Specialist Armando Clark, covered an arc to the front. Warren controlled the patrol in B31, the trail vehicle, as his gunner, Sergeant Gary Dowd, scanned to the rear. Anything suspicious was to be dealt with by Sergeant Steven Sanders' squad supported by the Bradleys. An additional patrol with a tank and Bradley was in another part of the town nearby and could mutually support.

As the patrol headed south and neared the main mosque in Bayjii, an RPG hit the turret of Lieutenant Litherland's vehicle. The track commanders and gunners had been up in the turret scanning for roadside bombs. When the RPG slammed into B31, Gary Dowd had been leaning outward looking for bombs. A massive flash of flame and concussion rocked the Bradley. The warhead hit at an angle near the TOW launcher and then skimmed the sloped armor into Sergeant Dowd.

Gunfire peppered the Bradleys. Sergeant McGrath and Specialist Clark, also up and scanning the curbs for bombs, spotted the muzzle blasts of the enemy coming from a building in the distance. They returned fire immediately with their M-16s. The enemy recoiled, and Sergeant Sanders moved his squad toward the enemy location. Hearing the explosion and gunfire, the tank and Bradley on patrol nearby sped to the location and opened up on the building where the enemy was firing. Sanders and his men cleared the building, but the enemy had already escaped. This ended the engagement.

Warren was knocked senseless, bleeding and trying to get his bearings. He saw Dowd slumped awkwardly and hanging listlessly over the turret gunner hatch. The top of the turret was blackened from the blast. Dowd's body armor was shredded on the left side of his body. The Kevlar layers were spilling from it, looking like fiberglass insulation from a demolished home. The armored plate inside it was nothing but shattered ceramic held together by the outer coating. Litherland could see that Sergeant Dowd was in critical condition, if not already dead.

The Bradley, having been hit in the turret, was still drivable, and Warren managed to direct the driver to return to the outpost that they had come from so they could get medical attention. Sergeant Dowd had absorbed nearly all the blast. Lieutenant Litherland ignored his own wounds and ensured that Dowd, miraculously still breathing, received emergency medical attention. He called for the medevac that ultimately took Dowd to the 28th Combat Surgical Hospital.

After the hospital chaplain's alert, we followed him to the surgery prep area. Gary had just landed via helicopter and was wheeled in on his back, completely unconscious. As they prepped him for surgery, he struck me as one of the most mangled human beings I had seen still living. His face, though intact, was seared and bloody. His neck was pocked with various holes. From the lower neck to the navel he was clean and unharmed. His body armor delineated the portion of his torso it had protected. His diaphragm rose and fell as Gary fought for each breath. His left forearm from just below the elbow was missing, the wound seared and exposed. Silver dollar-sized holes oozed below his belt line on his left side, his internal organs and spleen severely damaged. The orderlies tended to him while the surgeons readied their operating room and instruments.

In the brief interval before surgery, I begged God to spare his life. I put my hands on his injured head, and the chaplain and I prayed over him.

Lord, You are the God of all creation. Life and death rest in Your hands. Spare this man. Give him the fight to live. Heal his wounds. Guide the hands of the surgeons. Save his life, Lord. Spare him for another day. We have nothing to come to You with other than our plea as soldiers and our faith in You. Spare this man.

I knew that he would face a very long recovery. I stayed with him until they wheeled him into surgery. By God's grace, he lived through the first surgery and was later evacuated to Baghdad and then Germany. If he survived, he would spend many months in arduous recuperation.

For now, Mike Rauhut and I stood there looking at each other for a few moments and reflected on a very tough day. I roamed around to find the head doc of the hospital and laid out the case to keep Brad in theater. I pledged to keep him in my headquarters and not release him for duty until the docs cleared him. Only the great working relationship we had with the combat hospital even permitted such discussion. It would be several months before Brad could return to the streets, but as he wished, he would stay with us. I felt the need to win the case, as I knew that Brad would likely go AWOL to be with his unit. Then we would all be in trouble.

The negotiation accomplished, Mike and I patrolled back to the command post, alert and on scan as always. It had been a long and grueling day, but it was not yet over. There were still phone calls to make. When I arrived, Command Sergeant Major Martinez had the phone ready—but was I ready? I took a deep breath and started calling the wives or mothers of our wounded, determined to answer their questions as best I could.

I was not required to make such calls. It would have been far easier to allow "the system" with its snail's pace and detached formality to deliver the details after the first official notification. I put myself in their place. What would my family want to know? Besides, we had the technology to accomplish it from the field. I had better information than someone detached from our world. I thought it best to tell the families everything they wanted to know about their loved one's condition. While tough for them to hear, I pledged to answer any questions they asked and tried to answer with sensitivity, dignity and honesty. Still, I would rather have attacked into a nest of Fedayeen than make those calls. At least this time I was not calling to explain how their soldier died. For that, I could be thankful. Regardless, no one really knows what to say.

CUCUMBERS AND CHRISTMAS

I slept soundly that night, body winning over mind. Up again at dawn, we patrolled a mostly passive city. Incredibly, the people smiled and occasionally waved. It was as though nothing had happened. Just the day before, five of my men had been wounded, three of them critically. A sense of disgust returned to the core of my being. Still, I had to remind myself to heed my own advice. Just as I had admonished Brad's soldiers, I could not allow myself to succumb to the temptation of seeing all Iraqis as the enemy. Most certainly were not.

In this spirit, I went to Auja to meet with Sheik Mahmood, still a prisoner of sorts in his own town, courtesy of our barbed wire. We had a productive discussion about the Auja fence, the future of the Tikriti people, and the larger issue of the manner in which the Sunnis must fit into a new Iraq. They needed to embrace the future and relinquish the past.

After this visit, my men and I continued our patrols about town and the surrounding area, checking the mood of the people and for signs of enemy activity. Back at the palace, I gave Chris Morris, our scout platoon leader newly promoted to captain, an idea for snaring the bomber in the white Mercedes who had wounded Brad. Chris would remain my scout platoon leader despite his promotion. He did not want to give up commanding troops for a staff job, and I needed him. We set to work planning an operation to set a trap with observation posts and snipers. The operation would last about four days.

Early activity was light. The night of December 17 produced a single roadside bomb. It was another cinder block bomb like the one I nearly stepped on just weeks earlier. Like that one, it boasted the phrase "Allah Akhbar" (Allah is powerful) hand drawn on the cement caps, as if somehow Allah hated Americans and wanted to see them all die. We could not negotiate with these people; they only understood force. Without their removal, innocent people would continue to suffer from dictatorial and religious tyranny.

Anyone who believed that we could sit down at Starbucks and work it out over a latte needed to walk an Iraqi mile in our boots. For the soldier, it was not an academic discussion. It was experiential, and the facts clearly demonstrated the need for a decisive defeat of these maverick insurgents. Without a doubt, emboldened jihadists seeing us flee Iraq would attempt to kill us in the cities of other nations or even on our own shores. We would, instead, kill them here to prevent them from enslaving twenty-five million Iraqi people.

The next day was calm. In fact, Tikrit was actually civil. Chris Morris had stealthily positioned his scouts for the ambush along the "Chevron." The rain fell in torrents. The temperature dropped. Tempers subsided. The merchants and the insurgents stayed indoors. Consequently, I stepped up my personal patrols of our area and checked on the guys out in the rain.

This was the type of weather in which our troops could get

lax. Even though we were soaked from head to toe in our open-topped vehicles, we still searched for signs of danger. Everywhere we patrolled, we found the morale of our soldiers to be very good. They sensed that we were winning this fight. I saw it weeks before when talking to several of the units. I gathered all the enlisted by company and listened to them in small groups. I then did the same with the sergeants. It was insightful to hear what was on their minds. They looked forward to Christmas and the New Year, realizing we were close to going home. I urged the soldiers to stay focused on their mission. Getting home would be when we got there. Not before.

December 19 was overcast and damp. The freshness in the air provided a relief to the normal stench of the land. Patrols were out, and movement appeared normal with the shops and markets full of activity. Jon Cecalupo's "Cougars" patrolling in Cadaseeyah passed one shop that caught their eye. Prominently displayed inside was a poster of Saddam. He and his men dismounted their tanks and checked it out. A cursory search of the vegetable shop revealed grenades and plastic explosives mixed with the cucumbers and tomatoes. While the vegetable disguises were novel, the Saddam poster decorating the wall indicated that they might as well have hung a sign proclaiming "Idiots Work Here" next to it.

Our men in the tank company searched every shop in the complex and found another merchant with a "garden variety" of explosives. As the situation developed, we sent some infantry support from First Lieutenant Mike Isbell's platoon of "Cobras" and ultimately arrested two men. We left an observation post to spy on the houses of the shop owners and pulled in two more men over the next two nights. One of them, Faris Amir Ahmed, was one of the insurgents who bombed Brad Boyd's convoy. We also found a detailed sketch plotting the June 7 attack on the CMIC that wounded several of our soldiers and killed Private First Class Jesse Halling.

The next few days were relatively calm. There was a lull in roadside bomb activity for several days following the harvest of exploding vegetable vendors in Cadaseeyah. We had sporadic contact but nothing significant. In fact, we actually had a little time to pause and reflect on Christmas. At a 4th Infantry Division prayer breakfast, General Odierno reminded us that we should be thankful to celebrate Christmas. He exhorted us to remember those who came to Iraq with us but would never celebrate again. That night, at a battalion candlelight service, the soldiers fashioned an American flag from some red, white, and blue Christmas lights they found.

Captain Craig Childs and I led in singing Christmas carols. Soon the soldiers took over, and I faded into the background, pensively contemplating the mind-boggling events since my last Christmas. We were separated from our families, but we had their love and prayers. We were separated from our homeland, but we had the best wishes of our countrymen, for the most part. We were separated from all we held dear, but we had the steadfast and loyal, unyielding bond of warriors in this harsh and desolate land.

It was an odd place to observe Christmas, but I quietly celebrated the birth of Jesus Christ, His salvation, and the hope He brings. I was grateful to command such exemplary soldiers who gave all they had day after thankless day. I was honored to be a part of our respected division, once viewed as having arrived too late to the war but now recognized as having delivered one of its greatest victories. Saddam Hussein was in captivity, and I was humbled to have been a part of his hunt and capture alongside fellow warriors in the special operations community and the regular "Joes" doing the tough work of soldiering. Despite the roller coaster of combat success and setback of the previous six months, I was truly thankful to be an American fighting man.

CRACKING THE WHIPS

The period immediately following the capture of Saddam Hussein had been interesting. The initial reaction locally was one of shock and, for a small number of dissidents, irrepressible anger that led to fatal action. We dealt with a broad range of response in the sure and steady way that characterized the work of our incomparable soldiers. We came with a clear objective and had always believed that we would prevail. Nothing we had experienced to date had changed that.

So much of our general mission had already been accomplished throughout Iraq in 2003. The overall task had been to defeat the Iraqi Army, overthrow Saddam's government, kill or capture the leaders of the Baathist regime, establish the foundation for a new government, and provide security until a new government could stand on its own. The only uncertainty was how long the last element might take. For us, it had never been a matter of whether, but when, we would achieve it.

My battalion would leave Tikrit better than we found it. We would cull those seeking to do harm to the people and to the institutions of the new Iraq. We were often questioned and criticized for employing tactics that seemed heavy-handed, but in truth, even the locals acknowledged that conditions were much improved because of our firmness.

As I reflected on our mission to that point, I likened the situation to that of a lion tamer who has cracked his whip frequently enough for the sting to be well known to the lions. They decide it best to sit calmly on their chairs. The lions understand that they could press their advantage and maul the tamer, but they realize that the cost is too high. Thus, they remain in their places. While the picture appears serene, the tamer knows that the air is fraught with tension and danger. The spectator knows nothing of the effort of rounding up the lions and establishing a disciplined regimen. The spectators see only the controlled result. The tamer knows all too well the hard work and consistency it took to achieve it.

After Christmas, the lions still desired to roam about in search of fresh meat. Unwilling to come at us directly, they roared with indirect fire attacks in an attempt to be heard. Our tank company received two such attacks on their compound on Christmas Day and the day following. During the second attack, the "Cougars" countered with .50 caliber machine gun fire at the attackers who were spotted in the distance launching 60mm mortar rounds from a residential area in the suburb of Cadaseeyah.

Our mortars worked up a counter battery mission, changed at the last moment to illumination by Jon Cecalupo. The scouts supported the "Cougars" in a search but were unable to get the attackers—this time. We discussed at length the dilemma of firing that mission and the type of munitions we used in a populated area. Risk of collateral damage had to be weighed against the risk of insurgents using the population to kill our soldiers. I tended to see it as a military target. The enemy was there, they were shooting us, and we needed to make it stop. Still, I was satisfied that the main reason Jon asked for illumination instead was that the shift from the mortar registration point had reduced the chance of the rounds landing on target in the residential area without a bracketing adjustment. Otherwise, we would have fired the explosive rounds.

The episode continued to illustrate the difficult task leaders faced when fighting an enemy that disregarded the laws of land warfare and hid behind the innocent. None of our soldiers were injured in this attack, and fortunately for us, the attackers were not first-rate mortarmen. Neither were those who attacked our compound on the night of 29 December. Those rounds struck the bridge across the Tigris River where our soldiers manned a checkpoint on each end. One round exploded harmlessly in the river while the other lodged in the base of the bridge without exploding.

The enemy, unable to inflict damage with his mortars, changed his approach to attacks we had not seen in some months. I believe this was due in part to having fewer willing to risk their lives for money alone or a Baathist resurgence that was now unlikely to materialize with the detainment of Saddam and so many of his leaders. Even so, we began to see more highly trained "diehards" emerge to engage us as they mustered what strength they could after our major advances during the last three months. We welcomed this in many ways, as we wanted to purge Tikrit of the most evil characters before redeploying in the next few months.

The first indication of a new round of street fights occurred in the late afternoon on 30 December. An infantry foot patrol led by Sergeant Jeff Allen from 2nd Squad, 2nd Platoon of C Company walked the streets in northern Tikrit around the "Chevron." Allen stopped to set up a flash checkpoint to search car traffic when a burst of gunfire interrupted the effort. Allen tumbled to the ground. A light blue car, unseen by the squad, had positioned itself by a corner, and a man had gotten out and shot at the patrol. The enemy immediately fled from the corner.

"I'm hit!" shouted Allen, as the soldiers scrambled for cover, scanning the area.

"Where you hit, sergeant?" called Private First Class Joseph Weaver.

"It's my back." Allen winced as he struggled for cover.

"Get down," yelled Private Robert Pena to a man moving along a rooftop. Gunfire began to pop from his M-16.

As his squad took cover and scanned the area, Specialist Gregory Sizer, the platoon medic, began to feel for Allen's wound. Carefully removing the body armor, he slipped his hand to Allen's back. There was a tear in the uniform but no entry or exit wound on Allen's torso. His body armor backplate was shattered. Two rifle rounds from an AK-47 had partially penetrated but were obstructed before they pierced Sergeant Allen.

"You're OK," informed Doc Sizer. "The plate stopped the bullets."

Allen slipped his body armor back on, heartened by the news but feeling as though someone had struck him in the back with a baseball bat. His soldiers moved cautiously along the houses where they believed the fire originated. As Specialist Patrick Belt led the squad to clear the suspect houses, First Sergeant Mike Evans arrived with reinforcements from the quick reaction force. Allen was evacuated to the battalion medics. Other than sporting an ugly, softball-sized bruise on his back, he was fine. Jeff Allen was truly a Regular, by God.

GET IT DONE

As 2003 came to a close, we pressed hard to secure intelligence on a number of Baathist individuals who were funneling money and weapons to finance attacks. Through signal intelligence intercepts, we were able to trace them to the inner city of Tikrit. It seemed that Saddam's capture had not collapsed the resistance. Now it was up to us to force the issue. We received orders from Colonel Hickey on 30 December to raid a large section of the city in attempts to find the individuals.

Information was scant, names were incomplete, and Colonel Hickey's patience was wearing thin. As I evaluated the situation, I believed that I could find the individuals by working the local intelligence networks, but I would need a little time. I went back to Hickey and laid out the situation for him.

"Sir, I need more time."

"Get it done, Colonel," ordered Hickey.

"Sir, you've asked us to raid a major portion of the city," I started apprehensively. "Far from dragging my feet, I want to accomplish the mission. But the prospect of finding a few individuals whose full names we do not know, living in an area containing 107 houses based on several ellipses drawn on a map from signal intercepts seems like a recipe for disaster."

"Are you saying you cannot carry out the order?" Hickey pushed back. He was losing patience.

"Sir, even if the scant information we have is accurate, these thugs would surely flee unless we hit the lottery on the very first house," I pushed back.

"You are an infantry commander with a large amount of resources," he started. "I will not have these insurgents freely moving about the city killing our soldiers. Get it done!"

"Sir, I fully intend to get it done," I said, sensing a confrontation neither he nor I would welcome. I tried one more tactic. "Sir, as your infantry commander, you expect me to make recommendations to you and provide my insight on how best to accomplish our missions.

"I'm not asking to call off the mission. I am asking for twenty-four hours to develop my intel sources so I can narrow this target from 107 houses to perhaps a few we can actually get. I need twenty-four hours."

Pausing and glaring, Hickey blurted, "You've got your twenty-four hours, Colonel, and I want this mission accomplished. Is that clear?"

"Yes, sir, it is," I shot back. "I will make good use of it."

We were all feeling the pressure. Colonel Hickey was fed up, as we all were, with the recent spike of activity and the wounding of several soldiers in the last two weeks. From his view, any lead needed to be relentlessly pursued. I agreed but realized that if we turned hundreds of residents out into the streets by raiding their houses in a single evening, there would be serious repercussions. We would create more enemies than we would find. My best hope lay in using the Mukhtar network that had proven invaluable to us in recent months.

Joe Filmore and I approached our secret source that night. We explained the need to find three men. If I could deliver the very negligible information we had to the Mukhtar, there was a chance of narrowing the targets for the raid. As the companies patrolled the city, we worked the intelligence piece hard. Tougher targets than these had been uncovered in the last few months. We had even hunted down Saddam Hussein successfully. We ought to be able to flush out a handful of rebels. We went to work refining the targets in order to minimize the impact on the unwitting locals they used for sanctuary.

The information we provided the Mukhtar and his son was thin at best. One individual we were seeking had a son of a certain name and the other worked in Jordan and they talked to each other on the phone. A different man who had a certain type of business in Tikrit talked to them both. That was it. That was all we had from the signal intercepts other than the attacks they were planning and the types of weapons they were moving. We knew that they were communicating by short wave radio transmissions, but I did not disclose this to our source. Incredibly, by the end of the following day we were in possession of the full names and locations of our targets. Our raids would commence on New Year's Eve and target just four houses instead of the 107 houses in the original plan.

Toward evening, as we prepared for these raids, Mike Evans, C Company's first sergeant, provided rations and water to his 3rd Platoon soldiers who were guarding the Civil Military Information Center. It was a routine task. He dropped off the rations and then left. Unknown to him, two men in a white Oldsmobile parked under cover of darkness in a back alley across the street drew pistols, and frightened away a local boy playing in the area. This was the same alley used in the CMIC attack on our soldiers the previous June. The insurgents, using the alley to mask their covert activity, placed a 107mm rocket on an earth berm used to cover a water main. The enemy crudely aimed the rocket toward the building where our soldiers were and hooked a motorcycle battery to it. Touching the terminals to the battery as they hid behind the cover of dwellings, the rebel rocketeers ducked as the missile popped, ignited its motor, and lurched across the highway like some child's bottle-rocket experiment from the Fourth of July.

Staff Sergeant Matt Lessau had placed his men in various positions to support the feeding of the soldiers. Specialist Radhames Camilo manned a machine gun on the roof of the CMIC, pulling security. He noticed two red flares launch into the sky toward the south and thought it strange when he heard the initial pop across the street. He saw a stream of flame heading his way and lunged for the floor. Private First Class Andrew Pollock left his position at the gate to climb back on his Bradley. He saw the flame shoot from the back alley, tracing its way to the second floor of the CMIC.

Lessau and the others in his squad were on the first floor preparing the rations when the rocket slammed into the building. The structure quivered as the rocket penetrated the wall and propelled through two more walls of the second floor before exploding. Flash and flame brightened the windows, followed by a gentle oozing of secondary smoke and dust. Miraculously, with soldiers on the lower floor, courtyard, and roof at that exact moment, no one was harmed.

Sergeant Ramon Esparza-Reyes, alerted to the enemy attack location by Camilo, organized his men, who began to pepper the alleyway with small arms and light automatic weapons. Specialist Bradley Burns supported them with his squad automatic weapon from the courtyard.

Captain Mitch Carlisle heard the explosion and gunfire from the location he had just left. He had been with the element that dropped off the chow to the soldiers. I had placed Mitch in temporary command of C Company while Captain Boyd recovered from his wounds. He was doing a superb job.

Carlisle and First Sergeant Evans turned their Humvees around, trying to determine the direction of attack. Meanwhile, Staff Sergeant Lessau's soldiers at the CMIC laid down a large amount of fire on the alleyway, opening up a general engagement. As they did, Carlisle's group spied three individuals fleeing the area near the alleyway where the soldiers at the CMIC were shooting. Mitch maneuvered his element slightly, hoping to cut them off. Seeing Captain Carlisle's group moving to cut off the enemy, Staff Sergeant Lessau ordered his men to cease firing.

First Sergeant Evans fired a flare pistol to warn the three escapees and to deduce their intentions. Seeing hostile intent, he maneuvered an element on foot, firing at the enemy. Specialist Sergio Cardenas and Specialist Jacob Lynn joined them. Specialists Byron Foster and Rodrigo Vargas oriented on their fire and opened up with their Hummer-mounted .50 caliber machine guns, dusting up the fleeing element until they disappeared from view into the densely populated residential block.

Captain Carlisle had the CMIC forces hold while he took the supporting element toward the neighborhood where the enemy had vanished. As they entered that street, Sergeant Mark Callahan noticed one of the three lay dead, hit in the jaw by .50 caliber machine gun fire. The "Cobras" then cleared the houses where they believed the other two had found safe harbor. They were not located.

As the "Cobras" checked their men and equipment following the attack, Bryan Luke and I readied the battalion for the evening mission. We still had a major raid to conduct. Captain Carlisle was able to consolidate his forces and ready them for the raid. Fortunately, none of Staff Sergeant Lessau's men had been hit in the CMIC. The enemy, however, paid a great price for their attack.

On New Year's Eve, we launched the raid for which I had requested a twenty-four-hour delay. Mark Stouffer's "Gators" and Chris Morris' "Commanches" joined Mitch Carlisle's "Cobras" to hit all four targets simultaneously. We found all three of the targeted individuals and, more importantly, were able to capture all the special transmitters and cell phones. They exactly matched the types that division intelligence forces had intercepted. As we searched the houses, we found a fair number of weapons, large amounts of money, and documents providing details that we would use to launch a very large raid in the weeks to come.

NEW YEAR, OLD FIGHT

Around the world, people awakened to January 1, 2004, with resolutions and hope for a better year, as if old habits, deep-seated desires, and human nature had loosened their grip on their daily lives. Usually, such lofty aspirations faded after a few weeks. For us, it was mere hours. New Year's Day was just another bloody, hard-fought day. Consistency and drive would make the difference in the success of our mission, not some folkloric tradition on a particular calendar date.

The enemy continued to find his courage, in spite of the colder weather and overcast skies. By early afternoon, suspicious activity had been spotted on rooftops near the "Chevron." Our soldiers on patrol, alert as always, had already discovered another cinder block bomb. By mid-afternoon, an MP convoy had been bombed, but the timing of the attack was slightly off, and the bomb detonated between two of the MP Hummers.

With our patrols meandering through much of the city, First Lieutenant Conrad Wilmoski, our medical platoon leader, assisted in the escort of a brigade medical element transporting an Iraqi man to the combat surgical hospital. The escort accomplished, he returned his "Blood Convoy" back to our headquarters. Slightly ahead of them, a white Mercedes dropped a wheat sack near the curb and then immediately accelerated to put some distance between them and the convoy. Despite the clearly delineated red crosses on the white background identifying them as medical vehicles, the enemy attacked them.

Lieutenant Wilmoski and his driver, Specialist Chase Cradeur, noticed what appeared to be a wheat sack near the drain recess by the curb. They saw the speeding car ahead but had only moments to process the information. They had just exited the Highway 1 overpass and were entering the city from the interchange. Before they could alert anyone to the danger, they were already past it.

Driving trail in the five-ton truck, Specialist Lovie Moran was thrown to the passenger side by a violent explosion. Keeping his foot on the gas pedal but unable to see, he focused on keeping the wheel straight toward the last direction he had been going. Riding shotgun, Corporal Reuben Nambo tried to focus on getting through the blast area. Private Ronald Bailey was pulling security in the five-ton cupola when the bomb went off. He blacked out completely.

Moran felt the truck shudder and wobble to a stop. Six of its tires were blown, holes littered the skirts and sides of the truck, and it was leaking badly. Only its substantial size and height prevented greater injury to our soldiers. Corporal Nambo called to Moran and Bailey to get out of the truck. Vaguely sensing Corporal Nambo's order through his dazed state, Moran pulled himself from the truck. His arm was bleeding and his uniform torn. Bailey came to and reflexively followed the others. Suddenly feeling dizzy, he soon found himself on the ground.

Lieutenant Wilmoski set up a perimeter. The wounded soldiers were fortunate that everyone in this convoy was a medic. Spurred into action, they placed Bailey on a stretcher and dressed his wounds. Specialist Moran, with his arm now bandaged, continued to pull security. Captain Jon Cecalupo's "Cougars" heard the blast and responded immediately, quickly followed by Captain Carlisle's "Cobras." They searched the area, gathered evidence, and assisted in the ground evacuation of our two wounded soldiers.

The enemy was becoming brazen. Short of garrisoning the entire city, we could not cover everything. We could not prevent normal life from happening, and the enemy exploited that normalcy to shroud their underhanded movement. They were shifting tactics from night to day and from indirect assaults to face-to-face attacks. The enemy was assailing soldiers from back alleys and side streets. He was dropping bombs in front of convoys. The white Mercedes plop-and-drop bomber was becoming a major nuisance. He had already accounted for several wounded men in my battalion, including Brad Boyd. Two more were added to his list that day. Chris Morris' scouts were still set up in the area of the city most likely to net him, and would be for several more days.

I had planned a series of raids in close collaboration with a detachment from the 10th Special Forces Group recently assigned to Tikrit. We hoped to shut down the trigger-pulling network reinvigorated following Saddam's capture. Having worked previously with the 10th Group in Kosovo and with the 3rd Group in Afghanistan, for me they were a most welcome sight. We were still refining our targets based on a large quantity of intelligence from the Mukhtar and his son. We would use this information along with the intelligence that "Pat" and his Special Forces element had developed to undertake a massive "roundup" raid that would catch them all by surprise. Pat and I had forged a strong working relationship. This would be our first big raid together.

Having expended a great deal of mental energy throughout the day working the intelligence for the raids, I was longing to get back on the streets to circulate among the men. Activity had been fairly heavy, and I felt it might continue into the evening. I dropped by to see Captain Mark Stouffer and his "Gators." They were doing great work in Auja and farther south, continuing to provide the quick-reaction forces as needed to parts of the city. We discussed the lifting of the lockdown as we were about ready to open the gates on the fenced-in village. I continued to be impressed with this fine officer. The entire southern area of our task force rarely caused me concern because of his skill and maturity. Mark would be leaving us very soon, and it was not something I wanted to think about.

Earlier in the fall, Mark had asked if I would write a recommendation for him to transfer to the 75th Ranger Regiment. He had served with them previously as a lieutenant, and I could think of no one more qualified to return. Unfortunately for me but good for the Army, he was accepted. Now we would lose him in a matter of weeks. Some would have advised waiting until our redeployment, but I recognized that opportunity does not always knock twice. I was very happy for him. Captain Mike Wagner could take the "Gators." I was confident that Mike would do well as he had worked for me earlier in III Corps operations.

After checking on Mark's men that night, I decided to visit the "Cobras" in the heart of the city. Heading toward the main intersection along Highway 1, I conferred briefly with Captain Mitch Carlisle and First Sergeant Mike Evans. While conversing, we were noisily ambushed by a pack of two dozen wild dogs. Attempting to gain our flank on the abandoned street after curfew, the dogs had good separation of forces and an impressive formation as they closed on us at about fifty feet. Mike Evans pulled his captured flare gun from his vest, cocked the hammer and sent a flare sailing on a red arc right through the middle of the pack. A brilliant flash of red magnesium light burst on the street. The unharmed dogs scampered in retreat, yelping as they fled in all directions. Observing us from the balconies of the main street apartments above the shops were several laughing Iraqi men who gave us the thumbs-up for the entertaining counterattack.

Though the attacks on us had certainly been intense since Saddam's capture, I perceived a sense of relief among the people even as they looked to an uncertain future. While they could not know what the future held, they were beginning to envision it without Saddam. Cooperation and even acts of kindness were initiated among the population of Tikrit. Unfortunately, much of that relief and cooperation would soon be shattered by an incident on the interchange loop of Highway 1 at the northern part of the city.

Ibrihim Allawi was transporting four passengers to the Mosul area in his blue Chevrolet Caprice taxi. Driving through Tikrit, he eased back his speed because a three-vehicle American convoy traveling the same direction was stalling the flow of traffic. Cars appeared to be passing safely, yet Allawi approached cautiously. Receiving a wave to proceed from a soldier in the trail vehicle, Allawi passed the first two vehicles. Just as he moved ahead of the lead vehicle, he felt sharp pain to his leg and heard loud bangs on his car. His hand was hot, and he felt excruciating pain to his stomach. Glass began to explode, the dash ripped open, and his passengers began to jerk and twist. Allawi lost control and the car went into the roadside ditch, where it came to an abrupt stop.

Struggling to gain his senses, he looked to the other passengers. Rasheed Hamoud Taha and his brother, Abdullah, were dead. Intisaar Khadem lay lifeless, clutching her seven-year-old son,

Ahmed. The boy's head had been ripped apart by the heavy caliber machine gun.

For Jon Cecalupo's men patrolling the Highway 1 bypass, the scene was horrific. Iraqi civilians, attempting to come to Allawi's aid, flagged down our soldiers. The men surveyed the carnage, immediately incensed at the scene played out before them. Whatever the perceived threat these innocent Iraqis posed, nothing on earth justified such wanton killing of innocents or the abandonment of them by the side of the road. Even if shot in error, the proper recourse would have been to stop and assist once the mistake was realized. Instead, the unknown unit convoy, among scores of others that passed along the main highway each day, left the tragedy to us.

Captain Cecalupo radioed our headquarters to request assistance with a translator. He also asked for the Iraqi civilian hospital to be alerted. Allawi was rushed to the hospital. Our soldiers began to ease the shattered bodies from the car. Iraqi provincial police chief, General Mezher, arrived at the scene, stunned by the occurrence. As the facts began to surface, I ordered Major Mike Rauhut to investigate the scene. I then alerted all commands that once the word of this tragedy unfolded, we would likely be seen as the perpetrators and would need to prepare for an increase in violence.

What Mike found was horrific. The car had been riddled with over forty rounds of .50 caliber heavy machine gun bullets. It was a miracle the driver survived. We quickly alerted Colonel Hickey to the tragedy and hoped whoever was responsible could be identified to get their side of the story. It never happened. No units would acknowledge responsibility. We opened an investigation that was later taken up by the 4th Infantry Division, but without evidence, the incident became an unexplained tragedy of war. For my soldiers handling the flesh and blood that day, it remains seared forever in their memories.

As might be expected, the press wanted the details surrounding the attack. I shared information with them freely, emphasizing that my soldiers were not involved. They could clearly differentiate between innocent civilians and the enemy. I was urged to play it cautiously, but I chose to state publicly my belief that the act of cowardice had been executed by a U.S. convoy. No other element had access to .50 caliber machine guns. Had an insurgent group been in possession of such weaponry, we surely would have noticed it on the road. I felt, as always, that speaking the truth as known when known would always be greeted with fairness. To the credit of the press, they could see that my soldiers were not involved and made no attempt to paint us as the perpetrators.

I met immediately with General Mezher to secure his assistance as well as the Governor's, to reinforce that neither "Tikrit's" soldiers nor my men were involved. While this eased the pressure slightly, it changed nothing in the hearts of those who hated us and viewed us all the same. This lesson (that the actions of one affect thousands) was about to be driven home.

DEATH THROES

Staff Sergeant German Sanchez moved about alertly with his squad as they walked their patrol from the Birthday Palace to the market area in Tikrit's city center. As they patrolled, his heightened senses told him that the temporary attitude of goodwill from the people had soured again. Men spat on the ground and narrowed their eyes as the soldiers passed by.

Continuing eastward to what we called Market Street or Cross Street, the soldiers heard an echoing pop and began looking intently for the source. Staff Sergeant Sanchez heard a man behind him screaming in pain. He spun around to see Specialist Will Gilstrap writhing on the ground, his Squad Automatic Weapon

(SAW) entangling him where he fell. A sniper's bullet had passed through the drum securing the weapon's belted ammunition, causing some of it to cook off. The bullet then passed into Gilstrap's pelvis and the secondary explosions made his midsection appear to be smoking.

Immediately the soldiers bristled their weapons in every direction, scrutinizing balconies, side streets, and bystanders. Specialists Jaime Garza and Jason Klepacz rushed to Gilstrap's aid, shielding him with their bodies, as he lay helpless in the street. Sergeant Michael Trujillo ordered a wider security as the soldiers fanned out. Using his squad radio, Staff Sergeant Sanchez alerted C Company to assist in Gilstrap's evacuation.

Specialist Garza tore open the wounded warrior's vest while Klepacz removed the SAW sling from around his neck. As Garza searched for wounds, he discovered a bloody hole in the pelvic area. The pain seemed almost unbearable for Gilstrap. Applying a bandage and pressure, the two soldiers comforted the exposed and wounded warrior as best they could while he lay on the street.

First Sergeant Evans arrived some minutes later with a Hummer for evacuation. Gilstrap was in extreme pain as the soldiers loaded him into the truck and rushed him to our battalion aid station. With his wounded man secured, Staff Sergeant Sanchez led his squad into the surrounding area where they reasoned the shot might have been fired. Searching several houses and probing adjacent alleys, they found nothing. The enemy scored on this one.

As soon as I was alerted to the casualty, I went to the aid station to see how serious Gilstrap's injury was. When they brought in Will Gilstrap, he was in excruciating pain. The bullet had perforated an area where the nerve endings were very sensitive. Doc Marzullo immediately set to work searching for the bullet as attendants gave the anguished soldier something to dull the pain. He began to calm but spiked with verbal assaults and stinging winces when probed.

To keep his mind off his condition, First Sergeant Evans began to tease and taunt Gilstrap. This seemed to work as he pushed back on his first sergeant with jabs and assertions of his toughness and manhood. After the doc stabilized him, Gilstrap was evacuated to the 28th Combat Surgical Hospital. He would suffer more than a dozen surgeries and limp with a cane, but he would make it.

It was time to strike back. We continued preparations for the upcoming raid, a large-scale operation. The locations for targeted individuals were shaping up nicely, but we wanted to snare as many of the enemy as possible. Having seen so many possible family connections over the past six months, we realized that each insurgent could literally bed down at one of three or four places each evening. That, compounded with the number of individuals being targeted, increased the possibilities exponentially and necessitated the utilization of the greatest part of my battalion for the raid.

Despite losing Gilstrap to wounds, we were able to contain the activity in the city. It appeared that the Tikrit Baathist resistance remaining loyal to Saddam was in its death throes. While there was indication that Baathists nationwide were shifting their allegiance to al-Qaeda operatives, we were not seeing it in our area. Nor did we wish to. With the ever-growing police force, the couple of hundred Civil Defense soldiers that were already patrolling with us, and the full cooperation of the Governor, we felt like we could get total control of the city now that Saddam was removed from the picture.

We dubbed the grand raid "The South 40 Roundup." It was a reference to most of the targets being in the southern portion of the city and along the Street of the Forty district that we called 40th Street. We would target twenty houses, three shops, and eighteen individuals. Most were in the "Trigger Puller" category but still had family ties to those who had harbored Saddam. Even with their leader gone, they still maintained their deadly allegiance.

The raid was set for January 8, 2004. With a tactical modification, we struck that night at approximately 11:00 p.m. That being the hour of curfew, we reasoned that most of the targets would just be settling down for the night, thereby raising the probability of our finding their security lax. I additionally reasoned that the large number of forces used in this mission might not immediately arouse suspicion as the enemy was accustomed to seeing increased patrols around curfew time.

Pat's Green Berets struck several of the targets related to a cell they had been tracking. We hit the ones related to bomb attacks against our soldiers and those attempting to infiltrate the Iraqi police. Striking with coordinated swiftness, we found twelve of the eighteen targets. Two were cell network commanders, seven were trigger pullers, one was a bomb maker, and two were manufacturers of fake police identification cards. We seized bomb-making components, stacks of fake IDs, the equipment to produce said IDs, and numerous photos that we would later find useful in tracking down those we missed.

Mark Stouffer's "Gators" were wrapping up their targets while Mitch Carlisle's "Cobras" continued to ransack the fake ID maker's house for evidence and clues. Chris Morris' "Comanches" assisted Pat's team while Jon Cecalupo's "Cougars" provided city security. I had positioned myself between the "Gators" and "Cobras." Command Sergeant Major Pete Martinez controlled the detainee evacuation, as he often did on larger raids, to provide a central battalion collection point for the companies. A few of my command group soldiers were assisting Martinez when one of the detainees broke free of his zip cuffs and lunged at Specialist Jeff Barnaby.

How the insurgent broke his cuffs became evident when he attacked Barnaby with a "Knuckle Duster" fighting knife sporting a blade with brass knuckles built into the hand grip. While Barnaby was frequently described as "pint-sized," he was one tough soldier. He not only contained the Iraqi but prevented injury to himself. Several other soldiers, seeing the struggle, subdued the insurgent, who was whisked away posthaste with his peers.

Several authorized reporters witnessed the attack and were amazed at the soldiers' restraint and presence of mind, as any one of us would have been justified in shooting this man point-blank. It irrefutably demonstrated that our targets were not poor innocents wrenched unjustly from their homes in the middle of the night. These evil men would sacrifice their own countrymen for their cause.

At the raid's wrap-up, Robin Pomeroy from Reuters asked for my assessment and the meaning of the evening's events.

"We're trying to get out the last remaining resistance in the city," I replied. "I think it was a good night. Tikrit will be a safer place tomorrow as a result."

Tomorrow came, and as predicted, a sense of relief permeated the city. The locals began to talk excitedly of the future and optimistically anticipated getting on with their lives. While I certainly believed that they were nearer that dream, I knew that we must remain focused and vigilant until the 1st Infantry Division relieved us in March.

HOW'S BUSINESS?

With the exception of a university school bus running over a landmine intended for Jon Cecalupo's tanks on 15 January, the coming days did appear safer. As tragic as that scene was, with the ensuing loss of life, the overall activity in our area fell sharply, yielding a well-deserved respite for our soldiers. Our patrols remained consistent, but the city seemed much more relaxed.

Hoping to take advantage of this lull, I asked Colonel Hickey about the possibility of obtaining startup funds for some small businesses in our area, particularly along 40th and 60th streets of Tikrit. Procurement of friendly young entrepreneurs would produce Iraqi men focused on profit rather than pandemonium and perhaps new sets of eyes and ears in the area.

Exploring options led us headlong into a typical bureaucratic morass. No worthy idea would go unpunished. Every proposal was routed through some unrelated group, agency, or system whose priorities had no relationship with troops fighting on the ground. At such moments, I was envious of British field commanders in Iraq and Afghanistan empowered to produce and fund credible projects. Our "assessment" teams were unable to follow up with financing for potential and promising enterprises. Sadly, field commanders were not trusted to invest small amounts of money where most needed. Commanders would later be sanctioned to directly coordinate "micro-grants." At this time in the mission, however, these options were not available.

Undaunted, Colonel Hickey and I were able to secure some subsidies earmarked for religious purposes and intended as relief aid to the area. The funds were intended for allocation to local imams who, in turn, would distribute goodwill through the mosques. In our experience, the only commodities distributed in the mosques of Tikrit were enemy weapons and propaganda.

I made the argument that underwriting small businesses in modest amounts of one hundred to two hundred dollars per venture rather than dispersing free "aid" to imams of dubious motivation would give the same result. General Odierno agreed. Fully comprehending the circumstances in Tikrit, he earmarked some discretionary funding for Colonel Hickey and the other brigade commanders across northern Iraq.

The allotment to my battalion amounted to approximately five thousand dollars, a seemingly insignificant sum. In Iraq, however, it had roughly thirty times the buying power it would have in the States. The difficulty would be in disseminating the funds judiciously. Indiscriminate distribution might well create a new dilemma. Further, Army bureaucracy required each transaction to be recorded and traceable to a known recipient. Getting "known recipients" to cooperate with the Army would be a challenge of its own.

There had been a time when I implored Colonel Hickey to close the Civil Military Information Center because it was an RPG magnet. One of our soldiers lost his life there, and many others were wounded during its tenure, including one the previous week. Colonel Hickey refused permission for closure, so it was guarded at our own peril. Nevertheless, Iraqis could interface freely with us at the CMIC with minimal risk. At last, it would redeem itself as an improvised "small business administration" distribution center.

Since Iraqis would often use the CMIC to lodge complaints and make claims against Americans, it seemed the perfect place to receive funds for cooperating with us without fear of suspicion. If the money were disbursed from the CMIC, a man could claim it was for damages or whatever other explanation he could concoct. Application needed to first be made at the CMIC before receiving the funds from the Finance Corps, who needed assurance that the Iraqi in question was one authorized by us for payment.

I considered a wide range of ideas from some form of battalion currency to some type of note "known recipients" could present to Finance Corps. Whatever we produced would, no doubt, be compromised eventually. Since I only had a $5,000 endowment,

I decided to use a deck of cards, assigning a value of one hundred dollars per card. Rummaging through my kit, I found a pack of National Rifle Association cards that I was certain would exist nowhere else in Iraq and would be difficult to forge. I could present a single card to a future businessman signed and dated in red ink on the face, explaining the value of that card was $100.00, redeemable at the CMIC to underwrite his business. He need only negotiate it in the aforementioned manner, and no questions would be asked. I could issue multiple cards if the situation warranted. It worked like a charm.

So it was in the coming weeks; we would simultaneously patrol and seek to promote local business development. Word quickly spread about American soldiers subsidizing small local shops. We helped a new barber secure chairs and equipment. Electronics shops, produce stalls, convenience stores, and the like benefited from our endowment. As we made the rounds on patrol, we also made note of positive activity and engaged the locals for their assessment of threats and trouble in each neighborhood.

On 17 January, we piled into our Hummers along with Matt Stannard, a reporter from the *San Francisco Chronicle,* to conduct a routine patrol during which we proposed to interact with local shop owners. It would be a good way to show him a different perspective of the progress we were making and for him to mingle with the population. I also used it as an opportunity to take my intelligence officer, Captain Clay Bell, along to get his appraisal of the population. Major Bryan Luke, who normally accompanied me on all combat patrols, was hip deep in alligators planning the transition for our relief in the coming weeks. Clay would assume his duties as my field operations officer for this patrol since Mitch Carlisle was temporarily commanding C Company.

We meandered south along 40th Street, making the loop north on 60th Street, while various patrols from the battalion scoured the city and surrounding villages. We found some new graffiti and quickly sprayed over it; we found what turned out to be an innocuous cinder block we had treated as a bomb. The city seemed pretty relaxed overall. Resuming our patrol, we pulled up to a small convenience shop. Several young Iraqi men were there along with the owner's children. I wanted to ask him how things were going.

"How's business?" I asked as a deafening explosion washed over us. Flashes of light flared to the north as gunfire began to pop.

"We've got a burning car!" shouted Sergeant First Class Gil Nail as a white Mercedes rolled from the side street, bounced the curb, and careened into a small palm tree short of the residential wall.

"All right, watch 360!" I ordered. "Let's go."

We rushed the Hummers forward to close up with our vehicle-mounted machine guns and leapt to the street, taking up positions on each side.

We ran toward the enemy, unsure of the situation unfolding before us. Gunfire seemed sporadic. We worked our way toward the scene with Gil Nail and Cody Hoefer on the left as I led out with Sergeant Jeff Mann and Specialist Michael Bressette on the right. Clay Bell radioed the contact to battalion to alert all units in the area. Intense flame gushed from the car. Gunfire popped on the left side of the street north of Gil Nail but seemed to be inaccurately aimed.

Acting on training and instinct, Gil and Cody watched my side of the street as I watched theirs. A flickering glow from the car lit the intersection, revealing at least one person on the street. Getting my first clear look at the car, I immediately registered "white Mercedes" in my mind. I found an injured man near the car who would surely burn if not moved, so I grasped his feet as Bressette lifted his torso. We moved him about twenty feet to the sidewalk, and a gate sprung open near us. Sergeant Mann covered it as all of our rifle muzzles locked on the head of a local resident peeking out in curiosity. Sensing his innocence, we gestured a thumbs-up to show no hostile intent. He gave a nervous smile and seemed to relax while watching our efforts.

Mike Bressette and I checked the injured man. He was a young Iraqi in his early twenties and appeared to be dressed for mayhem. While unarmed, he displayed all the other characteristics of the types that we typically encountered in street fights.

"Venegas, bring a stretcher! We got a live one who needs help," I yelled to Private Luis Venegas, a medic newly assigned to my command convoy.

As we checked the injured man for wounds, the curious resident pointed and spoke in broken English, "Why you no help him?"

Him? Who was "him"? I scanned the street and car. Gil Nail and Cody Hoefer were scouting the origin of gunfire and were focused west while the remaining men near the vehicles covered us and scanned south. Staff Sergeant Lonnie Hinton kept new traffic at bay as it advanced up the street.

Between Sergeant First Class Nail and me was "him." A badly broken human being was splayed on the street in a supine position. While Bressette covered the first man being attended by Venegas, Sergeant Mann and I checked out the newly discovered Iraqi. He displayed the obvious look of death. His face was seared, and his eyes were gray, glazed, and open as blood pooled around his head. He had been severely burned as well. Blood trickled from multiple wounds along his entire body. In the center of his chest was a silver-dollar-sized hole.

Kneeling beside him, certain he was dead, I grabbed his left wrist to check his pulse. As I did, he gurgled horrendously and twitched with life-struggling movement. The hole in his chest sputtered, and his jaw moved with attempted speech. He stared through visionless eyes at the sky above.

"Venegas, this guy is alive!" I called out. "Chest wound, severe burns to the face, and internal bleeding."

Diverting his attention from the slightly injured man at the sidewalk, now in the care of the Iraqi resident, Venegas rushed into the street with his aid bag. Sergeant Mann and Bressette helped with the stretcher. We lifted him onto it as Venegas tore into the bag for a venting chest tube and an IV bladder. He stuck the IV and tended to the sucking chest wound. The man was no longer making gurgling sounds, and in moments he lay still.

"He's gone, sir," the young medic informed.

"All right," I replied coldly. "Dump him. We need the stretcher."

I studied the area while Venegas worked to save the man's life. Plastic parts lay scattered about. An electronic bomb initiator lay near the dead man. The popping sounds of rounds cooking off indicated a smelting AK-47 or two in the vehicle. These were insurgents, and they had just tried to kill us. I morphed from compassionate to angry as reality washed over me.

This is THE white Mercedes. They were attempting to place a bomb in the road as we came up the street. These were the bastards who tried to kill Brad Boyd and had wounded a half dozen of my men in the last month. They were trying to kill us. My mind snapped back to reality when Gil Nail walked up to me.

"Sir, I think we have another one," he surmised, waving something in his hand. It was a human foot. "The other two have both of theirs."

I looked to the ground and saw that the dead man, while extremely mutilated, had both feet. The other insurgent was more or less sound as well.

"Let's look for the rest of him," I ordered. "He could be

anywhere. Look for more evidence like this, too," I added, holding parts of the bomb-initiating device.

"Roger, sir," acknowledged Nail as he moved with several other men who had closed in to help.

Clay Bell studied the area for an obvious bomb attack. It appeared that these men had been shadowing our patrol and diverted down a side street to lay a trap for us. They must have gotten their wires crossed prematurely and set off the device. The initial AK-47 firing was from a local resident on the corner who believed he was being attacked and fired bursts of intimidation to ward off the attackers. The later gunfire came from flaming AK-47s in the volcanic car.

C Company began to arrive with First Lieutenant Mike Isbell's 3rd Platoon. They secured the area. First Sergeant Mike Evans offered his medics to assist Venegas. Gil Nail relayed orders to contact the Iraqi Fire Department to extinguish the exploding and intensely burning car whose roof was split open by the blast. Combustion of burning elements emitted random but mild explosions. The tires were melting, but amazingly, the headlights were still beaming. You have to admire German engineering.

We assembled a collection of body parts, including a match for the foot. The missing torso would be discovered when fire hoses doused the remains of the car. A square chunk of black char emerged, topped off with what appeared to be the remnants of a skull near the open right side back door.

At this juncture, it seemed that the three insurgents had flanked us on the western outskirts of the city. When they saw us pause to talk to the local businessman, they came up a side street quite near to us and prepared to set a bomb fashioned from an artillery shell with plastic explosives stuck in the nose and a fuse inserted into it.

The young guy we found alive exited the car while the bomb layer prepared to emplace the device on the street. Sitting in the rear passenger seat with the bomb in his lap, Mr. Bomber swiveled to exit the open door. That's when the electrical circuit completed on the device he held. He was blown to bits, with portions of his arms and legs sailing outward while his torso stayed behind. The blast lifted a part of the roof off the car and immediately sparked the gas tank. The driver was burned and pierced with shell fragmentation, losing control of the car as it did a slow coast. The flaming Mercedes then struck the residential wall after bouncing up a curb. While the driver somehow managed to exit, he collapsed in the street and rolled over on his back. Stunned and injured by the concussive blast, the young guy also fell to the sidewalk near the car.

During this entire episode, I was oblivious to the presence of Matt Stannard from the *Chronicle*. Not only did he advance with us, but he also snapped some incredible photos of raw action as we were put through the paces of another act of combat.

With the car now doused and its entire complement or their remains collected, we gathered what information we could. The tag of the Mercedes was from Baghdad. Using our "Mukhint" contacts, we discovered that our would-be killers were well connected to Saddam. The driver was Bashar Sadiq Jassim, a nephew of Watban al-Hasan, better known as Saddam's half brother. We think that he was the man who died in the street. The man blown to bits was Ahmed Ayad Sachran and a neighbor of Jassim's. The young guy who survived was an unknown local insurgent named Ahmed Mohammed Juwad.

We resumed our patrol, leaving the recovery to the local Iraqis and the "Cobras" of C Company. It was good just to be alive. As I took it all in, I could not help but think again of the words found in Psalm 64:

> *Protect me from the plots of the wicked, from the scheming of those who do evil. Sharp tongues are the swords they wield;*

bitter words are the arrows they aim. They shoot from ambush at the innocent, attacking suddenly and fearlessly. They encourage each other to do evil and plan how to set their traps. "Who will ever notice?" they ask. As they plot their crimes, they say, "We have devised the perfect plan!" Yes, the human heart and mind are cunning. But God himself will shoot them down. Suddenly, his arrows will pierce them.

I was thankful on this night that business for us was very good indeed.

8. TORMENT

FIGHTING FOR A NATION

Roadside bombs were, without question, a major problem we faced in combat. We had developed tactics that reduced their effectiveness to only about 30 percent of those employed, and of those, less than half caused injury. Jon Cecalupo's "Cougars" would patrol the outer city loop while Mitch Carlisle's "Cobras" focused on the northern two-thirds of the city and Cadaseeyah. The "Gators," now under the command of Mike Wagner, covered the southern third of Tikrit as well as the villages of Auja, Oynot, and south along Highway 1. Linked in with Lieutenant Colonel Mark Huron's 299th Engineers, we were able to keep the area fairly clear of roadside bombs.

Even so, the injuries were usually severe when we missed one. A day after my latest close call, Scott Thomas' "Bears" in B Company had a close call of their own. A bomber in Bayjii had damaged another Bradley that escaped with holes and scars, but our first-rate mechanics were able to keep it in action. Fortunately, there were no injuries.

We were now getting closer to going home. Advance parties from the 1st Infantry Division had already visited our area, and our relief units were identified. While this was certainly good news, my mood was mixed. I knew that this was the most dangerous time we could face if we did not remain focused. There was so much work to be done, and we only had eight weeks left to do it. With Saddam gone and his Baathist insurgency network severely degraded in our area, we still had the responsibility to tighten up the local government, strengthen the police relationships, and continue to train more Iraqi Civil Defense troops who clearly would become part of the future Iraqi Army. We were already deploying over 200 of them in our daily operations.

By this time, not only had I been able to use these Iraqi troops as a fairly reliable augmentation force of company size, but we had enough of them to allow for platoon-sized augmentation on the patrol routes of our companies. That gave me a mobile force for battalion use, and the companies could use an Iraqi static force to pull their guys off of checkpoints.

The Iraqis demonstrated bravery equal to those we were fighting and were not afraid to fight for their new nation. We had already lost one Iraqi soldier who was gunned down in Cadaseeyah on 8 January. We gave him full honors.

Our Iraqi soldiers faced danger at checkpoints all along Highway 1 from north to the CMIC to south of the city near Auja, in sandbagged bunkers perched on the highway's center median. This effectively restricted the flow of insurgents when our patrols were not at a particular location.

Our wonderful CMIC proved yet again why I wanted it closed down, despite its usefulness to local business engagement. At dusk on the 19th of January, Corporal Patrick Tayfel led a small foot patrol into the surrounding area. After the patrol was complete, the small group of American and Iraqi soldiers wove their way back to the CMIC for drop-off and to link up with the Iraqi checkpoint there. Suddenly, a burst of fire let loose from the vicinity of the

"Lucky Panda" ice cream shop. C Company troops at the CMIC covered Highway 1 and sent a squad to reinforce, but the enemy could not be located.

Specialist Bradley Burns, at the trail of the patrol, held up his left arm and called out to the others. A bullet cut along the back of his left hand, tearing into several tendons and shattering bone. Corporal Tayfel covered Burns as an Iraqi soldier began to administer first aid to his hand. They were able to get the patrol and Burns back to the CMIC.

First Sergeant Mike Evans arrived to take Burns to the battalion aid station while patrols from C Company scoured the surrounding area. Confusion reigned as other insurgents made their way into the crowds around the market area of the city north of Cross Street. The "Cobras" spotted one man with a weapon and fired warning shots, trying to avoid the crowd. Others fired at a fleeing car, wounding one of its occupants. When the gunfire reached a peak, Specialist Jacob Lynn opened up with his vehicle-mounted .50 caliber machine gun on the wall of a building from which he believed he was receiving fire. That caused the entire crowd to part like the Red Sea.

After this firing crescendo, our men were able to search the area. Unfortunately, the attackers fled. Locals stated that the attack had been conducted by black-clad men wearing black kaffiyeh headdresses who sped along a back alley in a late '70s blue, four-door Chevy Malibu. The enemy scored a small victory on us with the wounding of Brad Burns, but the streets were still ours. Burns would undergo multiple complex hand surgeries. Eventually, his tendons and joints would deteriorate, causing him to lose a finger. He was a calm and brave man that day.

It was obvious that the threat of insurgent activity, while waning, had not fully abated. We even had indication in other areas of Iraq that pro-Saddam groups were aligning themselves with al-Qaeda operatives such as those led by Abu Musab al-Zarqawi. Our enemy still appeared to be the loyalists to Saddam. While the street fights had claimed a few wounded recently, the roadside bomb was still the greatest threat.

Despite the street fights, we did not stop our raiding, even with the major players suffering big losses. My soldiers continued to work closely with John's special operations team on small, pinpoint raids. My Scout Platoon, led by Chris Morris, usually participated in these combined raids. We also acted rapidly on free-flowing intel that greatly contributed to keeping Tikrit beautiful. The fruit of these raids in January included such notables as Hadooshis, Khatabs, Shehabs, and Musslits. If necessary, we were willing to collect the whole set.

John's team would transition back to the States by February. They would be missed and the bonds we felt with them cannot be described. In their place, a new SOF team led by "Liam" worked a few raids with us, but by and large, the major hunt for Saddam and his henchmen was now over. The special ops community began to shift its focus to the al-Qaeda connections farther south while we labored to strengthen the Iraqi civil and military structure in Tikrit and Salah ad Din province. The hope was that by the time we left, Iraqis would secure some of the void as the 1st Infantry Division shifted its resources to cover more ground.

In the meantime, I urged my commanders to not only remain vigilant but also realize that our actions against enemy threats could only mean fewer insurgents for someone else to face. I was very proud of my commanders and the way they handled the breakneck pace that all of our soldiers had been keeping for the better part of a year.

Every single day, these young soldiers woke to new tasks, new patrols, and new threats. To handle the risk, their alertness was punctuated by 100 percent adrenaline as the mind pushed the body to stay alive. While nineteen and twenty-year-olds back home were focused on carefree lives or youthful pursuits, our soldiers were becoming men acquainted with their mortality. Such high-gear, full-speed daily life begins to take its toll, even on young and healthy soldiers, but they were still holding up with very good morale.

Our Bradleys were also holding up to the breakneck pace. We were driving the road wheels and tracks off of them all day, every day to support the soldiers in their worn-out boots and faded uniforms. Night was the norm for our most intense patrols as the sun now sank around 6:00 or 7:00 p.m. each evening. The temperature would drop with it, and the soldiers could often be seen in various forms of wet weather gear and clothing to protect against the cold. It was still the rainy season in Iraq.

Command Sergeant Major Pete Martinez and our stable of tireless first sergeants kept the troops ammoed, fueled, and fed. Few soldiers worked harder. First Sergeant Delionel Meadows had the unenviable task of keeping the headquarters troops in order. He and Captain Chris Fallon, while not on the streets every day, did a marvelous job with "Hammer" Company, defending my headquarters against multiple attacks while supplying everything the vast variety of troops in this company needed. No enemy was ever able to penetrate our defenses, due to their superb work.

The line first sergeants were fighters, suppliers, ambulance drivers, administrators, and right-hand men to their commanders. Their task was enormous. Mike Evans carried a huge load when C Company lost its commander. Jaime Garza kept the A Company "Gators" fighting fit through their recent change in company commanders. My B Company in Bayjii had recently been sent a new first sergeant to replace the tough and able Louis Holzworth, who was due to take my headquarters company from First Sergeant Meadows.

Newly assigned First Sergeant Robert Summerfield was a

unique fit for the "Bears" of B Company because he was an engineer rather than an infantryman. When Pete put the notion to me that he and brigade Command Sergeant Major Larry Wilson were looking to put him in a rifle company, it just made good sense to give him the "Bears." He was a first sergeant of high caliber, and we were glad to get him.

First Sergeant Summerfield wasted little time getting the feel of his men and the environment around Bayjii. Not only did he keep the men supplied, but he also fought on patrols with them like all of our top sergeants.

On the 24th of January, Summerfield was leading a Bradley section on combat patrol with vehicle B23 and his own B65. While Sergeant Braden Sickles took the lead in B23, Summerfield covered the trail. The initial mission was to gain some information from an informant and follow it with a raid. On this night, there was no new information, so Summerfield gathered Sergeant Sickles and the rifle squad led by Staff Sergeant Dale Howell and Sergeant Jose Montenegro to establish some outposts in the city. Disgorging troops to their designated point short of the hot spots of Bayjii, the patrol cruised a loop north along Highway 1 and then swung south to support them. Another patrol was not far away, if needed.

Staff Sergeant Montenegro and Sergeant Howell set their elements on opposite sides of the highway and prepared for action. They received a tip from a local about a gray Opel with four men planning to attack Americans, using RPGs and small arms. Unfortunately, no time or date was specified. Still, the soldiers remained alert.

Sergeant Chad Stursma, at the gun of B65, did this kind of patrol often. He and driver Private First Class Ervin Dervishi had been on many a patrol. It was typically a top-notch crew to be selected to gun and drive for the first sergeant. They knew it, and they knew their jobs. They had been in tough scraps before and would take care of their new first sergeant. As they made their way south along Highway 1 into the heart of Bayjii, Stursma scanned the turret like a pendulum, covering the rear of the patrol from 4 to 8 o'clock if it were viewed on the face of a clock.

For Ervin Dervishi, it was a long journey that brought him to Bayjii and the Regulars of 1-22 Infantry. Dervishi loved American soldiers and never dreamed, when he was an Albanian boy in Kosovo, that he would emigrate to the United States with his family and become an American citizen. Now he was living his dream. It pained him that jihadists had taken Islam and twisted it to suit their lawless attacks. He was Muslim himself, but he could clearly see the evil that existed over the many months he had been in Iraq. Now he was making a difference, not only for himself and his family, but also for his nation and his faith.

As Dervishi guided the Bradley in a stagger behind the lead vehicle, Sickles' Bradley scanned from the 10 to 2 o'clock position. Stursma saw normal activity through the thermal gun sight. Pedestrians walked along sidewalks and men hung out sipping coffee in the cafes. First Sergeant Summerfield scanned about as well. They were approaching the Bayjii CMIC. While the city seemed fairly normal, Bayjii always had a tense feel.

A violent explosion crashed the calm and threw Summerfield into the brow pad of the commander's hatch in the Bradley.

"IED!" shouted Summerfield, not realizing that it was a ground attack with RPG-7 rockets and small arms from a blind spot to his left rear flank.

Sergeant Stursma had also been lurched forward, becoming completely dazed. Sergeant Sickles craned behind him at the noise and saw a fireball on the first sergeant's Bradley. It was still moving. A second explosion a couple of seconds later shattered any pretense of a good situation.

"IED!" shouted Summerfield again. "Are you OK?"

"Roger, First Sergeant," replied Stursma. His head now cleared a bit, he picked up his scan for the enemy through the gun sight.

"Lancer Mike, Bear 7, contact with IED vicinity the CMIC on Highway 1, over," called Summerfield as he overrode the turret controls from Sergeant Stursma to point him and the gun at the suspected enemy location.

Hearing the explosions and the radio transmission, Staff Sergeant Howell ordered his squad to make their way along both sides of the highway toward the Bradleys in an attempt to cut off the attackers.

"Dervishi, are you OK?" asked Sergeant Stursma as the Bradley continued to roll.

"Dervishi, are you all right?" asked First Sergeant Summerfield, noting that the Bradley seemed to be coasting and drifting across the highway median.

"First Sergeant, I think Dervishi's hurt," informed Sergeant Stursma.

"Dervishi. Dervishi!" called Summerfield. He then radioed that his driver was hurt. Suddenly the power went dead on the Bradley. Summerfield watched as the lights went out on all the controls in the commander's station and the tracking LED screen in front of him faded to a residual glow. Not knowing if the radio call transmitted, he hopped out of the turret and scrambled to the driver's hatch. Stursma was already there and had cut off the badly damaged engine. "Let's try to lift him out."

"Roger, First Sergeant," replied Sergeant Stursma.

It was no use. Dervishi was not responding, and the weight of his body, combined with the tight fit of the driver's compartment, prevented them from pulling him out.

"Go down the Hell Hole, and see if you can get to him," ordered Summerfield.

"Roger, First Sergeant," responded Stursma. Making his way into the small space on the left side of the turret inside the Bradley, affectionately known as "the Hell Hole," Stursma came up behind Dervishi.

"I see blood," discovered First Sergeant Summerfield as he shined his flashlight down from above while Stursma came in from behind.

Stursma saw it, too. He looked Dervishi over to see its source and saw it dripping from his left side, pooling onto the floorboard. Raising Dervishi's uniform, he saw a nasty hole. Clutching a combat lifesaver bag inside the Bradley, Stursma ripped open a bandage and slapped it up against the wound. The bandage sucked into the hole as an unconscious Dervishi struggled for life. Stursma tried to hold it there and attempted to wrap it around his body in the tight confines of the driver's compartment.

Staff Sergeant Howell's squad began to arrive and helped Summerfield pull Dervishi out the hatch while Stursma pushed him from behind. Dervishi's legs were caught in the seat, so Stursma unhooked them as they carefully pulled him out of the stricken Bradley.

First Sergeant Summerfield's call had been heard, and by the time Dervishi had been pulled from the Bradley, a mortar track and a scout Hummer from 3rd Battalion, 66th Armor arrived. They loaded Ervin onto it and rushed him to a helipad for air medevac to the 28th Combat Surgical Hospital.

First Sergeant Summerfield and the "Bears" immediately cleared the area surrounding the attack. It appeared that a small cell had attacked them with a volley of rocket-propelled grenades, one hitting and one missing, followed by small arms fire. The rocket that connected hit from an angle on the port side of the Bradley, causing a slag of molten metal to penetrate the skirt, hull, Private First Class Dervishi, the engine access compartment, and the engine.

The soldiers regained contact temporarily with the assailants, or perhaps their accomplices, and poured fire on a rooftop spotted by Sergeant Sickles' Bradley and Staff Sergeant Howell. Several Iraqis were detained, along with some small arms and propellant.

At 3:04 a.m. on January 24, 2004, Ervin Dervishi slipped away on the operating table at the 28th CASH. He fought and died for a nation that had freed his family.

A CHANCE TO SAY "GOODBYE"

Dervishi's death pained me as we drew closer to our redeployment. How many more would we lose? Questions such as "Why couldn't he have died early on rather than fight a year and fall at the end?" were foremost in my mind. Such questions were not mine to ask. I was not bitter. I blamed no one but the enemy for his death. Still, the pain of losing such fine young soldiers cut through me like a knife.

When a unit takes casualties, the natural reaction is to recoil. We could not, and I would not, allow it. The worst strategy would be to adopt a defensive mind-set in the final weeks of our mission. Such a course would only make things worse. I had to keep the men focused on the enemy rather than ourselves. We would continue to raid his leadership and ambush him in his cities and villages until we were formally relieved of duty or ordered home.

The insurgents were fully aware of the troop rotation due to our free and open press reporting. They knew the designations of the units coming to Iraq and could even deduce specific battalion locations and unit commanders. It was a simple matter of reading news clippings from the towns from which they deployed.

Colonel Hickey and Major General Odierno were naturally concerned for the safety of arriving troops. The new troops would not see the environment through the same eyes we did or with the same alertness born from the experience of a year's worth of combat. Jim Hickey was adamant that we step up the pace to clear the highways and streets of roadside bombs. The area for which our brigade was responsible along Highway 1 from Samarra through Tikrit to Bayjii was cleared to such an extent that no newly arriving unit traveling through or taking up station in our area suffered a single casualty from either a roadside bomb or direct attack until the day of our departure.

For the next eight weeks we gave it everything we had, though we had close calls of our own, such as when we nearly lost an A Company vehicle to a bomb on the 26th of January between Tikrit and Auja. Thousands of newly arrived troops passed through unmolested. This was a remarkable achievement, born from incessant patrolling and fighting on the part of Colonel Hickey's Raider Brigade soldiers.

Confident that we could control our area, I still felt the threat of the open space beyond it. To our west, there were literally hundreds of miles where no soldiers patrolled. What lurked there was a great mystery. To the east of us, along the Tuz-Tikrit Highway, a stretch of some 50 unsecured miles greeted our soldiers who would sometimes have to travel the route to make spare parts runs for our large number of vehicles. Such supply runs were not without risk.

Our Army was forced to create islands of security concentrated mostly on populated areas along the Tigris and Euphrates rivers. It was the best of the worst arrangements, as securing people and infrastructure in a new Iraq was more important than securing expansive terrain. While about 40,000 more troops would arrive later in the war and would combine with hundreds of thousands of new Iraqi security forces to connect these islands, such reinforcement was completely foreign to us. We accepted the situation as we found it.

So it was when our mechanics found some critical parts we needed to keep the fleet rolling; they did not hesitate to go into the less patrolled territory between Tikrit and the Jabal Hamrin Ridge on their way to Kirkuk to get them. Well aware of the no-man's-land between our area and the ridge, Captain David Muller, leading a 4th Forward Support Battalion convoy, put together a sizeable force of five vehicles to beef up his security that included a medical vehicle.

When my support company soldiers working on vehicles in the brigade's support area were asked if they could support the convoy, Sergeant Eliu Mier and Corporal Juan Cabral volunteered to add their Hummer as trail security. Their cargo Hummer, A-17, was a welcome addition, boasting a Mark 19 40mm grenade launcher in a makeshift mount in the back. Volunteering to man that grenade launcher, Private First Class Holly McGeogh again jumped at the chance to go out on patrol.

To crew A-17 and take up rear security, a more veteran roster of fighting mechanics could not be found. Sergeant Mier was levelheaded and perhaps the ablest wheeled mechanic in our entire task force. Corporal Cabral had already received a Purple Heart for actions in June when he had gone forward to work on C Company vehicles, being wounded by an RPG rocket. As for Holly McGeogh, I had to mildly reprimand her for sneaking onto my command convoy during combat patrolling more times than I could count, although this did allow her to introduce "Duck, Duck, Goose" to throngs of Iraqi children on one of our more civil liaisons.

With only a handful of wheeled mechanics in the task force, I could not risk their skills on routine combat patrols. Now three of them, jumping at the chance to cover their fellow support soldiers and needing to acquire parts for our own vehicles, departed on a fairly routine mission. They could not have imagined the results of their decision. Tough soldiers all, they would need everything they could muster as they prepared for it.

On the last day of January, this convoy wove the streets of Tikrit a short time after 8:00 in the morning. Crossing the Tigris, they clipped along at a vigorous pace on the Tuz-Tikrit Highway with about 50 meters' distance between vehicles. For Captain Muller, it was another chance to obtain parts needed for the mission. He had traveled the road before, always a little concerned about the territory and that naked feeling of venturing beyond the security provided by the Regulars.

Corporal Cabral drove the road with alertness, mindful of the potential ambushes on the flanks of the road that could be launched from the farmland. Sergeant Mier kept a strained eye on the surrounding territory, maintaining a respectable distance from the rest of the convoy vehicles. Private First Class McGeogh panned the big 40mm grenade launcher from side to side at suspected threats.

The area was sparsely populated between Tikrit and the eastern mountain ridge. Captain Muller was pleased with the time they were making after they passed through the last checkpoint on the outskirts of Tikrit. With any luck, they would be in Kirkuk in no time.

After traveling little more than an hour, they spotted a small, white pickup coming up a side road from an insignificant cluster of dwellings to the south. As the pickup pulled into the intersection, it seemed to go around something. Entering the road, it crossed into the opposite lane and then diverted back, traveling in the same direction, just ahead of the convoy. This temporarily slowed the convoy. As the pickup did not appear to gain any speed, Second Lieutenant John Lopez, driving Captain Muller's vehicle, passed it.

Corporal Cabral spotted the convoy diverting around both a

spot on the road and the pickup. As Sergeant Mier looked to the south, he scanned ahead and north for any trouble. Private First Class McGeogh continued to cover the rear with the grenade laun . . . Blackout.

Checking his six in the rearview mirror, Lieutenant Lopez saw the tall medium truck called an LMTV successfully pass the white pickup. Initially, he was unable to see behind it due to its size, but he soon saw a mushrooming cloud of smoke fill the rearview mirror.

"Sir, I think somebody got hit," he warned.

Captain Muller looked behind him and saw the same cloud in the short distance. He began to count vehicles. One . . . two . . . three . . . Where's the fourth? he thought.

Private First Class Agundhi Copeland, in the vehicle just ahead of A-17, heard a massive explosion. Instantly glancing in the rearview mirror, he saw flame mixed with a dirty brown cloud. To his horror, he could see the vehicle gunner being propelled north through the air a great distance from the Hummer, still sitting in the makeshift seat used to mount the gun. He immediately pulled the vehicle off the road and ran to offer assistance, along with Sergeant First Class Gary Kent.

The scene was horrific. The Hummer was not recognizable as a type. The blast was so powerful that it had launched the Humvee skyward 25 yards and flipped its remains on its back, sending them skidding another 25 yards. Only a single spar connected what remained of the Hummer's frame. The tires were ablaze, dripping pools of rubber. The engine was missing entirely. So were all of the occupants.

Sergeant First Class Stephen Arnold raced the considerable distance to what was left of the burning vehicle. As a combat medic, he began to look for the soldiers, as did the others now collecting there. Corporal Cabral was discovered a short distance from the

Hummer, limbs contorted in impossible positions. There was not much hope, but Arnold took his pulse. Nothing. It seemed certain he died instantly.

McGeogh was spotted after a quick search about 75 yards northeast of the blast crater. There was little doubt looking at her horrible injuries that she was dead. As Arnold checked her pulse, he noticed her staring up at the sky through lifeless eyes.

Sergeant Mier could not immediately be found. The soldiers made concentric circles from the blast crater, and he was eventually located with his shattered and mangled weapon still in hand about 100 yards to the east, across a berm. Mercifully, there was little doubt that he, too, had been killed instantly.

Trying to manage the situation, Captain Muller made repeated attempts to raise his unit. The distances were too great for transmission. Concerned for the soldiers' safety, out of contact and quite exposed, the sergeants tightened security, but the entire convoy had been deeply affected by the scene and by the loss of friends. The white pickup was caught and searched, but little could be deduced from it. It was possible that it was a point vehicle to pace the convoy and expose it to ambush, but little evidence could be mounted for such speculation.

The soldiers did find a long wire leading back toward the little village. From studying the large crater, it appeared that a heavy caliber artillery shell, or perhaps a sizeable sack of explosives, had been burrowed under the asphalt, concealing it and enhancing the force of its blast. The wire connecting the fuse had been hidden with dirt. This appeared to be what the pickup was skirting as it entered the roadway.

Some fifteen minutes later, the convoy received their first assistance from a group of British contractors who happened by on a trek to Kirkuk. They relayed to their contacts in Tikrit, by phone, what had happened so the military could be notified. Word passed both to the 4th Infantry Division and to the 1st Brigade. Our Assistant Division Commander, Brigadier General Mike Barbero, was in the air on one of his frequent trips to field units. He, along with his aide, First Lieutenant Pete Nunn, a Regular officer who was selected for that duty from my battalion, diverted their helicopter to find the scene of destruction.

General Barbero spied the wreckage in the distance and approached for landing. Finding the officer in charge on the ground, he directed Captain Muller to increase his measures to secure the area and to provide leadership to the shattered convoy. With kind firmness, he urged them to pull themselves together, recover their weapons and equipment, and focus on the tasks at hand. He was then able to get an element from the 173rd Airborne Brigade, who was responsible for the territory, to come and recover the scene. General Barbero then ordered the shattered convoy back to Tikrit after making arrangement for the remains of my soldiers to be recovered by the airborne unit.

I received the news at about noon. It had the impact of a baseball bat to the head. One minute we had a combat Hummer with three great mechanics, and the next minute Mier, Cabral, and McGeogh were all dead. The news sent ripples through our entire task force. Nearly everyone knew these soldiers because they worked on the entire battalion's wheeled vehicles.

Needing to educate myself as quickly as possible, I located the "Aggressors'" company commander, Captain Curt Kuetemeyer. He informed me of what details he had.

"Curt, what were they doing out there?" I demanded.

"Sir, they were making a parts run and offered to provide security for the convoy," he explained.

"Who authorized it?" I pried angrily.

"Sir?" responded Curt somewhat confused by the question.

"Who authorized the mission?" I demanded.

"Sir, it was part of a Packhorse convoy," he offered, Packhorse being the nickname for the 4th Forward Support Battalion. "It was cleared by their battalion."

Sensing my frustration and anger, Curt brought me back to reality.

"Sir," he said, treading carefully, "if they had been successful and got the parts we needed for our vehicles and helped protect a Packhorse convoy, would you be upset then?"

I didn't like the question. I wanted to be angry. I wanted someone or something to blame, to make some sense of it all, to find some explanation for the realities of combat and loss.

"No . . . I guess not." I thought it through. "I'm sorry, Curt. You're right. They were doing what we trained them to do . . . to take initiative and not shy away from the fight. I'm sorry. It just comes as such a blow. Let me know what you need. I know you are as deeply upset, if not much more affected by this, than I am."

The remains of our soldiers were taken initially to the 173rd Airborne area, the beginning of a long journey back to the nation for which they gave their lives. As for me, once I was certain that their families had been officially notified, I made calls to give them what comfort and information I could.

I called Paula Zasadny in Michigan, the mother of Holly McGeogh, and introduced myself. She appreciated the call. She wept, as would be expected, and then asked me a question I had not been prepared for.

"Will I get to see my baby again?" she queried.

"No, ma'am, I am sorry, she is gone," I replied, not certain of her meaning.

"Will I be able to see her face again?" she clarified, inquiring about an open casket arrangement when buried. "She was my only child."

"I would not recommend it." I treaded lightly.

"But why?" she pursued.

"You need to remember her the way she was, ma'am," I managed in the most delicate way I could muster.

After a long pause of weeping, she continued to question.

"How do you know?" she pressed as a loving mother would.

"Ma'am, she was hit by a roadside bomb with a force that killed all three soldiers in the vehicle," I explained. "The blast was very devastating."

"But how do you know? Were you there with them? Did you see her?" she queried in succession.

"I am certain of it, ma'am, but no, I was not there," I explained. "They were killed on a road outside of our area."

"I want you to find someone who was there and you ask them," she continued. "Promise me you will do that."

"I will, ma'am," I replied. "I'll call you back as soon as I can."

I hated these calls. The pain of the parents was so raw, and their hurt was so much to bear. Still, if it were my child, I would want to know. Lack of information creates more stress than to just have it straight, as the mind will play over a thousand things that do not apply. It is better to know the truth.

After disconnecting the line with Mrs. Zasadny, I called Brigadier General Barbero. I explained to him about the call.

"Sir, she wants to know if she can have an open casket and if she will be able to see her again," I informed. "I explained to her the devastation involved."

"Absolutely not, Steve," General Barbero said without hesitation. "I cannot imagine anyone putting themselves through that. Tell her I saw her and I could not agree with you more that it would be best to remember her the way she was."

I appreciated General Barbero even putting up with such conversations from commanders. At the end of the day, we were all human and had hearts. These were, after all, America's sons and daughters entrusted to our care, and we all felt a deep personal responsibility for them. He gave me the confirmation I needed to fulfill a promise to a mother.

Calling Mrs. Zasadny back, I relayed my conversation with General Barbero. After more weeping, but without any anger toward those of us who served with her daughter, she said, "I never got to say goodbye."

These were words that landed on me heavily. I had no response for them. How true it was of all loved ones who suffer the loss of a son or daughter in battle. No chance to hold them one more time; no opportunity to see their face, to touch their skin, or hear their voice; not even one last chance to say, "Goodbye." Just heartbreaking news and then . . . gone. Forever.

How many more? It is best to not ask such questions. As I reflected on our casualties, compared to America's wars of the past, we were fortunate. My regiment, the 22nd Infantry, suffered over 800 casualties in the first three days of Normandy in the Second World War. In the Hurtgen Forest, the unit had 210 percent casualties in 18 days. We had not suffered like that. Thank God.

Still, we knew these soldiers. We served alongside them and heard their laughs, knew their stories, and shared their burdens. What we lacked in scale, we felt in intensity. To a soldier in a fight, the combat is still just as real and so are the costs to those involved, even if fewer in number.

Unlike previous memorial services honoring our fallen, the honoring of Mier, Cabral, and McGeogh affected us a bit more. I think there were several reasons for it. For one, we lost three soldiers in a single attack, and the enemy had not paid a price for their actions. No friendly soldiers from our unit were even able to come to their aid like we had been able to do in our other actions. For us, they simply went out and never came back.

Another reason was that because these mechanics worked on

every single one of the wheeled vehicles in our task force, we all personally knew them. They worked hard, got dirty, shared risks, and made their best effort to support our combat operations. As infantry, we were supposed to protect them while they did their job. We never got that opportunity on the 31st of January.

Lastly, McGeogh made it tough. I don't care what anyone says. Losing female soldiers in battle is different. We had now lost two. People can try to talk themselves into any type of theory they wish, but to the average infantrymen in battle, losing a female soldier is different.

As we gathered that first week of February to "say goodbye," we did so the best we could. With three pairs of boots standing beside three M-16 rifles crowned with Kevlar helmets, we honored their lives. When I spoke, I reflected about Sergeant Mier's example, commitment, and dedication. The Mexican-born 27-year-old gave everything he had to his adopted nation. I extolled 25-year-old Corporal, now promoted to Sergeant, Cabral's bravery and un-wavering commitment to get the job done. He had been awarded a Purple Heart in June for that. The additional one he received in January was final. He would leave behind a wife, a seven-year-old son, and an eighteen-month-old son.

McGeogh's death was particularly hard for me for one reason. Back in the late summer, it was almost as if I could sense the danger to her. I ordered her off of my combat patrols, mostly because she was a mechanic, but partly because I did not think I could for-give myself if she should be hit while on my convoy. I took solace back then that she would somehow be safer. Now she was dead.

When it was time to speak about 19-year-old Private First Class, now promoted to Specialist, Holly McGeogh, it came with the baggage of her actions on my patrols, of her playing with the Iraqi children, and of her mother tearfully asking why she could not see her again. I am only human. My voice broke. As a commander, I did the unthinkable. I cried before my soldiers. I suppose I could have shown more sternness as a commander. Still, the Army tradition goes that memorial services are the place to say your goodbyes. Maybe they just don't want the goodbyes to be felt too deeply. If we could not show our love for our fellow soldiers there, then where could we? My soldiers knew me. They knew I would lead the fight for them, and now they knew I was also capable of mourning along with them. I don't regret it.

After the memorial service, amidst stern reminders to "get a hold of ourselves," we returned to the tasks of taking the fight to the enemy and making the area better for those that would relieve us and, most importantly, for the Iraqis who lived there. We had ongoing offensive operations still in play and even had ambushes in place that very day during the service. We did it with the same high standard and skill as we always did. Our brief brush with the feelings of humanity would not change that toughness or dedication.

The cruelty of war is that, while you survive in life's greatest extremes, there is little time allotted for emotion. Anger, yes, but not that other stuff. You really cannot dwell on it. The hurtful things quickly give way to the humorous, the routine, or even the mundane. The macabre is made light of. Memories and feelings are suppressed, buried perhaps for another day . . . or year . . . or decade.

People back home, other than combat veterans, cannot understand it. The soldiers you serve with do, but they often would rather not bring it back up. So we carry the memories of our fallen friends that Americans will never get to know. They were the finest and most selfless citizens that our nation produced, sacrificing so people could live in ignorance of them in a future of peace and freedom. We know them and see them every day. You never really get a chance to tell them "Goodbye."

INSIDE, OUTSIDE

While we were mourning our fallen, an Iraqi man exiting a taxi and discreetly carrying a toolbox approached the turnoff intersection leading to our main compound. Looking to his left and then right, he slowly and cautiously gathered tools and a large object, placing them in the median of the turnoff on Excellency Street. His taxi-driving accomplice parked nearby. This was a favorite bombing spot, and we had participated in dozens of episodes on this bottleneck turnoff.

Specialist John Hartline spied the man from his little C Company outpost on the second floor of a bank overlooking the troubled intersection. Observing him carefully, he could not believe what he was seeing. Since many of our early morning patrols were attending the memorial service at the Birthday Palace, the enemy was taking an opportunity to fill what they believed to be a void in security.

Seeing a large object and wires, Hartline lifted his M-16 rifle and looked down the iron sights. Mindful that a bomb had killed three more of our soldiers two days before, Hartline took careful aim at the device, instead of the man, and pulled the trigger.

The enemy working in the median heard an earsplitting crack. As he reflexively looked about, he heard another and then saw his toolbox explode before him. As the instinct for survival kicked in, he dropped to his knees and placed his hands on the back of his head. Wires and debris lay scattered around him.

Hartline saw the man take a submissive posture and ceased firing. He and his buddy ran down to the street after calling C Company and took the man and his driver prisoner. Hartline was very disappointed that he had been aiming at the toolbox, thinking it was a bomb. Behind it, though, was an olive green 120mm artillery shell with a prepared fuse. The insurgent also had a wireless car alarm to be used as the initiator.

Arriving at the scene from the Birthday Palace and thankful that we were not the new victims of another attack, I commended Hartline for his alertness and quick thinking that had resulted in the capture of the enemy and the bomb.

Responding to an AFP reporter who was riding back with us from the service, Hartline said, "I was on duty today, and I couldn't attend the memorial service. I knew two of the killed soldiers well. Catching these criminals doesn't change the fact that they're dead, but I'm glad I was able to do my job today."

The would-be attackers worked for the fire department, and several interviews of local traffic police in the area revealed a bad case of the Sergeant Schultz syndrome from *Hogan's Heroes*—they knew nothing.

When pressed by the AFP reporter about the traffic cops I replied, "I don't know if the Iraqi police were involved in this, but they were definitely trying to cover it up."

The concealed bank location we used for observation of that intersection was now blown but had provided us the necessary cover the day we needed it. It was not long until attackers shot up the second-floor windows of the bank, a few days later. In typical reaction, locals complained to the chief of police that our soldiers had vandalized the bank and shot up the windows—from the inside!

To reassure General Mezher, the provincial police chief with whom we had good relations, I stated that my men would do no such thing. I agreed to go with the plaintiffs to get to the bottom of it. Walking up the stairs of the bank to the second floor, I immediately noticed several bullet holes in the thick window facing a side alley to the north. I placed my fingers in the divots on the glass and felt that something was not quite right.

"These holes came from the outside," I proclaimed, explaining that glass will spall in the opposite direction of the bullet's impact, creating a divot. It is such useless little knowledge packed in our heads that sometimes proves valuable.

"No, mister . . . inside!" argued the chief plaintiff standing beside General Mezher, who was now considering my plausible explanation with crossed arms and cocked head.

"No, outside," I countered. "The glass. Look at it. It is smooth on the outside of the window and caved in on our side where the glass flew into the room."

"No, mister . . . inside!" asserted the bank man, convinced that my soldiers had fired shots from inside the room.

"Excuse me," I warned, motioning for everyone to step back some distance from the window. Taking a knee, I flipped my M-4 carbine's safety to fire, took aim, and put two bullets through the window, spaced about a foot apart. Everyone around me looked stunned, eyes blinking in amazement.

Walking up to the window, I placed my fingers on the glass and compared them to the other holes. They were totally opposite in shape to the original suspect holes. The plaintiffs approached and felt the holes for themselves.

"Ah, yes, mister! Outside!" the now-convinced banker said with a broad smile.

With apologies to my men accepted, the locals assured us that they would be more careful to look out for insurgents in our area.

Inside, outside, every side. In the last two weeks before our relief arrived, we were hunting down the latest lead on the lingering Saddam loyalist clan that were purported to be behind some of the most recent insurgent activities. Chris Morris had our scouts out in the Cadaseeyah area planning that raid against a member of the Shehab family, and we successfully executed it. We not only captured Nazar Shehab, a relative of Izzat Ibrahim al-Duri, aka the King of Clubs, but we also found more information that led us to a raid the next night that netted four more members of the Musslit family. With these two raids, the last active vestiges of the network we had pursued for eight months had been erased.

The resistance we now faced was more akin to those insurgents pledging to fight regardless of motivation. Such malcontents began to align themselves with al-Qaeda, with further ties leading to Fallujah. For the first time, we heard the name of Abu Musab al-Zarqawi in connection with this forming network. We maintained pursuit for one such Tikriti individual connected to the Fallujah network that had killed D.J. Wheeler in October—Abbas Mahdi. We staked out several of his possible family connections with our snipers. Meanwhile, Mike Wagner's "Gators" and Jon Cecalupo's "Cougars" continued combat patrolling of the outskirts of Tikrit. Brad Boyd was able to return to command of C Company after a two-month absence, and had the Cobras in tight control of the city center.

Brad was still recovering somewhat and had even tried to convince me earlier to let him return to command. I told him when he could do an exercise called a Squat Thrust—involving bending at the knees, leaning forward into a push-up, and then springing back up—I would consider it. It took him some time, but he eventually did so. I returned him to command. Mitch Carlisle came back to the headquarters, and we were all grateful for his handling of the company in Brad's absence.

With this array of forces keeping Tikrit fairly civil, Sergeant Joseph Dalessio's team from our sniper squad took up an infiltration route in Cadaseeyah to pursue an important lead. The objective was none other than Abbas Mahdi, who was purported to be visiting his uncle's house. I gave orders to my snipers that if Abbas were spotted, he was fair game.

By 8:00 p.m. on February 7, Sergeant Dalessio's team had reached the objective area. Corporal Anthony Venetz and Specialist

James Kelly worked their way over a wall following Dalessio and soon laddered their way onto the roof of a two-story residence near Abbas's uncle's house. It was not far from where we had captured Saddam Presidential Secretary Abid Mahmood al-Khatab the previous June. The whole neighborhood was unfriendly.

Pulling up the ladder, securing the rooftop, and blocking the door, the soldiers began a planned watch for a 24-hour period. As they proceeded to work out their position inside the compound, a bullet suddenly smashed into the wall near Corporal Venetz's head, spewing bits of plaster.

"Close impact! Close impact!" Venetz warned, instinctively falling back on his sniper training and diving for cover.

Dropping their equipment and themselves to the rooftop, Venetz crawled toward the opposite ledge for a better position while Kelly crawled to cover the opposite side. While Sergeant Dalessio attempted to radio Chris Morris, Venetz could spy two individuals with AK-47s coming up from the south.

"AK! AK!" Venetz warned as he popped up into a firing position. The soldiers shouted to the suspects below in a pidgin Arabic call to put their hands up.

The enemy put their rifles up instead. Gunfire erupted at each location, both inside and outside. As Corporal Venetz and Specialist Kelly returned fire at the enemy to the west, the woodline across the street to the south erupted. Bullets smacked and licked the plastered concrete block forming the low wall on the flat rooftop.

Taking in the situation, Sergeant Dalessio could see several individuals now firing from the southwest and south. Crawling along the rooftop to get a better position, Kelly then fired a dozen rounds at the insurgents in the woodline, forcing their fire to slacken. As he did, another insurgent at the gate of the target house to the southeast opened up with an AK. Dalessio shifted his fire to the gate and dropped the enemy with his M-16.

"Put a frag in that woodline!" ordered Dalessio to Specialist Kelly. He and Venetz provided cover as Kelly prepared to throw a fragmentation grenade.

"Frag out!" alerted Kelly, sailing a grenade across the street and into the woodline. All three soldiers hit the deck until the grenade exploded. KABOOM! The firing was now sporadic and seemed to be coming from the east as two men were seen fleeing in the distance.

A short time later, another individual approached, walking down the street. Venetz shouted at him to put his hands up (in an Arabic phrase he had learned). The man smiled and walked forward. Venetz fired a warning shot in front of him and repeated the phrase. The man smiled and walked forward again and was greeted with another warning shot.

"Venetz, what are you doing?" asked Kelly.

"I am telling him to put his hands up," answered Venetz.

"Dude, you are telling him we are Americans and to not be afraid," jabbed Kelly.

With laughter breaking the tension among the snipers, the man was correctly instructed by better pidgin Arabic and he fell to his knees and put his hands up. The snipers did not see a weapon and he did not appear to be involved, perhaps just happening upon the firefight. He was later released.

Sergeant Dalessio relayed the contact to Chris Morris, who then informed me. Chris and our scouts vectored into the location after the soldiers "painted it" with an infrared device and, once reinforcements arrived, the soldiers began clearing the area. I arrived as the soldiers began clearing Abbas's uncle's house, capturing two wounded enemy and several enemy rifles.

When the smoke had settled, Abbas's uncle lay dead at the gate, a four-foot puddle of blood slowly advancing around him on the carport drive. Abbas's father had one of his legs blown off by Kelly's grenade and was being tended to by a woman at the house. A third relative had wounds to the shoulder and chest. We provided what medical assistance we could, and I called for one of our own ambulances to evacuate the men that tried to kill ours. Both the enemy wounded survived. Such is the difference between Americans and terrorists.

Abbas was believed to be one of the two men seen fleeing to the east toward the Tigris River. Locals said that he was definitely there. The price his family paid to protect him was steep. While he managed to escape us yet again it was to be short-lived. Later in the year, he would be killed fighting Americans in the 2nd Battle of Fallujah.

LONG BEARDS

That cool February 2004 brought more than rain. Mortar rounds fell on the Birthday Palace and the "Gator" compound in Auja while huge SS-30 rockets rained on the main compound of the 4th Infantry Division. The enemy launched them from dirt ramps with a crude aim at the bluffs of the Tigris River from the wheat fields and orchards due east. The counter battery fire from our own 120mm mortars kept these attacks to a minimum.

Along with the rain and rockets, thousands of soldiers began to pour into our area as the 101st Airborne Division departed from Mosul and the 1st Infantry Division arrived to take over our sector in Tikrit. With such an enormous temporary increase of troops, things became fairly quiet, but there were still occasional ambushes. On 18 February, one of our patrols was attacked with an RPG from a great distance in a back alley near the Fruit Loop Apartments on Highway 1. The rocket missed and plunged into a playground, killing a five-year-old boy. Such incidents only served to galvanize Iraqis against the insurgency.

With the influx of relief troops, each patrol had now doubled in strength. We gave the 1st Battalion, 18th Infantry "Vanguards," led by Lieutenant Colonel Jeff Sinclair, an official tour of Tikrit. We could not have asked for a better trained or more ably led unit to build on the foundation we had established. My focus was now divided between pursuing the final leads on known enemies in our area and making introductions to the locals to ensure the same or enhanced level of cooperation with Sinclair's new task force in Tikrit. We launched one final raid on the farmland south of Auja with the "Vanguards" also participating.

For the most part, our pursuit of Saddam Hussein and his henchmen had been completely successful. As we readied our forces for the return to Kuwait and eventually to the United States in March and April, we did so with a certain pride in our accomplishment. Still, Tikrit could be a very dangerous place. We tried to convey the sights and sounds of normal activity versus danger signals to our replacements. On a level of competency, our soldiers and our relief were on equal footing. In terms of experience and combat savvy, our relief could not yet recognize threats that were blatant to us.

Gradually, the Vanguard soldiers replaced our troops. Mike Wagner's A Company pulled out of Auja and temporarily occupied a spot on the "Packhorse" compound near them until they could load vehicles and equipment for Kuwait. Brad Boyd's C Company pulled out of the city, joined by Scott Thomas' B Company, which had finally rejoined us from Bayjii. With Jon Cecalupo's tanks and Curt Kuetemeyer's support troops completing the assembly, the task force was gradually being relieved of its duties.

By the first of March, I would maintain command of the city, but the majority of troops now belonged to 1-18 Infantry rather than to me. The designated time to switch control of our entire area would be midnight on 12 March. Mike Rauhut, Bryan Luke, and Pete Martinez worked fervently moving troops and vehicles over hundreds of miles through hostile territory to reassemble in Kuwait. Mike and Pete had already departed for Kuwait. Bryan Luke and Clay Bell remained with a skeleton staff until I was relieved of combat duty.

The final day of combat patrolling was one of mixed emotions. I had no concerns about the "Vanguards" or Lieutenant Colonel Sinclair, but it was difficult to relinquish the mission in which we had invested so much of our lives. Scores of my soldiers had shed blood on these streets, and some lost their lives here. As I surveyed each street and farm field, I sincerely prayed that we would one day return to walk them in peace. Perhaps we would dine in restaurants as old men with our families and point out things that locals could not conceive having happened in their peaceful neighborhoods. It was a nice dream anyway.

By the evening of that last patrol, we began to notice some things that did not feel right. It was no secret that new troops with bright clean uniforms were replacing ours. The locals noticed, too, that the new troops did not wear the burlap on their helmets that had so distinctly marked my men. Still, we were out there on a final patrol showing we had not yet left.

Driving north up 40th Street, I spotted some trouble brewing at the Huda Mosque. The gates were open, and a fair-sized gathering of men milled about. They were soldier age, with piercing eyes full of hatred. Most notably, they all had beards. Beards were uncommon among Sunni Arabs in Iraq. If they wore them, they were usually neatly trimmed and close-cropped. It was very unusual to see the free-flowing unkempt whiskers typically worn by the most radical elements of Islam.

Rounding the corner east on Cross Street, we saw more of them by the "Evil" Mosque (or Saddam Mosque). A few even dotted the market area, watching us warily as others went about their normal business, paying us no attention.

"Hoefer, how do we look on fuel?" I asked my driver, Specialist Cody Hoefer. "We're good, sir," he answered.

"Three, we're gonna patrol until midnight," I said, tossing my words back to my S-3 Operations Officer, Major Bryan Luke. "I don't like what I am seeing."

"Roger, sir," he acknowledged. "You mean the guys with the beards?"

"Yeah," I replied. "Something definitely doesn't feel right."

"I noticed that, too, sir," chimed in Cody Hoefer. "Did you see how they seemed to follow us from point to point?"

"Roger," I agreed. "Bryan, alert the rest of the convoy on the internal," I ordered.

"Wilco, sir," Bryan responded, cautioning our dozen remaining Regulars on patrol to expect the worst until midnight and take nothing for granted.

The night proceeded uneasily. It is difficult to explain. Law enforcement officers have told me that they have a "sixth sense" about areas with which they are familiar. I now knew what they meant. They just know things are not quite right without being able to say why. Apart from the obvious long beards in town, there was little else I could pinpoint, but I knew things did not look or feel right.

Midnight came, and I signed off the radio forever as commander of combat forces in Tikrit. My task complete, I decided to go to 1-18 Infantry's headquarters to pass along my concerns about the 40th Street district of Tikrit.

"Something's not right with the city," I offered to the task force Executive Officer, finding him in the ops center.

"What makes you say that, sir?" he asked.

"Watch 40th Street and the area around it," I continued. "We saw men with long beards at the Huda Mosque, and that whole area just did not feel right. You guys need to be careful."

"Got it, sir," he replied. "But do you think that maybe it is just partly because it's your last patrol and turning it all over to us?"

"No, it's because something is not right with the city," I allowed. "I'm serious. Watch 40th Street. Something is not right. I can think of no one we'd rather turn our mission over to, but I am concerned about what we saw on patrol."

"Understood, sir," he acknowledged. "I'll pass it along to Colonel Sinclair and the units."

We bunked one final night in our old headquarters location. My crew fueled the vehicles and would grab some rack time until morning. Then we would make our way to the battalion relocation point and ready our eventual trip to Kuwait. Jeff Sinclair, ever the professional, offered me a place to sleep in the command hooch. He and his Command Sergeant Major, Doug Pallister, were exactly the kind of men we had hoped to get for our relief.

Accepting his offer of hospitality, I began to relax. The weight of command in combat relaxed a little, although I had troops scattered under various commands from Tikrit to Kuwait. I worried very little about them, as they were ably led. In minutes I was out, descending into a deep sleep.

Waking abruptly at approximately 4:45 a.m. on March 13, I thought I was dreaming.

"Colonel Sinclair, sir," interrupted the 1-18 Infantry battle captain.

"Yeah . . . " answered a gravelly voice.

"Sir, B Company has been attacked," he continued. "Captain Kurth is dead, and so is Specialist Ford. There are some wounded as well."

"What!?" he answered, bolting straight up in his bed, as did Command Sergeant Major Pallister and I.

As he repeated the devastating news, I went into instinctive drill. In five minutes I had my gear, rifle, and crew assembled on our Hummers ready to roll. Jeff's men were trying to piece together what had happened. We waited and then waited some more. I made sure to withhold criticism in my mind. We had been through this so many times before. I would assist if he needed us.

"Sir, we gotta get out there to help them," urged Sergeant First Class Gil Nail.

"Sergeant Nail, I am no longer in command," I countered. "If they need our assistance we will help, but we have to let them work it out."

"Roger, sir," he grudgingly acknowledged.

After a twenty-minute wait, we joined Colonel Sinclair's convoy. I had gathered what info I could and learned that Captain John "Hans" Kurth had been leading his company's first early patrol when they were hit by a roadside ambush on 60th Street. I miscalculated the scene of trouble by a single block, but the prediction of the previous night was, unfortunately, very accurate on that early morning.

Arriving at the scene, I pointed to the location; we knew it well. Then my guys pulled security in the area. Jeff had already sent combat forces into the area to provide a wider security. The scene was one I had hoped never to witness again. It would serve instead as one more heartless send-off from the city of Tikrit.

At approximately 4:42 a.m., B Company Commander Captain Kurth had been leading a two-vehicle combat patrol north along 60th Street near the east-west road leading to the Birthday Palace. An insurgent had apparently planted a powerful roadside bomb on the back recess of the curb designed to allow streetside parking. It also concealed the bomb efficiently until it was too late. We had often countered such tactics by driving in the opposite lanes and direction of traffic. It would throw the enemy off and allow us to see ahead.

When the bomb exploded, the blast ripped into Captain Kurth. He probably died instantly. Specialist Jason Ford, a team leader from 1-18 Infantry's B Company, was also killed in the blast. Kurth's driver, Specialist Michael Press, escaped with fragmentation to the arm. Ford's squad leader, Sergeant Alfored Kalous, would suffer a broken left leg and later lose his left foot. SAW gunner, Specialist Rafael Lovell, would escape with less severe wounds to the face and left leg.

Fuel dripped from the ruptured tank of the stricken Hummer. The tires were blown, and the vehicle lay broken and undrivable on the street. Bandages, syringes, and other medical waste lay scattered about, mingled with blood, concrete, rubber, and oil. The time was approaching 5:30 a.m. In a mere half hour, Tikrit would spring to life as curfew lifted. We had very little time.

"Jeff, would you like me to raise the fire department to assist in cleanup?" I offered.

"I got it," he snapped with a radio receiver in his ear. He was not so much mad at me as he was mad at losing men.

I had been there. I decided to give him a wide berth and walked back over to the shattered vehicle. We have to get this vehicle outta here, I thought. We gotta wash the blood off the streets. When the people wake up, it needs to appear as if this never happened.

Feeling helpless and watching the unit respond like a duck whacked on the head, I started picking up stuff from the street. I grabbed bloody bandages and syringes and pieces of shattered gear. I tossed them into the broken Hummer. My men caught my lead and followed suit. Colonel Sinclair's ops sergeant walked over and joined in.

"Sir, what is going through your mind right now?" he queried in a polite but roundabout way of asking how I would respond in this situation.

"Sergeant, you gotta get this vehicle out of here," I began. "We've got thirty minutes before the whole town comes alive. When they wake up it needs to look as if none of this ever happened and you are still in charge and on the streets."

"Roger, sir," he said and wandered off.

"Steve, I'm sorry, man," called out Jeff Sinclair. "What was that number to the fire department?"

Jeff immediately went into action. We suggested they drag the vehicle with a Bradley tow bar to the Birthday Palace. A fire truck appeared to wash the blood off the street. The scene was cleaned up in short order.

That night, Lieutenant Colonel Sinclair dropped 120mm mortar rounds directly into the fields in the heart of the city near the "Evil Mosque" and the scene of the bombing. It had a terrifying effect on the locals and calmed the city considerably. I already liked Jeff's style and knew that they were going to take Tikrit to the next level. Still, it was a terrible first day for him in command of the city.

At 11:00 that morning, a ceremony officially transferring command from the "Regulars" to the "Vanguards" had been scheduled. Lieutenant Colonel Sinclair asked that we cancel it. I agreed to cancel the formal one but still wanted to properly case our battalion and regimental colors with the respect they deserved. I told him that we would do it with or without him.

"I've lost men, too, Jeff," I offered. "We'll support whatever you want, but we will case our colors with the honor and dignity they deserve."

Sinclair and Pallister agreed, easily able to identify with our situation. We held a small and abbreviated ceremony in which we rolled up our colors and placed them in slipcases to be unfurled again on arrival at our duty station at Fort Hood. Our mission was now over.

9. TRIUMPH

RAT PATROL

I spent the final days in Iraq addressing clusters of my men as they departed for Kuwait. I urged them to conduct themselves with the same professionalism upon return as they had in performing their duties in combat. Our fallen comrades would forever be associated with the unit they served in when they gave their lives. They deserved to have that unit known for its good conduct and deeds. I explained such honor could be soiled if we "let fly" at home. They got the message.

Colonel Hickey was also departing for Kuwait to assemble the brigade for redeployment. We had a conversation by phone on 14 March 2004.

"What are you still doing in Iraq?" he asked.

"Sir, I still have some troops here and will leave when the final group departs," I answered.

"More than two-thirds of your unit is already in Kuwait," he countered. "You have competent officers to get the remainder home. The majority of your command is there. Leave Iraq."

"Wilco, sir," I acknowledged.

With that, we prepared for the drive of our command element

out of Iraq. The hundreds of miles' journey would be an adventure all its own as we drove south along the ancient river valley to Kuwait. My last day in Tikrit was spent giving an interview to Peter Jennings at the request of ABC News. My command group soldiers, tough young men all, were the highlight of that interview, and it was great to see the media coverage as I looked on with pride. Mr. Jennings was the consummate professional. I had dealt with larger-than-life media personalities before, but Jennings was first-class all the way. He produced a nice story revolving around the question "With Saddam captured, what now?" Time would tell. We had given our all; now others would take up the fight.

Assembling the three Humvees of my command convoy, we strapped on spare tires and multiple five-gallon fuel cans, and soon the trucks were bristling with guns and soldiers. The fourteen of us would make our way through hundreds of miles of unfamiliar territory. We resembled a desert "rat patrol," not unlike those from the old television series. Bryan Luke remained a few days longer to ensure that the very last group pushed out. Clay Bell's Hummer would replace Bryan Luke's in my convoy.

I said goodbye to many Iraqi friends made along the way and was able to pin Bronze Stars on American citizens Joe Filmore and Alex Mikhaiel for their irreplaceable service to our unit and nation as translators. Alex, an Egyptian Coptic Christian who had emigrated to the United States and given selfless service, had worked mostly with the intelligence section. He also filled in when Joe Filmore was unavailable. We shared many exciting episodes together. I cannot imagine how any of our successes would have been possible without the eyes, ears, and voices of these two dedicated Americans.

After gathering the latest intelligence information for the journey ahead, I was somewhat disturbed by the dozens of attacks along the designated convoy route to Kuwait. While it was imperative to remain on these routes for security concerns and medical evacuation access, I believed that they were equally dangerous because the enemy could take advantage of small vulnerable elements as they passed. The daily number of roadside bombings on those routes was alarming. I could not bear to lose a man on the trip out. Nothing could be more cruel or hateful to my mind.

We set out on the route to Baghdad without incident until we encountered a small Military Police unit's roadblock. We were approximately three vehicles back in traffic when they began to set up the blockade. All six lanes of highway were beginning to back up in both directions as far as the eye could see. Unlike the minor irritation of commuter inconvenience a driver might experience back home, we instinctively went on high alert and battle drill, dismounting our vehicles.

"What's the problem?" I asked, walking past the MPs to the sergeant in charge who was talking on a radio in his Humvee.

"IED." He pointed toward a roadside bomb.

"We can take care of it if you like," I offered. At this, Sergeant First Class Nail began to take up a position to shoot the initiating device in front of the large artillery shell set up on the side of the road some 75 yards away.

"What, sir?" asked the MP staff sergeant.

"We can take care of it and get the road clear," I continued. "You're going to have a tight spot here pretty soon with all this traffic and angry, waiting people."

"Roger, we have EOD coming," he offered, hopeful that explosive ordnance disposal troops would soon arrive.

"How long till they get here?" I asked.

"Well, sir, yesterday we waited for three and a half hours," he lamented.

"Three and a half hours?" I repeated.

"Roger, sir," he confirmed. "Maybe they will be quicker today."

"Sergeant, I know this is not our area, but look, we do this all the time. Look over there at the little box in front of the device." I pointed. "It has an electrical initiator of some kind hooked to the fuse in the nose packed with plastic explosives. Shoot that initiator and you break the circuit. Break the circuit and there is no way it will go off. It is just like any other artillery shell packed in a crate. There is no way it can go off unless you have a spark to the fuse."

"Well, sir, let me make a call," he reasoned, looking about at all of us and seeing that we probably had done this before.

After he raised his unit, they were adamant that we not interfere. I understood and expected as much. Too bad for them. Equally unfortunate for us was our situation on an enormous bridge. We could not edge forward or backward due to the densely packed traffic. Forget this, I thought. We're gonna sit here all day and have our troops get hammered in some ambush or get sniped at like sitting ducks for nothing.

"Hoefer, you think you could make it down there?" I asked, pointing to the embankment just short of the gap on the bridge.

"Roger, sir," he stated confidently. "It sure beats sitting here."

Sergeant Nail located a spot in the guardrails just wide enough to traverse. We threaded our Hummers down the steep embankment like Mr. Toad's Wild Ride. Finding a side street, we made our way back to the highway and were off again. I felt terrible for that poor sergeant and his men stuck in limbo. I had no authority or command in that area, so if they did not wish to exploit our skills, we were powerless to help. We could not waste valuable time waiting for them to follow military protocol. For the moment, my direct command encompassed the safety of fourteen soldiers, and we had a date with Kuwait. It was a date I intended to keep.

Arriving after dark at a midway base for refueling, it looked as if we had entered a prison. Mazes of concrete "Texas Barriers" separated this penitentiary of our own making from the outside world. After uppity instructions from junior guards directing us to an area to draw linen and cot space for our men, I immediately gave my men other orders. Once I found the fuel point, we gassed up our tanks and cans. I then instructed our mini convoy to locate a spot between the outside wire and the inside barriers. We circled into a little laager and slept on vehicle hoods, the few cots we had, and the ground. At first light, we fired up the Hummers, grabbed some chow, and prepared to head southward.

While the troops ate, I checked the latest intelligence reports. They were not good. There were more bombings yesterday than the previous day. One soldier had been killed and others wounded. Most of the contact seemed to span an eighty-mile stretch of dirt road. Pulling out the map, I looked for a safer route. Common sense had to prevail at that moment. What was the point of driving through blinding dust and getting ambushed for the purpose of sticking to the "safe" convoy route?

I gathered my men and explained the strategy to divert potential disaster by detouring on a giant dogleg around the trouble. While it seemed a no-brainer, I reminded them that in doing so, we would be venturing into an area where no troops had been in any numbers since the initial invasion. It would also invite some risk, but I banked on the element of surprise outweighing any impending danger. Should a vehicle break down, tow straps would allow us to press forward. We agreed. Any positive plan was better than playing roadside roulette with the enemy.

Threading our way through the city of Diwaniyah and countless other small towns, we inched our way toward Nasiriyah. There were many surprised looks cast our way, but as our tough, hardened appearance conveyed we meant business, most had more fear of us than we had concern of them. We finally reached a military base near Nasiriyah, where I looked up First Sergeant Kevin Blake, who had once been my driver when I was a company commander and he a Private First Class.

Spotting a phenomenal historic structure in the distance as we approached, I shouted to my soldiers.

"Check that out! That's the Ziggurat of Ur!" I exclaimed to the men in my truck.

"The what?" they asked.

"The Ziggurat of Ur," I continued. "You know, where Abraham was born."

"Abraham who?" a soldier asked.

Some things are better left unsaid, I suppose.

It was late afternoon in southern Iraq when I decided that we needed one last drain of fuel cans before proceeding on to Kuwait. Spying a little oasis about a mile from the road, we drove up to the spartan farm amid lush palms and bushes. The concealment would shelter us while we paused to fuel should someone become wise to our presence and decide to ambush us.

The local family was terrified as we pulled into the knot of trees. We smiled broadly and pointed to our fuel cans. Using pidgin Arabic, we successfully conveyed our fuel stop to our reluctant hosts. The guys enthusiastically passed out candy to the children. We left beef jerky, chips, and army rations with them as well. Several of us had Iraqi currency we would no longer need and offered it to the family. Their initial terror was replaced with smiles and waves as we departed. I often hoped that this family's experience with Americans might someday serve as a good "campfire" story in the future to counter all the propaganda about our inhumanity.

For the last leg of our journey, about a dozen of us donned motorcycle riding gloves fashioned in the pattern of American flags. They had been shipped from a chopper shop on the Texas Gulf Coast. After seeing our unit on television, the owner and his buds boxed up a huge care package for us unlike any we had ever received. It contained novelties, from Harley gear to pinup biker calendars to the patriotic biker gloves. The soldiers loved it. We even discovered a fifth of Jack Daniels tucked in the bottom of the box. How that contraband passed through military channels was a great mystery to us. The gloves from that box were the ones we sported on that final leg of our journey through Iraq.

After another hour or so, we spotted a checkpoint on the horizon indicating the Iraq-Kuwait border. It is hard to describe the feeling that overcame us at that moment. We felt as if we were really going home. Crossing into Kuwait after a perfunctory stop, we drove down clean superhighways with modern structures on all sides. Honking cars full of grateful Kuwaitis gave us the thumbs-up and many covered their hearts with their hands to show gratitude. They had firsthand knowledge of the terror that Saddam Hussein could invoke. Children waved to us with broad smiles. For the first time, it became real to me that we were no longer at war.

WISH THEY WERE YOU

Rejoining the troops was exhilarating as we milled about, finally out of danger and working to redeploy. My executive officer, Mike Rauhut, had things in top order for the uploading of vehicles and the manifesting of troops on airliners to go home. Command Sergeant Major Pete Martinez convinced me to catch some rest. I slept as I had not to that point of the deployment.

After standing around idly trying to make myself useful, Rauhut and Martinez finally spoke bluntly.

"Sir, it's time for you to go home," Mike said flatly.

"Roger, sir, I agree," chimed in Pete. "Sir, we know you want to help and you are an out-front leader, but you are just holding things up here."

"What do you mean, Sergeant Major?" I asked.

"Sir, when you show up to be with the troops, you are slowing us down," he explained. "It's not like you can help them fix engines, clean vehicles, or load their stuff on planes. When you show up, things slow down."

"Well, it's nice to be so wanted." I smiled.

"Sir, we got this here," Mike assured. "We need you to use your command influence in the fight back home."

"Sir, he's right," tag-teamed my sergeant major. "There are lots of battles back at Fort Hood . . . our barracks . . . our headquarters. You can call and make things happen that we need."

"I guess I ought to listen to my command element," I answered. "But first I want to make sure the S-3 makes it out safely, and then I'll grant your wish and leave."

With that, I turned in my weapons and prepared to depart. I felt naked. No Colt M4 carbine, no battle gear, no loaded magazines, no Beretta M9 pistol strapped to my leg. I wandered around attempting to be useful, but my men were on autopilot and doing a fine job on recovery of our equipment.

Bryan Luke made it out of Iraq a few days afterward, and with that, all of my soldiers were either safely in Kuwait or already in Texas. I was manifested to one of the civilian airliners chartered to transport troops back to the United States. This one was an American Airlines jet. I stepped on board and was immediately whisked away by flight attendants to first class. My protests were met with "captain's orders" from the crew. To my surprise, our troops had recovered weapons and equipment efficiently enough that many of them were on board. Many more were already en route to freedom. So many were homeward bound that even Pete Martinez decided to join our flight. It was good to have my battle buddy along for the trip home.

American Airlines crew members volunteered for these freedom flights. A surplus of volunteers necessitated a rotating duty roster, though they would hardly have called it "duty." They assured us that the duty was considered an honor. During the flight, they dressed some of the soldiers in outrageous flight attendant attire and pressed them into service to attend to their fellow soldiers. We were even permitted into the pilot cockpit, the cabin door never closing. It was so unlike any post-9/11 flight I had flown on. I will never forget how well the airline treated us that day. The undue attention made me feel a bit guilty.

Finally arriving at Fort Hood, we were bused into a gymnasium where our families were waiting to welcome us home. My wife, Cindy, our five children, my parents, my brother, and my sister were all present. It was a very moving and emotional time being reunited with my family. Embracing my wife, I breathed in deeply the smell of her hair and warmed with her hug while my children swarmed like bees at chest, waist, and leg height. How good to finally be home.

In the following few weeks before a thirty-day block leave, we closed up on our barracks and sent soldiers to reintegration classes. The reintegration was a good concept, but the instructors left much to be desired. The class dealing with combat stress was led by a 100-pound female psychology major who had never deployed or been in battle. My leathered, combat infantry veterans were polite, but I am glad their thoughts could not be read. A woman with a degree taught the reentry-to-marriage class, but she had never been married, had no children, and had a live-in boyfriend of two years. What a joke! My sergeant major (married for over two decades) and I (nearly so) just shook our heads in bewilderment.

Eventually, we would turn to local veterans of World War II, Korea, and Vietnam for help. They may have lacked scholastic credentials but certainly had more experience reintegrating from battlefront to home front.

As we prepared for leave, I wanted to ensure that every soldier received his campaign decorations for service in Iraq. A new medal for expeditionary service had been recently authorized. Scores of my men would separate from the service when our block leave began. If their decorations were not issued before leaving the service, they would never receive them properly. Because the Army supply system could not act quickly enough, I instructed my staff to find where the medals were being made. As luck would have it, they were manufactured in Texas. I authorized the unit credit card to buy medals for every single soldier. My supply officer, Captain Troy Parrish, purchased the awards in person and had them in time as a result.

Two key ceremonies would leave a lasting memory. The first was in honor of the division's fallen at an outdoor memorial dedication service attended by families of soldiers killed in battle. I had asked permission to perform a song that I had written to my fallen soldiers and felt might be appropriate for the division's ceremony. After hearing the song, Major General Odierno readily agreed. With more than four thousand guests present, plus our soldiers, I was able to pay tribute with this song.

I'll Think of You

I wait for your face
To return from a distant place.
I seek your words,
Mental speeches that are never heard.

Refrain:

And today I thought of you,
Of the full life that you never knew;
Of the world that passed you by;
Of your loved ones, you never told "Goodbye."
So today, I'll think of you.

Free souls, steep price,
Proud flags draped on sacrifice
Of youth, now gone
But the memories carry on.

Refrain:

And today I thought of you,
Of the full life that you never knew;
Of the world that passed you by;
Of your loved ones, you never told "Goodbye."
So today, I'll think of you.

In the audience were several families of my fallen soldiers. It was a moving tribute to them. Present that day was Paula Zasadny, mother of Holly McGeogh. The phone conversation we shared the night after she was killed was the inspiration for the song.

Having purchased thousands of medals for my soldiers, we now readied for one final assembly of our troops. Individual companies would also have ceremonies, and we would take group pictures of the units, knowing that these exact groups of men would never be together ever again.

Captain Scott Thomas' B Company had a special soldier they wanted to honor. Sergeant Gary Dowd had come from Florida to reunite with our unit. I was privileged to pin a Purple Heart on his chest. As I did, I remembered the night he lay bleeding and dying and how prayers for God to spare his life were answered. He stood before me to receive his award with an arm missing and a face set full of determination. All eyes were riveted on him waiting to hear his words. He started slowly.

"It is an honor to be back," he said, holding back the tears. "I'm . . . I'm . . . sorry I let you all down by not finishing the mission with you."

With that, no man with a heart could contain his tears. How is it he could believe he had failed anyone when he had sacrificed so much? It is something only the battlefield soldier can understand. All war veterans instinctively understand and feel a kindred bond with one another. What Gary was trying to articulate is how we all felt about each other and our unit as well.

After pinning thousands of medals on my soldiers for their campaigns, service, valor, and wounds, I was honored to look each one in the eye, shake his hand, and express thanks on behalf of a grateful nation. I truly hoped that our nation would be grateful, yet I feared what most of these soldiers had achieved would be forgotten, if ever really known.

We assembled for the last time that May of 2004 with our military brothers and sisters who served together in Iraq and the historic hunt and capture of Saddam Hussein. As I endeavored to convey my love for them and the swelling pride I felt for what they had achieved for the United States of America, these words poured from my heart:

" . . . Someday your peers will look back on their lives and wish they were you. When your nation called, it was you who answered. Regardless of what people make of our service or this war, no one can take away what you have achieved. Ever.

"As the decades pass and we grow old together, we must remember not only what has been accomplished but what the cost was as well. Only we can carry the memory of our fallen. It is we who knew their faces, their smiles, their stories, and their sacrifice. They are now just a name, but as long as we have breath, they will live."

SADDAM'S SOCIAL NETWORK

CARDS FROM THE DECK
HVT#1 Saddam Hussein—Ace of Spades
HVT#4 Abid Hamid Mahmood al-Khatab— Ace of Diamonds
HVT#11 Barzan Sulayman al-Majid—Queen of Hearts
HVT#52 Adil Abdullah Mahdi al-Duri—Two of Diamonds

THE MUSSLIT FAMILY
Omar al-Musslit (questioned, released)
Rudman Ibrahim Omar al-Musslit (died of cardiac arrest)
Mohammed Ibrahim Omar al-Musslit (captured)
Adnan Ibrahim Omar al-Musslit (captured)
Mawlan Ibrahim Omar al-Musslit (captured)
Nazhan Ibrahim Omar al-Musslit (captured)
Birhan Ibrahim Omar al-Musslit (captured)
Salwan Ibrahim Omar al-Musslit
Telfah Ibrahim Omar al-Musslit (captured)
Abid Ibrahim Omar al-Musslit (captured)
Kalil (Khalib?) Ibrahim Omar al-Musslit
Faris Yaseen Omar al-Musslit (captured)
Nasir Yaseen Omar al-Musslit (captured by INP)
Taha Yaseen Omar al-Musslit (captured)
Ahmed Yaseen Omar al-Musslit (captured by INP)
Adnan Abdullah Abid al-Musslit (captured)
Bashar Abdullah Abid al-Musslit (captured)
Finar Khatab Omar al-Musslit—Tikrit insurgent leader

THE HEREMOS FAMILY
Rashid Abdullah al-Heremos (captured)
Muthama Rashid al-Heremos
Rafa Ali Hussein al-Heremos
Nafit Ali Hussein al-Heremos (captured)
Ghalib Selfij al-Heremos

THE HADOOSHI FAMILY
Mohammed al-Hadooshi
Mahmood Kareem al-Hadooshi (captured)
Amer Abdullah al-Hadooshi (captured)
Sabir Abid al-Hadooshi (captured)
Abdu Samad al-Hadooshi (killed)

THE MAJID FAMILY
Barzan Sulayman al-Majid—HVT #11 Queen of Hearts (detained after surrendering)
Hussein Ali Ibrihim al-Majid (captured)
Kareem Jasim Nafoos al-Majid (captured)
Saddam Hussein—HVT #1 Ace of Spades (captured, tried and executed)

THE HASAN FAMILY
Munther Idham Ibrahim al-Hasan
Rafa Idham Ibrahim al-Hasan (captured)
Yada Idham Ibrahim al-Hasan (captured)
Omar Idham Ibrahim al-Hasan (captured)
Saad Abdul al-Hasan (captured)
Raad Abdul al-Hasan

THE KHATAB FAMILY
Abid Hamid Mahmood al-Khatab—HVT#4 Ace of Diamonds (captured, tried and executed)
Ghalib Mahmood al-Khatab—married Saddam's half sister Bissan, also HVT#4's uncle

Abdullah Ghalib Mahmood al-Khatab—
led 7 Jun ambush
Kaied Ghalib Mahmood al-Khatab—
(KIA—9 Nov)
Abid Ghalib Mahmood al-Khatab—(KIA)
Shuja Ghalib Mahmood al-Khatab—
Jordan
Fuaz Ghalib Mahmood al-Khatab—
(captured) daughter married to Abid
Mahmood HVT#4
Amer Kalid Abdullah al-Khatab—1 Oct
bomber
Hayid Hamid al-Khatab—(captured)
student

THE GHANI FAMILY
Mahmood Abdul Ghani—married
Saddam's half sister
Ryad Mahmoud Abdul Ghani—
(captured)
Adnan Mahmood Abdul Ghani—
(captured)
Saddam Mahout Abdul Ghani—
(captured)
Sa'ad Hythem Abdul Ghani—(captured)
Mo'ad Hamoud Abdul Ghani—(captured)
Saqr Ghani—7 Nov helicopter witness

THE AHMED FAMILY
Mohammed Yunis al-Ahmed—Bayjii to
Tikrit resistance chief, Baathist rank just
behind Saddam—helicopter shooter
Munther Mohammed Ahmed—(captured)
19 Nov
Omar Hadel Mohammed Ahmed—
(captured) 28 Dec
Faris Amir Ahmed—(captured) 16 Dec,
bomber Brad's convoy

THE RASHID FAMILY
Maher Abdul Rashid—Qusay father-in-
law (captured)
Ali Maher Abdul Rashid—(KIA—23 Jul),
Qusay brother-in-law
Yasir Maher Abdul Rashid—cell leader,
Qusay brother-in-law
Abdullah Maher Abdul Rashid—courier,
Qusay brother-in-law

THE KHADER FAMILY
Mohammed Khader—harbored
Mohammed al-Musslit (captured in
Baghdad SOF 12 Dec)
Abdel Khader—8 Dec target Cadaseeyah,
possible brother to Mohammed
Sofian Abdel Khader—son of Abdel
Khader
Kalil Abdel Khader—son of Abdel Khader

THE ALI FAMILY
Haji Amin Ali—saved Saddam in 1959
Thaier Amin Ali—(captured) harbored
Mohammed al-Musslit, sisters married
to M. Hadooshi, Thamar Sultan &
Sami Sharif
Mahsin Amin Ali—harbored Mohammed
al-Musslit
Thamer Jassem Mohammed Ali—
(captured) cell leader
Hardan Ali—Sabawi's bodyguard
Arkan Hardan Ali—(captured) cell leader

OTHER ASSOCIATES
Hussein Ahmed Mohammed Hazaa—
married to Rudman's daughter
Tariq Ibrihim Farash—Bayjii & Awija
chief, elevated in rank by Saddam
Salaam Sheban—(captured) mayor's
security chief
Adris Yunis Noori—(captured) arrested in
Ad Dawr

TASK FORCE
1-22 INFANTRY "REGULARS"
ORDER OF BATTLE

HQs, 1st Battalion, 22nd Infantry

Headquarters Company, 1st Battalion, 22nd Infantry

A Company, 1st Battalion, 22nd Infantry

B Company, 1st Battalion, 22nd Infantry

C Company, 1st Battalion, 22nd Infantry

C Company, 1st Battalion, 66th Armor

74th Engineer Company (Bridge)

A Company, 4th Forward Support Battalion

362nd Psyops Detachment

DST-1, 418th Civil Affairs

TPT-1692

THT-44

Iraqi Civil Defense Troops

Attachments for Various Missions

G Troop, 10th Cavalry

A Company, 299th Engineers

A Battery, 4th Battalion, 42nd Field Artillery

Detachments, 401st Military Police

Detachments, 720th Military Police

TASK FORCE ROSTER

Note: This roster is as complete as possible given the flow of replacements, the discharge of soldiers who completed their enlistments while in theater, and with the evacuation of those wounded. It is inevitable that someone will not be listed who served in the task force. Others served in more than one company but may be listed only in the first one. Spellings were copied from the deployment rosters and may be incorrect. The valor and casualty lists are not complete but the known ones are listed.

(v) = valor   (w) = wounded   (k) = killed in action   (ks) = killed in later tour

HHC

OFFICERS

Woempner, Mark S
Russell, Steven D (v)
Rauhut, Michael W
Reed, Brian J
Luke, Bryan
Bell, Clayton T
Bell, Jahme D
Billoni, Philip
Carlisle, Mitchell C
Cashaw, Frederick
Childs, Craig S
Fallon, Christopher
Burguetechapa, Armando
Camp, Andrew J
Carter, Daryl A
Franklin, Douglas
Linkous, Roy, Jr
Lojka, Jason R
Lusk, Casey
Martin, Timmy R
Morales, Alex
Morris, Christopher J (v2)
Morrow, Timothy J (w)
Nunn, Peter P
Pacheco, Antonio L, Jr
Parrish, Troy S
Price, Jason D
Saul, Nathan C

Thomas, Scott (v)
Tran, Xuan N
Weber, Matthew W
Wilmoski, Conrad R

ENLISTED

Martinez, Salvador M.
Dikes, Dwayne, D
Castro, Cesar
Adrian, Eddie J, Jr
Aiken, Andre D
Alokoa, Fritz F
Antolik, Andrew J
Arredondo, Juan C
Bach, Sean A
Bailey, Ronald (w)
Ball, Terrance L
Banks, James G
Barnaby, Jeffery P
Barr, Patrick R
Bear, Thomas
Behnke, Christopher L
Benson, Milton
Bledsoe, Matthew N
Bocanegra, Jesus
Bournazian, Steven M (v)
Branscome, Sean
Brog, Justin D
Brokish, Andrew J
Brown, Thomas W
Cantu, Juan (w)

Cardenas, Franscisco J
Carvajal, Alejandro A
Castanodelgado, Roberto A
Cherry, Michael S
Cline, Pierre F
Cloe, Roy F, Jr
Correa, Angel L
Cradeur, Chase J
Crowe, Mitchell D
Cruz, Daniel
Dennis, Brian L
Dunning, Corey D
Eisenbraun, Kyle P
Eschenbacher, Robert W
Evans, William C
Ewings, Willie E, II
Fasulo, Richard
Ferguson, John T
Feucht, Scott J
Flores, David
Fox, Gerald W, Jr
Garcianaranjo, Gersain
Gardner, Christopher L
Gaspard, Christian C
Giardine, Richard (v)
Giles, Leundrea, T
Gillman, Todd, A
Goodwin, Claude J, IV (v) (w)
Graham, Matthew P
Gretton, Rueben A
Gross, Tyler, D

TASK FORCE ROSTER

Haggerty, David E, Jr
Harper, Brandon, M
Harris, Noah, K
Harris, Danny (w)
Haten, Duston, D
Herrera, Jeremiah, E (v)
Hines, Ricky, D
Hoefer, Cody J (v)
Ipatzimendoza, Oscar
Jablanski, Jared E
Jenkins, Steven A
Kadar, Christopher M
Kelly, James P
Kesner, Bryan L
Lance, Kevin M
Larde, William III A
Larson, Jason T
Lawrence, Carl S
Lay, Michael J
Lazen, Felipe A
Lee, Ronald E, II
Liban, Gregory A
Lloyd, Brandon E
Lopez, Gilbert R
Lugo, David
Luke, Kino A
Lyons, John A (w)
Mack, Austin W
Madrid, Felipe A (w)
Maduro, Rudolph R
Maennena, William A
Mahon, Michael B
Maldonado, Erik E
Mann, Jeffrey S
Martinez, Pedro J, Jr
Mason, Delton H, III
Mastro, Ian L
McBean, John H
McCrary, Eddie, III
McFarland, John M
McKnight, Andrew A
Meadows, Delionel B
Mitchell, Shaun E
Moran, Lovie V, Jr (w)
Morris, Jean C
Morris, Waylon B
Nambo, Ruben R
Pate, Lamont T

Pena, Heriberto L, Jr
Phillips, Percell E, Jr (w)
Pinedalopez, Jesus, A
Pollock, Jason
Pollock, Steven M
Pulliam, Muhammed
Riveraantuna, Pablo F (v)
Rodriguez, Moises, III
Rodriguez, Carlos
Rushworth, Robert S
Russell, Dustin, W
Salas, Daniel
Salas, Gary J
Sample, Jesse A (v)
Sanders, Jeremy L
Santos, Colon V
Scott, Michael A
Serba, Brian J
Seto, Dennis Jr, D
Shaw, Matthew
Shoffner, Sean C (v2)
Simmons, Stewart, G (v) (w)
Sims, Jerel V
Sims, Santino M
Sizer, Gregory K
Smith, Jourdan B
Smith, Kurt B
Soden, Robert E
Stewart, Randall S
Stewart, William G, III
Su, Andres, Jr
Takahashi, Masataka
Tate, Will D
Tatro, Jason E
Tenorio, Cesar (v)
Thomas, Dwayne, A
Thompson, Raymond, M
Tignor, Stewart, D
Traver, Daniel, R
Trujillo, Michael, R
Truong, Mai, V
Valdovinomendez, Simon, S
Venetz, Anthony, Jr (ks)
Venegas, Luis
Vickers, Christopher, J
Walker, Brandon, K
Walker, Robert L, III (v)

Webb, Gregory A
Wells, Jason D (v)
Werts, Jason S
West, Bobby (ks)
White, Anthony E
White, David R
Wiese, Brendon R
Williams, Alfred
Yslas, Stephen S
Zarate, Lorenzo

A CO.

OFFICERS

Coffey, Riley
Crow, Colin D
Guzman, Israel
Harrington, William B
Myer, Matthew R
Oliver, Ramsey
Tapp, Eric E
Roberts, Shane
Stouffer, Mark W
Wagner, Michael P

ENLISTED

Ackerman, James W, III
Adams, Adam N
Adams, Eric L
Alaniz, Joshua L
Alexander, Dana L
Allen, David B
Allen, Jason R
Arrieta, Roman III
Armida, Joshua
Bales, Christopher L, II
Barron, Robert H, Jr
Barton, John W, Jr
Beebe, Michael A
Bobella, Cory A
Booth, Brannon N
Brown, Justin A
Brown, Matthew
Brown, Robert J, III
Brown, Thomas W
Bullard, Gary A

Burns, Justen E
Caballero, Daniel
Caffie, Earnest L
Cameron, Dieter D
Chapman, Bryan S
Chapman, Joshua L
Chenault, Charles E (w)
Clark, Steven S
Contreras, Benhor
Cooper, James R
Cummings, David R
Curry, Ryan S
De Los Santos, Miguel
Deal, Edward L
Dent, Timothy L
Dornbush, Mark B
Eastwood, Matthew
Ervin, Eric C
Fay, Erland A
Feliz, Luis D
France, William R
Fuentes, Mario A
Fyffe, Craig R
Gamboa, Edgar
Garay, Byron R
Garcia, Benito M
Garcia, Juan A
Garcia, Noel E
Garcia, Orlando J
Garza, Jaime, Jr
Goodwin, Bill
Goodwin, Donald A
Goodwin, Jason L
Gordon, Marcus
Guy, Dwain A
Hart, Randy L
Hartwell, Paul W
Henao, Ruben D
Henson, Roy A
Hernandez, Daniel V
Hernandez, Eduardo L
Hernandez, Isaac
Herrera, Joseph L
Hill, Mark R
Hinojosa, Rolando A
Hoy, Bradley J
Hubert, Eric J
Hubert, Jeffrey W

Iribe, Erbert
Johnson, Edward
Johnson, Joshua C
Johnson, Nicholas B
Keith, Brian H
Keltner, Curtis
Kopp, Eric J
Lam, Gabriel S
Lapre, Jamie R
Larocque, Matthew W
Lavina, Jerry K
Lee, Eric J
Leemon, Benjamin D
Lewis, Roy R
Little, Mark J
Livingston, Andrew V
Long, Eric F
Lott, Jason D
Lusk, James P
Machuca, Rolando I
Macias, Jose D
Mallory, Cletus E
Manley, Benjamin E
Mann, Stephen
Martinez, Michael
Mason, John M
McCoy, Joshua L
McDougal, Michael L
McNabb, Ian R
Medina, FNU MNU
Missildine, Joe K
Morgan, David A
Morris, Jean C
Muhammad, Dwyer
Murphree, Waylon L
Meyer, Jason J
Nava, Jose A
Neptune, Chad A
Newkirk, Kyle W
OlverallIja, Hugo
Owens, Brad, T (v2) (w)
Pagnello, Robert R
Parker, Daniel A, Jr
Parker, James D
Parrish, Ranger B
Patenge, Bryan L
Payne, Jason
Phillips, Andy C

Pineda, Jesus A
Pirnat, Anthony R
Poncedeleon, David
Poore, Daniel
Porcher, Reginald L
Portillo, Chris
Poynor, Mark E
Putnam, Timothy A
Racine, Eric N
Ralston, Eric A
Ramirez, Gabriel
Rankin, Matthew P
Ransom, William
Rice, Timothy R
Richards, Bramwell K
Rivera, Daril A
Robinson, Kenwaski U
Robles, Jesus D
Rodgers, Thomas W
Rosales, Christopher
Rosales, Rudy
Salcedo, Esequiel
Saxby, Caleb R
Saxton, Lindsay R
Saylor, Barrye A (v)
Schneider, Michael P
Schwartz, Robert D
Schwope, Christopher A
Shields, Jason R
Shoaff, Wayne A
Sick, Colin R
Spears, Michael
Stevens, Derik
Strong, Kenneth C
Sucsy, Joshua
Summers, Matthew L (v)
Tilley, Johnny E
Torres, Joseph G
Valentin, Miguel A
Valle, Alberto
Vasquez, Zenon C
Voll, Kevin E
Walker, James D
Ware, Charles E
Waters, Michael R
Watson, Presely S
Weise, Brendon
Wells, Christopher J

White, Tommy J
Whitson, Phillip S
Witt, Jeremy D
Wolfe, Scott A
Wycoff, Ronald A (v)

B CO.

OFFICERS

Claycomb, David
Lannan, Ford M
Litherland, Warren S. (w)
Love, James B
Peters, Charles D (v)
Scott, Clarence C, Jr
Sheils, Jeremy K
Thomas, Scott (v)

ENLISTED

Alejandro, Stephen A
Alexander, Jay
Allen, Andre L
Azua, Carlos Jr,
Bahruth, Daniel A
Banks, James G
Bass, Joseph G
Baxter, Anthony W
Bennett, Paul W
Berry, Christian
Blalock, James P
Bressette, Michael J
Brown, Benjamin E, Jr
Burfitt, Adam J
Canine, Robert D
Carter, Nickolas J
Chhim, Kear
Chisolm, Antquawn D
Choeum, Chanthorn
Christy, Andrew C
Clark, Armando, Jr
Cole, Brett M
Craven, James P
Dalessio, Joseph M (v)
Deguzman, Joel S (w)
Delacruz, Gilbert D, III
Dervishi, Ervin (k)

Dorrity, Dennis, O
Dowd, Gary, L (w)
Duncan, Jason A
English, David
Ferrell, Timothy C
Fields, James H, Jr
Fink, Stephen R (w)
Finley, Willie
Flanagan, Joshua D
Garcia, Hector, Jr
Garza, Gary W
Gillis, Joseph A
Gomez, Keith R
Gonzalez, Edgar E
Greenhow, Todd
Gross, Jason
Gutierrez, Oscar X
Gutierrez, Sean E
Halley, Sedric W, Jr
Harden, Robert L, Jr
Harris, Raymond S
Hartman, Brian A
Henton, Lonnie
Hickman, David A
Holzworth, Louis A
Hoskins, Trent S
Howell, Dale
Howell, Dustin M
Hsia Ming, Ming K
Huffaker, Keith D
Johnson, Leonard T (w)
Jones, Timothy K
Judd, Richard
Keel, James M
Lahner, Steven G
Lewis, John, A (w)
Lichnovsky, Tyler G
Lugo, David
Marler, Paul A
Marrison, Ryan C
Mattison, Troy R
McCue, Matthew R
McGrath, Michael E, Jr
Mickens, Aaron J
Minzer, John D
Mishkoff, Marc D
Molina, Rodson C
Montanez, Isreal

Montenegro, Jose L, Jr
Moon, Benjamin B
Moore, Timothy M (w)
Morales, Luis E
Moreno, Jose, I
Moreno, Manuel
Morris, Andrew C
Myers, Charles, A (w2)
Nail, Gilbert E
Navarro, Jose M
Neal, John T
Neria, Joseph D
Ortega, Mark A, II
Ortiz, Vicente C
Padilla, Carlos H
Pater, Jason R
Patterson, Seth L
Payne, Ranger T
Perdue, Charles C
Perez, Carlos R
Pierce, Devon E (w)
Poirier, Sheldon D
Powell, James E (k)
Ransom, William
Rhoades, Scott M
Ridlon, Robert A, Jr
Rivers, Patrick L, Jr
Sanders, Steven R
Schmaltz, Jason A
Schoellman, Joshua M (w)
Sellers, Scott B
Sickles, Braden K
Simpson, Larry C
Smith, Brian B
Smith, Henry L, Sr
Smith, James O
Soto, Orlando Jr
Stoak, Matthew D
Stursma, Chad A
Summerfield, Robert H, Jr
Summers, John
Surdam, Zeb F
Techur, Michael
Teisher, Johnathan
Thomas, Mack A
Upshaw, James C
Valentin, Raheen
Wagner, Kurt E

Walden, Joseph T (w)
Wale, David L
Weatherall, Willie J
Wedderburn, Ricardo I
White, David M (w)
Whitlock, Adam J
Whitson, Joshua L (w)
Wilke, Kyle J
Woods, Ronald E, Jr (w)
Wright, Dustin P
Zachary, Curtis D, II
Zamora, Jorge M, Jr (w)
Zern, Aric S

C CO.

OFFICERS

Boyd, Bradley L (v) (w)
Deel, Jason R
Orozco, Osbaldo (k)
Calderwood, Don
Isbell, Michael J
Taylor, Randy L

ENLISTED

Anderson, David M
Andrade, Francisco, III
Arispe, Abel A
Atkinson, Marcus D
Axline, Travis, M
Barbosa, Jose, B
Belt, Patrick R
Blystone, Ronald C (ks)
Bohrn, Joshua A
Booth, Mcgregor J
Bordes, Michael J
Burns, Bradley (w)
Butcher, Eli J
Caballero, Daniel J
Callihan, Mark E
Camilo, Radhames (ds)
Cardenas, Sergio (w)
Cardona, Keith
Carpenter, James E
Certain, Carlton, A
Colbert, Marcus, B

Combs, Richard, L
Conway, Jonathan, D
Cordero, Fabian,
Cornette, Ryan, A
Crawford, John, L
Crayton, Anthony, C
Cruz, Felieciano, R
Davidson, Laveto, E
Davis II, Rodney L,
Durand, Eric P
Elkins, Brandon J
Esparza-Reyes, Ramon H
Euresti, Michael A
Evans, Michael F (v)
Fillippino, Quinn M
Flores, James W
Foster, Byron R
Garcia, Miguel A
Garcia, Roger (v) (w)
Gardner, James A
Garza, John A
Garza, Jaime H
Gellerman, Milton E
Gibson, Jarvis G
Gilbert, John D
Gilstrap, William (w)
Greem, Joseph D
Griffiths, Andre D
Guerrero, Julian
Guerrero, Sanzabeedee
Hamilton, Thomas P
Hammett, Mark R
Hann, Adam T
Harrison, William J
Hartline, John B
Hartman, Shaun J
Hayden, A J
Hebert, Nathan W
Hernandez, Marco A
Hoffman, Justin E
Hood, Tyler C
Hornyak, Eric J
Jackson, Jason D
Jenkins, Kenneth A (ks)
Jordan, Christopher M
Kammer, Kevin D
Klepacz, Jason R
Krause, Jason L

Kuenzel, Kenneth K
Lam, Gabriel S
Latch, Stephen W
Leasau, Matthew K (w)
Loehr, Jeffrey A
Lucas, Kelly W
Lynn, Jacob V
Marfell, Timothy P
Masih, Simon P
Mays, Chris G
McDermott, Patrick M
McKnight, Andrew A
Mead, Don J
Merritt, Harry T, Jr
Morrical, Thomas L
Morris, Joseph A
Morris, Robert W
Munoz, Joe V
Nilsson, John M
Nolan, Anthony
Norris, Jerry
Nota, Peter
Oliva, Edgar
O'Quin, Braedon S
Ortega, Daniel
Parker, James D (w)
Peebles, Richard D
Pena, Robert T
Perry, Steven A
Pollard, Andrew H
Prahl, Matthew, L
Rawlins, Harvey E
Reddish, Dennis J
Reed, Joshua C
Reeves, Willie C
Rose, Matthew L
Ross, Kermet L
Sanchez, German M
Sanders, Benjamin L
Schroeder, Mickey H
Siqueido, Samual C
Soria, Jeremiah
Steckler, Ryan W
Stephenson, Edward M (w)
Stewart, Jackie A
Stuck, Mitcheal W
Sukel, Robert E
Tayfel, Patrick R

Thompson, Marcus B
Trainer, Joe C
Trujillo, Michael P
Turner, Gregory M
Turner, Patrick J
Uhlenhake, Ryan J
Uribe, Ricardo M
Vargas, Rodrigo (v) (w)
Vargas, Omar D
Vega, Joshua S
Velez, William A (w)
Waldman, Rogero
Weaver, Joseph A, Jr
Webb, Christopher A
Weivoda, Collin R
Wheeler, Donald L, Jr (k)
Wold, Jason M
Wulf, Vincent J
Wygal, Marcus L
Zamaniego, Anthony T

C CO. 3-66 AR

OFFICERS

Bishop, Marty
Boytim, Justin
Cecalupo, Jon
Choi, Eugene
Cooper, Matthew
Durney, Janson
Holloway, David
Noll, Charles E
Redden, Nathaniel S
Thompson, Philip C

ENLISTED

Aguilar, Eli
Andrada, David D
Arnaudo, Matthew R
Baker, Nicholas S
Ballou, Timothy J
Barcomb, Raymond E
Bourland, John A
Brigance, William C
Calderon, Geroge
Cano, Felix

Casey, Sean Z
Cavaner, Jonathan D
Christophe Sr., Channing C
Coates, Anthony R
Corey, Herman L
Daisley, Anselmo J
Dano, William B
Davis, Christopher
Dearmas, David
Deatley, David
Dennis, Anthony
Dick, Jacob
Dombroskas, Jesse C
Ervin, Nicholas
Fletcher, Marvin E
Foster, Curtis E
Frazier, Jeremy A
Friman, Alexander
Garza, Michael
Gonzalez, Elton
Goodson, Elton A
Hall, Benjamin
Harper, Derrick
Heilman, Daniel E
Hernandez, Antonio (w)
Holgate, Kevin
Hornsby, Chad
Hurtado, Juan F
Jago, Joseph A
Kalugdan, Raymond
King, Derell L
Kingman, Christopher
Kirschke, Matt D
Kline, Shawn A
Kohlhaas, Jeremy R
Laroche, Leighton
Lee, Alexander
Lewis, John L
Longmore, Travis J
Lucas, Irving
Makin, Barrie
Matlock, William
Mclian, David
Metacarpa, Garrett
Miranda, Pedro
Montgomer, Travis
Moore, Vincent A, Sr
Morgan, Terry

Nickolai, Jeremy
Partida, Austroberto B
Pierlioni, Nicholas D
Platero, Darian R
Rheinschmidt, Brett
Ricker, Robert
Riedlinger, Dylan T
Rodgers, David
Rodgers, Jefferey
Rodriguez, Francisco
Rogan, Brian
Rosales, Angel
Rountree, Shawn
Serna, Michael E
Shanley, Michael T
Shirley, Wesley C, Jr
Shreve, Douglas W
Smith, Carl
Snow, Adam J
Solano, Jose
Starkey, Brian
Stauty, Christopher
Stewart, Steven F
Syverson, Branden K
Talley, Curtis
Tandriff, Ryan
Thomas, Marcus D
Vanacker, Stephen
Venardos, Peter M
Werry, Brandon
Wilkinson, William H, III
Williams, Bobby J
Wynn, Donald
Yanez, Isidro
Zamarripa, Jamie

A CO. 4 FSB

OFFICERS

Adnan, Ali (w)
Alexander, Matthew D
Cruz, Richard
Eagling, Christopher J
Kuetemeyer, Curt (w)
Rottman, Matthew W
Pisani, Joseph

ENLISTED

Araujo, Chad
Artiga, Rodric
Ault, Matthew
Bailey, Ronald
Bates, Roy W
Behlin, Ricardo
Bemak, Jason A
Bentancourt, Carlos
Bounds, Michael W
Brooks, Malcolm I
Brunner, Raymond A
Burgess, Lamel D
Burman, Justin L
Burto, Shawn A
Cabral, Juan C (w) (k)
Carlisle, Michael P
Childress, Michael D
Cisneros, Celina
Coles, Raymond R
Coombs, Heather M
Cruzartud , Miguel A
Dahl, Clayton O
Davis, Charles F
Davis, Ronald E
Demorest, Dale W
Dorn, Katie A
Dorty, Anthony D
Downs, Travis W
Dunbar, Damion T
Esparza, Analaura L (k)
Finn, Justin
Fitzgibbon, Daniel M
Flores, Christopher M
Flournoy, Ronald E
Foreman, Kelly
Foster, Ronnie L, Jr
Franklin, Delores J
Fry, Steven
Fuentes, Andres
Gabriel, Gilbert
Garcia, Carlos A
Gibson, Temu M
Goldwire, Mark K
Gomez, Jose
Grant, Marcus J
Grimes, Charrod

Guckert, Karen L (v)
Hames, Thomas R
Hanger, Jeremy D
Hattaway, Michael
Howard, Jeffery
Hubbard, Henry Jr
Jaramillo, Karl Jr,
Jarvis, Terry
Jimenez, Arturo
Johnson, Michael
Jones, Todd
King, James
Koski, Christopher
Laymance, Michael
Le-Bisenieks, Ngoc T
Lee, Tabitha M
Lee, Walter
Lerma, Raul
Lobo, Joseph D
Lopez, Veronica
Lopez, Aldolfo (w)
Maddox, Felissa
Magana, Felipe
Magdaleno, Bonifacio
Martinez, Ismael
McBroom, William G (w)
McCellon, Eugene
McCoy, Reginald L
McDaniel, Rickey
McDermott, Leighton
McGeogh, Holly (k)
Meketa, Michael
Mier-Sandoval, Eliu (k)
Miller, Nicholas
Mitchell, Carl A
Morehouse, Allen
Morgan, Kendrick M
Nettles, Kregg
New, Lindsey
Newsome, Daniel E
Northington, Shauna S
Nolan, Paula
Ott, John L
Overturf, Mark A
Parnell, Niya
Patton, Darrell W (v) (w)
Pitts, Gregory J
Proseus, Jason R

Pulido, Jeffery B
Ramos, Cipriano
Rautenburg, James B
Reed, Urie L
Reese, Herman
Regehr, Micheal L (w)
Ricks, Regina G
Robinson, Remirus J
Robinson, Del
Rodriguez, Mike
Rose, Manuel
Rzhevskiy, Anton
Sanders, Charles
Scruggs, Matthew S
Sheldrick, Joseph A
Silva, Joseph A
Sims, La-Vincent
Spann, Shirley L
Stephens, Angel T
Stewart, Ronnie W
Stinson, Tyronne
Sucsy, Jayme
Swift, Earnest
Taylor, Larry A
Taylor, Jeremy D
Theiss, Peter J
Thompson, Curtis Y
Thompson, Richard S
Trejo, Christopher
Trimble, Shem H
Urrutia, Christopher D
Vakselis, Dennis
Venoms, Jeremiah
Washington, Alonzo
Webb, Job W
Williams, Carl A
Wolgemuth, Jason A
Yates, Jeremiah

74 EN CO. (BRIDGE)

OFFICERS

Herbst, Karl F
Muller, Stephen
Rogers, David L

TASK FORCE ROSTER

Scott, Ann M
Shaw, Peter
Williams, Marc H

ENLISTED

Anderson, Chad C
Babcock, Robert
Babcock, Stephanie
Bailey, Aileen C
Bamsberger, James
Banks, John
Beal, Latesha
Beltran, Wendy L
Bennett, Jayson B
Bienemy, Dalven
Bittner, Kieth J
Bonnett, Raymond J
Brookshire, Justin
Burgoyne, Max
Burton, Danjanira
Campillo, Alexander
Campos, Mario
Carrasquillo, Joaquin
Carswell, Brian
Castro, Eric
Cheatham, Darryl M
Christensen, Kenton
Cleary, Alston
Codogan, William S
Collin, Zachary
Corrigan, Timothy
Cortez, Jimmy
Craig, Shawn K
Creppel, Richard L
Cuffy, Franklyn
Dailey, Floyd C
Daniels, Thomas A
Davis, Antonette
Davis, Hayward
Dickson, Kevin A
Eanes, Adrienne D
Eller, David W
Ellison, Ernest
Enriquez, Eleazar
Estes, Brent
Ewell, Laparis T
Ferguson, Anderson

Fletcher, Richard T
Franco, Roberto
French, Robert
Gallup, Kristi
Garcia, Benjamin
Garner, Lakesha
Germain, Emily
Gibson, George R
Gilley, Kevin J
Grant, James R
Gregg, Steven R
Gustafson, Robert S
Hambrick, Cory
Hamby, John R
Helvey, Ryan T
Hemingway, William J
Herman, Steven M
Hightower, Jason L
Hofmann, Damian A
Howdahl, Jesse L
Intong, Khanhthong
Jennings, Billy
Johnson, Patrick
Jones, Lameka
Jordan, Adam R
Kabelman, Andrew R
Kallhoff, Tyrel J
Keller, Nicole L
Kidwell, Charles T
Korbal, David E
Krick, Joseph R
Krick, Melissa J
Labuda, Kurt J
Leanos, Azucena
Liendo, Antonio
Mallet, Robert
Martin, Michael
Martinez, Miguel A
Matthews, Keenan
Maybin, Timothy
Mcdaniels, Bryan
Mckee, Robert
Mcrae, Daniel B
Mercado, Jose L
Merriman, Anthony J
Moore, Edwin
Moore, Klysta
Mower, Kevin D

Murdock, Eric M
Nicho-Diaz, Caesar
Nielsen, Zachary R
Norng, Dy
Otis, Aaron
Padilla, Felipe E
Parker, Reginald
Parks, Tiffany M
Payne, Alice O
Paynther, Brandon
Person, Chentell
Peters, Terrance
Pinion, Charles W
Powell, Jason A
Putman, Pheama L
Randall, Timothy H
Replogle, Christopher
Rice, James W
Rivas, Jason
Rivera, Manuel
Robinson, Brian
Rodger, James
Rogers, Reginald
Sanchez, Jaime
Scovill, Todd L
Showman, Craig A
Simm, David
Skelton, George
Smith, Stephanie
Soennichsen, Amanda
Soennichsen, Casey J
Sokolowski, Jason
Spain, Jacob P
Steele, Clennon E
Steele, Jennifer L
Stendel, Shawn M
Stevens, Marcus
Stevens, Renee
Stroman, Cory
Tjersland, Scott
Tye, Adam P
Uchel, Hammurabi
Vanpoorfliet, James M
Vargo, Michael
Vega, Jose A
Vodehnal, Nicholas J
Ward, Joshua J
Warren, Quent R

Weatherton, Curley
Whitby, Akins
Williams, Christopher
Wilson, Frederick
Wilson, Lance R
York, Thomas
Yuhas, Lorraine

362ND PSYOPS DETACHMENT

Darrah, Charles P, Jr (w)
Carrizales, Antonio R (w)
Mosely, Malcolm X (w)

DIRECT SUPPORT TEAM 1, 418TH CIVIL AFFAIRS BATTALION (USAR)

OFFICERS

Ailslieger, Kristafer R
England, Jerry

ENLISTED

Groefsema, Daniel V
Weaver, Daniel D
Ponder, David R
Wistrom, Ronald
Erickson, Sean D

AUTHOR'S NOTE

Acknowledging those who helped me shape and form this book has been extremely difficult. It is inevitable that my appreciation can never be adequate to the men and women of Task Force 1-22 Infantry who served in Tikrit, Iraq, from 2003 to 2004. I, along with the nation, owe them a debt of gratitude that can never be repaid. Some soldiers I fought with and led may have been at my side, while others performed crucial duty elsewhere materially shaping the outcome of our mission.

This memoir is a depiction of the life I knew during my service in Iraq. It has been extremely difficult to write as I have drawn up raw emotion from the well of traumatic experience and have attempted, with the use of words, to convey what it is like to live on a battlefield. As a trained Army historian, I recognized at the time the importance of where we were and the historical significance of our service. I attempted to record events in my journals and notes the best I could, and implemented procedures in our task force to help us document the fight. The events listed in this book are drawn from my memory, from my journals, from the period combat action reports of our task force, from contemporary news reports, and from interviews of others present. Many of the conversations and details in this memoir were a result of our witness statements and combat action reporting procedures from the participants themselves, fresh after the battle. Even with all that effort, I have found it still possible to omit some key player or some key action. My hope is that I can be forgiven and that this story shall serve as the basis of memory for those who were there.

Among the soldiers to thank, I am grateful to General Raymond T. Odierno for his kindness and encouragement to finish the book and for his battlefield leadership that I believe saved many of our lives. His writing of the foreword is, to me, both humbling and more than I deserve. To the skilled leaders of the 4th Infantry Division, I say thanks. Men like General Mike Barbero and General Don Campbell made a difference and always kept the field commander foremost in their minds. I also count myself very privileged to have had the encouragement and enthusiastic support of fellow Oklahoman and extraordinary leader General Tommy Franks.

I don't have adequate words to say thanks to Colonel Jim Hickey. His toughness and standards paled in comparison to his focus and understanding of what we must achieve when our nation asks. I knew him as one of his main battle commanders and I can think of no one I would ever want to serve under or fight with more where so much was asked and times were uncertain. More than that, we became brothers in the bonds of battle, differing from many in that we fought in the streets and fields while also carrying the extreme burdens of commanding large bodies of America's soldiers. Thanks, Jim. We, and our nation, owe you much.

I want to say thanks to Command Sergeant Major Larry Wilson for his humor, his dedication and his great treatment of our soldiers as a part of 1st Brigade. Many times the brigade sergeant major can be a burden to the battalions. Larry was anything but. He will always be my brother.

To Jack, Matt, Doug, John, Kelly, and many others—the bonds cannot be described. Thanks.

Nothing could have been executed in Task Force "Regulars" without Bryan Luke, Mike Rauhut, and Brian Reed. Nothing. These iron majors were not only professionals, but sought to understand what was in my tired mind and passionate heart. They not only carried out the plans and orders but they pursued them as their own with the same excitement and drive. More importantly, we fought together, dodged bullets and bombs together, ate together, cried together, and celebrated the success of our great soldiers together. I dragged them through much and at times felt a bit of guilt for the risks I placed upon them, but knew they had to be taken. I am grateful for their lives and their friendship. Thanks, my brothers.

To my battle buddy and hardened confidant Command Sergeant Major Pete Martinez, thanks for keeping me straight. No two humans can share the same food, hooch, work, and burdens of being in charge together in war and be anything less than family at the end of it. Again, words are not adequate. Pete knew my every burden, secret, and concern and kept me focused through it all. Thanks seems so inadequate, Pete—as long as we have breath.

To my commanders in Task Force 1-22 Infantry who carried out the fight and shed their blood and sweat on the streets and in the fields of Tikrit, Iraq, I will be eternally grateful. Their friendship and commitment will be forever burned in my memory: Chris Fallon, Mark Stouffer, Scott Thomas, Brad Boyd, Jon Cecalupo, Curt Kuetemeyer, Mitch Carlisle, and Mike Wagner. I still see them and think of them every single day.

Our soldiers who returned home are alive due to the efforts of First Sergeants Delionel Meadows, Jaime Garza, Louis Holzworth, Mike Evans, Robert Summerfield, William Matlock, and Ron Davis. The nation will never know how many wounded, bleeding soldiers you transported on Hummer tops, how many weapons, how much ammunition, fuel, and food you delivered, and how tough you were in a fight rallying the young and inexperienced in shocking episodes of war. But I will. And I am forever grateful.

To my field surgeons, Phil Billoni and Bill Mazullo, and to my physician assistants, Alex Morales and Armando Buerguete, who saved our lives on the stretchers in the dank kitchen converted to handle battlefield surgery. How can thanks ever be expressed to those who handled the trauma of hurting, broken, bloody young men and women and do it at a moment's notice, day in and day out? We owe them, the surgeons at the 28th Combat Surgical Hospital, and all of our Task Force 1-22 Infantry line medics, medical platoon, and attending chaplains, so very much.

One of the surprising bonds to have developed from our time in Iraq was with the field reporters and photographers who recorded our story, one filing at a time. I came to respect combat reporters such as Brian Bennett, Kim Dozier, Greg Palkott, Kevin Sites, Robin Pomeroy, Alexander Vasovic, D'arcy Doran, Paul Garwood, and Andrew Cawthorne, to name a few of the many who embedded with our task force. These reporters endured enormous hardship and risks to file their stories, complimented with the artistic work of combat photographers such as Efrem Lukatsky, Yuri Kozyrev, Shawn Thew, Ivan Sekretarev, Jewel Samad, Mauricio Lima, Stefan Zaklin and Rob Griffith. Because of the risks they bore, armed only with pens, recorders and cameras, we have an incredible and almost daily record of many of the actions relating to the hunt and capture of Saddam. For that I am ever grateful.

To my friends who took up the fight upon our return home to convey the truth of our service in Iraq and Afghanistan, I wish to particularly say thanks to David Bellavia, author of *House to House*; Marcus Luttrell, author of *Lone Survivor*; and Jeremiah Workman, author of *Shadow of the Sword*. The friendship we formed on tour with Vets for Freedom and Pete Hegseth is something I count as a privilege. As long as we have breath we will tell of our soldiers' gallantry and the service they rendered to our nation. Thanks for your encouragement to complete this work and for your continued friendship.

Although this tale is personal and much of the thanks has been expressed to soldiers and combat field reporters, I am reminded that turning a soldier's tale into the reality of a book is the work of many professionals and volunteers in civilian life. To my agent, Frank Breeden of Premiere Authors, thanks for sticking with me and believing in the work. To Emma Conaughty, none of this would even have made it to the page without your encouragement and incredible editing ability. To Deb Purinton, who handled myriad calls and schedules, many thanks.

To 1-22 Infantry Vietnam veteran, Bob Babcock, your friendship is priceless. We have a history because of you and your team at Deeds Publishing. I am also grateful to Mark and Jan Babcock for poring through the manuscript, presenting the layout, and editing the text. Their efforts have made the work professional.

To my incredibly tough and beautiful wife, Cindy, and my five wonderful children, Jessica, Matt, Chris, Patricia, and Hannah; to my parents, Gene and Donna, and my sister, Janelle, and brother, Rusty: your love is a bond that sustained me in battle and tolerated me through the emotional roller coaster of writing this book. I love you all more than anything in this world.

Now to the King eternal, immortal, invisible, to God, who alone is wise, be honor and glory forever and ever.

SDR

Oklahoma City, Oklahoma
March 2011

INDEX

Note: Arabic family names that begin with "Al" are sorted by the letter that begins the second word of the name. For example, "al-Musslit" can be found in the "M" section.

ABOUT THE AUTHOR

STEVE RUSSELL served 21 years in the United States Army as an infantry officer, deploying operationally to Kosovo, Kuwait, Afghanistan, and Iraq. During his command of the 1st Battalion, 22nd Infantry Regiment, 4th Infantry Division, he was widely covered during the first year of the Iraq war by TIME, CNN, Fox News, ABC, CBS, NBC, AP and Reuters. He and his unit were featured in BBC Panorama's *Saddam on the Run* documentary as well as Discovery's *Ace in the Hole*. He has also been the subject of numerous books and publications. Russell retired from the Army in 2006 to return to his native state of Oklahoma, where he has advocated nationally for veterans of Iraq and Afghanistan. He has been a featured speaker at events across the United States, in Canada, and in Europe. Russell lives in Oklahoma with his wife and five children.

SONOMA
COUNTY
LIBRARY

to renew • para renovar

707.566.0281
sonomalibrary.org

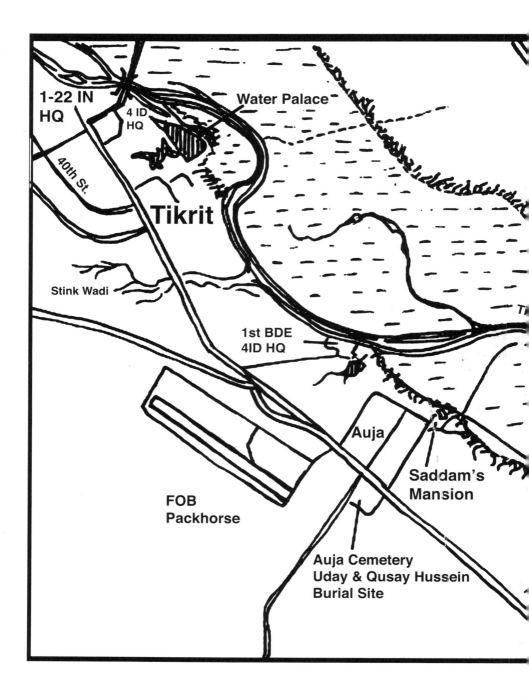

1-22 IN
HQ

4 ID
HQ

Water Palace

40th St.

Tikrit

Stink Wadi

1st BDE
4ID HQ

Auja

Saddam's
Mansion

FOB
Packhorse

Auja Cemetery
Uday & Qusay Hussein
Burial Site